# Bois-Brûlés

# Bois-Brûlés

*The Untold Story
of the Métis of Western Québec*

MICHEL BOUCHARD,
SÉBASTIEN MALETTE, AND
GUILLAUME MARCOTTE

**UBC**Press · Vancouver · Toronto

29 28 27 26 25 24 23 22 21 20    5 4 3 2 1

Printed in Canada on FSC-certified ancient-forest-free paper
(100% post-consumer recycled) that is processed chlorine- and acid-free.

**Library and Archives Canada Cataloguing in Publication**

Title: Bois-Brûlés : the untold story of the Métis of western Québec / Michel Bouchard, Sébastien Malette, and Guillaume Marcotte.
Other titles: Bois-Brûlés de l'Outaouais. English
Names: Bouchard, Michel, author. | Malette, Sébastien, author. | Marcotte, Guillaume, author.
Description: Translation of: Les Bois-Brûlés de l'Outaouais: une étude ethno-culturelle des Métis de la Gatineau. | Includes bibliographical references and index. | Translated from the French.
Identifiers: Canadiana (print) 20200193783 | Canadiana (ebook) 2020019397X | ISBN 9780774862325 (hardcover) | ISBN 9780774862332 (softcover) | ISBN 9780774862349 (PDF) | ISBN 9780774862356 (EPUB) | ISBN 9780774862363 (Kindle)
Subjects: LCSH: Métis – Québec (Province) – Gatineau River Valley – History – 19th century. | LCSH: Métis – Québec (Province) – Gatineau River Valley – Genealogy. | LCSH: Métis – Québec (Province) – Gatineau Region – History – 19th century. | LCSH: Métis – Québec (Province) – Gatineau Region – History – 20th century.
Classification: LCC FC126.Q3 B6813 2020 | DDC 971.4/22400497—dc23

Canadä

UBC Press gratefully acknowledges the financial support for our publishing program of the Government of Canada (through the Canada Book Fund), the Canada Council for the Arts, and the British Columbia Arts Council.

This book has been published with the help of a grant from the Canadian Federation for the Humanities and Social Sciences, through the Awards to Scholarly Publications Program, using funds provided by the Social Sciences and Humanities Research Council of Canada.

Printed and bound in Canada by Friesens
Set in Galliard and New Baskerville by Artegraphica Design Co. Ltd.
Copy editor: Camilla Blakeley
Proofreader: Helen Godolphin
Indexer: Margaret de Boer
Cover designer: George Kirkpatrick

Cover images: *front (top)*, Mary Keith Taylor, ca. 1850s or 1860s, HBCA 1995/43/2; *front (bottom)*, Cornelius Krieghoff, *Hunters Pulling Dead Moose*, ca. 1860, LAC 1950-14-2; *back*, Thomas Taylor Jr., ca. 1850s or 1860s, HBCA 1995/43/6

UBC Press
The University of British Columbia
2029 West Mall
Vancouver, BC V6T 1Z2
**www.ubcpress.ca**

*To the memory of*
PRIVATE PATRICK "PADDY" RIEL,
*1876–1916,*
*a First World War Métis volunteer from Maniwaki*
*(#1295 of the 8th Battalion, Canadian Infantry)*
*who made the ultimate sacrifice*

# Contents

# Illustrations

# *Foreword*

I READ AND REREAD *Bois-Brûlés* with passion. This ethnohistorical study sheds a dazzling light on my ancestors, the Métis of the Gatineau Valley. It allowed me to recognize myself as never before and to understand with greater clarity where I come from and who I am. Through the words, I saw once again the beautiful landscapes of my childhood. I vividly recalled times spent on the shores of the majestic Outaouais, Gatineau, and Lièvre rivers, and at the Cabonga reservoir near Grand-Lac Victoria. This rich telling reminded me of the exceptional men, women, and children I knew then. They were larger than life and forever dwell in my memory. In *Bois-Brûlés*, I recognize the names of my family – grandparents, uncles, aunts – and friends. I discovered facts and locales that give comfort to my identity. *Bois-Brûlés* is in many ways my biography, and the characters who inhabit this work are central to my lived past, my family tree, and that of hundreds of inhabitants of the Gatineau Valley.

I am privileged to have existed for close to three-quarters of a century. In my childhood, I lived in tents and log cabins; I knew the life of traplines, dog teams, feasts of moose, beaver, and pike, and evenings passed in drumming. I also witnessed the devastation brought by the clear-cuts of lumberjacks. I observed the yellow tractors ripping the stomach of the red earth, the stripped logs despoiling the white waters of rivers. I saw my people impoverished, cowed, and I watch them rise today, breaking their silence, emerging from their clandestinity. The pride and the strength of my people grows and I hear their voices rise up anew.

My father, like all men of the forest, cultivated a love of the woods and respect for animals. Like those who belonged to preceding generations, he had a poetic gift as he transformed the smallest facts, the most fortuitous encounters, the most banal incidents into epic narratives. He let himself be carried away by words as a boat, its sails inflated by the wind, carries its cargo along. I was his most diligent listener and I burned into my memory everything that I saw, heard, and felt, telling myself that one day, I would bequeath these fabulous stories to my children. These remembrances, these accounts of hunting and fishing, these tales and legends, I have not only recounted but written and published them so that parents and their children can share them in turn.

At a very young age, I had the privilege of regularly visiting the last authentic trading post of the famed Hudson's Bay Company. The post was located in the Algonquin reservation of Rapid Lake in Québec. Its trading activities, even in decline at the end of the 1940s, remained a crucial component of my family's lifeblood. My father brought me there regularly. I keep a vivid memory of this post, as we lived a few kilometres from the Algonquin community and our cabin was a gathering place open to and attended by all. The manager of the HBC post, Mr. Whiteduck, was a friend of my father. On each of our visits, I was intoxicated with the pungent odours of raw beaver pelts, dried apples in wooden cases, and tea sold in bulk from bulging burlap bags. I loved to travel by canoe with my father on the long journey that took us to the village of Grand-Lac Victoria. Sitting at the stern, my father seized this opportunity to educate me, to introduce me to our traditions, as his father had done when he was a child. As the water flowed by, he shared with me his knowledge of the configuration of the mountains, the campsites on the banks before coming to a portage. Sitting at the bow, I learned to read nature and I discovered my story, my history.

Grand-Lac Victoria's post is sacred land and we set foot on it with the greatest respect. We were setting foot on the very spot where François Naud, our venerable ancestor, had worked a hundred years before. He was married to Élisabeth, daughter of Andrew McPherson and Marie Pinesi-okijikokwe. Andrew McPherson, an experienced trader, was the manager of the HBC post at the time. Today, I often say *kitshi miguetsh* to my two ancestors Marie Pinesi-okijikokwe and Élisabeth McPherson. I am grateful because I owe to them who I am today. I now understand why my father felt in his element when he was treading these lands or navigating those waters. These sacred lands had seen our ancestors! The ground we covered had been trodden by their footsteps. It sheltered the dust of their bones.

My Métis ancestors are not ghosts, abstractions. They existed in flesh, bone, and action. They formed a nation by the sweat of their brow, a nation that persists. What we are as Métis is a historical fact. I am the product of a long history. I knew it in childhood, a known fact so integrated into my extended family that we did not feel the need to talk about it. However, I was not as fully aware of it as I am today. Rather, I always had the deep feeling that my ancestors had chosen me to become a carrier of tradition, a cultural smuggler of sorts.

The role of a Métis in today's society is to build bridges between peoples so that they live in harmony, with the greatest respect for one another. To accomplish this role of cultural mediators, we must know who we are and where we come from. To recognize ourselves as Métis is simultaneously to become ambassadors for the nation, to commit ourselves to promoting our history and our traditions while standing and speaking out. This is what I have worked tirelessly throughout my life to achieve as a creator, promoting the rich culture that my ancestors left me and that I have cultivated all this time.

I have shared many beautiful, long, and intimate hours with my ancestors, and now I understand why I have always held them in immeasurable esteem. My Métis ancestors were brave, resourceful people. They helped to make our Canadian and Québécois societies what they are today.

My grandfather would probably have liked me to become a renowned hunter. Instead, I became a writer. My work is autobiographical and is inspired by my experience. I am no less Métis because of it. I am part and parcel of an unbroken ethnohistorical continuity. I take pride in being from the Métis Nation of the Gatineau Valley.

My belonging to the Bois-Brûlé people is a badge of honour and nobility.

*Michel Noël, Métis of the Gatineau Valley and Homme de Plume*

# A Note for Readers

MANY TERMS USED IN this book have fallen into disuse or now have pejorative connotations. We have nonetheless used the terms found in the primary documents in order to give readers a fuller understanding of the phenomenon of historical Métis identity. The following terms appear: Indian, *Sauvage/Sauvagesse*, Half-breed, mixed-blood, white, and Canadien (for French Canadian). This terminology was widely in use in the nineteenth century, including in communications authored by First Nations, Inuit, and Métis people themselves, as well as in the correspondence of colonial authorities, commercial elites, and clerics.

Also, the term *Outaouais* as used in this text goes beyond the administrative frontiers of the region in Québec that carries this name. To remind readers of this distinction, we occasionally refer to the greater Outaouais. This use of Outaouais encompasses the watershed of the Ottawa River (Rivière des Outaouais), while references to the Gatineau Valley refer to that river's watershed plus that of the Lièvre River. These designations trace the territory occupied and travelled by the inhabitants of a few Métis hamlets in the nineteenth century, a community tied together by a common history and culture.

# Acknowledgments

WE WOULD LIKE TO thank the Métis community of Maniwaki for their support as we penned this account of their history and the lives of their relations: their grandmothers and grandfathers and other ancestors. While striving to be accurate and to meet the highest standards of academia, we always kept in mind that this story belongs to Maniwaki.

We sincerely thank the institutions that provided archival documents essential to the research and writing of this book: the Archives Deschâtelets-NDC in Richelieu, Québec; the Diocese of Pembroke Archives, Ontario; the Archives of Ontario, in Toronto; Library and Archives Canada in Ottawa; the Bibliothèque et Archives nationales du Québec, via archival centres in Gatineau, Québec, Rouyn-Noranda, and Vieux-Montréal; the Genealogical Society of Utah, in Salt Lake City; the Hudson's Bay Company Archives in Winnipeg; the National Archives in Washington, DC; the Société historique de Saint-Boniface in Winnipeg; and the Société d'Histoire du Témiscamingue in Ville-Marie, Québec.

We extend our thanks to Professor Denis Gagnon of Université de Saint-Boniface for granting us access to research compiled for Justice Canada and for the transcriptions of interviews that were provided with the permission of the Métis community of Maniwaki. We also thank Youri Morin, Stéphane Jobin, and Claude Hubert for sharing diverse information, including genealogical data and photographs.

We thank our families and friends for their patience and support, especially our children, whose playtime with us was occasionally disrupted by writing and editing: Sophie and Louis-Philippe Bouchard, Kali and Médérik Malette-Godbout, and Léonie and Clovis Marcotte.

As writing is only one component of publication, we would like to thank the professionals who facilitated and enhanced our work. They include the anonymous peer reviewers and members of the UBC Press publications board, who provided valuable suggestions and support. We also thank Joanne Muzak for her early editorial interventions, as well as the copy editor, Camilla Blakeley, the cover designer, George Kirkpatrick, and others at the Press. Finally, we extend a warm word of thanks to Darcy Cullen, who skilfully guided us through the many steps. We are grateful for her encouragement and expertise. Merci! Meegwetch! Thank you!

We wish to acknowledge the financial support of the Social Sciences and Humanities Research Council of Canada and the Fonds de recherche québécois – Société et culture, whose funding facilitated the research, writing, and dissemination of research results, as well as the University of Northern British Columbia for providing a publishing grant for this book.

# Bois-Brûlés

# Introduction

THE MÉTIS, OFTEN DEPICTED as fierce bison hunters of the plains, are less well known for driving logs down the eastern rivers. Yet in his handbook for travellers to the central regions of the continent, Moses Foster Sweetser (1876, 132) describes a perplexing view from a steamer ship heading down the Ottawa River from Aylmer to Ottawa at the height of the nineteenth-century lumber boom: "Long lines of lumber-booms are found on this reach; and the steamer passes timber-rafts bearing low square sails and numerous huts, and great islands of logs drifting down to the Ottawa saw-mills." Though this description certainly fits into the conventional history of the region, the following sentence hints at a past that jars historical conventions: "These rafts are managed by French Canadians and Indian half-breeds, – hardy, powerful, and semi-civilized men, who still chant the old Norman boatsongs amid these wild forests." The "Indian half-breeds" chanting French (i.e., old Norman) songs would have been Métis.

Sweetser's handbook, published close to a decade before Louis Riel's execution, alludes to the presence of a Métis people in the larger Outaouais region, including in what is now the province of Québec. This nascent community, far from the Red River, was tied to a larger cultural complex that emerged from the fur trade and the battles that had raged between the Hudson's Bay Company (HBC) and the North West Company (NWC), which HBC eventually swallowed up into its trading empire. Historical documents highlight that the so-called Half-breeds of this region shared a common ethnonym: they were "Bois-Brûlés" (burnt wood), like Métis elsewhere, and they even shared kinship ties to communities far to the west and north. They also looked to Louis Riel as a martyred leader. Riel, in their oral history, had even sought refuge in the valleys of their region.

By all accounts, the Métis formed a historical community that can be traced to the present;[1] our rereading of overlooked archival documents reveals a community hidden in plain sight, a Métis community at the core of French-speaking Canada.

The scions of the fur trade had become raftsmen, and Sweetser is not alone in his description of the men on the massive log vessels. Percy St. John (1867, 254), this time in a work of fiction, describes "the timber men, who being generally Canadians, half-breeds, and Irish of the lowest description, had actually been in the habit of receiving eighteen or twenty dollars a month, besides their keep at the shanty." Though fiction, this description was inspired by the reality of the era, but it also imitated an earlier work. A nearly identical passage appears in *Letters from America,* John Godley's (1844, 115) firsthand account of his travels from Bytown (now Ottawa) to Kingston. In both cases, we see the Half-breed distinguished from the French Canadian, and Half-breeds were numerous enough to catch the attention of the era's writers as they described the timber trade – real and fictive – on the north side of the Ottawa River. Godley applies racial characteristics in distinguishing populations, noting that those in Lower Canada "comprise of course infinite gradations of colour and feature, from the dark copper hue, high cheek-bones, and underlimbed figure of the full-blooded Huron, to the pure white and muscular proportions of the European race" (67–68). In addition to physical features, he notes, "The French Canadians, too, fraternise with them [the Indians] far more than the English race; indeed the extent of the intercourse which exists is proved by the numbers of the half-breeds, almost all of whom speak French and Indian promiscuously" (67). The Métis then in Lower Canada were thus also distinguished in terms of culture, in that they spoke both European (French) and Indigenous languages.

St. John, who had translated the works of Gustave Aimard, would certainly have been influenced by the latter's descriptions of Bois-Brûlés as well. The Métis raftsmen he describes would have been the descendants of earlier generations of fur trade company employees and "freemen" – independent traders or hunters – seeking to make a living through beaver pelt commerce. Though their history is overlooked, like their Métis or Bois-Brûlé kin in Manitoba and on the prairies, Métis from the Outaouais did not disappear. They see themselves as a distinctive people, and this book recounts their untold history, excavating the long disregarded role of the fur trade in the larger Outaouais region before and during the expansion of the forestry industry in the nineteenth century.

This affirmation of a Métis presence raises many hackles in our era. A case in point: at the 2018 Métis Nation General Assembly, the Métis National Council (MNC) adopted the Homeland Map Resolution, explicitly stating that there were no Métis communities east of Rainy Lake in western Ontario, and released a map of the historical homeland of the Métis Nation to that effect. The MNC categorically denied that six historical communities identified by the Métis Nation of Ontario (MNO) were legitimately part of the Métis Nation (Métis National Council 2018). The six communities identified by the MNO as existing outside of the Rainy Lake/Lake of the Woods region (see Map 1) include those on the eastern border of Ontario, notably the Abitibi Inland Historic Métis Community and the Mattawa/Ottawa River Historic Métis Community, both in the region bordering our area of study (Métis Nation of Ontario 2017). Citing the 2002 definition of citizenship, the MNC placed the MNO on probation for failing to remove these other Métis groups from their membership list. The decision conformed to ideas set out by Chris Andersen (2014), as the policy forum at the assembly reviewed "the rise and proliferation of groups in eastern Canada who are falsely claiming Métis rights, misappropriating the symbols of the Métis Nation, encouraging tax fraud and using their claims to Métis identity to attack legitimate rights-holding Indigenous nations including the Mi'kmaq of Atlantic Canada and the Innu in Quebec" (Métis National Council 2018). Darryl Leroux was invited to speak and "briefed the policy forum on the evolution of these groups, some of which are rooted in the white rights, white nationalist movement" (Métis National Council 2018).

The Métis of Maniwaki find themselves in the same position as these derided communities of eastern Ontario. Not only the MNC but also the provincial and federal governments refuse to acknowledge the existence of any Métis community in Québec. It is thus up to legislators, and the courts as cases are litigated, to weigh the evidence and decide whether communities such as Maniwaki meet the criteria set out by the Supreme Court – the *Powley* test – to qualify legally as right-bearing historical Métis communities in this province. To do so, a community must have existed both before and after the effective integration of the territory under state control. This work seeks to provide the evidence needed to properly evaluate the history of the Maniwaki community, in the hope that facts will

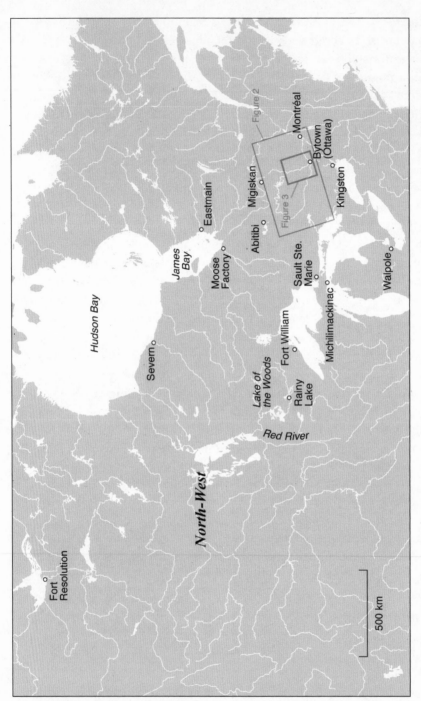

*Map 1* Key fur trade locales mentioned in this book. Note that the fur trade posts shown here did not necessarily exist concurrently. The large rectangle represents the greater Outaouais region (see Map 2), while the rectangle within it shows the regional community that is studied in finer detail in this text (see Map 3).

prevail over innuendo. It is part of a much larger research project to develop a better understanding of the continental Métis, a rhizomatic network of interconnected communities united by a shared fur trade economy and culture (Foxcurran, Bouchard, and Malette 2016). When we were approached by the community of Maniwaki we were happy to share research documenting the history of their region as part of the larger continental diaspora. Métis need not form one homogeneous nation but can instead comprise a continuum of distinct peoples, with overlapping histories and destinies. Community leaders were happy that we heeded their call. Not only are governments disinclined to accept the existence of any past and present community but, as we shall explore, scholars and activists alike have offered vocal resistance to the proposition. As geographer Étienne Rivard (2017, 2) phrases it,

> The situation of the Métis in Quebec is a highly sensitive matter. For some
> – politicians, scholars or mere citizens – calling the Métis in Quebec an
> Aboriginal people is heresy. Despite the fact that the only Francophone
> province in Canada is one of the regions of North America where the *métissage*
> of the French and Aboriginal populations goes back furthest, the Quebec
> Métis, unlike those of Western Canada, have never had the right to a chapter
> in the national historic grand narrative. Thus, contemporary Métis are, from
> a strictly demographic perspective, marginal to say the least.

From an ideological standpoint, the suggestion that there are Métis in Québec is thus often met with accusations of cultural appropriation, opportunism, and even identity fraud. Despite this charged context, we believe it is necessary to examine the evidence to establish whether there was truly a community identified as Métis, or its equivalent designation of Bois-Brûlé.

A careful review of the historical record – reams of HBC records, letters, Oblate archives, and reports – demonstrates that there was a Métis population in the Gatineau River region, and that this population was distinctly identified as such by the Algonquins who resided at Maniwaki, as well as by various priests, colonial officials, military officers and, after Confederation, government officials. Though the Outaouais is remembered for its white pines – and the forestry industry that thrived for decades in the valleys of the Ottawa and Gatineau rivers and their tributaries – the region was also a major artery for the fur trade dating back to the French regime. The Ottawa River led to a network of rivers that opened up the Great Lakes and points farther west. Even after the HBC eliminated its competition, the NWC, following a merger negotiated in the imperial capital of London, it expanded its claim on the fur trade in this region. It established a number of forts and sought to squeeze out free traders, many of whom had grown up in the shadow of the fur posts. Much like their distant kin farther west, they had established a culture that integrated Indigenous and European markers, often marrying Indigenous women and having Indigenous heritage themselves. The same structural forces and processes that had encouraged the emergence of a Métis community at Red River and other points west had promoted a Métis ethnogenesis in the Outaouais, but it did not happen in a vacuum. The historical evidence underlines how the Bois-Brûlés of the larger Outaouais region were related to families in western and even far northern communities that are now unequivocally recognized as Métis by both academics and government officials.

Before we turn to that historical record, we must ask how Métis identity is defined and what evidence would substantiate the existence of a historical Métis population in Québec, and more precisely in the Gatineau Valley of western Québec. To paraphrase Chris Andersen (2014), to be Métis is more than simply being biologically mixed; it is a social and cultural phenomenon. But unlike Andersen, we do not reduce Métis identity to large-scale political activity that would prove some kind of national spirit cast in stone, a reified *Geist* by which one could then discriminate against other Métis as nothing more than mere mixed-bloods whose ancestors were not cognizant of belonging to a people with a distinct heritage. Rather, we argue that political experience, solidarity, and mobilization large and small are invariably contingent on forging a shared sense of belonging and identity that may differ from one region to another. Notions of community and identity emerge in specific social and cultural contexts, often tied to larger networks with shared symbols and beliefs, and this occurs without the need to fit them within a larger national framework that necessitates absolute cultural homogeneity. The evidence presented throughout this text demonstrates how individuals and families were identified as Bois-Brûlé, Métis, or its older variant, Métif, and how this community and identity persisted over time.

Given the controversy surrounding our subject, historical documents are front and centre in this analysis. To borrow Gwynneth Jones's wording (n.d., viii), the current work can be read as a study of the documentary evidence as opposed to the creation of a "smooth historical narrative" of Métis "in which the sources are buried in supporting roles to the story." This choice is motivated by the need for transparency and objectivity, as the conclusions we draw challenge some pillars of Québécois and Métis historiography. Wandering into the minefield of controversies over the question of the Métis of Québec, this work aims to present information that is relevant to a meaningful conversation on the topic of the Métis in the East. The first part of the text establishes the framework by articulating our theory and positioning our research within the field of Métis studies.

The second part then examines the fur trade in the Outaouais region in the nineteenth century. Though the fur trade was active before then, this century yields plentiful documentary sources – notably, the writings of clerks and other HBC officials – as a network of fur trade posts was established from Fort Coulonge in the south, some 100 kilometres from the contemporary city of Ottawa, to Abitibi in the north. More than 400 kilometres separated these two posts, and it would have required two weeks to travel from one to the other via the waterways. This stretch of terrain covering what is now western Québec is also part of what we define as the greater Outaouais region. As was the case elsewhere, the HBC insisted that company clerks and factors record their daily activities with precision. This has left a rich archive of fort journals, letters, and accounting records, dutifully saved by the company. The correspondence exchanged between employees stationed at forts across the continent, as well as with their superiors, offers researchers a panoply of written sources that describe life in and around the fur trade posts. Thus, mundane bookkeeping records noting the purchase or sale of *ceintures fléchées* (sashes), vermilion, or moccasins by certain Métis families provide insights into the daily lives of individuals and their communal ties. These documents and those left behind by government and church officials highlight a number of Métis identities. We also analyze the use of the term *Bois-Brûlé*, an appellation used across the continent to designate Métis individuals, communities, and populations. Not only was the term being used in the far reaches of the Outaouais but it was also tied to a cohort of cultural markers, implying a shared sense of identity among those who were known as Bois-Brûlés.

Moving deeper within the larger Outaouais region, the third part of the text focuses on the much smaller area of Maniwaki, and in particular on three historical settlements: Rivière Désert (Maniwaki), Lac des Sables, and Lac-Sainte-Marie (Maps 2 and 3). The Maniwaki region attracted a number of retired voyageurs, Métis, and other freemen who became quite active in petty trade and contraband. To make our case more salient, we compare historical descriptions of the communities of Sault Ste. Marie in Ontario and Lac-Sainte-Marie in the Gatineau Valley of Québec and then analyze an account based on oral testimony about Louis Riel being given refuge in the Gatineau while in exile. The documentary and oral history of the region complement one another, in that both attest to the existence of a community with a comparable culture to that of other Métis communities, and even with familial ties. Riel's sojourn in the Outaouais region demonstrates how he became a central figure in the historical lore of families that still identify themselves as Métis today.

The fourth part of the text reviews evidence of the cultural and historical continuity of the Métis population in the Outaouais region. This section includes an examination of the role that Métis played in forestry from 1843 to 1873, during a period of growing demand for labour in that industry. We also analyze the creation of the Maniwaki Reserve in 1853, a crucial moment in a history fraught with conflict, to document the challenges faced by the Métis community and the pressure to conform to either white or Indian identity. We uncover intriguing and enlightening historical artifacts, overlooked in historical accounts: namely, three petitions suggesting the existence of a Métis community, the Bois-Brûlés, that saw itself sometimes as neither white nor Indian, sometimes as both simultaneously. We also trace the community to the contemporary period, examining how community members have fought for recognition of their identity and to have their rights recognized.

*Part 1*
# Theoretical and Methodological Considerations

# 1

## *Studying Métis Identities*

LIFE IS LIVED LOCALLY, in both the bright lights and the shadows of neighbourhoods, villages, and counties, where family secrets are known by all but publicly acknowledged by few. There may be no need to record the known while whispered memories still linger across generations. But such secrets become problematic when accounts must be disclosed to state institutions, bureaucracies, and legal systems that require written documentation to prove the existence of the known. Unfamiliar with lives lived in distant locales, and lacking knowledge acquired over generations, outsiders often doubt the veracity of accounts that do not conform to what they know and expect. Such is the dilemma faced by the community of Maniwaki in western Québec. For generations, many of its families have known who they are – Métis. They knew of their fur trade past, as quite often their grandparents had traplines and neighbours whispered that they were a bit too "Sauvage" to conform fully to the settler ideal, whether "Canayen" (as "Canadien" was typically pronounced) or "English." For decades, they suffered the stigma of a public secret, and holding neither power nor authority, many managed to survive by supplementing paid labour with traditional practices such as hunting, fishing, and gathering. The state cared little about these cottage industries so long as they did not interfere with logging and other industries that were central to the economy. Even publicly stating they were Métis would have advantaged community members very little or not at all, as Métis were not recognized by either the province of Québec or the federal government. Keep in mind that only status Indians had recognized rights under the Indian Act. Thus, the Métis of Maniwaki and surrounding communities simply lacked official recognition.

In the late 1960s, as the world witnessed decolonization and the Canadian state wrestled with its past and the rights of its citizens – notably debating issues of bilingualism and Indigenous rights – communities mobilized. In Québec, French Canadians had become Québécois and were challenging the vestiges of colonialism and inequality. In parallel, Métis of the Outaouais joined forces with non-status Indians to press their concerns, forming provincial and local organizations to lobby for recognition and rights. The efforts of communities and associations across the country led to the inclusion of Métis as Aboriginal people in the Constitution Act of 1982, along with First Nations and Inuit. This constitutional victory did little to help Métis communities such as those in the Outaouais, which remained poor and marginalized. Though Métis had been included in the Canadian Constitution, neither Métis people nor Métis rights had been truly defined. At that time, the provinces and the federal government had little interest in recognizing the existence of Métis outside the Prairie provinces. In 1983, the Métis National Council was formed, later coming to lobby for recognition of descendants of the Métis communities of the Red River region in Manitoba as the only true Métis. Facing this resistance, communities often had to turn to the courts to define who could be Métis and what rights, if any, they had, notably harvesting rights. This came at great financial cost.

One successful court case, *R. v. Powley*, did lead to the recognition of a historical Métis community in Sault Ste. Marie in Ontario, though certainly at no small price.[1] This is the challenge faced even by legitimate communities: the state can afford to pay legal teams and researchers when making their case, while communities simply cannot match the state's resources. This is true of Maniwaki. When we were approached to undertake a study, the only data the community had found that was suitable for court scrutiny consisted of a few historical fragments. For example, a report written by the Oblates of Mary Immaculate in the 1840s notes that alongside a chapel at Lac-Sainte-Marie, built under the supervision of Father Joseph Desautels, lived sixteen families comprising French Canadians, Métis, and *Sauvages*. Though striking, the information was insufficient for a paragraph, let alone a book. Fortunately, we had already been actively researching Métis across the continent and had accumulated considerable material. As the community lacked the means or government support to finance a large research project, we decided to share our ongoing research at almost no cost, believing that every Indigenous community should have a fair access to information and to justice. Michel Bouchard and Sébastien Malette (Foxcurran, Bouchard, and Malette 2016) had published *Songs upon the Rivers*, which demonstrated that much Métis history was buried south of the forty-ninth parallel. Guillaume Marcotte had spent a decade studying Hudson's Bay Company archival documents for work on the fur trade of western Québec. This book weaves together years of collective research and disciplinary expertise in anthropology, history, and law. Though inspired by theories of ethnonationalism and by Gilles Deleuze and Félix Guattari's (1987) work – which provides a rhizomatic framework for understanding a Métis identity that is diasporic rather than rigidly located – it was nonetheless inductive research, the accumulation of evidence to illustrate the existence of a Métis community in one part of Québec.

## Defining the Research Problem

Though local communities were certainly aware of their families' histories, this book ventures into new academic territory, as little research has been published on the history of the Bois-Brûlés, or Métis (or Métif) of the Gatineau Valley and how it fits into a larger regional and continental history. We began this project by generating a number of questions to guide our research.

The research first necessitated an analysis to identify any families with Métis origins: with both European and Indigenous heritage. Then, it was essential to see whether shared accounts had similarities. Were there markers of socialization and an emerging identity and culture in the historical context of the fur trade? It was also necessary to pinpoint any designations of community and identity, either used by individuals to describe themselves or applied by others. Potential ethnonyms indicating the mixed ancestry of individuals would include, among others, terms such as *Métis, Métif, Bois-Brûlé, Half-breed, Half-Savage.* The term *Half-breed* was used throughout the nineteenth and well into the twentieth century to designate those who today are called Métis. Did individuals use such terms to name themselves, or did others designate individuals of mixed ancestry in this way? If so, what indicators of social structure linked these individuals? Such structures would include kinship ties, occupational networks, and ties to the trading posts and religious missions.

Likewise, it was necessary to examine residence patterns. Were there any indicators of community settlement in specific regions or around forts and missions? Given that individuals and families would have lived in the region before the arrival of state surveyors, what documentary evidence of petitions or other forms of collective action conducted by the Métis ight exist? The final interrogation concerned the existence of a shared culture. Were there distinctive cultural traits pertaining to material culture – the building of canoes, the fabricating of moccasins and other material goods – or symbolic and religious culture, or preferences when it came to lodging and occupation? Simply put, our goal was to determine if there was evidence that a distinctive Métis community existed, and if it existed, whether evidence showed continuity with contemporary individuals and families.

Our research questions are thus both historical and anthropological, as they involve the study of cultures and communities, past and present. To ensure the robustness of our analysis, our work builds on research undertaken in ethnological reports on Métis in Ontario, including the *Review of Reports and Cartographic Representation Pertaining to Historic Métis in Ontario* (Reimer and Chartrand 2002), which uses seven criteria to establish whether there was a historical Métis community in Ontario. To these seven, we add an additional one pertaining to the use of ethnonyms tied to Métis identity (see Table 1). This last criterion was deemed necessary to add greater precision to the analysis. Ultimately, the goal was to determine whether there is a historical Métis population in western Québec, and more specifically one centred in the vicinity of Maniwaki.

## Community and Culture

Community and culture are slippery concepts, their contours ever changing. In the case of Métis, definitions of culture and community are tied to political and legal struggles as some individuals and communities seek to have their rights recognized by governments and courts. Since 1982, Métis have been one of the three Indigenous peoples recognized by the Constitution of Canada in generic terms. The inclusion of Métis in section 35 of the Constitution Act led to the famous court case *R. v. Powley,* the first victory in Canada when it comes to the recognition of these constitutionalized rights. The *Powley* ruling did not, however, offer a definitive definition on the concept of community. In line with precedents from Aboriginal jurisprudence pertaining to section 35 rights, it nevertheless insisted on the collective foundation of Aboriginal rights and their source in cultural practices. In other words, Métis defendants have the burden to demonstrate that their constitutional rights are fully anchored in historical Métis communities with a distinctive culture, determined by being neither Euro-Canadian nor First Nations (or Indian).

*Table 1*  Criteria for the Study of a Métis Ethnic Community

| Criteria | Explication and Examples |
|---|---|
| 1 Mention of mixed origins, Indigenous ancestor necessary but not sufficient on its own | Exogamous and endogamous relations during the fur trade and/or Métis cultural context |
| 2 Shared experiences as individuals | Bicultural parentage, cultural intermediary between Europeans and First Nations, socialization in the historical context of the fur trade |
| 3 Cultural recognition | By others (alter-descriptive): description of a "distinctive" individual identity (he/she is Métis/Half-breed), identity type, or collective identity (they, the Métis/Half-breeds) By Métis (auto-descriptive): use of a "distinctive" self-referent (I am Métis/Half-breed) or one that is "distinctive" and "collective" (we are Métis/Half-breeds). |
| 4 Social structure(s) such as kinship | Social and cultural organizations tied to the fur trade, trade outposts, missions, kinship ties, etc. |
| 5 Political and ideological elements | Petition(s), negotiation(s) for different causes, claims of rights, political organization(s), historical expressions of such demands |
| 6 Geographic elements, including proximity | The fur trade was marked by great mobility for the Métis but historical observers noted the existence of communities/missions, which included Métis residents, next to trade posts. |
| 7 Cultural elements, including material culture, language, music, celebrations | Voyageur clothing, ornaments, artistic traditions drawing from both European and First Nations, moccasins, wooden cabins, religion, the sash *(ceinture fléchée)*, violin, etc. |
| 8 Métis ethnonyms | Use of terms including, but not limited to, Bois-Brûlé, Métis, Métif, Half-breed, sang-mêlé, mixed-blood. |

In addition to assessing possible extinguishment or justified infringement of the right claimed, the court asks that Métis implicated in a *Powley* cause demonstrate that their community existed post-contact but prior to the territory coming under the effective control of European laws and customs. This is the cut-off date for the existence of historical Métis communities in Canada. That is to say, the Métis had to exist in a territory prior to the Crown or the state exerting real power over the territory. The state's claim alone is insufficient if it did not have effective control over the territory and the communities within it were independent and self-governing, in effect retaining most of their sovereignty over the land.

One of the challenges posed by scholars who adhere to the thesis of Métis evanescence or assimilation – reached through observation of classical sociological forces and expressions of collective behaviour, such as population density, collective affirmations, and so forth – is that they often share with us the same theoretical suppositions and the same ethnological criteria in defining a Métis community. However, our reading of the historical record differs from theirs in the definition and application of the concepts of *distinct* versus *distinctive* in relation to elements attributed to the historical Métis. To succinctly define the difference between these two concepts, we call upon the *Van der Peet* (1996) decision of the Supreme Court of Canada. To establish an Aboriginal right under section 35 of the Constitution Act, 1982, the court ruled that a practice, custom, or tradition in question must be distinctive but not necessarily distinct:

> To be an aboriginal right an activity must be an element of a practice, custom or tradition integral to the distinctive culture of the aboriginal group claiming the right. A number of factors must be considered in applying the "integral to a distinctive culture" test. The court must take into account the perspective of the aboriginal peoples, but that perspective must be framed in terms cognizable to the Canadian legal and constitutional structure ... A practice, custom or tradition, to be recognized as an aboriginal right need not be distinct, meaning "unique," to the aboriginal culture in question. The aboriginal claimants must simply demonstrate that the custom or tradition is a defining characteristic of their culture. (R. v. Van der Peet, [1996] 2 S.C.R. 507)

It should therefore be clearly understood that the practices, customs, and traditions we document as best defining the historical presence of Métis cultures and communities do not need to be unique to the Métis; they may also be at the centre of many Indigenous cultures or Canadien culture. In other words, our ethnological criteria (see Table 1) highlight *distinctive* cultural elements, which in turn provide us with a better insight into the culture of the Métis people in question: a culture that may not have any distinct markers but rather a cloud of distinctive features that together differentiate between the Euro-Canadian and Amerindian cultures from which the historical Métis community originated (Ray 2011). Indeed, due to the syncretic and cumulative nature of Métis culture, as well as to the diversity of Métis populations across North America, if a strict condition of distinct cultural features were required, almost no historical Métis community would be observable. Indeed, an in-depth and nuanced study of documentary sources shows that historical Métis communities combine practices, traditions, and customs from both Aboriginal and European cultures. Because of their dual parentage and their role as cultural intermediaries between Amerindian and Euro-Canadian societies, Métis individuals borrow from the two "mother" cultures, forging a syncretic culture that makes it difficult, if not impossible, to identify strictly Métis elements.

This subtlety in the analysis of the evidence for a distinctive Métis culture is quite relevant, as is the caution the researcher must use when considering Métis acculturation in a colonial context, in which being tinged with the *Sauvage* was often stigmatizing. As is discussed in the following sections, several factors may lead the researcher to mistakenly believe that a Métis community does not exist, such as when several seemingly contradictory ethnonyms are in use within the community. A Métis population may face state and social structures that actively seek to assimilate them, whether as whites or as Indians. Quite often, demographic shifts favour Euro-Canadian identities and Métis populations may be pressured to conform to broader society. These shifts and pressures can be exacerbated when the Indigenous ancestor is genealogically remote and few endogamous marriages exist within the family. It can be quite easy for researchers to misguidedly seek cultural traits that are distinct or unique to the Métis alone, as opposed to a distinctive culture comprising a new combination of traits drawn from a number of cultures.

Thus, to identify a historical community and its continuation over time, it is necessary to take into account fluidity of identity, the occasional need to identify with another identity, and thus truly to understand the historical complexity that shapes the actions of individuals and the contours of communities. To seek a strictly defined, unchanging, homogeneous historical identity that clearly does not and could not exist would be setting a standard that few cultures or communities could attain. Indeed, the ability of individuals and families to shift identities and social ties in a pragmatic fashion is a remarkable feature of the historical Métis community, permitting it to persist in spite of the movement of individuals in and out of identities over time.

Legal considerations surely add to the challenge of defining community for Métis who assert Aboriginal rights. For the purpose of this book, however, the notion of community will be analyzed purely from an anthropological and social science perspective. The intent is *not* to evaluate whether the current Métis community in the Outaouais has legal standing as a historical Métis community in conformity with the *Powley* test discussed above. That being said, we assert that there is a historical regional community in the vicinities of Maniwaki, but, we insist, this conclusion is based on ethnographic standards, not legal precepts. We leave such qualifications to the proper judicial authorities.

The analysis of community from a strictly social and cultural perspective is complex in its own right, in that one must develop theoretical and methodological tools to meet the challenge of identifying, for example, if a community has a multi-ethnic or a homogeneous composition. These considerations can be added to the complexity associated with the notion of a community already present in the academic literature. By the mid-twentieth century, George Hillery (1955) had gathered at least ninety-four different definitions of community. A contentious and lasting debate within the social sciences is whether a community must have a precise geographical locale to be so defined, or can exist across dispersed locations (as in the case of a diaspora), and thus whether the concept of community is necessarily fixed in geography or in social interaction. If the latter is the case, are those interactions tied to larger political expressions of social solidarity, or can they be grounded in the most mundane vicissitudes of daily life? Nonetheless, a community can be understood as a social entity that can exist with different forms of attachment, including the sentiment of belonging tied to past or the vision of a shared destiny, shared values and beliefs, and/or familial or ancestral relations that are prized by its members. A community is a collectivity that shares a commonly defined space and/or geographic locale (neighbourhood, city, coastal zone, etc.), and/or commonly held traits or characteristics, and/or a sense of belonging leading to a shared identity, for example within an ethnic, religious, or professional community (Azarya 2003). A community is thus not necessarily tied to geographic proximity (Azarya 2003; Calhoun 2002). This is particularly relevant to Métis, as their ethnogenesis is historically tied to the inherent mobility of the fur trade, whereby employees or freemen had to travel great distances through a network of trading forts and posts over the course of a year and over their careers.

In the field of Métis studies, at least three different types of community have been described. The village settlement is characterized by a concentration of individuals and families living together in close proximity, such as around a fort or trading post. The regional community comprises a more dispersed population that shares familial, professional, or cultural allegiances. Finally, the national community is often understood as highly politicized, with the goal of establishing political institutions. The national category of community with respect to Métis is currently subject to acrimonious debates as there is no consensual definition of the Métis Nation. As Gerhard Ens and Joe Sawchuk (2016, 380–82) and the Royal Commission on Aboriginal Peoples (RCAP 1996, 189–90) highlight, there is no agreement on the territorial delimitations, unity, and/or exclusive use of Métis identity. In fact, Ens and Sawchuk suggest that a nationalist definition of Métis community emerged only in the 1930s, with a consequent recent shift from *racial* to *ethnonational* conceptions of identity (Ens and Sawchuk 2016, 13). That, in turn, led to a much more politicized ethnonational discourse, which is now tied to groups in western Canada that claim exclusive right to the Métis ethnonym, especially since the inclusion of Métis among the Aboriginal peoples specified in the Constitution Act of 1982. With that development, resources and institutional privileges flowed to organizations that lobbied and are now increasingly accepted by government ministries as official representatives of the Métis Nation. Yet a growing number of cases clearly demonstrate the emergence of Métis communities that were not tied to grand national political circumstances. Among them are the communities of Sault Ste. Marie (Ray 1998), the Labrador region (Kennedy 2014), and Great Slave Lake (Jones, n.d.). The peril is that formal recognition of only one real cultural entity within the "Métis Nation" may threaten recognition of the diversity of Métis communities and histories across Canada, and of their willingness to conduct their own political affairs and negotiations.

The concept of culture, equally central to issues surrounding Métis identity, also has multiple and varied definitions. Here again, we concentrate on debates within the social sciences, leaving aside the judicial treatment and definitions of Indigenous culture, which have already been criticized for reductionist and static tendencies (Grammond 2013, 9–10). Social science debate focuses largely on what should be included or excluded as properties and characteristics of culture (D'Andrade 2003). Kroeber and Kluckhohn inventoried more than a hundred definitions of culture in the 1950s (Kroeber and Kluckhohn 1952). Included among them is E.B. Tylor's classic definition of culture as "that complex whole which includes knowledge, belief, art, morals, law, custom, and any other capabilities and habits acquired by man as a member of society" (Tylor 1871, 1). Tylor's model implied a universalist and comparative lens through which to study culture. It was tinged with an evolutionary assumption whereby cultures continually progress toward civilization and can thus be placed on a continuum. Such understanding was criticized as ethnocentric, including by Kroeber and Kluckhohn's mentor, Franz Boas (1911). Later generations of anthropologists have developed more nuanced interpretations of culture that are not tied to the ideas of progress and evolution.

The universalist approach to the study of culture was ultimately succeeded by a new methodological relativism, notably in the work of Clifford Geertz (1973) and Parsons and Mayhew (1982). Their work centres on thick description, the goal of which is to produce in-depth ethnographic accounts that privilege singular cultural expressions, not in order to produce a cultural typography but to compare synchronic cultural tableaux in which all cultures are inherently valuable (Kuper 1999; Stocking [1968] 1982, 195–233). Such research attempts to avoid the evolutionary determinism of Tylor, seeing each culture as rooted in its own cultural and linguistic categories, which in turn shape the behaviours and actions of individuals in the collective who, through traditions and customs, reproduce its essence or inherent characteristics (Descola 2005, 111–12). Though critical of the evolutionary model, Geertz (1973) and Parsons and Mayhew (1982) still essentially search for what is invariable and consistent. Indeed, they seek to define the contours of complex and diverse cultures, which are seen as sufficiently autonomous one from the other. Although subject to possible criticisms (including the danger of reification and excessive rigidity attached to any universal definition), such considerations are particularly relevant to the ethnographic identification of a historical Métis culture.

We argue that it is necessary to find a balance between atomistic models of culture that catalogue its smallest constituent parts and models that postulate absolute fluidity, in which the lack of identifiable cultural contours makes the conceptualization of any culture nearly impossible. A balanced approach to studying culture can certainly incorporate a number of elements from Tylor's model while also putting forward a methodology that permits a comparative framework. Thus, it is possible to assemble a list of cultural markers that point to the existence of a Métis community without reifying culture. In marrying an analysis of discrete and identifiable cultural markers and the study of culture as fluid and ever changing, one should also consider the more recent work of Yochai Benkler. Benkler (2006, 283) suggests that culture should be understood as founded in the experience of being the "Other," with identity defined as relational and evolving and thus without an inherent and fixed essence. Benkler's work echoes the older, groundbreaking work of Fredrik Barth (1969, 15), who argues that it is the "ethnic boundary that defines the group, not the cultural stuff that it encloses." In other words, culture is not the final product. Rather, it is always contingent on multiple dynamic and symbolic interactions and negotiations that allow – most significantly in the case of historical Métis across the continent –' a series of local acculturations that led to a process of historical cultural syncretization. Our challenge is therefore to generate an understanding of culture and community that strikes a reasonable balance between what has been derided as the shopping-list approach and the other extreme, which leaves culture as a nebulous entity impossible to circumscribe, let alone define. Thus, the goal is to provide a means to recognize the existence of a distinct Métis culture via a number of culturally *distinctive* practices and customs, while avoiding the traps of essentialism, purity myths, teleology, Eurocentrism, and overly fluid and ambiguous definitions that would impede our understanding of communities past and present.

In our account of Métis in the larger Outaouais region, we analyze the object of a Métis culture both historically and comparatively, considering the dynamic nature of culture that counters the essentialist models of Métis community highlighted above. In search of that balance, we understand the emergence of a Métis community as a process of cultural syncretism in a specific sociohistorical context, that of colonization tied to resource extraction, notably furs and forests. This process implicates societies that originated in Europe and implanted themselves on Indigenous lands. Our analysis is therefore in line with academic literature that locates the emergence of different historical mixed communities of European and Indigenous heritage when the fur trade was the principal occupational niche (Ens and Sawchuk 2016, 65–66). In other words, the fur trade provided the ethnocultural matrix for different mixed populations that were highly mobile and were of great utility within these commercial networks (Ray 2005, 21; Thorne 1996, 64–68). It is thus possible to identify a series of ethnocultural markers for the communities of mixed heritage that emerged in this specific context, all the while knowing that any identity relation remains in constant flux. As Tanis C. Thorne reminds us (1996, 250–51), this fluidity is particularly salient when it comes to Indigenous and so-called mixed-blood historical communities:

> Ethnic identity, in both the past and our own day, has less to do with genetic or cultural "purity" than with the complex interplay among a number of variables, such as individual choices, language, community and kinship ties, residency patterns, customary practices of reckoning descent, and fluctuating historical forces that periodically separate or bond people together for survival. Far from being static or homogenous, native communities and kin networks have continuously engaged in the dynamic process of forming and redefining themselves as "new" peoples.

This is certainly true when examining a French-speaking community in western Québec that defines itself as Métis, as it is necessary to be attuned to subtle ethnocultural markers and familiar with the culture in order to ascertain the contours of this potential community.

### The Contested Eastern Métis

As mentioned, the possibility that a historical Métis community could exist in Québec has many detractors. The main argument against such a possibility hinges on the notion that the only true Métis people are the Red River Métis, as all others lack the cultural and social cohesion, as well as a national consciousness in their past, to call themselves Métis with a capital "M". They are perhaps "mixed" according to this reasoning, but can never be truly Métis. Adam Gaudry and Darryl Leroux (2017, 118) articulate this idea as they argue why only some descendants of Europeans and Indigenous peoples qualify as Métis, quoting Chris Andersen's article "From Nation to Population: The Racialisation of 'Métis' in the Canadian Census":

> Red River Métis collectively created, borrowed and combined elements to form a distinctive culture and lifestyle separate from both their Euro-Canadian and First Nations neighbours, including a new language, form of land tenure, laws, a distinctive form of dress, music, a national flag and, in 1869–70,

distinctive political institutions. Indeed, by Canada's formal establishment in 1867 the Métis constituted an indigenous nation of nearly 10,000 people possessing a history, culture, imagined territorial boundaries, national anthem and, perhaps most importantly, a sense of self-consciousness as Métis. (Andersen 2008, 350)

We concur that being Métis is more than a simple question of being mixed, and having a distinctive culture is certainly a crucial element of any historical community. But our goal here is to determine if there is any evidence for both a distinctive culture *and* a sense of self-awareness. That is not an easy task, as not all communities are fortunate enough to have a literate leader such as Louis Riel, who produced a prolific quantity of material in his lifetime that attests to his Métis identity. However, we suggest that it is necessary to judge history based on the evidence, not necessarily on contemporary national narratives (or history re-imagined through the prism of nationalist narratives). Historical evidence may give nuance to what such narratives take as indisputable truths. For instance, due to the overwhelming numbers of Métis with Canadien parentage, evidence shows that the predominant language of Métis across the continent was in fact French, or to be precise a popular form of French derived from the language of the voyageurs, a *lingua franca* spoken also in the Red River region. Because a majority of Métis had mothers from different First Nations, it was not uncommon for individuals to speak many languages, making the assertion that Michif was the single national language for Métis across the North-West Territories quite problematic. Likewise, the land tenure system of long river lots found in the St. Lawrence and as far away as the Oregon Country was evidently not unique to Red River Métis. Thus, it is necessary to examine historical assumptions critically, based on the written evidence. The existence or non-existence of a historical Métis community should not be denied a priori based on theoretical assumptions, particularly theories of nation and nationhood.

Although the cultural markers that Andersen lists are now understood as Métis, it is very unlikely that these same markers of identity would have existed in 1885 or 1870, let alone in 1815. As Ens and Sawchuk (2016) discuss in detail, the symbols of Métis identity have changed over the decades, even within the Red River region. They highlight that the Métis infinity flag was chosen in the late twentieth century by the Red River leadership to represent the Métis Nation. Notably, "the Métis leadership of the later twentieth century eschewed the flags Riel had used in 1869–1870 (featuring a fleur-de-lys and a shamrock) and at Batoche in 1885 (featuring the Holy Virgin). Instead they chose the flag given to the Métis by the NWC in 1815" (Ens and Sawchuk 2016, 83). They affirm that from 1816 to the twentieth century this flag was nowhere to be seen. As for the Métis national anthem, "Chanson de la Grenouillère," they note that it too was a "product of North West Company propaganda" (87) as the song, composed by Pierre Falcon shortly after the Battle of Seven Oaks, or la Grenouillère, was rushed to Fort William by the NWC to ensure that it arrived before news of the battle made it to Canada. The song caught on more than the flag and was sung well into the 1870s.

Pierre Falcon's epic song was popular beyond the Red River and far eastward. One of the oldest recordings of it, on a wax cylinder in 1916, comes from Québec's North Shore at Tadoussac, where the Saguenay River flows into the St. Lawrence. Here, Marius Barbeau (1942) recorded Edward Hovington, an eighty-nine-year-old former HBC employee, performing the song. Like the men employed by the HBC, songs travelled widely. Given his advanced age, Hovington no doubt learned the anthem in the distant North-West in the second half of the nineteenth century. Barbeau met Hovington while collecting the folklore of Québec's North Shore. As well as Falcon's "Grenouillère," which he titled "Les Bois-Brûlés," Barbeau (1942, 18–19) recorded other songs that would have been central to the Métis, including "Le 6 de mai" and "Épouser le voyage," which he describes as "chansons du voyageur." Annette Chrétien (2005, 132) explains that Barbeau "corrected" the song lyrics to a standardized French using François-Alexandre-Hubert LaRue's (1863) older published text (which we analyze in Chapter 3), noting that the wax cylinder recording is sung in Michif-French. In the stanza that Chrétien (2005, 132) refers to, the Michif-French is not the bilingual mixed Michif language but a French vernacular that is still quite close to the French spoken elsewhere on the continent. As Robert Papen (1984, 136–37) notes, unlike the bilingual mixed Michif language, Michif-French features few words borrowed from Cree.

Chrétien also addresses the question of language in her research on Métis music. She confronts what she describes as two myths: that there is an authentic Métis or real Red River style; and that "Métis sound traditions, especially those involving the mixture of languages, are largely dying or already extinct" (Chrétien 2005, 107). Papen (2009), who has conducted extensive linguistic research on the Michif language, highlights that the bilingual mixed language of French and Cree was spoken by only a minority of Métis and even only a minority of Red River Métis, and even these mixed bilingual speakers of Michif would have invariably spoken French as well as Cree. He highlights that using the bilingual mixed Michif language was a political choice, not necessarily founded on nineteenth-century linguistic reality but politically determined, much like the choice of flag to represent the Métis Nation. It is not surprising, then, that existing Métis songs are invariably in French, even in the heartland of the Red River district. Confirming this point, Chrétien (2005, 119, 120) notes that in Turtle Mountain in North Dakota, community members were invited in the early 1990s to sing traditional songs, including a number of French songs sung by both Elders and children in Michif-French. If one were to take use of the bilingual mixed Michif language (as opposed to Michif-French) as a criterion for membership in the Métis Nation, it would exclude not only nineteenth-century Métis born in "Indian Country" (who spoke English and Cree) but also most Red River Métis, whose ancestors would have spoken either Canadien or Michif-French.[2] In general, Métis spoke numerous languages, which was one of their most remarkable cultural characteristics (Bakker, 1997).

Having reviewed the history of the symbols that represent the contemporary Métis Nation, Ens and Sawchuk (2016, 507) note that they serve the present, although they do not suggest that these traditions are inauthentic or invented: "This analysis of Métis political representations of the past has not been to suggest that they are distortions of a 'real' past, but to emphasize that the Métis, like all ethnic groups and nations, are always reinterpreting (or 'inventing') the past in the interests of the present, and that there is no primordial nation or identity." We concur, adding a cautionary note that scholars should not use arbitrary markers of nationhood, selected in the late twentieth century to affirm a primordial nation, when they attempt to determine if any past or present Métis community is real. The political representations of the past selected by a particular political elite may not be a faithful representation, and they may exclude some who would be legitimately Métis were other criteria selected to represent the nation.

Despite compelling historical evidence testifying to the existence of Métis communities outside the Red River district, Gaudry and Leroux (2017) keep affirming that only the Red River Métis can be truly Métis.

They criticize the very idea that Métis could value their dual heritage in ways other than adopting a strict nationalist identity founded on fixed territorial boundaries and forged by large-scale political mobilization. Citing Andersen once again, they put forward a definition of Métis identity that seeks to mute alternative explanations:

> Andersen makes the case for an understanding of the Métis as an Indigenous people in the same sense as the Anishinaabe, the Plains Cree, the Mi'kmaq, or the Sylix. In this way it is not mixedness that defines Métis people but rather their Métisness – belonging to a particular Indigenous social and political formation called the Métis Nation from what is now primarily called Western Canada. (2017, 118–19)

In this framework, no other community, historical or contemporary, could ever be Métis, as to be Métis is circularly defined as being of the Métis Nation, understood through a structuring of definitions of identity to emphasize symbols put forward as exclusive and universal to the nation, a "monological grammar," positing retroactively a linguistic and territorial unity to justify the contours of a contemporary nation or ethnic group. Such constrained definitions of Métis identity, we argue, are problematic as they ignore much historical evidence, including from Louis Riel himself, who recognized the existence of Métis in British Columbia and the eastern provinces of Canada (Foxcurran, Bouchard, and Malette 2016; Malette and Marcotte 2017).

Driving the point home, Gaudry and Leroux (2017, 119) refer to the works of Jacqueline Peterson to affirm that no population outside the Prairie provinces could truly be classified as Métis: "In a similar manner, one-time proponent of a broadly placed 'Métis' existence Jacqueline Peterson now argues that only historical communities that understood themselves as Métis should be considered as such by contemporary observers, which for her means Red River as a site of Métis emergence, as opposed to either the Great Lakes or locations further east." They continue, citing Peterson (2012, 27) as she disavows her previous research and denies that self-consciousness of Métis or Bois-Brûlé identity existed prior to the Red River Métis: "Even as the terms Half-breed, métis, and metif [sic] began to appear in fur traders' journals and travelers' accounts after 1800, only along the Red River after 1814–16 did the term Métis come to connote a separate ethnic group – the bois-brûlés [who would become the Métis Nation] – who viewed themselves as a new tribe or nation" (Gaudry and Leroux 2017, 119). Gaudry and Leroux end by affirming, as Peterson does, that even when the term *Métis* is used by non–Red River Métis, it is invariably an outsider ascription as opposed to insiders defining themselves as Métis (119).

Another aspect of the Métis identity debate relates to the term *Métif.* The assertion that it appeared only after the 1800s does not conform to the historical record. By the 1720s, French colonial records were using the term to refer to individuals living in the Pays d'en Haut – the territory of New France covering regions west of Montréal and including most of the Great Lakes area – and resisting the authority of the French governors and officials. Although Métif living in the Great Lakes region often had close relationships with Indigenous people, they represented a distinct social and political force within those communities, as is evident from the description of a Métif trader named Chartier written by the governor, Beauharnois, in 1739:

> They [some Indigenous representatives] replied to me that they were happy and they had noticed that I had spoken of the true Father, that they liked him and they apprehended that no accident would become of them, that they would carry to their village the necklace that I had given them ... and that from their side they were willing to do my will, that there were many among them of the same opinion and they had heard of the one named Chartier, French Métif, who has considerable assets among the English, who was capable of turning a faction, even if he was not a chief among them, as he had a lot of credit, tied to the presents he made either from the English or from himself, to respected chiefs on order to succeed in his enterprises. I let them know that they should not listen to him, to which they seemed to consent, they nonetheless asked me to give my orders to S. [Sieur or Lord] De La Saussaye, to engage him to go down with them the next spring, and that there was reason for them to believe that once I had spoken to him, he would change his mind, I gave my instructions in consequence to S. de La Saussaye and recommended to him to do all that he could to bring Chartier with him.[3]

Note the reference to Métif, and this is not an exceptional case. Clearly, the French were using the term long before they reached the Red River.

In her exhaustive analysis of the French colonial record relating to New France, Devrim Karahasan (2006) notes that Peterson overlooks references to Métis and Métif. She writes, for example, that Father Vivier remarked in 1750, "The inhabitants [of the Pays des Illinois] are of three kinds: French, Black and Savages, without speaking of the Metis who are born of both of the former for ordinary, against the law of God [i.e., illegitimately]." She notes another case dating to 1749, in which an officer speaks of the "sang mêlé" (mixed-blood) when referring to individuals from Michilimackinac, and yet another in 1751 when the French marine officer Bossu encounters a man he refers to as a "sauvage métis," also referred to as a "mi-sauvage" (Karahasan 2006, 188). Building upon Peterson's earlier work, Karahasan (2006, 211) affirms that by 1757 a Métis identity had emerged in the Great Lakes region, shaped by both attachment to indigenous soil and ancestral memory. In other words, Métis had formed distinctive communities.

Clerics also used the ethnonym. In 1738, Father Tartarin describes the mixed population of Kaskaskia as Métif, even labelling children born of Christian marriages as "legitimate Métifs" (Havard 2016, 336). The use of terms such as *Métif* during the French regime calls into question Peterson's later assertion that no true Métis ethnogenesis occurred in the Great Lakes region and the terms came into play only with the rise of the North West Company. It also casts doubt on Gaudry and Leroux's historical assumptions, as they rely on Peterson's later work to uphold the notion of Red River Métis as the only authentic Métis. Here, too, it is necessary to ensure that arguments are substantiated by the historical record, or at the very least not falsified, and that there is no adherence to false explanations because they conform to favoured ideological arguments that fit recent national tropes. It follows that if theories of Métis ethnogenesis are disproved by new evidence, arguments built upon these theories and consequent assumptions must be re-evaluated.

The example of Chartier confirms that some individuals were identified as Métif, distinct from other Canadiens in New France (although identities may sometimes have overlapped). Analysis of the significance of the Métif ethnonym calls for historical nuance. Some Canadiens might have had Indigenous heritage but conformed to social norms and the authority of the governor; others may also have had Indigenous heritage but not been fully incorporated into the social and political structures of the colony. In either case, political behaviour does not necessarily nullify distinct ethnicity for either the inhabitants of New France or their descendants. Chartier was flagged as a troublemaker by the governor of New

France because he was a free trader who used the proceeds of this trade to sway his Indigenous allies to his benefit, not that of the colony. The case of Métis leader Louis Riel, on the other hand, who self-identified as both a French Canadian and a Métis over the course of his life, suggests the possibility of cumulative ethnic identity, whereby an individual will have two or more shared identities that do not negate each other and can be emphasized or downplayed in varied social settings (Flanagan and Campbell 2013, 264).

Clearly, New France was not a homogeneous society. Gaudry and Leroux (2017, 125) refer to the work of demographer Bertrand Desjardins (2008, 72) to demonstrate that the "old stock" Canadien had little Indigenous ancestry:

> Through analyzing the marriage contracts signed during the French Regime, Bertrand Desjardins deduces that French (mostly Norman, West, and Parisian metropolitan) ethnicities made up 97 percent of the overall ethnic composition of the population of New France by 1765 [sic] (the end of the French Regime). By contrast, Acadian ethnicity accounted for 0.6 percent; English was 0.9 percent; other European ethnicities were 1 percent; and Aboriginal was 0.4 percent.

Though this data is accurate overall, it does not account for individuals such as Chartier and others who were important actors in the history of New France yet were not always recorded in official censuses and church records and thus not factored into Desjardins's analysis. Desjardins (2008, 71) draws upon the Registre de la population du Québec ancien, a record of Catholics living in the St. Lawrence Valley in the seventeenth and eighteenth centuries. Given that marriages and births in the families under study occurred in the nineteenth century, beyond the frontier of the St. Lawrence Catholic parishes, the registry is incomplete for our purposes. Métis families from western Québec were not included in the registry, nor were any Métif who lived in the Great Lakes area or points farther west. Gaudry and Leroux's assertions perhaps apply to Canadiens living in the St. Lawrence heartland of New France, whether in towns or inside forts, but not to those living outside the forts and in "Indian Country" in or alongside Indigenous communities. Thus, it is necessary to examine the historical record to understand these nuances and the variation that existed even within pre-1763 New France.

When Métis are exclusively defined as tied to the Red River community, any other Métis can be construed as inauthentic, leading to accusations that their descendants are engaging in cultural appropriation. Or, in the words of Gaudry and Leroux (2017, 125),

> The more one looks at the available "evidence" of historical métissage, the more it seems that the claim is based in the evocative realm of twenty-first-century political expediency. Whether in the form of a decade-old body of research reevaluating French colonial policy or of detailed demographic information provided by digitized written records from the period, seventeenth- and eighteenth-century métissage seems largely fantastical.

This affirmation, however, does not rest on an examination of the historical record but on the statement of a historian who made and then later recanted a powerful argument for the existence of Métis historical communities in the Great Lakes in the late seventeenth and eighteenth centuries (Peterson 1981, 2012). Peterson's new conclusions certainly do not contradict the writings of Chris Andersen – which culminate with his publication of *Métis: Race, Recognition, and the Struggle for Indigenous Peoplehood* in 2014 – and they fall in line with the rhetoric of the Métis National Council.[4] In her doctoral dissertation, however, Peterson (1981) provides a thoughtful and cogent overview of the historical record, developing a well-reasoned argument for Métis ethnogenesis outside the Red River Valley. This laudable work demonstrates how communities emerged from a collective of individuals, such as the French Métif Chartier, before the fur trade reached the Red River. In line with Peterson's doctoral research, our review of the history of western Québec has led us to conclude that a community that identified as Métif and Bois-Brûlés emerged in the Great Lakes region. Although a French fur trade existed in the Outaouais prior to the 1760 Conquest of New France, our examination of the historical record focuses on the emergence of a Bois-Brûlé community in the last decades of the eighteenth century and first decades of the nineteenth.

As stated earlier, the individuals and families in question did not always have a political leader to record their identity and articulate a grand political vision. Researchers must therefore patiently piece together traces of auto-identification both directly (when feasible) and indirectly via the writings of outsiders. As we do so, complex relationships between Métis families across regions are revealed, along with different realities formed by micropolitics and communal schemes that do not necessarily match any grand national political expression, such as is found in the letters of Riel. The historical record attests to multiple and distinct yet intertwined moments of Métis ethnogenesis, through which a cultural identity emerged. This identity was not tied to evolutionary national assumptions or the desire to achieve a predetermined level of political maturity, and it was not contingent on arbitrary levels of blood quantum.[5]

A cultural consciousness can develop and persist based on prior unions with Indigenous kin: a cultural consciousness that under favourable circumstances can become mobilized as a political movement, even a national one. This consciousness can be based on a shared ethnosymbolic world view forged in daily interaction, and with a common set of identitary referents that travelled by canoe and York boat from fort to fort across a continent. As Ens and Sawchuk (2016, 65) affirm,

> Although there are divergences in the process of Métis ethnogenesis in different regions (Great Lakes, Lower Missouri, Northern Plains, and the north) there are common patterns related to the fur-trading economy. Occupational and economic aspects of ethnogenesis have been emphasized not because the cultural or kinship aspects of Métis identity are unimportant, but because it was the fur trade economy that created the social and economic space wherein a distinct culture and identity could develop.

If anything, the regions Ens and Sawchuk enumerate are actually quite constrained, as the evidence presented by Foxcurran, Bouchard, and Malette (2016) highlights. Nonetheless, Ens and Sawchuk (2016) do recognize the existence of Métis ethnogenesis beyond the Red River and contiguous plains. It is in the painstaking analysis of historical documents that one can assemble evidence for both a historical Métis community and a Métis ethnogenesis. We are in effect expanding the territory covered by Ens and Sawchuk to include the nineteenth-century fur trade frontier of western Québec as part of the larger Métis ethnogenesis.

This work thus diverges from that of Gaudry, Leroux, and Andersen in that we do not accept a definition of Métis as tied solely to the Red River and a presumed awakening of Métis nationhood that culminated in the creation of the Métis Nation during the resistance of 1870 and 1885. Rather, we argue for the analysis of culture based on direct and indirect evidence that individuals and families came to see themselves as a Métis, or Bois-Brûlé, collectivity, with a shared distinctive culture. This was also the case in Sault Ste. Marie, which is examined here as well. Clearly, this position counters Gaudry and Leroux's (2017, 126) argument that

> In both Quebec and Mi'kma'ki, the common claim of self-identified Métis is a long-ago mixedness with an Indigenous ancestor. However, this mixedness and its equation with "Métis" identity belie a reduction of this identity to a racial hybridity that results in "Métis" peoples forming wherever European colonists (usually French) may have procreated with Indigenous women. The reduction of Métis to such a bio-historical process is at odds with recent scholarship that situates the emergence of the Métis Nation in a specific time and space well away from large-scale European settlement.

Our research focuses on the early decades of the nineteenth century, which is no more "long-ago mixedness" than either the Red River district or Sault Ste. Marie. We analyzed reams of archival documents to determine if there was any evidence for the emergence of a distinctive culture in a place that was both close to yet distant from large-scale European settlement – distant in that the ethnogenesis proposed occurred in lands still referred to as "Indian Country" by fur trade company employees and colonial officials. We then analyzed later historical records for traces of continuity between a historical community and the contemporary community. The evidence suggests that the community is not merely evoking a Métis identity based on seventeenth-century mixedness with an Indigenous ancestor; rather, a transmitted identity exists, founded on a historical community that had numerous kin ties with multiple Indigenous nations in both the immediate region and more distant locales. Patrick Riel, the soldier from Maniwaki who identified as "Métis" in 1915 during the Great War, and the descendants of Marie-Louise Riel, who did so later in the same region (Roberts 1917, 111), attest to this reality.[6]

Given the bias inherent in the production of documents tied to the fur trade, little information was recorded concerning the Indigenous wives and partners of the fur traders who, with their husbands, founded the Métis families of the Outaouais. Jennifer S.H. Brown's (1980) research focuses on the families of fur trade company officers, literate men who left a written record that mentions their wives. By contrast, the voyageurs and freemen of the Outaouais left little behind that would help us to understand the lives of their mothers, wives, and daughters. The role played by fathers and sons – the employees or competitors of fur trade companies – is described in the correspondence and journals of the fur trade, and their lives and work are consequently better documented in our analysis. The activities of these men directly affected the revenues and profits of the trading companies, and thus are the subject of documents preserved in the archives. In these accounts, women are mentioned in passing at best. Further research to show the crucial role of women, the mothers of the Métis, is an essential academic exercise but one that is beyond the scope of the current project.

## Living Métis Communities

In a 2018 article, Adam Gaudry reiterates the points he made with Leroux and elaborates on the notion of non–Red River Métis identity as a form of appropriation. Here too, Gaudry's work is premised on the assumption that individuals who are not descendants of Red River Métis are not part of a living community grounded in a historical Métis community, as the article title – "Communing with the Dead: The 'New Métis,' Métis Identity Appropriation, and the Displacement of Living Métis Culture" – makes clear. Gaudry (2018, 165) writes,

Anchored almost entirely in amateur genealogical studies and in New Age notions of blood memory and hypodescent, "new Métis" self-identification downplays the need for substantive connections to living communities of Métis people grounded in generations of cultural continuity and political struggle. The result is an attempt by these "new Métis" to define Métis identity almost exclusively through long dormant ancestral connections – the dead – rather than the still-living Métis communities throughout Western Canada and in [diasporic] communities beyond.

In keeping with his earlier article with Leroux, Gaudry here defines the Métis as the prairie Métis Nation, though he allows for a somewhat extended community with a Red River diaspora. Yet again, the assumption undergirding the analysis is that there is no living community outside the Métis Nation. Gaudry (2018, 166) reaffirms this definition: "This identity is grounded in a common culture, common historical experience, and a common sense of self that emerged in the historic 'North-West,' the prairies and parkland in what are now Manitoba, Saskatchewan, and Alberta and whose diaspora put Métis farther afield." Building on this narrow definition, Gaudry then argues that non–Red River Métis are practising "race shifting" if they claim a Métis identity.

Gaudry (2018, 170) borrows the term *race shifting* from Cherokee scholarship: "Cherokee race shifters in the United States have developed nearly identical narratives to 'new Métis' in Canada. According to Circe Sturm, race-shifting Cherokees locate their history in 'a painful ... hidden history,' where their families were forced to publicly disavow their Cherokee identity due to intense racism while supposedly maintaining some unspoken elements of Cherokeeness in private, often coded ways." He explains that in this narrative, self-identification and identity are constructed through "a connection to an oft-distant Indigenous ancestor" (171). Such statements ignore the fact that quite often Métis were indeed persecuted and did have to hide their history. The Métis of Montana, for example, often claimed to be French Canadian to avoid the threat of deportation (Foster 2006). Another example is the testimony of Elder Rose Bortolon, daughter of Alice Cunningham and George Gauthier, whose Métis roots are in Alberta. She notes that she used to identify as French in order to hide her "Halfbreed" heritage (Evans et al. 2007, 205–9). On the other side of the coin, a steady stream of news articles depict descendants of Red River Métis "discovering" this identity and their eligibility for Métis citizenship. Terry Fox's brother, for example, recently embraced his "Indigenous ancestry" (Laskaris 2017). Nonetheless, the notion of race shifting rests on the premise that no living Métis communities exist outside of the Red River Métis and their diaspora.

According to Gaudry (2018, 169), "Such an identity is largely rejected by Métis intellectuals because it lacks a historical basis and it undermines Métis self-determination in matters of citizenship." The intellectuals here, Gaudry indicates in footnotes, are Chris Andersen and Larry Chartrand. Examination of the historical evidence is missing from the analysis. Likewise, Gaudry refers to the Michif language and does not take into account the distinction between Michif, the mixed bilingual language, and Michif-French: "Linguists classify Michif as a language and Acadian French as a dialect. For instance, Peter Bakker describes Michif as a mixed language, not a dialect of either Plains Cree or French or as a pidgin or creole spontaneously pieced together by its speakers" (180–82). Michif-French, spoken in the past by the majority of Métis, both Red River and otherwise, was a dialect of French in the same way that Acadian French was. Gaudry thus relies on a constrained definition of Michif (the language, as opposed to the Michif-French dialect) to discredit the potential existence of Métis in Acadia and elsewhere. With respect to the Métis of western Québec, few if any would have spoken the Michif language, but they would have spoken a Michif-French quite understandable to Métis of the nineteenth-century Red River.

In the early 1980s, Violet Lalonde, one of the descendants discussed in Chapter 8, wrote an unpublished family history in which she recounts how Louis Riel was given refuge in western Québec by her family in the nineteenth century. This account, recorded before the inclusion of the Métis in the Constitution Act of 1982, testifies to the presence of a small "living community" in the Gatineau Valley forty years ago that exhibited continuity with events from some 150 years ago. Clearly, this history cannot be reduced to a mere question of "race shifting," and it is necessary to develop a nuanced and detailed analysis of the historical record to verify the existence of a historical Métis community and the ways in which culture and memory were transmitted over the generations.

## Weaving the Sash of History

To understand the history of the Métis, we need to better understand the contours of the fur trade in North America, and specifically in the northern reaches of the continent, as well as the role the French played in establishing the foundations of this trade. In the sixteenth century the French, having obtained the consent of the Pope to seeks new lands across the Atlantic that were not yet claimed by either the Spanish or the Portuguese Crown, sent Jacques Cartier sailing across the ocean and up the St. Lawrence River. He was seeking gold and other riches, and a route to China. Attempts to establish a colony failed in the 1540s, and the riches Cartier brought back to France proved to be nothing but fool's gold and quartz. With the country riven by religious wars, French interests in overseas colonies would be distracted until the following century, though fishing boats from France would continue making the crossing, bringing back boatloads of cod and some furs traded with the Indigenous people they met while salting their catch on shore.

In 1600, an expedition established a small trading post at Tadoussac, but the first concerted efforts by the French to establish a permanent presence in the continent began with Samuel de Champlain. After a few missteps, he founded the first permanent settlement at Port Royal in

Acadia, now Annapolis Royal in Nova Scotia, and then another at Québec in 1608. Unlike Cartier, he attempted to develop relationships with Indigenous peoples, quickly entering into alliances with the Innu (Montagnais), the Anishinaabe (Algonquins), and later their trading partners the Wendat (Huron). Though efforts were made to establish an agricultural colony, the truly profitable industry was the fur trade. A fashion craze for felt hats made the trade in beaver pelts, which provided the highest-quality felts, a lucrative affair. Champlain and successive governors sought to control the trade, but free traders known as coureurs de bois set out on their own to seek furs. Two free traders, brothers-in-law Pierre-Esprit Radisson and Médard Chouart des Groseilliers, headed deep into the continent and heard tales of a northern salty sea where the beaver were plentiful and of exceptional quality. When they returned, they were arrested and their furs were impounded. Furious with the governor, they made their way to London where they shared the information they had collected. Based on their reconnaissance, the English sent an expedition to discover a route to Hudson Bay, trading alliances were forged with the Indigenous nations encountered on the coast, and a first trading post was established. When the ships returned, the Hudson's Bay Company was incorporated in 1670, with a royal charter granted by Charles II.

For over a century, French and English traders would compete to control the fur trade. The French pushed deep inland and established forts throughout the Great Lakes and down the Mississippi to the Gulf Coast. Seeking to cut off the flow of furs to Hudson's Bay Company posts, they had travelled as far as what is now Alberta by the 1740s. To fully comprehend Canada's fur trade, one must appreciate that the initial process of colonization rested on collaboration with and protection by Indigenous peoples (Trigger 1992, 409–10). Building forts and posts often required the consent and cooperation of the nations that inhabited those territories. Hunting, fishing, and gathering also required the approval of Indigenous peoples. This context favoured the emergence of a mixed-ancestry population, as Europeans and newcomers sought Indigenous kin ties to sustain trade and resource use on the territory inhabited by their new kin. These unions – known as "country marriages" in English and "mariages à la façon du pays" in French – came to produce a Métis population that spanned much of the continent, as Métis identity and culture were carried along the fur trade routes. Already during the French regime, the distances were too great to allow traders to travel from the St.

Lawrence to distant posts in one season; the *hivernants* (winterers) there-fore stayed year round in the trade territories, while the *mangeurs de lard* (lard eaters) would go to a central locale by mid-summer with trade goods to be distributed farther inland and then return to the St. Lawrence Valley before the waters froze (see Foster 2001, 182–84).

As was the case farther west, most voyageur winterers did not settle in the Indian Country of the Outaouais. Rather, they were hired by fur trade companies on two- or three-year contracts before returning to pursue other occupations in the St. Lawrence Valley (Marcotte 2017; Podruchny 2006). Ens and Sawchuk (2016, 65) suggest that there were three essential steps in Métis ethnogenesis. The first was to winter in Indian Country in the employ of a fur trade company; the second was to become an in-dependent trader, trapper, or tripper; and the third was for the various families of these freemen to join together, usually close to trading posts. As can be seen by the relatively small size of the regional Métis community in the Outaouais Valley, the process of wintering and then forming unions with Indigenous women and finally settling in Indian Country was ex-ceptional, but sufficient numbers of people went through these steps to form a small congregation at Lac-Sainte-Marie. As agricultural colonization pushed into the hinterland of the region later, some former voyageurs also settled there with Euro-Canadian wives and children. Of course, the notion that Métis ethnogenesis is tied to one location, along with the as-sociated idea that communities need discrete settlements, is challenged by an understanding of the continental distribution of Métis culture as a rhizomatic network forged by the fur trade occupations and shared lifestyle of the Métis. And this culture, much like the old Canadien culture, was a continental phenomenon (Foxcurran, Bouchard, and Malette 2016).

Using their status as intermediaries to their advantage, Métis acted as interpreters, guides, and diplomats to further their interests as they en-couraged trade relations between Indigenous peoples and European traders. The growth of these Métis populations came to worry French colonial officials, who doubted their loyalty and castigated their free com-merce as well as their mores. Samuel de Champlain's perhaps utopian dream had been to create a new society in which French and Indigenous inhabitants lived together in "amity and concord" (Fischer 2009, 7). The French, however, had to address the reality that instead of Indians inte-grating into French culture and society, some men abandoned the French colonies and became much closer to Indigenous peoples culturally. A number of regulations were adopted to stem the exodus of Frenchmen from the fur trade forts and thus counter the growing number of mixed marriages (Delâge 2011).

The historical trajectory of the growing Métis community – the older term *Métif* was in use in the French period – was deeply affected by the British Conquest of 1759–60 and the Treaty of Paris, signed in 1763, which transferred the territory of New France to the British Crown (Calloway 2006). As French forces abandoned forts across the continent, the HBC hoped to finally exercise the monopoly it had been granted a century earlier. The peace was short lived, however. Indigenous leader Obwandiyag (Pontiac), from the Odawa Nation, led a resistance against the British, who now sought to control the new territories under its dominion. His actions pushed the British Crown to issue the Royal Proclamation, 1763, which recognized Indigenous rights and claims and required the Crown to negotiate treaties with Indigenous nations before land was ceded. This proclamation, along with the British North America Act, 1774 (also known as the Quebec Act of 1774), which conferred rights on French-speaking Catholics and levied taxes to pay for the Seven Years' War (1756–63), in turn pushed the thirteen colonies to revolution and eventually republican statehood. The Métis descendants of the French saw themselves plunged into this simmering conflict as they inhabited what would become the contested borderlands of the British and later Americans, having to negotiate their place as new borders were continually drawn. The War of 1812, as a case in point, often pitted Canadiens and Canadien Métis against each other, as they were recruited by both the British in what is now Windsor and the Americans in the region of Detroit to wage war for the respective states (Aboriginal Affairs and Northern Development Canada 2012; Barkwell 2012). All the while, the fur trade to the north and south of the forty-ninth parallel was being reorganized to deal with the new political frontiers.

Even in territories far from the eventual United States of America, the HBC was not granted much of a reprieve. Scottish and some English traders moved to Montréal and sought their fortunes in the fur trade. Relying on the labour of the French-speaking Canadiens, these petty traders followed the old French fur trade river routes. Eventually, their individual trading interests coalesced under the NWC banner, and the NWC waged a bitter battle with the HBC to control the fur trade in the interior. The NWC often called upon the children of the *hivernants* in distant territories who had remained behind after the Conquest. The conflict between the two rival companies certainly helped to cement Métis identity. In response to Lord Selkirk's creation of a colony in the Red River area, to which he brought in Scottish Highlanders, the NWC encouraged its Canadien and Métis employees to organize themselves against this intrusion of settlers, particularly as the governor of the Selkirk Settlement, or Red River Colony, sought to restrict the trade of pemmican from the Red River to distant outposts.

Pemmican was a vital source of food for the *hivernants*, most of whom were Canadien and Métis, but in 1814 the Selkirk Settlement governor issued a proclamation prohibiting the pemmican trade. The Pemmican Proclamation precipitated a series of events that ended with the fusion of the HBC and NWC. Ens and Sawchuk (2016, 80) argue that the Pemmican War must be understood in the context of a battle for the Athabasca fur lands. When the Selkirk Colony curtailed the movement of pemmican out of the Red River Valley in order to provision either HBC employees or those who had been brought in to settle the colony, NWC engagés were left with limited food supplies, challenging their dominance in these lands. Selkirk was thus a "strategic settlement in the reorganization plans of the HBC" (80). Although the Pemmican War simmered for several years, the battle of "la Grenouillère," known as the Battle of Seven Oaks in English, was pivotal. In 1816 a company of Canadiens and Métis seized a shipment of pemmican from the HBC that was then in turn stolen from them. Indeed, this company of men was intercepted by a force of HBC employees and colonists who intended to seize the pemmican. In the clash that followed, Selkirk settlers were led by the inexperienced Governor Robert Semple. Semple and twenty others were killed.[7]

The conflict raged until 1821, when the companies were merged in London – to the HBC's advantage. The merger left the Métis families who lived in proximity to the fur trade posts in turmoil once again. Under the North American direction of George Simpson, the HBC sought to cut costs and restructure by merging forts (often HBC and NWC forts were located adjacent to each other) and developing new trade routes that relied on York boats, as these required fewer employees to ship furs and trade goods. Métis and Canadien employees were effectively blocked from climbing the ranks of the HBC, as the new corporate structure favoured the English and Scottish clerks. Even highly literate and erudite men such as Noel Annance, an Abenaki clerk, were also blocked from advancement because of their Indigenous identity (see Barman 2016). A number of voyageurs and company employees retired after the merger, and though some settled at Red River, others returned to Lower Canada, occasionally with their families, to become petty traders or to work in the thriving lumber industry.

Around this time, liberal and republican sentiments that would lead to the Rebellions of 1837–38 were growing. Like the flow of trade and human migration, these ideas flowed westwards. Patriote flags were raised among the Métis of the Red River as republican ideas gained ground there as well. The idea of founding a free state was not completely unknown to the Métis. A band of Métis who piloted a schooner from Buffalo, bound for California and passing through Sault Ste. Marie in 1836, for example, wanted to create a republic for the benefit of those with "Indian blood." In 1836, California was still Mexican territory, but it was seized by the United States in war a decade later; the territory to the north, the Columbia Department, was under the shared jurisdiction of the British and Americans. Jennifer Brown (1980, 190–92) recounts the tale of sons of the NWC who set out with an "Indian Liberating Army," whose stated goal was to take California and found an "Indian Kingdom." George Simpson described the ragtag force as "wild thoughtless young men of good education and daring character, half-breed sons of gentlemen lately and now engaged in the fur trade" (Arthur 1973, 42). This expedition was under the command of the Métis Robert Dickson, a "brigadier-general" from Minnesota, and included the son of John (Jean-Baptiste) McLoughlin. The younger McLoughlin, also John, had earlier been refused hire at the HBC in spite of his father's prominent status as the head of the company's Columbia Department. Dickson and some sixty recruits left Buffalo on August 1, 1836, with the goal of reaching the Red River to get new recruits among Métis there. Only eleven men reached the Red River. Once they were there, the HBC undermined the expedition by bringing into the fold some of the wayward sons, notably John McLoughlin, who was hired as a clerk. Though the expedition came to naught, it remains significant as it highlights a grand political agenda for those with "Indian blood," including Métis across the continent, not solely those of the Red River.

## Other Political Events

One of the significant events discussed in the following pages is the October 1842 decision by the governor general of British North America,

Charles Bagot, to commission a study of the administration of Indian "affairs across the united Province of Canada." Bagot sought to implement reforms that would improve the living conditions of Indians under his charge while reducing the expenses of administering Indian affairs. As we will see, the study demonstrates significant interest in possible distinctions between Métis and Indians. The presence of Métis in several locations is noted, and the study recommends reducing annual expenditures by no longer offering them "presents."[8] The descriptions articulated by the Bagot Commission help us to understand not only some of the distinctions between the Indian and Métis or Bois-Brulé populations but also the cultural markers Métis shared across territories.

Technological innovations and the growing global demand for raw materials such as copper also pushed colonial officials to negotiate new treaties with Indigenous peoples, which implicated Métis in eastern parts of Canada. Copper deposits were found on the northern shore of Lake Superior, but the challenge was bringing the copper to market. By the 1840s, the HBC was transporting goods by sailboat and paddle steamers were navigating Lake Huron. With the spike in global copper prices and the means to move the raw copper to market, mines were established in the Great Lakes region (Jones 2013, 111). The first licences for copper mines on the British side of Lake Superior were issued in 1845 on unceded Indigenous lands, surveyors having been sent to the region prior to the negotiation of treaties. Government surveyor Alexander Vidal compiled a list of thirty-two individuals who had settled on the north (British) shore of St. Mary's River (112). From the colonial perspective, they were "squatters." T.G. Anderson, the Indian agent overseeing this territory, stated to the Province of Canada Executive Council in 1845 that "these poor Canadians and half-breed settlers ... [at Sault Ste. Marie] located themselves without other authority than a permission from the Natives" (112).[9]

As colonial officials were preparing a round of treaty negotiations, tensions began to mount. Ojibwe chiefs Shinguakonce (or Shingwaukonse, also known as Little Pine) and Nebenagoching protested against the surveying and mining underway on their territory. Government officials tried to disqualify Ojibwe demands by asserting that the group had relocated from the United States. Janet Elizabeth Chute (1998, 237) argues that the Ojibwe chiefs sought managerial control over lumber and mining operations and wanted to promote farming. They would certainly have expected royalties to be paid to them from the mines operating on their territory. The goal was not to block mining and forestry but to ensure Indigenous rights and oversight over these industries. To achieve their aims, alliances were sought, notably with the Métis and others: "To aid in securing his goal, Little Pine surrounded himself in 1848 with Native allies, interpreters, Métis and French [Canadien] traders, and, in the case of Allan Macdonell [McDonell], a lawyer and entrepreneur" (Chute 1998, 237). Colonial officials resisted such calls as they could not imagine First Nations as managers of industry, claiming that there would be chaos and wastage (237).

Following the failure of the Ojibwe to get their claims recognized, the chiefs called for Métis and Canadiens at Sault Ste. Marie to join them and Allan McDonell in seizing mining operations at Point aux Mines, or Mica Bay (Chute 1998, 237; Jones 2013, 115). McDonell had raised a force of some hundred armed men and stolen several boats to carry them to Point aux Mines and Michipicoten Island. As the Ojibwe chiefs had leased this locale to McDonell, the force was trying to evict other government licensees (Jones 2013, 115). As Jones reminds us, the colonial reaction was swift: "The 'Indian war' quickly came to an end with the dispatch of soldiers from Canada West and the arrest of Shinguakonce, Allan McDonell, Pabinacochin [Nebenagoching] and 'two other half breeds' (Pierrot Lesage and Charlot Boyer)" (115). Though the Robinson Treaties were successfully negotiated with the Ojibwe, and the Métis excluded, colonial officials strove to ensure that no similar event would recur; in June 1853, a bill introduced by Attorney General Robert Baldwin and passed by the legislature of the Province of Canada "provided for harsh legal action against any instigator of Native discontent within the Algoma district" (Chute 1998, 237).

Though Métis had participated in the so-called Indian War, they were divided. Métis Elders recalled in the 1890s that although Shinguakonce had met with the Métis of Sault Ste. Marie prior to the seizing of the mines and promised them a share of treaty proceeds if they should "side with them in the Point of Mines affere," the response had been tepid (Jones 2013, 116). While some joined the fray, others answered that "they were already Indians enough without binding themselves to be under an Indian Chief." This passage suggests that the Métis considered themselves not only distinct but also as having a legitimate claim to the land based on their Indian ancestry. Their refusal to submit themselves politically to the Ojibwe chiefs implies a sense of being a distinctive political community, even as the Robinson Treaties enjoined Métis to become either white or Indian.

At Red River and points farther east, there are other precedents for Métis taking up arms or otherwise seeking to have their rights recognized by government officials, but the conflict following the case of Guillaume Sayer illustrates that they were not immune from division and political turmoil. In 1849, the Métis Sayer was arrested in the Red River region and charged with possession of contraband alcohol. Ironically, Cuthbert Grant, Métis hero of la Grenouillère, sided with the HBC against Sayer. Grant had been appointed by George Simpson as "Warden of the Plains of the Red River" in 1828, and thus served as the region's sheriff under the HBC's umbrella for decades (Woodcock 1985). Under the leadership of Louis Riel Sr., a faction of the Métis opposed Grant's stance on Sayer, took up arms, and threatened to break away from British authority. Sayer was liberated, while Grant eventually lost his position. The French Métis and Canadiens of Red River saw opposition to Grant as the end of the HBC monopoly in the colony (McLean 1987; Woodcock 1985). Twenty years later, Riel Sr.'s son, also Louis, would lead resistance to the entry of surveyors sent by Ottawa, eventually resulting in the creation of the province of Manitoba in 1870. Again, historians have noted tensions between French Métis and English Half-breeds in this political process, giving the lie to any romantic notion of a past and unified single Métis nation marching under one drum or one flag (O'Toole 2012). Under close scrutiny, the politics of the everyday and its inherently inchoate nature often resist our desire to shape complex realities into a grand nationalist narrative.

With a bounty on his head for the execution of Thomas Scott, who was tried and convicted of treason by the provisional government led by Riel in 1870, elected parliamentarian Louis Riel sought refuge in a number of places in Canada before finally relocating to the United States. There, he would become a naturalized US citizen.[10] Tellingly, while Riel was in exile, the Canadian state would also negotiate with Nicolas Chatelain (also Chastellaine, Chatelaine, Chatelan, Chattelaine), who was representing the Métis of Lac à la Pluie, later baptized anew as Rainy Lake in what is now Ontario. The case of Nicolas Chatelain offers yet another example of the complexity that tainted political rapport within the Métis community, as it was Chatelain who facilitated the passage of the Wolseley expedition sent by Ottawa to seize Riel and pacify the Red River Resistance (Lytwyn 2012, 206).[11]

Chatelain is known for acting on behalf of the Lac à la Pluie and Rivière à la Pluie (Rainy Lake and Rainy River) Métis after they were excluded from Treaty 3. He signed a memorandum of agreement with the surveyor general of Canada, John Stoughton Dennis, known as the "Half-Breed Adhesion to Treaty No. 3" (McNab 1990). By virtue of their Indian blood, Métis were to have two reserves set aside for them and to receive benefits from the Canadian state, including annuities, cattle, and farm equipment (McNab 1990). This memorandum was never ratified and was ignored by the Department of Indian Affairs. Chatelain pushed ahead, lobbying to get the annuities owed to the Métis. The case highlights how a community defined itself as Métis and sought to have its rights based on Indian blood recognized by the state, using all the political levers available to it. Notably, they used the same arguments that Riel had done when he claimed Indigenous title rights for the Métis, although they were independent from his politics, which were tied to the Red River community.

These few but notable examples demonstrate that the notion of a single Métis identity forged on the prairies after the battle of la Grenouillère and in the Red River and North-West resistances led by Louis Riel is an oversimplification of the cultural, social, and political complexity of Métis histories and local cultures. Undeniably, from the French regime to British rule and eventual Confederation the spirit of independence displayed by the Métis was a constant – but it was evident in multiple areas of Canada and the United States. Colonial authorities of all stripes were disturbed by this population, which could be prompted to revolt not solely in the Red River region.[12] A quick review of broad Métis history reveals a collective consciousness tied to distinct ethnic identity (based, in turn, on various distinctive practices and customs), but that identity cannot be confined to one geographic location.

That said, the Métis diaspora of the North-West and Manitoba certainly faced difficult days following the execution of Louis Riel. The fragmentation of Métis communities under the weight of endless immigration led to the quasi-disappearance of the Métis variant of the French language in the Canadian West: Michif-French, a language that had long served as the de facto *lingua franca*. French-Canadian Métis culture maintained itself, as communities in the Saint-Boniface region and other areas of Manitoba turned to the Catholic Church and the French language as a vector of social cohesion. Farther away, with the waning of the continental fur trade and consequent weakening of the structural force that had united distant communities into a larger network, linguistic forces were local and regional. Under these circumstances, English rapidly became the dominant language, although Indigenous languages at times predominated in particular Métis families and communities, whether Cree, Saulteaux, or other. In some places, the mixed bilingual Michif language was maintained. These various linguistic shifts occurred as Métis found themselves living in communities also containing status and non-status Indians, recent immigrants, and French Canadians.

While the Métis community were dispersed and marginalized in the West, the execution of Louis Riel contributed to the rise of a French-Canadian nationalism in Québec. Clearly, his death was seen as the political execution of a compatriot. Riel had openly identified himself as French Canadian as well as Métis in 1869, at the outbreak of the first resistance. Although he emphasized the necessity of distinguishing the people he called "Métis Canadien-Français," Riel nonetheless underscored in a letter to his cousin Paul Proulx in 1877 that the term *Métis* should be inclusive:

> It is a name that signifies mixing. Up until now, it has served to designate a race issued from the mixed blood of Europeans and *Sauvages,* but it is also proper to designate a race of man that drew upon the mixing of all the bloods living among them and cast in the French Canadian mould conserving the memory of its origin in calling itself Métis. The name Métis would be acceptable to all, because it is not exclusive and would have the advantage of mentioning in a convenient fashion the contingent that each nation contributed to forming a new people.[13]

Rejecting a monolithic and exclusive definition of what it means to be Métis in 1877, Riel here demonstrates the impossibility of applying a homogenizing nationalist formula that would restrict the Métis Nation unduly. Moreover, as the patron of Métis people, Riel clearly states that there is a Métis population in the eastern provinces of Canada: "As for the eastern Canadian provinces, many Métis live scorned under Indian guise. Their villages are villages of indigence. Their Indian title to the land is nonetheless as good as the Indian title of the Métis of Manitoba" (Riel 1985a, 121; our translation).

Louis Riel's affirmation of a Métis presence in the eastern provinces is not a misstatement or a flight of fancy, as the transcription of his trial does the same (Anonymous 1886, 158). Riel calls for help to ensure that the eastern Métis can secure the same rights as the Métis of the North-West. The evidence demonstrates that Riel embraced an inclusive vision of Métis identity and rejected the notion of a minimum threshold of "Indian blood" or a specific geographical frontier for the Métis:

> Very polite and amiable people may sometimes say to a Métis, "You don't look at all like a Métis. You surely can't have much *Sauvage* blood. You could pass anywhere for pure White." ...
>
> It is true that our *Sauvage* origin is humble, but it is indeed just that we honour our mothers as well as our fathers. Why should we be so preoccupied with what degree of mingling we have of European and Indian blood? No matter how little we have of one or the other, do not both gratitude and filial love require us to make a point of saying, "We are Métis"? (Riel 1985c, 278–79; our translation)

Thus, Riel does not define Métis in terms of blood quantum, nor limit the Métis to Manitoba (or even the prairies), nor endorse a strict patri-linear model when it comes to the transmission of Métis identity.

# 2

# *Métis Identities and Ethnonyms*

IF NEO-NATIONALIST HISTORICAL explanations that conflate Métis ethnogenesis and nationhood are to be abandoned, how can the contours of a Métis community be identified? Already, in 2004, Étienne Rivard recognized the importance of not seeing Métis nationalism as the sole expression of a Métis identity, particularly when studying historical communities. He goes further, evoking the possibility of national identities existing outside of models based on political action and claims:

> In spite of what Oliv[e] Dickason says, it is not impossible that the Métis of Quebec developed a "national" identity – which remained invisible to the outside observer, namely colonial or state authorities. Insofar as it has a special meaning for the ethnic group itself, an identity does not have to be recognized by the Other to exist. National identities are therefore not all expressed in the same way. Some result from an active nationalism and putting forward claims. By contrast, others exist despite a silent or even non-existent nationalism ... In any case, the lack of direct evidence has not prevented ethnohistorians from documenting Métis ethnogenesis in the remote North-West far from the Red River ... Métis ethnogenesis theory could also apply to several peripheral regions of Quebec. (Rivard 2004, 200; our translation)

In the absence of nationalism tied to active claims, it is possible, even likely, for a national identity to be known only to its members, as there is no incentive to seek external validation. Thus, Rivard mentions in passing that theories of Métis ethnogenesis could be applied to peripheral regions of Québec. This raises an additional question: can we conceive a Métis identity outside the parameters of a strictly nationalist imagination (inside or outside Red River)? It has been demonstrated that Métis in the Great Lakes area and in the Red River Colony shared political practices, such as the filing of petitions. A comparison of the Great Lakes and Red

River Métis also reveals patterns of interrelated kinship networks spread across vast distances. Shared religious practices were also a vehicle of social cohesion and cross-territorial political consciousness (Pigeon 2017). These structural forces facilitated the rise of a Métis identity outside the narrow nomenclature of Métis modern nationalism, and in particular a nationalism that is conflated with a theory of sovereignty mapped to the European grammar by which it became perceived as the apex of political consciousness.[1]

In reviewing historical evidence from the region of Maniwaki, our primary goal is therefore not to determine if there was a distinct Métis nation or culture in that area – one entirely different from other Métis cultures across Canada and the United States. In fact, the evidence indicates that there were many connections between diverse Métis communities, as well as unique expressions of Métis cultures tied to the different regions and ecosystems of Canada, including the Outaouais. The use of a primordialist explanation to justify a single Métis nation as the source of a unitary Métis identity and culture thus seems inappropriate as a model to explain such complexity (Foxcurran, Bouchard, and Malette 2016). To avoid the trap of an artificially narrowing notion of the political, limited to the nationalism found in Red River, we extend Émilie Pigeon's (2017) argument that petitions, lived religiosity, and kinship ties between Métis families provided social cohesion and a collective political identity to include the Outaouais, of which the Métis of Maniwaki are part. It is indeed through practices such as drafting petitions and having the community rally around more mundane political affirmations, as well as lived Catholicism (and other cultural practices), that we can better understand the contours of a Métis people who emerged in various locales and communities.[2] Such political communities can be situated within a larger continuum of Métis culture.

In the context of the Maniwaki region, our research focused on whether it was possible to identify a community of mixed Indian and European ancestry that demonstrated distinctive cultural practices that were also shared with the Indigenous and Euro-Canadian cultures from which it emerged. We also sought to understand, if this was a named community, whether it was identified as such from within or from outside. This distinction is essential, as it guides both our understanding of Métis culture emerging in different communities and our methodological approach to archival documents. It is apparent in the literature on the historical Métis culture that Métis communities and individuals combined traits and cultural practices drawn from European and Indigenous antecedents. Such cultural syncretism confounded many observers and bureaucrats alike about the exact contours of Métis identity. Likewise, it shaped Métis strategies when it came to identity, as they were often pressured to choose to become solely white or Indian. As the weight of demography shifted to benefit Euro-Canadians, government policy increasingly sought to regulate Indigenous populations, often at the cost of Métis identity. This explains why we use eight analytical criteria (see Table 1) to detect the emergence of a community of mixed European and Indian heritage, taking stock of shifting identities and the presence of a historical synthesis marked by the distinctive cultural practices that characterize the evolution of Métis cultures in different regions of Canada. These criteria guided our research as we attempted to determine whether a historical Métis community existed in the Gatineau Valley.

**Ethnonymic Nuances**
Not only is Métis culture characterized by cultural markers that sometimes overlap with Indigenous and European cultures, but the ethnonyms used to identify Métis were diverse and interchangeable, making it even more challenging to identify whether individuals, families, and communities were in fact Métis.[3] Similarly, ethnonyms can have different connotations in English and French, as is evidence by the term *Sauvage/Sauvagesse.* While the English word *savage* and the French term *sauvage* derive from the same root, the two are not perfectly synonymous, as the French is much closer to the original meaning. The term is derived from the Latin *silvaticus,* or that which belongs to the forest (*silva* in Latin), a place where there was no cultivation; thus, *sauvage* is used in French to refer to plants and animals that have not been domesticated. By extension, a *Sauvage* is a person living in the forest, and it can also connote being free of the constraints of society. The term at the outset was not inherently pejorative, and the original meaning and connotation have lingered in the French language. Although the word has become pejorative in both languages, and its meanings overlap, the French does not have precisely the same connotations as the English *savage.* As Nancy Senior (2004, 464) explains, "With time the meanings of words and of constructions change. The fact that some meanings of a word are different while others remain the same can pose problems for translators." *Sauvage* is one of these problematic

words. Senior continues, "The French word 'sauvage' and the English 'savage' are not symmetrical. The meaning of the French word has changed less than the English one" (466). The phrase "vivre en sauvage," for example, signifies living as a recluse and is not inherently pejorative, while in English to "live as a savage" has an entirely different connotation as *savage* is a loaded term. In French, *sauvage* can still signify "uninhabited" or "not domesticated" (467), so a parent might say that a child "fait son sauvage" to indicate that he or she is skittish, much like an undomesticated animal that doesn't want human contact. In the nineteenth century, *sauvage* was most often used without derision, and at times even had a positive nuance. Given the disparity between the English and French connotations, we retain the original *Sauvage* and, where applicable, the feminine *Sauvagesse* in our discussion. As a case in point, the Indian Act was first known in French as the Acte des Sauvages. Métis, Louis Riel among them, also used *Sauvages* and *Sauvagesses* to refer to Indians and, by extension, distant kin.

Unfortunately, diversity in naming and cultural overlap are still often interpreted as a lack of cultural maturity, or as confirmation of the assimilation of the Métis to either First Nations or European communities. Both the literature and examples drawn from the archival sources caution against such interpretations, however (Foxcurran, Bouchard, and Malette 2016; Gagnon 2009; St-Onge and Podruchny 2012). Clearly, as identities emerge and shift they do not necessarily fall into static, fixed, and mutually exclusive categories. Historically speaking, it is worth noting that celebrated Métis historical figures have identified themselves in ways that would be viewed as contradictory today. It is also essential to take into account that Métis communities existed precisely because of the cohabitation of families that may seem to us to bear mutually exclusive identities, such as Indian, Canadien (French Canadian), or Métis. We must keep in mind that ethnic labels are fluid and that identities can hardly be reified in any definitive manner.

An example of this kind of fluidity is found in the overlap between the Métis and Canadien ethnonyms underlined by Monseigneur Alexandre-Antonin Taché, who uses "French" and "Canadian Half-breeds" interchangeably in his *Sketch of the North-West of America* (1870).[4] This is not to suggest that such fluidity makes identification impossible; Taché takes great care to distinguish Métis Canadien identity from that of *Sauvages,* while underscoring the existence of various subgroups of Métis based on their spoken language. Riel also mentions this fact in his correspondence when trying to recruit English Métis to his national project in opposition to Ottawa (Canada, Parliament 1886). Despite the different ethnonyms and interchangeable identification used in documentary sources, Taché's description suggests a number of precise ethnocultural criteria that make it possible to recognize the existence of subgroups within the larger Métis community. In that regard, the English version of Taché's work, published in 1870, uses the term *Half-breed,* while the French version, published in 1869, uses *Métis:*

> We use the word *Half-breed* to designate all who, not being pure Indians, are related to them in any degree. It matters not from what tribe the mother may spring, no allusion is ever made to such a distinction. With reference to paternal descent, however, the Half-breeds of the Northern Department, just as is the case with the foreign inhabitants, are divided into two classes distinguished as "French" or Canadian Half-breeds and English Half-breeds. (1870, 98)

As the evidence indicates, the term *Métis* (and the older *Métif*) was standard in French over a century prior to its common use in English, when the French term came to be used by the descendants of those who were identified as English Half-breeds by Taché, George Simpson (Rich 1938), and the 1870 census of the newly created province of Manitoba.

Another telling example of such fluidity lies with the case of Métis James King, who distinguished himself from Indians in commemorating and valuing his Canadien origins and European ancestry (Marcotte 2017, 203–6). Though of Indigenous ancestry, born in the James Bay region at a time when no white women were residing there, James King introduced himself to Catholic priests as a Canadien born in Montréal. What makes this particularly interesting is that many descendants of James King were identified as Indians or Half-breed or Métis over several censuses. Thus, even though King identified as Canadien, successive generations could literally choose to identify as Indian or Métis, ethnonyms that would, by all appearances, be contradictory to Canadien.[5]

Another revealing case is that of the Polson/Lévesque family of the Lake Abitibi region. William Polson, an Anglo-Cree Métis from James Bay, spent much of his life as a clerk and interpreter at the fur trade post at Abitibi. His wife, the Franco-Algonquin Métis Flora Lévesque, or

Otenimakwe, is described by the missionary Bellefeuille in 1838 as a *Sauvagesse,* all the while being classified among the Métifs of the region (Du Ranquet [1843] 2000, 114).[6] The Polson family moved in the 1850s to the Lake Témiscamingue region, where William retired. Another cleric, Father Mourier, describes these new arrivals as the first white family of the region.[7] This same couple is also labelled Indian in the 1871 census.[8] Most of their descendants will be described as Algonquins of the Lake Témiscamingue region in the 1901 census.[9] This case demonstrates the vagaries of identity and ethnonyms from a historical and documentary perspective.

The Powley family of Sault Ste. Marie provides another well-known example of the non-linear transmission of identity and the use of multiple ethnonyms across generations. Father and son Steve and Roddy Powley (the defendants in the *Powley* case), were descendants of the marriage of a voyageur named Lesage and Madeline, a woman of Indigenous ancestry who was born in the 1790s in what is now Wisconsin.[10] The Powleys were identified by multiple ethnonyms in historical documents over the genera- tions, including French, Indian (Eustache Lesage), and white (Éva Micks). There was no evidence of endogamous marriages, as each member of the Powley family had married a spouse who was neither Métis nor First Na- tions (see Armstrong 2003). Adding to this complex family lineage, it has been suggested that Steve Powley's grandmother lost her Indian status when she married a man who did not have status. This case highlights that identities can vary quite drastically, as the Powley line had been de- fined as Indian, white, non-status Indian, and Métis at different times. Like the King and Polson families, the Powley family does not feature a direct and continuous transmission of the Métis identification from gen- eration to generation but a Métis identity that was subsumed under diverse ethnonyms.

In the Gatineau Valley, Élisabeth McPherson (File 13) presents a similar case.[11] Daughter of HBC trader Andrew McPherson and Ikwesens or Marie Pinesi-okijikokwe, an Indian woman from the Grand Lac trading post, Élisabeth left the region with her voyageur husband, François Naud, in 1838. On the river on their way toward Montréal, they met the missionary Bellefeuille, who described Élisabeth as "métisse."[12] Five years later, in 1843, when the couple was living in the Lac-Sainte-Marie region, Father Du Ranquet was welcomed by a James Now. Now, it turns out, was François Naud, who had been going by the name Jacques Naud (as his daughter's marriage certificate shows), which would be anglicized to James Now.[13] The missionary in question identified Naud's wife and mother-in-law as "Algonquin" (Du Ranquet [1843] 2000, 239). Nonetheless, the 1861 census takers, who were trained in identifying the presence of visible minorities, classified Élisabeth as white.[14] Of course, one document alone is insufficient to ascertain the likely lived identity of any individual from the past. Rather, the fact that an individual is classified as Indian or Métis or white in different instances is itself a good indicator of a historical Métis identity.

In addition to differences attributed by outsiders in censuses, reports, and so forth, Métis themselves quite often use different ethnonyms over the course of their lives. As we've seen, Riel identified himself as a Métis and, then in 1869, as Canadien-Français (Flanagan and Campbell 2013, 264). Similarly, the personal identity of the celebrated Métis Johnny Grant varied from the older French-Canadian ethnonym Canadien to Métis and Indian over the course of his life (Ens 2001, 174). Thus, it is not possible to speak of a consistent use of a single ethnonym over successive generations. As demonstrated by the King, Polson, Powley, and McPherson families, as well as Grant and Riel, the use of a sole ethnonym at any given moment does not sufficiently define a family or, by extension, a community. It is necessary to look at the community ethnonyms used over the years within the larger historical and ethnocultural context. With a robust methodology, a nuanced analysis of the cultural contexts that frame observed facts, practices, and traits is possible. Drawing on the definitions of culture presented earlier, a thorough analysis requires the compilation of a thicker description of past cultural practices to ascertain the meaning of Métis culture and identity – and thus to trace the contours of a potential Métis historical community.

## The Transformation of Sociodemographic Forces
Although they are valuable, documented cases of auto-identification and identification by others that use meaningful ethnonyms should encourage researchers to seek additional criteria by which to identify the contours of a Métis community or culture more precisely. In seeking these criteria, one should be careful to avoid the pitfall of privileging the grand nationalist stories – or worse, giving proof of a grand political story as a necessary condition of Métis identity. As Nicole St-Onge and Carolyn Podruchny (2012, 61) remind us, even if some communities had to mobilize politically and

articulate a very strong ethnic self-identification, the evidence indicates that this was certainly not the case for all historical Métis communities: "Most inhabitants and descendants of fur trade communities did not need to mobilize in such fashion or take on an overt identification on a continuous basis, but we think they could have if they needed to." St-Onge and Podruchny also highlight that there was often no pressing need for Métis to publicly express their identity: "They lived a Metis life even if they did not have the need, time, or inclination to articulate it loud or brand it with a label" (80). This applies to many Métis communities.

When it comes to identifying communities, St-Onge and Podruchny therefore invite researchers to consider a suite of ethnocultural markers that are typical of Métis communities that arose out of the fur trade:

> Métis are distinct from neighbouring communities because of the sheer size of the area over which they travelled, lived, and worked; their emergence out of the fur trade; their close economic relationship to mercantile capital; their reliance on fur trade networks in the eighteenth and nineteenth centuries; and cultural practices passed down over generations. All these factors combine to give shape and coherence to their kin-structured communities. (2012, 80–81)

For our purpose, to understand the sociocultural context in which Métis of the larger Outaouais region in Québec emerged and developed over time, we take into consideration how changing social and demographic forces conditioned communities in the nineteenth and twentieth centuries, and how these forces advantaged non-Indigenous populations. We have been particularly careful not to hastily conclude that Métis populations were simply immature given the multiple ethnonyms that appear in the records, or, just as mistakenly, to assume that Métis populations were assimilated due to intermarriage with non-Indigenous peoples. A cursory examination could indeed lead to the conclusion that the Métis and Indigenous populations were assimilated, notably as a consequence of exogamous marriages over generations or the disappearance of the main economic drivers characterizing their culture (i.e., the fur trade). A prevailing and sometimes misleading assumption remains that a Métis community will disintegrate if the Métis become too few among the larger settler or non-Indigenous populations.

In a case study submitted to the Royal Commission on Aboriginal Peoples, James Morrison (1993, 26–27) highlights the modest number of families on the Canadian side of Sault Ste. Marie in 1847: some 50 families or roughly 250 people, many of them Canadiens who had arrived after the War of 1812 to work for the HBC and married either Anishinaabe or second- or third-generation Métis women, such as the Cadottes, Nolins, and Birons. Of the 51 families recorded in the 1850 "census," only seven still lived in Sault Ste. Marie in 1881 (Jones 1998, 17, 29–30; Lytwyn 1998, 30).[15] In the *Powley* court case, the Crown alleged that by 1900 Métis had either joined Indian bands, dispersed, or simply assimilated into the rapidly growing Euro-Canadian settler population (see Driver 1893). In short, it was believed that no Métis community existed in Sault Ste. Marie outside the reserves between 1920 and the end of the twentieth century. Yet evidence presented by expert witnesses for the *Powley* case has convincingly shown that Métis communities in the area adapted to these cultural pressures and in effect regularly integrated new members from surrounding Euro-Canadian and Indian communities. The resilience in Métis families to keep knowledge of their heritage alive, despite marrying non-Métis people over many generations, prevailed in what became the first constitutional case victory for Métis people in Canada. Simply put, strictly linear endogamy and a concentrated mass population are not prerequisites for the continued existence of either Métis or Indian identities.

## Legislation, Treaties, and Exclusion

The example of the historical Métis community of Sault Ste. Marie helps to illustrate the impact of government laws, regulations, and measures on Métis communities and individuals. Métis were confronted with the choice of making themselves Indian or white, by either signing onto a treaty and/or moving to a reserve or adopting the lifeways of whites in exchange for title to the land they occupied as squatters. This helps to explain why bearers of Métis culture and their communities may have become quasi-invisible over time, offering an extra challenge to researchers seeking evidence of their existence. According to evidence presented at trial, the Powley family did integrate into reserves, while other Métis families were dispersed. Only a small number stayed put, becoming a tiny minority in a growing Euro-Canadian community. The academic literature supports these findings and highlights that many Métis communities or individuals faced similar challenges and choices, thus contributing to the marginalization of their identity (Ens and Sawchuk 2016, 215–16; Lytwyn 2012; McNab 1985).

Besides the assumption of cultural superiority, supporters of measures to "civilize" Indigenous peoples had the ulterior motive of wanting to minimize state expenditures, notably on gifts given annually to First Nations.[16] One of the first measures civilian colonial officials took to curtail costs was to cease distributing gifts to Métis, who were excluded from treaty obligations that forced government officials to define who was Indian, or not, based on often very arbitrary criteria. It was also decided that any Indian woman who married a non-Indian would lose the rights and privileges tied to her status (gifts, treaty rights, and Indian title), as would her descendants. The correspondence of Samuel Peter Jarvis, the chief superintendent of Indian affairs for Upper Canada, specifies that the avowed goal of this practice was to discourage marriages between French Canadians and Indian women, a phenomenon that was seen as impeding the civilization of Indians because French Canadian husbands assimilated into Indian society rather than Indian wives assimilating into non-Indian society, and because the fur trader husbands brought alcohol into First Nation communities (McNab 1985, 60). All the while, Jarvis recognized the difficulty of distinguishing Métis from Indians in many cases. Métis were also judged on the basis of their way of life, their affinities with whites and Indians, and their potential for integration into a sedentary farming life. Add to this the fact that Métis, the majority of whom were French speaking and Catholic, were viewed as a nuisance by British colonial officials who sought to settle a growing number of Loyalist immigrants in these lands. The exclusion of the Métis from treaties, presents given to First Nation communities, and later from reserves, has therefore been a central aspect of the segregationist policies of the colonial government of Canada, as it was a means to eradicate nascent Métis cultures while assimilating other Indigenous communities whose members married exogamously.

Métis also encountered great difficulties when negotiating historical treaties. For the most part, early treaties with Indigenous peoples sought to ensure peace, friendship, and commerce or the neutrality of First Nations during times of war or armed conflicts between colonial powers (Grammond 2013, 50). Originally, such treaties did not call into question

Indian title, and they guaranteed the protection of Indigenous ways of life, presumably including among Métis populations. In 1850, a significant political shift occurred: any new treaty henceforth required the ceding of all territory in perpetuity in exchange for a reserve and some promises to be negotiated (Sprague 1996, 341–43). The precedent was set with the Robinson Treaties, which became the model for the negotiation of future treaties, notably the numbered treaties that would follow. The numbered treaties were undertaken to ensure the expansion of the dominion in the face of the potential threat of American annexation of these lands (Borrows and Rotman 2012).

The ceding or reduction of territory, which began in Ontario, was problematic for many Métis inhabitants because they were deemed non-Indians and therefore excluded from the negotiations. In response to the new measures, many Métis signed petitions demanding that their familial lands be secured or that they become signatories to treaties, as Indian blood also coursed in their veins (McNab 1985, 66). Again, most Métis of Sault Ste. Marie were excluded from the negotiations by William Robinson, in spite of the petitions and entreaties of Chiefs Shinguakonce and Nebenagoching (Morrison 1993, 168–72; Ray 1998, 69). Robinson affirmed that his only duty was to negotiate with Indians, suggesting that the chiefs adopt the Métis in question into their bands. The message was clear: Métis would not be included as signatories and beneficiaries of treaties unless they became Indians. This stance placed them at the mercy of the internal politics of Indian bands and the Indian agents appointed to oversee their affairs. As historian Douglas Leighton summarizes,

> The Metis population of the province fell into legal limbo between the status of citizen and that of Indian. Unrecognized in legislation, they were sometimes included in treaty discussions. One of the concerns of the Indians signing the Robinson Huron Treaty in 1850, for example, was the fate of their half-breed relatives. W.B. Robinson felt that if band leaders wanted to include such people on their lists, they should be free to do so. His position in a sense reflected the legal and social reality of the Metis: they had to choose whether they would be Indian or White. Once the choice was made, they in many ways ceased to be a people "in between." Their dilemma was not an enviable one: either choice meant giving up something of their unique inheritance. Politically, they remained extremely vulnerable, being utterly dependent on

the goodwill of the band leaders for their positions on the band lists. Legally, they had no distinct existence. (Cited by McNab 1985, 63)

Approximately sixty Métis out of just over 200 estimated to be living in the region were admitted to the list of beneficiaries of the Robinson Treaties in 1852. Moreover, Métis did not succeed in securing the same right to live on reserve as Indians did, which also contributed to the marginalization of their cultural identity.

A similar process of exclusion emerged on the legislative side. Comparable to the initial treaties, legislative definitions up until 1850 included Métis as "Indians," recognizing any individual married to any Indian, or with an ancestor who had married any Indian, as fully Indian (McNab 1985, 63). By 1857, the legal definition of Indian began to tighten to specify that an individual must be recognized as Indian by a tribe or band living on a reserve or on unceded lands. The Indian Act of 1876 goes much further, explicitly excluding all Métis as legislatively defined as not being Indian (Lytwyn 1998, 7; McNab 1985, 64). In short, the legislation deprived Métis of any and all legal protections afforded to those defined as Indian.

This changing political and legal landscape, however, was not necessarily uniform in its application. For example, it did not hinder governments in negotiating with certain Métis in Ontario, whether on a collective or an individual basis. Collective negotiations were undertaken at Lac à la Pluie (Rainy Lake) in 1875 and at Moose Factory in 1906. Government officials also negotiated individually with Michel Morrisseau, a Métis who secured 160 acres by arguing that he had been residing on the land before it was ceded by Treaty 3 (McNab 1985, 67). These examples show that the government did in fact recognize the existence of the Métis, both collectively and individually, and on occasion attempted to negotiate their rights as Indigenous peoples. Unfortunately, many of the rights demanded or negotiated by Métis in Ontario remained unaddressed, as negotiators invariably followed the same identity rule set out by the Honourable Alexander Morris (1880, 69):

I am sent here to treat with the Indians. In Red River, where I came from, and where there is a great body of Half-breeds, they must be either white or Indian. If Indians, they get treaty money; if the Half-breeds call themselves white, they get land. All I can do is to refer the matter to the Government at Ottawa, and to recommend what you wish to be granted.

Increasingly, in light of ever decreasing legal recognition, Métis were thus faced with an untenable choice between being Indian or being white. Even when Indian negotiators demanded the inclusion of Métis families – for example, during the Treaty 3 negotiations – Morris was adamant that treaties were not negotiated with whites, and as such the Métis had to become fully white or Indian, but not both (McNab 1985, 66).

This erosion and gradual extinguishing of Métis rights was amplified by Indian bands' successive rejection, as they sought to expel Métis from their territories. In a petition dated November 20, 1923, for example, the Mississaugas demanded that Métis signatures on the William Treaty be rescinded because the signatories had white blood in their veins. As David McNab (1985, 72) demonstrates, Métis were forced to leave the reserve and relocate to Burleigh Falls as a consequence.

Given the mitigated success that Métis have had in Ontario, particularly those near the Ottawa River, we should note the absence of any treaty with Algonquins of the larger Outaouais region. Elsewhere, Métis often manifested interest in ensuring the protection of their rights when treaty negotiations were undertaken with the relevant Indian bands. But in the Outaouais region, no known treaty has ever been ratified by the Algonquins, whose traditional territories cover southwestern Québec and include the Gatineau Valley. This is despite the fact that the 1845 Bagot Report clearly mentions the difficulties faced by First Nations in the area:

> The situation of the Algonquins and Nipissings is still more deplorable: their hunting grounds on the Ottawa, which were formerly most extensive, abounding with deer and other animals, yielding the richest furs, and which their ancestors had enjoyed from time immemorial, have been destroyed for the purposes of the chase. A considerable part has been laid out into townships, and either settled or taken possession of by squatters. The operations of the lumber-men have either destroyed or scared away the game throughout a still more extensive region, and thus as settlement advances, they are driven further and further from their homes, in search of a scanty and precarious livelihood. Their case has been often brought before the Government, and demands early attention. (Province of Canada 1845, EEE20–EEE21)[17]

The Bagot Report was compiled as part of the work of the Bagot Commission (1842–44), which sought to document and report on the living conditions of Indians under the charge of the United Province of Canada, created after union of Upper and Lower Canada in 1841.

The lack of a historical treaty process is important because it suggests that the conditions that might have provoked a stronger expression of ethnocultural identity in Métis communities, notably in the larger Outaouais region, were lacking (St-Onge and Podruchny 2012). Had a treaty been proposed for Algonquins east of the Ottawa River, Métis in the region would probably have put forward their claims, as was the case farther west, in Ontario. Yet in spite of the lack of treaty negotiations, we find historical descriptions of Métis of the greater Outaouais and Gatineau Valley that are nearly identical to those of Métis in Ontario; petitions and other correspondence mention the presence of a collective and distinctive Métis presence in the Maniwaki region. As we shall see, the evidence shows that many Métis families in the Outaouais had connections with Métis from Sault Ste. Marie and elsewhere. Therefore, they were most likely informed of the failure to include Métis in treaty negotiations in Ontario, which may have resulted in the apparent lack of political claims brought forward by the Métis of the Outaouais region to colonial authorities.

### Evidence over Prejudice

The literature on Métis ethnology certainly cautions against relying on singular expressions of ethnic designation in any historical analysis of archival documents (Kennedy 2014; St-Onge and Podruchny 2012; Thorne 1996). As we have seen, the primary sources clearly indicate that different ethnonyms were used cumulatively over the generations, and that the same individual was quite often labelled as white, Métis, and First Nations (Indian) in different locales at different points in his or her life. This complexity necessitates a methodology that can accommodate the social and cultural contexts of ethnonyms, the effect of demographics on assimilation, and the pressures endured by Métis due to racist legislation and policies. Guided by such considerations, our approach has been anthropological, looking for subtle clues of continuity and cultural transmission over generations in spite of major demographic changes, increasing marginalization and stigmatization of Métis identity, and dispersion and exogamous marriages. In a pivotal essay entitled "When Ethnic Identity Is a Social Stigma," Harald Eidheim (1969) illustrates that an identity can be maintained privately even when it is masked publicly. A Métis identity could thus be maintained even when government practices encouraged public denial, and when no treaty was negotiated with the Indigenous peoples of the Outaouais region.

In the chapters that follow, we analyze the contours of a Métis ethnogenesis from a historically mixed community within a framework that seeks to disentangle the knotted use of sometimes contradictory ethnonyms. We privilege primary sources in order to afford accuracy and transparency in our analysis. Following the model put forward by Gwynneth Jones (n.d.) for the Great Slave Lake Métis community, we refer to these sources without trying to create an overarching and necessarily chronological narrative. The goal is not to create the story but to provide a series of data points that trace the contours of community and belonging. We wish to ensure precision even if at times we must sacrifice elegance.

Having articulated the cultural markers that indicate the existence of a Métis historical community in the greater Outaouais region (see Map 2), Part 3 reviews the local history of Rivière Désert (Maniwaki), Lac-Sainte-Marie, and Lac des Sables (see Map 3), leading us to conclude that a historical Métis population emerged and took root in this western region of Québec.[18] Part 4 then examines evidence of cultural and social continuity to ascertain whether this Métis community persisted over the decades. This process allows for a dispassionate analysis, one divorced from the too often fiery rhetoric that claims there are no Métis in Québec. One of our goals is to give local Métis of the Outaouais region greater pride in their heritage and history. We hope to have a small hand in bringing recognition and perhaps reconciliation to the Métis of western Québec.

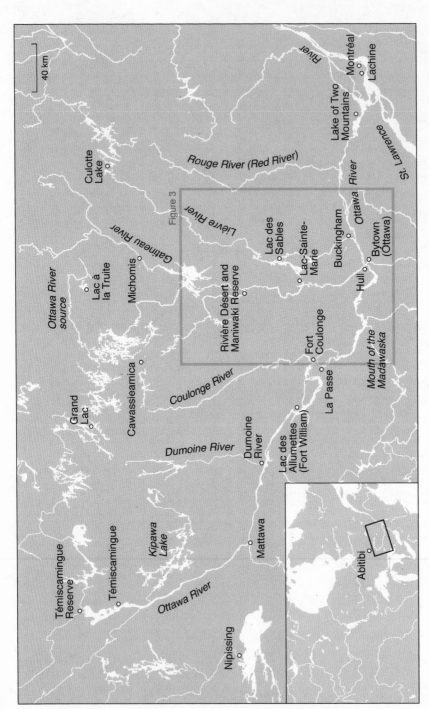

*Map 2*   The greater Outaouais region, its principal trading posts, and other important locations. Note that the trading posts shown here did not necessarily exist concurrently. The rectangle shows the region evaluated in the text to determine if it represents a historical Métis community that still persists (see Map 3).

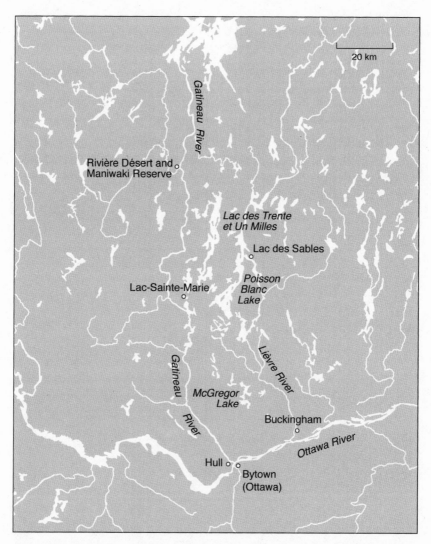

*Map 3* The historical and regional Métis community of the Gatineau Valley. Community members traded and lived across a larger territory over the decades, but the map situates the area within which the Métis collective has resided primarily.

*Part 2*

# The Métis Presence in the Outaouais Region

# 3

# *The Outaouais Fur Trade of the Nineteenth Century*

THE GREATER OUTAOUAIS REGION was shaped by the fur trade and by the same forces that facilitated a Red River Métis ethnogenesis. While the Red River is seen as a Métis heartland, the evidence suggests that a Métis identity, or more precisely a Bois-Brûlé or (French) Canadien Métis identity, emerged across the continent wherever the fur trade was thriving. In dispersed locales, the fur trade provided employment and economic opportunities that allowed for the emergence of a distinctive culture, as the Métis tended to live separately from their Indigenous kin. They pursued an occupational niche as guides and interpreters, intermediaries between the fur trade companies, and between the HBC and First Nations.

Even as the forestry industry pushed into the Outaouais region at the onset of the nineteenth century, the HBC kept open a number of less profitable trading posts. The company did so to better track free traders and block their access to the much more lucrative fur-bearing regions farther north. By the end of the 1820s, as the growing population of the St. Lawrence Valley began to face land shortages and the British colonial authorities tried to provide land for decommissioned soldiers, surveyors criss-crossed the greater Outaouais region to identify potential arable lands for agricultural settlement. The surveyors provide descriptions of the Métis individuals and families they encountered, even using the significant term *Bois-Brûlés* to identify Métis. This ethnonym is not accidental; it is used across the continent as far as the Pacific Coast to refer to French-speaking Métis. As we shall see, the greater Outaouais region had not only a named community but also a distinctive culture, one that can be distinguished from both First Nations and Euro-Canadian cultures.

**The Fur Trade on the Ottawa River in the Nineteenth Century**
The fur trade involving Europeans, Canadiens, and First Nations on the Ottawa River dates back to the French Regime and New France (Havard

2016, 130). The Ottawa River provided a quick canoe route to the Great Lakes and the rich fur-bearing regions beyond this hydrological basin. The route took French expeditions up the Ottawa to the Mattawa River and then crossed Nipissing Lake to reach Rivière des Français (French River). Little is known of the Métis who may have travelled up the river or lived in the region during the French period. However, in all likelihood there was a Métis presence here, given that a Métis population in the Illinois Country already travelled freely between the Great Lakes and Montréal after La Grande paix de Montréal (the Great Peace of Montréal) was concluded in 1701 between the Iroquois Confederacy, the French, and about forty other nations, represented by some 1,300 delegates.

Gilles Havard's (2003, 2016) meticulously researched work provides telling insights into the emergence of the Métis in the Pays d'en Haut, the vast western regions of New France. Though his work provides useful data about the larger context, Havard does not delve into detail on the history of the fur trade in the Outaouais. His book *Empire et métissages* (2003) covers 1660 to 1715, ending more than half a century before our historical analysis begins. This work provides a helpful account of the rise and dissemination of a Canadien identity, and of how this identity often overlaps with a Métis one. Though his later *Histoire des coureurs de bois: Amérique du Nord 1600–1840* (2016) covers in part the historical period with which we are concerned, Havard does not dive far into the Hudson's Bay Company Archives, relying instead on secondary sources. As the fur trade in the Outaouais was seen as peripheral to the HBC, it has received little attention in most secondary sources, which is perhaps why Havard does not cover in depth the nineteenth-century history of the Outaouais Valley and neighbouring regions, leaving the impression that the fur trade no longer existed in this region.

The British Conquest of New France in 1760 fundamentally altered the Franco-Indian trade networks that covered much of North America (Borrows and Rotman 2012). In the aftermath, the American adventurer Alexander Henry was one of the first English speakers to venture, via the Ottawa River, past abandoned French forts to Fort Michilimackinac in 1761, witnessing what was left behind. In his account of the trip, Henry underscores the existence of an ancient trading post at Fort Coulonge, to the south of the Outaouais region. He also mentions another post close to Barrière,[1] and yet another at the entry to the Lièvre (Hare) River, probably operated by the Foubert family, who were later employed by the NWC (Newton 1991, 1). Although Henry noted only a few outposts, the trade posts would become much more numerous and active in the greater Outaouais region on the eve of the nineteenth century.

Joseph Mondion, for example, established a busy trading post at the Chutes des chats (Cat Falls) in 1796, although it was later absorbed by the NWC (Newton 1991, 1–2). Various competing trading posts were operating at the time in the valleys of the Lièvre and Gatineau rivers (Cormier 1978, 108–11). In 1819–20, the NWC established a trading outpost at Lake of Two Mountains, today's Kanesatake, followed by another post at Lac des Sables, on the Lièvre River above Buckingham, with an outpost at the Rivière Désert, or Desert River (Newton 1991, 1–2). Thus, the Ottawa River route and its tributaries was also part and parcel of the fur trade territory of the NWC, which was called the Grand River Department as the Ottawa was also known as the Grand River. Most hunters here were Anishinaabe, along with some Canadiens and Métis. Moreover, traders and forestry workers existed side by side here. The fur trade continued unabated, and the posts at Lake of Two Mountains and Lac des Sables operated until 1848 and 1849, respectively, though after 1821 under the HBC flag. The Fort Coulonge trading post was maintained until 1855, and another post at Lac des Allumettes continued until 1869. As for the outpost at the Rivière Désert, it seems that it was operational until 1878, and a post at Grand Lac (established in or before 1788) was not closed until 1956 (Bond 1966, 16–17, 21; Marcotte 2015, 82).[2]

The fur trade did not, however, reign supreme in the Outaouais region at the onset of the nineteenth century. Philemon Wright, an American entrepreneur who established himself in the Ottawa River area at the close of the eighteenth century, exercised largely unfettered control over all the important commercial activities of the region where the Gatineau flows into the Ottawa, and was granted rights over part of the township of Hull. Wright's influence blocked any and all competing commercial enterprises from establishing themselves in the region (Newton 1991, 1; Ouellet and Thériault 1988). Consequently, neither the NWC nor its competitor HBC after the merger of the two companies in 1821 were able to open a trade post in the region of Chaudières and Hull. Because the companies could not effectively monopolize trade in the Ottawa watershed, a class of freemen were able to establish themselves as "petty traders," and this in spite of the fact that the HBC successfully opened a number of posts elsewhere in the Outaouais region and acquired the posts that had been under the NWC flag (Bond 1966, 7; Newton 1991, 1).

River mouths were favoured locations for trading posts because it was relatively easy to intercept hunters from here as they canoed down the riverine passages. The mouth of the Gatineau River, where it flows into the Ottawa, was a strategic locale that had escaped the control of the fur trade companies. But the HBC had a strategy: it set up outposts next to the hunting grounds of the First Nations to meet them *before* they went down the Gatineau and came across the free traders who had established themselves in the region. The trade post at Lake of Two Mountains also formed a barrier to the northward movement of independent traders (Bond 1966, 8; Du Ranquet [1843] 2000, 132).[3] Archival documents testify to the activities and competitive climate in the larger Outaouais region. Having perhaps learned the danger of such free traders after the Conquest – free trade had grown in size and strength and coalesced to become the NWC, pushing the HBC toward bankruptcy – the company was diligent in seeking to choke out any small individual competitors.

The historical context of the Outaouais fur trade can thus be understood as a theatre of commercial conflicts and efforts by the HBC to establish a monopoly. Despite the fact that the posts at Mattawa and along the Ottawa River were not profitable, the HBC maintained them in order to check the movement of petty traders and block their access to the rich fur-bearing regions of Témiscamingue and Rupert's Land farther north (Anick 1976, 150; Newton 1991, 3). In the 1820s, the mission of the posts at Lake of Two Mountains, Fort Coulonge, and Lac des Sables was to scope out the operations of independent traders along the Ottawa River and up to Lake Nipissing under cover of their own trade activities. HBC posts also served to prevent canoe access via the Lièvre to the back country inhabited by *Sauvages* (First Nations) and Bois-Brûlés (Métis), where there was an appreciable supply of furs.

Although the Outaouais was close to Montréal and the growing populations of both Lower and Upper Canada, the region remained part of the Pays d'en Haut. In the upper back country, settlement was slow, marked by a few hamlets around the trade posts inhabited by Métis, First Nations, and Canadien squatters. This same regional circuit of rivers navigable by canoe was travelled by missionaries who sought to convert the First Nations and Métis; missionary activities increased in the 1830s and particularly 1840s on the Gatineau and Lièvre rivers (Inksetter 2017; Marcotte 2014). This was a period of great change in the region, but the fur trade persisted as a substrate upon which were deposited new economic enterprises – notably forestry and farming – in the southern zones. As the regional economy was being transformed, Métis families adapted as well as they could in terms of occupational and cultural mobility. They became important actors in their own right in this transitional period, during which the fur trade withstood profound socioeconomic upheaval. (See Appendix: Principal Métis Families of the Gatineau.)

Despite the prevalence of water transportation – be it canoes on the secondary rivers or steamships, which make their first appearance on the Ottawa River during this period – travel between outposts was at times slow and gruelling, but not enough to deter either missionaries or free traders. A personal account by the missionary Bellefeuille highlights the practicability of such travel: "I left the twentieth of August from *Témiskaming* at one o'clock in the afternoon and happily arrived at the post of the *Allumettes* the twenty-fourth at nine o'clock in the morning, therefore in a matter of *less than four days,* this which passes as a rapid voyage" (Bellefeuille 1840a, 86; our translation). His account offers an important detail of Métis ethnogenesis in the greater Outaouais region, revealing the feasibility of travelling between the various regional posts not only for missionaries but also for individuals and their families. The relative ease of travel between posts following the river system, which connected hot-spots of permanent settlement, suggests that such communities did not evolve in a vacuum. A canoe trip of ten or so days was considered routine at the beginning of the nineteenth century. Mail, news, merchandise, and people moved from one locale to the next naturally. As the life trajectories of individuals demonstrate, the Métis families who inhabited the Gatineau region maintained multiple levels of relations within a notable occupational and cultural mobility.

### Explorers and Surveyors: Mapping the Outaouais Region

By the end of the 1820s, available agricultural land was running short in the St. Lawrence Valley. The growing French-speaking Canadien population had filled the seigneuries of Lower Canada, and land was being sub-divided even as the fertility of the soil waned. To push the agricultural frontier, expeditions were sent to identify land that would be amenable to farming, and this included surveying the land to encourage its colonization by agricultural settlers. With this aim, the Parliament of Lower Canada commissioned a study of the lands between the Ottawa and Saint-Maurice rivers. Commissioners were appointed to oversee the work and budget, and a team was assembled to set out by canoe and report back to the provincial Parliament. Two British officers volunteered, Lieutenant Frederick Lenox Ingall of the 15th Regiment and Ensign Henry Nixon of the 66th Regiment, and they were granted leave to undertake the task.[4]

The members of this expedition generated rich documentation that gives necessary nuance to the history of the Métis of the greater Outaouais region. Foremost is the *Report of the Commissioners Appointed under the Act 9th George IVth. chap. 29, for Exploring that Part of the Province Which Lies between the Rivers Saint Maurice & Ottawa, and Which Still Remains Waste and Uncultivated*, which was submitted to Parliament (Ingall, Nixon, and Adams 1830). In it, Ingall provides a firsthand account not only of the geology of the region but also of various individuals encountered and events that occurred during the expedition. He truly provides a "thick description," to borrow Geertz's (1973) expression, of the history of the region, with detailed information about the inhabitants as well as the expedition itself.

The second notable document is John Adams's (1831) "Sketches of the Tête de Boule Indians, River St. Maurice." Though this work looks specifically at the Têtes-de-Boule, today known as Atikamekw, Adams also finds it necessary to refer to the Métis and their trading practices, describing them in vivid terms:

> I was even informed that should these engagés of the fur companies find parcels of furs at an encampment when the owners are absent, they will seldom scruple to take them, and leave a tally for the amount, indicating to which of the posts they are indebted for the kindness of saving them the trouble of carrying their own goods to market. The men employed to visit the Indians in this manner are always Canadians, or half-breeds, and mostly daring fellows and skilful *voyageurs;* they are known by the *(patois)* appellation of Gens Derrouine, and they always put me in mind of bees returning to their hives, or posts, laden with plunder, and ready for another excursion, as soon as they have safely deposited the treasure with which they were laden. (Adams 1831, 29; emphasis in original)

Adams thus defines Métis not only as Half-breeds but also in occupational terms as "Gens Derrouine," or, to be more precise, *gens de la dérouine*. *Dérouine* is an archaic French term that refers to venturing out to the back country to engage in trade directly on Indigenous hunting grounds.

As Ingall, Nixon, and surveyor John Adams travelled from the Saint-Maurice to the Ottawa River, Alexander Shirreff was exploring the lands between the Ottawa River and Lake Huron. Shirreff was a long-time inhabitant of the Outaouais region. His father, Charles, came from a Scottish family of merchants and shipbuilders, but he was also tied to the Baltic timber trade, which was curtailed under Napoleon's continental embargo against trade with Britain, the same event that led to a timber boom in the Outaouais region. (Napoleon's army controlled access to European and Baltic ports, restricting exports to Great Britain in order to suffocate its economy.) Shirreff Sr. was granted 5,000 acres in the upper Ottawa Valley, and moved there in 1818 (Allen 2011, 11). William Allen (2011, 11–12) notes that Charles Shirreff had authored a report proposing that a direct route be established between the Ottawa River and Georgian Bay, based on information received from "Indian traders." His son, Alexander, who had worked under Colonel By in building the Rideau Canal, was sent to see if the proposed route would indeed be viable. Coincidentally, Alexander Shirreff published an article in the same scholarly periodical as John Adams. In this work, "Topographical Notices of the Country Lying between the Mouth of the Rideau and Penetanguishene, on Lake Huron," Shirreff (1831, 265) wrote, "la Bosse settlement, consist[s] of a narrow entrance, about a mile in length, with eight or ten huts. The poor unprogressing appearance of the place, at once marks it as a nest of old trading people – French, or Bois Brulées." The settlement in question was La Passe, across the river from Grand Calumet Island and a short distance from Fort Coulonge.

The work of Joseph Bouchette Sr. also attests to the Métis presence in the region. The elder Bouchette was born in Québec in 1774. Son of Jean-Baptiste and Marie-Angélique Duhamel, Joseph was clearly a French speaker, but he acquired great facility in English. Although not all of his academic history is known, his surveyor's diploma indicates that he was fluent in both spoken and written English. In 1790, he was working as an assistant draftsman for the Surveyor's General Office in Québec, before being appointed Surveyor General as confirmed in 1804 (Boudreau and Lépine 1988). He then served in the War of 1812, applying his expertise to the service of the British forces.[5] In 1824, he was commissioned by Lord Dalhousie to survey the Crown lands of Lower Canada in order to help resolve the question of land grants to decommissioned military men. The results of the survey were published as a report in 1825, which was lauded in a letter by the governor. Between 1826 and 1829, Bouchette was collecting data for a new set of books that would provide a detailed description of Lower and Upper Canada, and incidentally generate income for their always indebted author: the two-volume work *The British Dominions in North America; or a Topographical and Statistical Description of the Provinces of Lower and Upper Canada* ... (see 1832a for vol. 1); and *A Topographical Dictionary of the Province of Lower Canada* (1832b). In this work, Bouchette describes the Métis "squatters" he encountered. With French as his mother tongue, he would have fully understood what was said in French and the nuances of terms such as *Bois-Brûlés,* but given his class ambitions, he may not have empathized much with their plight.

Taken together, the works of all these men, based on firsthand research done at the end of the 1820s, provide a rich understanding of the fur trade frontier before it was opened up to massive agricultural settlement.

## The 1830 Ingall Report

Ingall and his fellow commissioners recorded a Métis presence in their official 1830 report of the zone between the Ottawa and Saint-Maurice rivers, a region that the title characterizes as "waste and uncultivated." The leaders of the expeditions relied on experienced voyageurs and birch-bark canoes in their reconnaissance of the territory. Commissioner Ingall recounts a sordid affair that occurred in the region, a murder at Pointe des Tombeaux, near Lake Kempt:

> Near the graves are the remains of a log hut, which had been erected as a temporary receiving place for furs, until a sufficient quantity had been collected to send to the post at Wemontachinque. This hut was in charge of a man named Tifoe, an Indian, who was married to a woman belonging to the tribe inhabiting the Lake of the Two Mountains. One day in the year 1816, while Tifoe was absent, a brother of Menisino, named Ke, ne, cab, an, nish, cum, accompanied by his wife and mother, went to the hut, and demanded of Tifoe's wife some provisions, which she refused. He insisted upon having

some; a scuffle ensued, and the villain shot the woman dead on the spot. They then departed, taking with them a young boy, the son of old Flamand, the Canadian hunter, who had given us so much information at Wemontachinque ... The mother observed, that if the boy met any of the half breeds, who were in the habit of going round to collect furs, he would certainly tell them in French of the murder. (Ingall, Nixon, and Adams 1830, 192, 194)

The authors refer to "métif" in the French version of the report and "half breed" in the English version. The term *Métif* was the standard before it was supplanted by *Métis*. This passage is telling as it shows that Métis were recognized as fur trade employees, or petty traders, who went around to collect furs, and also that they spoke French. Additionally, there were evidently sufficient numbers of Métis in the area for the murderers to fear that they would encounter some. For that reason, the young boy in Ingall's account is killed to prevent him from telling the tale.

This account not only highlights the presence of Métis but also positions them between the trade post of Weymontachie on the upper Saint-Maurice River and that of Lac des Sables in the Outaouais region – a strategic corridor between the two trading places. To top it off, Ingall then states, "Lake 'Culotte' [is] a name translated by the Bois Brulées, from the original Indian" (Ingall, Nixon and Adams 1830, 196). His identification of Bois-Brulés rather than Canadiens as the translators means that the name wasn't a recent invention or a translation by French-Canadian engagés; rather Ingall is cognizant of its origins and the role played by the Bois-Brûlés. His use of the French "Bois Brulées" is also noteworthy; the term is also used in the French version of the report but is corrected to "Bois-brûlés," as the adjective *brûlés* (burnt) has to be masculine to match the French word *bois* (196, 197). We see, then, a triad of terms used in English and French to refer to the same population: Half-breed = Bois-Brûlé = Métif. Around the same time, "Bois-Brûlés" were recorded by Alexis de Tocqueville (1860) farther away on the shores of the Saginaw River, and even earlier by Ross Cox (1832, 298) in the Pacific Northwest. Evidently, the same term was also current in the greater Outaouais region. Ingall would have heard the voyageurs, and most likely the Métis themselves, referring to the Bois-Brûlés. The demonstrated use of *Bois-Brûlés* and *Métif* is significant, as some researchers still assume that these terms did not exist east of the Great Lakes, or even east of the Prairies (see Peterson 2012).

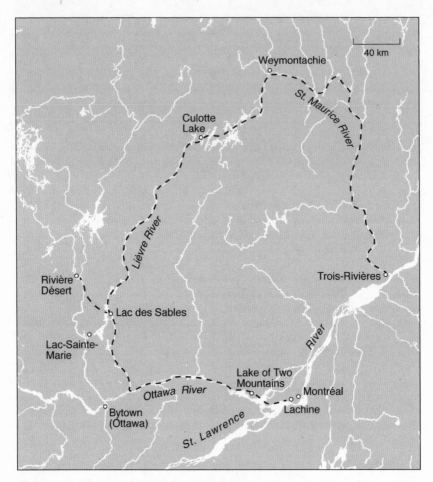

*Map 4*    Canoe routes mentioned in the Ingall Report

It is also possible to deduce that the Métis presence observed by Ingall was not limited to a set locale – namely, Culotte Lake or Pointe des Tombeaux – but rather that it extended along the entirety of the route connecting Weymontachie to Lac des Sables (see Map 4). The two trade posts were indeed commercially interconnected (Gélinas 2000, 68). Later, the canoe route that linked the two regions was also used by the missionaries (Payment 1842, 86–89). The fact that the Métis are credited with the translation of a topographic feature in the middle of this route and that they knew its original name, demonstrating a familiarity with the First Nations inhabiting the region, testifies anecdotally to their presence, but Ingall goes further by indicating that Métis were in the region.

Though the terms *Métif, Bois-Brûlés,* and the English *Half-breed* are used interchangeably in the English version of the report, Ingall does not confuse any of these terms with *Indian,* which is invariably translated as *sauvage* in the French version. In one revealing passage he describes the murderous impulses of a man named Macootogan:

> An Indian, a mountaineer, whose name is Macootogan, or "Crooked Knife," in a drunken fit, confessed having in the course of his life, killed and eaten several Indians and "Metifs," or "Half Breeds." When sober, he attempted to deny it; but upon being closely pressed, he acknowledged the fact, but said starvation drove him to kill and eat the first man, and that he slew and eat the others from a decided preference to any other kind of flesh;[6] and finished his statement by declaring that he would kill any "Metif" and eat him that he should meet alone. (Ingall, Nixon, and Adams 1830, 134)

Here, Ingall signals that Métis are not Indians – a distinction that Macootogan also apparently makes. In this passage and others, Ingall refers to "Métif" and "Métifs," implying both an individual and a collective identity distinct from First Nations and European heritage.

This distinction between Métis and Indians is observed not only in the northeastern Outaouais region but also at the departure point of the Ottawa River trade route, at Lake of Two Mountains. Two notable HBC officers, Angus Cameron and James Keith, exchanged letters concerning the presence of a certain Longmore and a group of Métis (a "Half Breed Party"): "Longmore's account has been presented to him and he pretends that he has not been credited with all the Furs which he delivered ... himself & his Half Breed Party are expected to start in a few days."[7] Here again, the Métis group does not seem to be associated with either Algonquin or Iroquois hunters. The 1828 account books of the HBC specify that Andrew Longmore is a "petty trader" rather than a hunter, an occupational term generally reserved for "Indians."[8] In fact, in 1831 Longmore is reported to be leading an independent trade expedition composed of "Half Breeds" up the Ottawa River, as recorded in the correspondence of the two HBC officers two months later: "I am informed that the Band of half Breeds who went up on a Trading excursion some time ago, have divided into two parties, one of which proceeded to Fort Coulonge, & the other have established themselves in the Bonnechere alongside of Siccard."[9]

The distinctive character of the Métis in the region is expressed even more clearly in another letter that Angus Cameron composed in 1835 at Témiscamingue, in which he evokes two ethnic categories as particularly efficient for combatting the implantation of new petty traders in the region: the (French) Canadiens and the Métis (Half-breeds). Cameron affirms that the best way to counter the competition is to hire both groups: "the required reinforcement of canadians they (and half Breeds) being the only hands fit to contend with opposition."[10] Such descriptions buttress Ingall's affirmations that Métis occupied the larger Outaouais region in an organized fashion between 1816 and 1838. Many groups of free traders and Métis seem to be present and active in the region, as Angus Cameron confirms in 1837–38 when he describes yet again a "party of half Breeds" – this time in the sector of Lakes Témiscamingue and Matawagamingue.[11] Many other independent traders, such as Aeneas Daniel McDonell and Charles Thomas, shared the trade route that Andrew Longmore took on the Ottawa River (Rich 1983; Stone Circle Consulting and Know History 2015, 60–61).

### The "Bois-Brûlé" Ethnonym

That a collective and distinct Métis or Métif cultural presence was observed at the beginning of the nineteenth century in diverse corners of the greater Outaouais region is certainly important. But the Ingall report carries an extra layer of significance when we consider its use of the term *Bois-Brûlé*. A review of the context ascribed to the term across the continent is useful here. One of the most significant uses occurs in the "Chanson de la Grenouillère," the song composed by Métis Pierre Falcon the day after the Battle of la Grenouillère, or Seven Oaks (LaRue 1863). Now regarded by many as a Métis anthem, the song merits closer analysis. We translate its lyrics as follows:

> Would you like to hear sung
> A song of truth?
> Would you like to hear sung
> A song of truth?
>
> On the nineteenth of June, the band of Bois-Brûlés
> Arrived as brave warriors
> Arriving at the frog pond [*grenouillère*]
> We took three prisoners:

Three prisoners from the Orkneys
Who are here to pillage our country.

Getting ready to dismount,
Two of our people cried out,
Two of our people cried out:
Here is the Englishman who comes to attack us.

Right away we turned around,
We had gone to meet them.
We spotted a band of grenadiers.
They are immobile, they are dismounted.

We acted as honourable people,
We sent an ambassador.
Governor, do you not want to stop for a moment?
We want to talk to you.

Falcon did not produce a written version of this song, and the lyrics produced here are therefore based on a version sung by a voyageur and recorded by François-Alexandre-Hubert LaRue, and subsequently published in 1863 in *Le Foyer canadien* in Québec. Though some of the turns of phrase and grammar appear archaic to a modern French speaker, the song is nonetheless in French.

In the first verse, the song defines Métis as Bois-Brûlés, and in the verses that follow they are set in opposition to both Englishmen and Orkney Islanders. The battle that raged in the Red River region in 1816 resulted in the Bois-Brûlés successfully fending off a company of Selkirk colonists and HBC employees who were under the leadership of Governor Semple (Ens and Sawchuk 2016, 87). This battle occurred against the backdrop of a fur trade war that pitted the NWC against the Selkirk Settlement and the HBC. Gerhard Ens demonstrates, however, that the nationalism voiced by Métis leader Cuthbert Grant was instrumentalized by the NWC so that blame for the disturbances – which the NWC in fact encouraged among its employees against the Scottish newcomers and the HBC – could fall squarely on the Métis "new nation" rather than the company once the dust settled (Ens 2012, 103–4). At the apex of the conflict, Governor Semple was killed, and Lord Selkirk wished to prosecute those involved in the Pemmican

War. We should note that Canadiens and First Nations warriors also took part in the conflict on the side of Cuthbert Grant, so his group was not ethnically homogeneous. That said, the term *Bois-Brûlé* seems to have been adopted by French-speaking Métis to designate themselves, at least during the conflict that ensued following the pemmican trade prohibition.

Eventually, the supremacy of Selkirk was restored with the help of Chief Peguis and his warriors, while lands continued to be redistributed to Scottish settlers in accordance with a treaty that Selkirk had ratified with leaders of various Indigenous nations in 1817. The treaty makes no mention of the Métis as a people who should be included in negotiations over Red River land (Ens 2012, 106). Evidence nevertheless suggests that the Bois-Brûlés formed a distinct group. For instance, in an 1818 statement to W.B. Coltman, William McGillivray wrote, "the half-breeds under the denomination of *bois brulés* and *metifs* have formed a separate and distinct tribe of Indians for a considerable time back" (Ens and Sawchuk 2016, 81). It seems clear, however, that this "tribe" was diasporic, their presence being noted in different areas of North America along the fur trade routes.

Furthermore, the Bois-Brûlés were distinguished from English or Scottish Half-breeds as Canadian Métis, which reveals the importance of the French language, Catholicism, and other cultural markers shared with French-Canadian culture. The equivalence of *métis canadiens,* or (French) Canadian Métis, and Bois-Brûlés is evident in the comments of Monseigneur Alexandre-Antonin Taché of Saint-Boniface:

> The death of Governor Semple and his people, killed in 1816, has been the theme of many accusations against the Canadien Métis or "Bois-Brûlés."
>
> We will say later, in speaking of the history of the country, what we think of this deplorable event, and who bears culpability. Suffice it to say, at this time, this fact does not prove anything as to the character of our population and even less against the Catholic religion practised by the largest number of Bois-Brûlés. At the time, not one among them had been baptized, not one had the opportunity to be influenced by religion, and, in any case, an isolated incident is never proof of the character of this people or any people. (David 1883, 90; our translation)

This synonymy of French-Canadian Métis and Bois-Brûlé identity is also noticeable in reports on the Red River by George Bryce (1885, 6), in which he uses the terms *French Half-breed, Métis,* and *Bois-Brûlés* interchange-ably. Bryce was a Presbyterian minister, scholar, and prolific author who settled in Manitoba after the collapse of the provisional government in 1870. Similarly, Richard Henry Bonnycastle's (1846, 144) *Canada and the Canadians in 1846* describes the mixed ancestry of the Bois-Brûlés:

> To this day, where, in the interminable wilderness, all trace of French influ-ence is buried, the Indian reveres the recollections of his forefathers respect-ing that gallant race; and, wherever the canoe now penetrates the solemn and silent shades of the vast West, the Bois Brulé, or mixed offspring of the Indian and the Frenchman, may be heard awakening the slumber of ages with carols derived from the olden France, as he paddles swiftly and merrily along.

Likewise, the term *Bois-Brûlés* was used in both Upper and Lower Can-ada, according to the 1834 *Revue britannique,* a compilation of periodical articles from Great Britain, translated into French. One of the articles, entitled "Statistique – Du Commerce et de l'usage des pelleteries chez les anciens et les modernes," explains the origins of the Bois-Brûlés:

> More than once, this natural instinct, which brings the sexes together, made them overcome the disgust which the vulgarity of Indigenous women must inspire in civilized men. It is from this union that is born this Métis race, designated in the two Canadas under the name of Bois-Brûlés. We have even seen some, having cut all their ties to their family and their country, adopt the life and mores of the *sauvages,* and affiliate themselves with one or another of their tribes. (*Revue britannique* 1834, 370, our translation)

In this usage, the term *Bois-Brûlés* is equated with Métis and race, whereas in its earlier sense it would have been equated in turn with nation. But more striking is the suggestion that it is applied in both Upper and Lower Canada, which included the Outaouais region. The passage also suggests that while some Métis integrated fully into Indigenous populations, others did not.

Indeed, English writers increasingly adopted the term *Bois-Brûlé* in their work during the first half of the nineteenth century. In *Tales of the Northwest,* William Joseph Snelling calls one chapter "The Bois Brule." Published in 1830 and based on his travels across the continent in the 1820s, Snelling specifies in a footnote that "BOIS BRULES, is the name given to the half-breeds, in the Indian country" (Snelling 1830, 285). He indicates that the Bois-Brûlés speak French as well as the language of their mothers' tribe, and notes that "they receive just enough religious instruction from their fathers, to despise the belief and superstitions of their savage kindred, but are as ignorant of Christianity as Hottentots" (85). He also provides a description of the physical appearance of one Bois-Brûlé during a meeting with Governor Semple:

> He was dressed in the costume of the *bois brulés*... His nether man was invested with a pair of elk skin trowsers, the seams of which were ornamented with fringes. Over these he wore a capot, or surtout, of coarse blue cloth, reaching to the mid leg, and bound round the waist with a scarlet woollen sash, in which was stuck a dague, or broad two edged knife, used in that country to divide the carcass of the buffalo. Buck skin moccasins, and a *capuchon* of one piece with the surtout, completed his attire. (89)

The cultural description of Bois-Brûlés in the Red River region in the 1820s parallels those of other authors across the continent. Ross Cox (1832, 309), an Irishman who spent the first years of the 1810s in the Pacific Northwest, defines Half-breeds as follows: "They are called Les Bois Brulés – but why, it is difficult to ascertain." Thus, by the 1830s, *Bois-Brûlés* was being used from the Pacific to the Red River and the Great Lakes, and beyond to the larger Outaouais region. In all these locales, the term refers to a population with mixed ancestry who generally spoke French and were tied to the fur trade.

It is also found in *Forestiers et voyageurs,* published by Joseph-Charles Taché in 1863, and based on real life stories. He describes voyageurs married to First Nations women *(Sauvagesses)* and living as freemen or as independent hunters in the Pays d'en Haut, as well as their "Mitis" or Bois-Brûlés descendants. Taché was a medical doctor and politician before undertaking a long writing career. His brother, Alexandre-Antonin Taché, became the second bishop of Red River (Saint-Boniface) in 1853 and the first archbishop of Saint-Boniface in 1871, where he served until his death in 1894. Joseph-Charles Taché's somewhat romanticized account of the North-West was therefore based on documentary sources, conversations with voyageurs and freemen in the Pays d'en Haut, and information shared by his own brother, an influential cleric in Red River. Taché makes no distinction between Métis based on where they lived, applying the term *Bois-Brûlé* to all:

> Before the arrival of the Hudson's Bay Company in the upper country [Pays d'en Haut], there had never been settlers in these regions: the population was composed of different *sauvage* nations, freemen and hired men. The freemen were ancient voyageurs married to *Sauvagesses;* they lived on what they hunted and the work they did from time to time for the North West [Company]. It is the descendants of these freemen that we named and name Mitis or Bois-Brûlés ... The majority of the bourgeois and clerks were Scottish or English, but almost all the interpreters and voyageurs were Canadiens. (Taché [1863] 2002, 206–7; our translation)

Taché thus employs the same terminology as Snelling, Tocqueville, Ingall, and Shirreff. Though he uses *Bois-Brûlé* with reference to Red River, he does not imply that the word applies solely to this population. Rather, the implication is that all the descendants of Canadiens and Indigenous women are Bois-Brûlés, and his descriptions of the Ottawa River explicitly indicate that the region was part and parcel of the Pays d'en Haut. Furthermore, Bois-Brûlés across the continent are described in terms of similar ethnocultural markers.

The entanglement of Canadien and Métis identities is also highlighted in the work of the renowned French political philosopher Alexis de Tocqueville. While sojourning in North America, he spent a fortnight in the "desert," or wilderness. Venturing from Detroit to the forests surrounding the settlement in the 1830s, Tocqueville described a man he encountered on the shores of the Saginaw River:

> As I was preparing myself to get in, the so-called Indian came to me, placed two fingers on my shoulder and told me with a Normand accent [French from the region of Normandy, in France, prevalent in Québec] that made me quiver: "Ah! You come from the old country of France! ... Wait, don't go too quickly; there are some who sometimes drown here." Had my horse spoken to me, I would not have been less surprised. I studied the one who had spoken and whose figure bathed in the first rays of the moon glowed like a ball of copper: Who are you? I asked him; you speak French, yet you have all the airs of an Indian? He answered that he was a bois-brûlé, that is to say the son of a Canadien and an Indian woman. I would often have the

opportunity of speaking about this singular race of Métis who cover all the frontiers of Canada and part of those of the United States. For the moment, I did not think more than of the pleasure of speaking my mother tongue. (Tocqueville 1860, 594–95, as translated in Foxcurran, Bouchard, and Malette 2016, 176)

As in the writings of Ingall and Shirreff, the reference to "bois-brûlé" here is not limited to the Red River or even the North-West. Rather, Tocqueville specifies that the man he meets is part of a race that spans the frontiers of the United States and Canada. The historical meaning of frontier, as used by Tocqueville, designated the geographical transition, or border-land, between territory that had a majority of European settlers and zones said to be Indian, or part of the Indian Country. Indeed, the greater Outaouais region of the 1830s was still a borderland, where the majority population was Indigenous.

By the 1840s, the term *Bois-Brûlé* had seeped into the lexicon of the bureaucrats of the now unified Canadas. In the 1847 "Report on the Affairs of the Indians in Canada," submitted to the Legislative Assembly, Superintendent J.W. (John) Keating reports,

But on Lake Huron and other places where I have had an opportunity of meeting the *"Bois brulé"* and full bred Indian, a marked difference is to be seen between the two. The former are mostly of French origin, a cross be-tween the numerous Canadians employed by the traders. The half breed is a species of Pariah from his own people, and assumes over the Indians a superiority they are unwilling to concede; he is beside generally dissipated, and unprincipled, and in all commercial intercourse, takes advantage of his knowledge of Indian character and habits, more effectually to grind down and impoverish the wretched dependants on the trader. These people are the curse of the Aborigines, and in all cases mislead them. They excite them to dissipation, rob them when under the influence of the ardent spirits they take among them, and in fact the synonymous word to "good trader" is "great rascal." (Province of Canada 1847, T-133)

Here "Bois brulé" is used to describe the Métis population of the Great Lakes region, notably that of Lake Huron. For better or for worse – and from the perspective of the Indian agent, definitely for worse – the

Bois-Brûlés are distinctive, forming a separate population from Indian nations.

## The Bagot Commission Testimonies

The 1847 report, published two years after the Bagot Report, provides a wealth of data illustrating how terms such as *Half-breed* and *Bois-Brûlé* were understood. The document starts with Section III, seemingly to highlight that it is a continuation of the earlier report, although that purpose is not specified. The 1847 report contains an appendix comprising fifty-three questions (as listed on pages T-63 to T-65) for the Indian agents who were overseeing reserves and settlements, and another twenty-four questions for the "Missionaries and others acquainted with the Indians" (T-65). The questions for the Indian agents include, for example, "Are [your charges] improved during that time in their moral and religious character, and in habits of industry?" (question 2) and "Do any of the Indians under your superintendence, from choice live in Wigwams? If so state the number" (question 5). The questions focus on whether agriculture is being successfully practised (questions 6 to 15), whether Indigenous "fondness for fishing, hunting, &c. [is] as great as formerly" (question 19), whether Indians have been converted and are faithfully practising Christianity (questions 23 to 32), whether their children are attending school (questions 33 to 36), and whether they have adopted any trades (carpentry, blacksmithing, and tailoring among others). Yet more questions inquire about the health of and prevailing diseases among Indians. One question specifically asks about marriages between Indian women and whites (question 45), and another asks about the presence of Half-breeds in the English version and Métis in the French version (question 46).

Historian Ted Binnema (2014, 5) has argued that the first pre-Confederate legislation to define "Indian" was adopted with the intention of protecting Indigenous people from exploitation and dispossession: "Officials only reluctantly decided to define Indian in law in 1850 in efforts to protect Indian land in Lower Canada." Binnema notes that in the case of the territory formerly known as Lower Canada, the primary threat was from "plausible insiders" – that is, those who had First Nations and European ancestry (9–10). He provides as an example the Gill family, descendants of two captives taken in New England and fully integrated into Abenaki society. He explains: "Because of intermarriage, all of Lower

Canada, including cities like Montreal and Quebec, as well as Indian reserves, was inhabited by people whose genetic heritage was mixed," yet because of lifestyle and relationships, others considered these individuals outsiders (10–11). Binnema's work highlights the need for nuanced research that takes into account the agency of all social actors and the changing political and social landscape. What may have been true in 1880 may not have been true in 1850, and thus it is necessary to avoid applying reductive principles that homogenize history. Likewise, the forces shaping one community may differ from those in another locale and/or at another time. Thus, our goal is to ensure a detailed analysis of ethnogenesis in one particular place, with particular attention to the actions of all the relevant social actors. The concept of "plausible insider" does resonate in the region that Binnema examines, the St. Lawrence Valley, but would not necessarily be applicable to other communities, like those in the Outaouais.

Reinforcing William McGillivray's idea that the Bois-Brûlés "have formed a separate and distinct tribe of Indians for a considerable time back," the testimony of Chief Superintendent of Indian Affairs Samuel P. Jarvis in the 1847 report emphasizes that Half-breeds ("Métis" in the French translation) see themselves as different from their Indigenous kin and have different lifeways:

> The half-breeds residing with the Indians, who are known to be the offspring of Indian women, and white men with whom they have cohabited, bear a very small proportion to the number of the Tribes, such half-breeds being generally the offspring of French Canadians, adopted as they grow up the manners and customs of their fathers, and become in fact more French than Indian in their habits and mode of life; they consider themselves a superior race to the full blooded Indian; to whom they apply the cognomen of "Savage" when speaking of them. (Province of Canada 1847, T-93)

Jarvis thus ascribes a distinctive identity to Half-breeds while affirming that the difference between them and the Indigenous populace is inherently cultural because they have adopted the "habits and modes of life" of their fathers. Nonetheless, Half-breeds are not to be confused with their Canadien kin. Jarvis highlights their knowledge of multiple languages and their disdain for agriculture:

The habits of the half-breeds resemble very much the habits of the lower order of the French Canadians, from whom they are principally descended; the most of them speak French, English, and their native language. I think the half-breeds are a more industrious class than the native Indian, except when the latter is in pursuit of game; they are exceedingly fond of music, dancing, and indeed any pastime which produces excitement at the moment. Their tastes for Agricultural pursuits is much on a par with the native Indian's, few of them doing more in that way than to raise a few vegetable[s] for their own consumption. (Province of Canada 1847, T-93)

Jarvis's account thus lends credence to the methodological model proposed, whereby a series of cultural markers can be used to determine the existence of a historical Métis community. His testimony underscores the ambivalence, if not hostility, of the Indian Department toward the Métis. He acknowledges, "They are generally stronger and more capable of enduring violent exercise and fatigue than the native Indian, and for that reason are generally preferred by the traders as canoemen," but adds, "They are, however, much addicted to the use of *ardent spirits,* and when in a state of intoxication become frequently very insolent and abusive" (T-93). While the Métis could be considered "civilized" by government officials, they were also perceived as immoral, dangerous, and thus a source of corruption for the Indians the department sought to manage.

Though the term *Half-breed* is used in these passages, elsewhere in the report are indicators that the term *Métis* was seeping into the lexicon of government officials, if only via French-speaking officials who were writing in English. The Reverend J. Marcoux, in his discussion of Sault St. Louis, writes, "If by the word Métis you mean those who are half or less than half Indian, they are very numerous" (Province of Canada 1847, T-69). As each of the accounts in the 1847 report follows the same numbered format in response to set questions, under the forty-sixth point Indian agents answered the following question: "Among the Indians under your superintendence, what is the proportion of half-breeds?" Marcoux's answer indicates that he had read the question in both French and English, and he uses the French *Métis* in answering the English question about Half-breeds.

Keating, however, clarifies his understanding of what it means to be Métis:

Among the Indians under my superintendence I am not aware of the existence of any regular half-breeds, that is to say, of our persons combining the
French or English habits with those of the Indians. That there may be a
mixture of the races I have no doubt, from the close and constant intercourse
with the numerous whites settled among them, but there are no recognized
children of mixed parentage; they all here alike yield the issues to the same
Chief, and differ in nothing from those whose red blood is uncontaminated.
(Province of Canada 1847, T-133)

Keating thus distinguishes "regular half-breeds" (i.e., Métis) from individuals of mixed ancestry; to be Métis in his understanding necessitates
the combination of European and Indian "habits," which is to say culture.
Though Keating brushes aside the existence of Métis of Walpole Island,
he does hint of it in the previous section, in which agents must comment
on the intermarriage of Indian women with whites: "Seldom or ever here,
although in the North among the traders is of every day occurrence"
(T-133).

The nuances expressed in these distinctions are important, as the Indian
agents in effect insist on the distinctive culture of the Bois-Brûlés (Canadien Métis). They are asserting as a matter of fact that to be Métis means
more than having mixed ancestry. The Jesuit priest Pierre Chazelle ([1844]
1973, 190, our translation), writing in the same period, also highlights
the "sauvage" nature of the Indian population of Walpole Island:

Our insulars, who see themselves as the model Nation, detest those half-
civilized *sauvages* as they hold on religiously to their ancient practices ... In
spite of their pretension to being faithful to the traditions of the life and the
family of their ancestors, I found among them fewer pure *sauvages* as I would
have thought. They offer to observers traits and nuances which announce
their European blood.

Here, too, culture is not a product of biology, and communities could
and did reject the integration of cultural practices from outsiders, even
if they had potential kin relations with those outsiders.

Following the same format of questions, the Reverend William, reporting on the Chippewas of Saugeen, emphasizes the importance of educa-
tional milieu in shaping Métis identity. Thus, children fall along a
continuum, some being wholly Indian and others comparable to whites:

It is my opinion, that this depends wholly upon their education. Those children, whose fathers are white men, who have been brought up among the Indians, are perfect Indians in every sense of the word, except complexion.

Those who have been brought up among the French Canadians, partake much of their manners and dispositions; and those who have been brought up in well ordered society, seem to lose nothing in a comparison with the white youth of the same neighbourhood and society. They, like other men, seem to derive their character from the spheres and scenes in which they move. (Province of Canada 1847, T-187).

William suggests that Métis brought up among French Canadians share some of "their manners and dispositions," but implies that they do not fully integrate and therefore remain somewhat distinct. (His testimony also reveals an Anglo-Saxon bias that sees French-Canadian society as not truly "well ordered" and thus unable to fully ensure all the presumed benefits of an education in a white society.) This third category – whereby Métis remained closer to French Canadians but were not fully like them – would thus presumably develop a cultural mix in children (rather than simply being of mixed blood), and this seems to be what Keating is alluding to when speaking of the Bois-Brûlés of Lake Huron and other locales. Likewise, this characterization parallels Ingall's discussion of Bois-Brûlés in the greater Outaouais region. In these primary sources, the interethnic parentage of the Bois-Brûlés, or Canadien Métis, emerges within a specific occupational context that in turn shapes a cultural complex from both European and Indian mores and considered by outside observers to be distinctive.

In short, a number of traits tend to characterize the Métis described in these accounts. Multilingualism is invariably highlighted, including mastery of Indigenous languages. The Métis are highly mobile, and their mobility is tied to the practices of the fur trade, which obliged movement between distant fur trade posts. They are also described as having subsistence strategies closer to Indigenous practices – hunting, fishing, and gathering, as opposed to intensive agriculture. Nonetheless, they demonstrate other cultural affinities that nullify their inclusion in the "pure sa(u)vage" category or even that of the Indians of mixed ancestry, who are not seen as "regular" – i.e., culturally distinct – Half-breeds, Bois-Brûlés, or Métis.

The 1847 report, along with the earlier findings of the Bagot Commission, brings to mind Binnema's (2014) discussion of the "plausible insiders" and the presence of "Métis" in the Indian villages of the St. Lawrence, east of the Outaouais region. D.C. Napier, the Indian agent responsible for filling out the questionnaire for Caughnawaga (today Kahnawake), specifies, "The Indians of Caughnawaga are nearly all half-breeds, or the children of Indians of mixed blood"; and responding to the question about any differences between the two, he says, "None whatever; their general conduct, habits, language, and pursuits are the same" (Province of Canada, 1847, T-67). The Reverend F.X. Marcoux, writing from St. Régis (today Akwesasne), also notes, "They are all half-breeds – it is difficult to find an Indian of pure blood," but this changes little as, in his words, "I see no difference between the *half-breeds* and the Indians of pure blood" (T-74).

The missionary J. Marcoux, priest at Sault St. Louis, concurs: "There is no difference; their education which is exactly the same, gives them the very same ideas, the same prejudices, and the same character, because they all speak the same tongue" (Province of Canada 1847, T-69). This Marcoux, too, affirms that most of the Indians at Sault St. Louis are Métis, but suggests that it is not blood quantum alone that defines identity: "At Sault St. Louis you would not perhaps find ten pure Indians. The annual Presents have a few years ago been unjustly taken from some of these half breeds, while they have been given to others who have less Indian blood, and in other villages no distinction is made" (T-69). Unfortunately, the priest states that he will not enter into great detail, but this telling statement again suggests that criteria other than ancestry determined identity and rights within the community. At St. Régis, the government bureaucrat S.Y. Chesley offers a similar response but notes a slight difference between Métis and Indians when it comes to drunkenness, which he suggests is more pronounced among the former than with respect to "the real Indian" (T-72).

At the third Iroquois community in Lower Canada, the Lake of Two Mountains (today Kanesatake), Superintendent J. Hughes specifies that at least two-thirds of the Indians are Métis, and further, "No difference whatever exists in the habits and ways of living of the half-breeds and the native Indians, but in general the half-breeds are far more addicted to vice than the native Indians" (Province of Canada 1847, T-76). Here the motif of the Métis as less moral surfaces again. Hughes reinforces his statement by noting that both men and women who marry into the community adopt its cultural practices: "In cases of intermarriages taking place with the whites, the condition of the Indian does not improve; white women who marry Indians adopt their manners and dress themselves like Indian women, and the generality of the white men who marry Indian women do the same, as well as their children" (T-76). Once again, no *cultural* mixing is apparent to the Indian agent. Having mixed heritage did not make the individual any less Indian, and many fully integrated into the community.

The same pattern holds true in observations about the Abenaki community of St. François (today Odanak). The priest P. Bélaud offers this observation about the presence of "Métis" in the community: "Not only the half-breeds fall into the habits of the Indians, but often also the whites who intermarry with them" (Province of Canada 1847, T-80). This idea echoes in the writings of Noel Annance, who defined himself as fully and wholly Abenaki, even if he was referred to as a Métif (Barman 2016). Affirmation of being pure Indian is also noted among the Abenaki of Bécancour (today Wôlinak) as well as the Algonquins of Trois-Rivières and the Têtes-de-Boules of Saint-Maurice. After mentioning and quantifying the limited number of Métis in the region – "One-sixth among the Algonquins, one-twentieth among the Abenaquois [Abenaki], and three among the *Têtes de Boule*" – M. De Niverville highlights that there is no difference between the groups: "No; for they are all considered as Indians of pure blood" (Province of Canada, 1847, T-82). Thus, having mixed ancestry does not make one any less "Indian" here either. Finally, the priest L. Fortier, in answering the same questions for the Hurons of Lorette, present-day Wendake, states that they are all Métis (T-83).

Clearly evident from the Bagot Commission testimonies is that the social and cultural contexts of Indigenous people varied in different regions of Canada (which included Lower and Upper Canada), and that local agents were grappling with how to define Half-breeds or Métis in their particular contexts. Some went so far as to provide definitions before proceeding to answer a specific question. In the minds of many agents, being Métis was more than simply being of mixed ancestry; a cultural component was also taken into consideration, with the expectation that "regular" Métis had a culture that was distinct from both Europeans and Indians.

## Distinguishing the Cultural Métis

The term *Métis* was therefore inherently polysemous, while *Bois-Brûlé* was much more precise. For Keating at Lake Huron and other northern locales with an active fur trade, Métis called "Bois-Brûlés" were distinct from "Indians" because of their "habits" (culture) and the occupational niche they occupied. They were not to be confused with those who were Métis or Half-breeds because of their mixed heritage, and who were culturally indistinct from their Indian peers and relations, such as those on Walpole Island. Our central question is this: which of the two potential definitions of Métis best fits the historical Métis community of the greater Outaouais region? Do they have a distinctive culture and lifeway that differs from Canadiens, Algonquins, and others and that would make them truly Métis, a distinct community from an anthropological perspective? Or are they Algonquins, or other First Nations, with mixed ancestry?

Had the Bagot Commission solicited an agent or other witnesses to report on the Indigenous population inhabiting the hinterland of the Outaouais at that time, it would have provided some data as a point of comparison. We do know that a number of Algonquins did not live at Lake of Two Mountains during the summer but spent the whole year in the Outaouais. They were referred to as Têtes-de-Boule, as distinguished from Algonquins who lived to the south during the summer (McLean 1849, 74).[12] It is therefore important to emphasize that not all Indigenous populations of Lower Canada were included in the Bagot Report, and to explore other documentary sources to determine if the Métis who were already known to be living in the greater Outaouais region were of mixed heritage but completely integrated into Indian communities, or, on the contrary, were comparable to the "Bois-Brûlés" described by Keating at Lake Huron and elsewhere – those who were active in the fur trade and had a distinctive culture and economy.

Historical documents depict these Métis as conforming to the second definition. Shirreff, Ingall, Joseph Bouchette Sr., and Allan McDonell (see Chapter 4) signal that Bois-Brûlés in the greater Outaouais region – notably those involved in the fur trade, who spoke French and were "old trading people" or "running here and there to get furs" – had a collective identity and distinctive culture. The documentary sources we analyzed demonstrate that Métis of the Outaouais region exhibit the same cultural markers seen elsewhere: interethnic Canadien Indigenous heritage (or occasionally British Indigenous), the use of French, the presence of French or British patronyms, and occupations as "intermediaries" tied to the fur trade.

Their hunting and fishing practices are described as different from those of Euro-Canadian settlers, who practised a more intensive form of agriculture. In many cases, it is reported that the Bois-Brûlés of the Outaouais region adopted agriculture tardily. Compared to the Bagot Report's descriptions of Abenaki, Huron (Wendat), and other Indians in the St. Lawrence Valley as largely mixed populations who followed First Nations habits and traditions, the documentary sources show that the ethnocultural composition of the Métis or Bois-Brûlés of the Outaouais region is more similar to that of the Métis of Lake Huron or even Sault Ste. Marie in the first half of the nineteenth century. Unlike the Half-breeds described as living among the Iroquois, Abenaki, or Huron, the Métis of the Outaouais region did not entirely share the habits and customs of the Algonquin and Atikamekw. Instead, they had a distinct culture that borrowed from both European and Indigenous sources. Passages from the Ingall Report provide an informative portrait of populations that correspond to descriptions of the Bois-Brûlés by Tocqueville, Taché, Bryce, Bonnycastle, Keating, Clapin (1894, 48), and Riel. It is evident that Métis in the Outaouais region exhibited cultural patterns and markers comparable to Métis in Sault Ste. Marie (Ray 1998), Ontario's Mattawa region (Stone Circle Consulting and Know History 2015), Great Slave Lake (Jones, n.d.), and Manitoba's Red River region (Havard 1880).

Whereas Indian agents in the St. Lawrence Valley writing reports for the Bagot Commission grudgingly used the term *Half-breed* to describe a population with mixed ancestry – while specifying that there were no real cultural differences between Half-breed Indians and those of pure blood – the historical sources attest that this was not the case for Métis in the Outaouais region. The fact that the Bagot Commission required Indian agents to comment on the presence of Half-breeds in the Indian communities of Lower and Upper Canada does not mean there was necessarily a Métis presence in these communities, nor that the Indian nations of the St. Lawrence were not fully Abenaki, Huron, or Iroquois. Rather, where individuals from other communities had been fully integrated into First Nations communities, they and their descendants were understood by both insiders and outsiders as indistinguishable in terms of identity and culture.

As the Bagot Report is largely silent on the Indigenous populations of the upper reaches of the Outaouais, we consulted other historical sources as well, and these underscore the originality of the Métis culture of the region in the first half of the nineteenth century. This comes to the fore when we compare these populations to the Bois-Brûlés of the Lake Huron who are described in the Bagot Report. It is culture that defines the shared traits of Bois-Brûlé communities – not solely having First Nations and European ancestors. Like other scholars, notably Andersen (2014), we suggest that the formation of a Métis identity depends upon more than a mixed heritage. A close reading of the reactions submitted by various Indian agents – both bureaucrats and clerics – reveals that, in the 1840s, distinctions were made between "regular" Half-breeds and those who were indistinguishable from the Indian populations among which they lived.

One of the best summaries of the Métis communities across the continent in the nineteenth century was compiled by a naturalized American citizen, Valery Havard. Born in 1846 in Compiègne, France, Havard studied medicine before immigrating to the United States. Once there, he served as a surgeon in the American military, appointed in 1871. He was active in the military throughout much of the three successive decades. In 1877, Havard was stationed with the 7th Cavalry in Montana. He was then posted with the 1st Infantry as it opened roads in West Texas. In the 1880s, he was under the command of Captain Livermore and stationed in the upper Rio Grande (Phalen 1939). Thus, Havard spent much of his career on the American frontier, and after his tour of duty in the American West, he submitted a report to the Board of Regents of the Smithsonian Institution entitled "The French Half-Breeds of the Northwest." His account appeared in the Smithsonian's 1879 *Annual Report,* which was published in 1880. It was quite thorough in its description of the continental Métis communities, and Havard specifies that he had personally known Métis individuals, writing, "Wherever I have met him, he has always appeared to me endowed with many qualities of heart and of mind which readily develop and ripen on contact with civilization" (Havard 1880, 320). Evidently, Havard spoke French and thus would have been able to speak directly with the French Half-breeds he describes. He uses the terms *Bois-Brûlé* and *Métis* in his account, even though its title uses *French Half-breeds.* Indeed, he understood the three terms as largely synonymous.

Havard (1880, 314) also underscores the vast geographical distribution of those he names collectively and distinctively as French mixed-bloods. Although he was writing a few decades after the publication of the Bagot Commission findings in 1845 and 1847, his work demonstrates the continued use of the term *Bois-Brûlé* across the continent. Furthermore, Havard was adamant that being Métis meant more than being of mixed ancestry:

> The term mixed-blood is too vaguely comprehensive. Métis, when referring to French mixed-bloods, seems the most appropriate name. The designation of French is often indifferently applied to Canadians, Métis of all grades, and even pure Indians who associate with métis and speak their *patois*. It should also be stated that in Manitoba and other places a certain proportion of mixed-bloods, from English and Scotch fathers, bearing such names as Grant, Grey, Sutherland, &c, are classified as French, from their language, religion, and associations, while occasionally such names as Lambert and Parisien are found among English half-breeds. (314)

Additionally, Havard refers to "'Bois-brulé' (burnt wood) [as] an appellation mostly used in the British provinces" (314), and thus not limited to Red River. He then proceeds to cover the continent, detailing how many Métis are found in each locale. The extent of the Métis presence, according to Havard, stretched to the "Indian Country" of New Mexico; he traces some thirty or so individuals who settled on the Canadian River, most likely, he suggests, "the descendants of the 8 Canadians, employees of the Hudson Bay Company, who at the beginning of this century, having wandered in a southern direction in quest of furs, were captured by a party of Mexicans and afterwards allowed to settle in New Mexico" (316). The Canadian River would have been named after these wayward fur traders, so, once again, "Canadian" meant French Canadian. Significantly, Havard asserts,

> If we could obtain the number of métis in Canada, New Brunswick, Nova Scotia, Labrador, and in the northern part of New England, as well as that of the French-descended families tainted with Indian blood in the States of Illinois and Missouri, I doubt not the total would reach at least 40,000 as the strength of the population of French-Canadian mixed-bloods in North America. (317)

Thus, he does not deny the existence of Métis in Québec and Ontario (here "Canada"), including the greater Outaouais region; rather, he laments that he cannot include their numbers in his survey.

As the following chapters describe, the distinct culture of the Métis of the Outaouais region is observed via a number of characteristic traits. In addition to those already noted – mixed heritage and the observed use of the French language – other markers emerge, including a particular relationship with Christianity, expertise in the industries of the *Sauvages,* the building and use of cabins (as opposed to tents), and expressions of collective identity. These markers substantiate our finding that Métis in the Ottawa Valley conformed to the "regular" pattern – that of Métis not living in an Indian community – as specified by Keating with respect to the Lake Huron district and elsewhere. Thus, the Métis of what is now western Québec had more in common with those of Sault Ste. Marie, Fort William, or even Red River than with individuals of mixed heritage on Walpole Island or the nearby Lake of Two Mountains.

# 4

# Shared Cultural Traits
# of the Bois-Brûlés

IN THE HISTORICAL SOURCES we examined, Bois-Brûlés' use of the French language appears closely tied to a specific Canadien parentage; not surprisingly, those whose fathers were French Canadian spoke French. The proximity of this bicultural people, "more at ease in the company of the French and native people than with the Anglo-Americans," has already been documented by Tanis C. Thorne in the area of St. Louis and the Missouri River (1996, 137). In the Outaouais region, the prevalence of the French language among the Métis is noted by geologist William E. Logan. As part of a scientific expedition, Logan passed through the region on his way to the HBC's Témiscamingue post in 1845, a trip for which he required assistance: "I have two new hands procured from Mr. Siveright [HBC officer stationed at Fort Témiscamingue], one Algonquin who speaks neither French nor English, the other a half breed [a Métis guide named Rakin ha] who speaks French very well" (Smith and Dyck 2007, 151). At La Passe, on the Ottawa River, Logan met a Métis by the name of Jean-Baptiste Bernard (File 3) who was working as a guide for the HBC and living in a clearing, and whom he also recorded as speaking French: "While at breakfast Mr. Bernard paid us a visit. He is Sir George Simpson's pilot, a half savage 60 years old. He is an Algonquin, & to our men speaks French not understanding the Iroquois" (Smith and Dyck 2007, 97).[1]

Fourteen years earlier, Alexander Shirreff, also passing through La Passe opposite Fort Coulonge, had described a community of retired voyageurs, Bois-Brûlés, whom he referred to as "French" but with the additional descriptor "Bois Brulées": "The poor unprogressing appearance of the place at once marks it as a nest of old trading people – French, or Bois Brulées" (1831, 265). This use of the term *French* by English speakers is comparable to the way it was used in the Red River region of Manitoba in the nineteenth century. Here, too, the appellation was applied indiscriminately to Métis of multiple origins and to French Canadians (Havard

1880, 314). In both regions, French was often the lingua franca, even among Métis with non-French origins.

### French Language in the Outaouais Fur Trade

With respect to the Outaouais region, references to "French" could include the Métis, emphasizing the importance of the French language among the Métis even with respect to those with English, Scottish, or Irish patronyms. A case in point: on a frigid night in 1833, as English-speaking HBC clerk John Lorn McDougall was getting ready to find a camping spot for the night with his Métis guide, he comments, "On discovering this spot my Indian asked me if I would be able to pass the night upon it. I answered in the affirmative asking at the same time where he was to lay himself. 'Pour moi je me sacre' [As for me, I couldn't care less] was his ready answer."[2] McDougall's guide, Thomas Brown – whose name suggests that he is an English speaker – preferred to speak French with McDougall the clerk. The clerks and "bourgeois" of the HBC invariably spoke French, as their labour force was predominantly French. Even George Simpson, governor of the HBC in North America and therefore its highest-ranking official, spoke French. Simpson was even more straightforward on the topic: in his journals he specifies that the language spoken defines the Métis, as they are either "[French] Canadian half breeds" (the majority being Catholic), or "English half breeds" (who are predominantly Protestant) (Rich 1938, 365). Not only does he distinguish the two but he sees the English as slightly superior to the (French) Canadians: "Five Interpreters and Runners English half breeds (as they are attached and trustworthy, whereas the Canadian half breeds are thoughtless, dissipated, and depraved in every sense of the word, secretly attached to their former employers the N.W. Coy. and in whom the smallest confidence cannot be placed)" (365).

Camille Derouet (1896, 614) also remarks that the language spoken by western Métis is unequivocally French, highlighting a cultural particularity shared by the "Métis canadiens-français." These observations spill across the continent, as Havard reports the use of French in the American West and even Southwest. As already cited, Havard also notes that there are Métis in Lower Canada and the Maritimes but that he does not have the data to provide their exact numbers. The use of the French language cannot be reduced simply to a trace of biological mixing; rather, it is a marked *cultural* trait that is found not only in the Canadian northwest but also among the Métis of the American Great Lakes, the Midwest, the Pacific Northwest, and, by extension, the greater Outaouais region.

Language was also tied to a number of cultural markers, including mixed heritage, a propensity for lived or folk Catholicism (or at the very least Christianity), and a way of life shaped by the fur trade (see Pigeon 2017). This is not to suggest that French was the *only* language spoken by the Métis, who were culturally diverse. (There were, for example, English-speaking Métis, who often referred to themselves as "Country born," Inuit-Métis, and Acadian Métis.) But French was spoken within Canadien Métis kin circuits, and they clearly constituted a significant portion of the Métis population across the fur trade network. Also, as argued in *Songs upon the Rivers* (Foxcurran, Bouchard, and Malette 2016), French was a continental lingua franca in the fur trade, spoken by Governor Simpson and all the way down to clerks such as the Irishman Ross Cox (1832, 218), who complained that "bad French and worse Indian began to usurp the place of English." French was used in petitions and in the practice of the Catholic faith, as almost all nineteenth-century Catholic clerics in the borderlands spoke French. Language and ritual thus served to ensure social cohesiveness across a vast region.[3]

These cases illustrate that not all French-speaking Métis were of French-Canadian extraction. Thomas Brown's name suggests that his paternal line was not exclusively French, and it is likely that Rakin ha had an Iroquois background. These two cases, along with that of Jean-Baptiste Bernard, help us to define the contours of the shared culture of the Métis of the greater Outaouais region. They worked in similar niches, often serving as guides or pilots, as Métis had an intimate knowledge of the territory and, given their spoken fluency in Indigenous languages, could also serve as interpreters or intermediaries with Indians (Du Ranquet [1843] 2000, 114, 204; St-Onge and Podruchny 2012, 61–62). The history of these individuals also functions as a microcosm of the collective history of the Bois-Brûlés, who were known as experienced fur traders and among whom the French language was a characteristic feature distinguishing them from the surrounding First Nations.

Allan McDonell, an experienced fur trader, was a key witness to the history of the Métis of western Canada and the Outaouais region, and he, too, refers to the Bois-Brûlés. McDonell possessed an intimate understanding of the Bois-Brûlés, having been at the very battle that inspired "Chanson de la Grenouillère," the anthem that mythologized the Bois-Brûlés in verse, as explained in Chapter 3. A partner in the NWC, McDonell was arrested by Lord Selkirk in the Red River Colony following the violent events of 1816 (Mitchell 1977, 239). A year later, he was transferred to the fort at Lake Témiscamingue, in the Ottawa River watershed. In a letter dated September 1830, McDonell explains how some HBC men under the command of Andrew McPherson (File 13) at Grand Lac were molested and robbed by other HBC men led by "Robertson a Bruller."[4] McDonell is referring to James Robertson, a Métis employee posted at the northern frontier of the Outaouais region,[5] and "Bruller" is derived from "Brûlé," the shortened form of "Bois-Brûlé." Thus, we see here a variation in phrasing but nonetheless the use of a term strongly associated with the Métis of the Red River region of Manitoba. Allan McDonell's letter also demonstrates that competition, even among HBC traders, was a common occurrence that frustrated company authorities. The letter shows that the cultural and social reality of the Bois-Brûlés, both in the Assiniboia Colony (Red River) and the Outaouais region, included often quite violent rivalries between fur trade employees, and the Robertson incident had raised the tension to an unacceptable level for McDonell.

The fur trade profession required a panoply of skills related to mobility and cultural expertise. Métis were often called upon to be guides, intermediaries, or diplomats in relations between company officials and members of First Nations. Their role as intermediaries, their use of French language inherited via the Canadian parentage, the presence of specific ethnonyms referring to Indigenous heritage, and shared Christian practices such as godfathering and godmothering at baptisms, all help us trace the contours of a distinct people with a continental distribution, found in various territories along the fur trading routes.

### Christianity and the Métis

Multiple historical sources reveal a rapid conversion or a significant attachment to Christianity as a significant cultural trait of Métis in Canada (Champagne, Beal, and Ghostkeeper 2005, 40, 42, 47; Cottrell et al. 2005a, 67; Cottrell et al. 2005b, 54; Donna Cona 2005, 56; Jones, n.d., 75, 83, 88; Scace et al. 2005, 92; Stone Circle Consulting and Know History 2015, 43–44). Louis Riel insisted that Métis attachment to Christianity was shaped by parentage, as demonstrated by their adherence to the biblical

*Chats Rapids, near Ottawa,* by Philip John Bainbrigge, c. 1838–41. Brigades of voyageurs of the Hudson's Bay Company travelled up the Ottawa River and its tributaries in the 1830s and 1840s. Here, the voyageurs navigate a birchbark canoe up a small rapid "à la cordelle," pulling it upstream with the help of rope.
*Credit: Library and Archives Canada, 1983-47-65*

command to honour it: "The Métis are Christians. Even when their Indian origins are modest, they are beholden to honoring their mothers as much as their fathers. The Métis hold to the name of their race. They are not preoccupied by the degree of mixed blood they possess as they have their Indian and their European blood" (Riel 1985b, 273; our translation).

The Catholic registers of Sainte-Geneviève-de-Berthier in Québec also testify to a significant historical relationship between Métis and Christianity. Baptismal documents reveal that many Canadien voyageurs travelled thousands of kilometres to have their Métis children baptized by Catholic priests in Lower Canada. Additionally, an 1817 petition, circulated among the "inhabitants of the Red River" and signed by Canadien freemen who identify their descendants born in the country as "métifs or bois-brûlés," demanded that the Bishop of Québec send a priest to tend to their spiritual needs. The signatories take care to distance themselves from the 1816 Battle of la Grenouillère, or Seven Oaks, in which the Métis were implicated. The petition emphasizes the need to return Métis to their faith, stating that they are the children of Christians and thus tying faith to their Canadian parentage.[6] Historians have explored the importance of such petitions and lived Catholicism as markers of social and political cohesion among Métis people (Pigeon 2017, 6–10). As Susan Sleeper-Smith (2000, 424) explains, Indigenous women were central to Catholic religious networks through which they traded goods, disseminated ideas, and forged kinship ties – notably, symbolic kinship ties through the practice of being godmothers when new believers were baptized in the Catholic faith (see also Pigeon 2017, 55).

The importance of Catholicism to the Métis was confirmed again when Lord Selkirk, who was judged "heretical" by the Sainte-Geneviève-de-Berthier parish historian and priest Stanislas Albert Moreau, nonetheless transmitted the demands of the petitioners to Monseigneur Joseph-Octave Plessis in Québec. Though neither Selkirk nor the HBC necessarily wanted the Catholic Church to be implanted in the Red River Colony, Selkirk probably acquiesced to stop the exodus of western Métis from the Red River lands for Lower Canada (Moreau 1889, 105). With the arrival of priests and the establishment of the Catholic Church in Saint-Boniface, it would no longer be necessary for the Catholic faithful to make the long journey to Lower Canada, notably to the Sainte-Geneviève-de-Berthier parish, to baptize children or be married following Catholic rites.

Significantly, among the "Métifs" from the fur trade territories baptized at Berthier was Jean-Baptiste Bernard (File 3). Louis Riel Sr. was also baptized there,[7] as were members of the McKay family – Amable and Marie-Angélique McKay, children of Neil McKay and "Thérèse Sauvagesse." Their baptismal records note that the father is a Protestant but that he has promised to "raise the two children in the Catholic Faith."[8] The McKay children are the cousins of the Métis John McKay of Lake Témiscamingue (Mitchell 1977, 236), who is discussed in greater detail below. Thus, baptismal records testify to the ties between the Red River region in Manitoba, the Berthier region of Québec, and the Outaouais region, as we find Métis families with direct ties to all three locations, underscoring the great mobility of the Métis as they travelled to Sainte-Geneviève-de-Berthier for baptisms and participated in the fur trade in far-flung locales. As Brenda Macdougall (2010, 130) explains, a Catholic baptism also reinforced Indigenous kinship ties by establishing family relationships beyond those of mother and father, which therefore consolidated political and cultural networks outside the confines of a strict definition of Métis identity based solely on descent.

With regard to the greater Outaouais region, the missionary Jean-Baptiste Dupuy also confirms the attachment to Christianity of the Canadiens who have relations with *Sauvages*. During his first itinerant missionary enterprise up the Grand River (another name for the Ottawa River), he comments on the work of the missionary Bellefeuille at the Dumoine River where it flows into the Ottawa, and describes the 1836 baptism of the Métis child of a certain Caillet and a *Sauvagesse:* "It is remarkable that the Canadiens, who have relations with the *Sauvages,* speak of the faith and its ministers with the deepest respect, but are unable to provide any explications of the truths it teaches, even if they are capable of easily speaking their language" (Dupuy 1839, 36; our translation).

Bellefeuille affirms these ties on August 24, 1838, when, at the Allumettes post in the south of the larger Outaouais region, he signs the baptismal records of "thirty-three *Sauvages* or Métifs" (Bellefeuille 1840a, 87; our translation), highlighting the presence of both Indians and Métis among his newly baptized faithful. At the Portage des Joachims, between Fort Coulonge and Mattawa, Father Du Ranquet notes an attachment of the same nature in 1843 while observing trilingualism in the Caillet household, the same Canadien Algonquin family described by Dupuy: "It was a Canadien (Mr. Cahier) who brought to us his two little boys aged six and eight years old ... These little children knew French, English, and Algonquin, the language of their mother. When they recited for me their prayer, I believed it was in a fourth language, so extraordinarily they pronounced the French" (Du Ranquet [1843] 2000, 147; our translation).

The Christian faith also occupied an important place among the inhabitants of the Lac-Sainte-Marie community on the Gatineau River, which included several Métis families. A chapel was built on land belonging to an influential Métis family in this community, that of François Naud and Élisabeth McPherson (File 13). The family had donated the land to the clergy expressly for this purpose (Barbezieux 1897, 436). A comparable event occurred at the Baskatong mission, where the Métis Joseph David (File 5), a native of Red River, left a parcel of land for the construction of a church.[9] The archives reveal a notable "Scottish Métis" presence in the greater Outaouais region, and these Métis also demonstrate an attachment to Christianity, as well as knowledge of both European, in this case English, and Indigenous languages. Farther north, on the shores of Lake Témiscamingue, a particular devotion is observed on August 7, 1881, by the missionary Proulx (1885, 42; our translation): "Several families of Scottish Métis got together; there is a night prayer as a group; under the starlight, all understand English; Mr. Robert begins his ministry in reciting the rosary."

During his travels north of the Outaouais region, Proulx (1885, 40) encounters the canoe men Stanger, Thomson, and Polson – who had accompanied the bishop Monseigneur Duhamel, on an official trip to visit the Catholic faithful at Abitibi – and refers to them as well by the ethnonym "Scottish Métis." Though there may be Scottish Métis among the crew, all join in singing "En roulant ma boule" and "Alouette," songs that figure prominently in the voyageur repertoire, suggesting that a common culture was shaping Canadien and Scottish Métis. Intriguingly, Proulx at one point describes *Sauvages* as singing "Un Canadien errant" in Algonquin (42). This song was probably composed after the Lower Canada Rebellions of 1837–38, and mention of it in this context demonstrates not only that new songs were being integrated into the regional culture but, moreover, that a sharing of culture occurred across ethnonational lines (Plouffe 2013).

When taking into account the role of the Scottish Métis in Métis ethnogenesis, it is important to keep in mind that most – but not all – of the

Missionaries heading to Abitibi via Témiscamingue, c. 1880–1900. These men of the cloth also relied on birchbark canoes deftly navigated by Algonquin or Métis voyageurs.
*Credit: Bibliothèque et Archives nationales du Québec, digital collection, CP 021571 CON*

Scottish Métis in the Outaouais region were fervent Catholics. Their religious faith, unlike that of the Protestant English "Country Born" in western locales, would have certainly eased and encouraged closer ties with the Catholic French-speaking Bois-Brûlés. Shared faith would have ensured that religion was less of a barrier to marriage between families, and members of different families could have served as godparents to one another's children. Also, as French was the spoken lingua franca of the fur trade across the continent, we can infer that many Scottish Métis would have spoken French in addition to English and Indigenous languages. Their history is part and parcel of the Métis history of the Outaouais and must be noted; their Catholicism, as well as their limited upward social mobility within the ranks of the fur trade companies given their status as Half-breeds, certainly facilitated the emergence of a shared community identity.

Proulx (1885, 78) confirms the presence of some thirty Scottish, Métis, and First Nations *(Sauvage)* families at Lake Témiscamingue in a letter addressed to his superior on August 14, 1881, making it clear that he distinguished Scottish families and Métis families even though there were also Scottish Métis. The mention of the Canadien and Scottish origins of the Métis in the Outaouais region is not mundane. Academic literature often mentions the amalgamation of these ethnocultural compositions when it comes to the subject of the Métis and Half-breeds: the Métis in effect originate principally from two ethnic compositions of European origin, having Canadien and Scottish roots (Cottrell et al. 2005a, 65; Holmes 1996, 72). The fact that nineteenth-century archival documents underscore distinctions between Scottish and Canadien Métis in the Outaouais region is thus significant, as it confirms the presence of the same ethnic origins found in numerous descriptions of historical Métis populations of European and Indian origins in other locales, which is to say the Bois-Brûlés (or Canadien Métis) and the Scottish Métis.

Geographically, this description of the ethnic particularities of the Métis population is found not only in the area of Lakes Abitibi and Témis-camingue but across the entire region. Bellefeuille, for instance, refers to "all these different posts," from Fort Coulonge all the way to Abitibi to the North. In reviewing his handwritten journal of the 1838 expedition, we discovered the following passage, not included in the later published account, in which he describes the Métif woman Flora:

> She is approximately 45 years of age and in addition to her baptismal name and her sauvage name, she also has the name of L'Évêque from her now deceased father, a former Canadien or Métif voyageur. There is also in this same post Sauvages or Métifs some named Gaucher and others going by the name Chénier. As was at Témiskaming there is a large family who are the descendants of an ancient voyageur by the name of Leduc. And in all these different Posts, there are Métifs who are for the most part the descendants of Canadien or Scottish Voyageurs or Clerks or Bourgeois. These Métifs are ordinarily more intelligent than the others, but also more susceptible to good or bad impressions.[10]

Interestingly, like Keating's narrative of Lake Huron Métis, the passage contains value judgments about the Outaouais Métis. For Bellefeuille, the Métis are "more intelligent than the others" (i.e., the *Sauvages,* or Indians), an impression that may have been tied to their greater openness to his missionary message (Marcotte 2014, 83). The excerpt illustrates not only that Métis practised baptism but also that they were distributed across the region, at many posts. Like Proulx, Bellefeuille also confirms the presence of both Scottish and Canadien Métifs.

Also interesting is that when Bellefeuille evokes the names Gaucher, Chénier, and Leduc, he signals that these descendants of voyageurs can be either *Sauvages* or Métifs. Using the logic expressed in the Bagot Report, he is in effect specifying that descendants of whites were found among both Indians and Métis. The former would certainly have adopted the culture of their community. The Métis have also become sufficiently distinctive that they merit being named. Thus, here too being Métis is not simply a question of mixed ancestry but one of culture. One can indeed have *Sauvages* who are not Métis, sharing the same ancestry but not the culture of their kin with the same name. It is therefore necessary to trace the contours of Métis culture in the Outaouais region, as we continue to do in the following sections.

## Métis "Sauvage" Industries

During his 1843 trip to the Outaouais region, the Jesuit priest Du Ranquet remarked upon the Métis skill in what he called the "industries of the Sauvages." Following an 1843 trip to Fort Témiscamingue, he described the cultural synthesis that represents the prototypical Métis of this period – a man working as a clerk in the fur trade posts of the HBC:

> The clerk, who conducts almost all the affairs of the post, Mr. McKay is a meritorious man in his duties ... He demonstrated great kindness, he gifted Mr. Moreau an admirably carved stone pipe, and as he overheard me asking many questions as to the country, he promised a map of the Ottawa that he would make himself. He has to a supreme degree a mastery of all the industries of the *Sauvages:* hunting, fishing, the making of canoes, pipes, maps of lakes and rivers, etc. (Du Ranquet [1843] 2000, 170–71; our translation)

The clerk here, known to be Métis, simultaneously masters accounting, cartography (Marcotte 2015), and other "industries of the *Sauvages.*" Even his cartography suggests a blending of both Indigenous and European perspectives. Following Indigenous practice, McKay's maps included rivers belonging to various watersheds that were fused by specific canoe routes, but they also adhered to Eurocentric conventions that emphasized fur trade posts and outposts (Marcotte 2015, 88–89). The maps are a telling example of syncretism, combining Algonquin map-making on birch bark and European conventions that served colonial interests and centred on the fur trade and commercial activity. McKay's skills as a clerk demonstrate how Métis who worked in fur trade posts engaged in intermediate cultural practices that were distinct from both European and First Nations practices.

In addition to the production of birchbark canoes (a task that requires much expertise and skill), stone pipes, and syncretic maps, Du Ranquet ([1843] 2000, 209; our translation) also notes the finely decorated moccasins that Mrs. Polson (a Franco-Algonquin Métis born Otenimakwe, or Flora Lévesque,) made for him and another missionary, Moreau: "Mrs. Polson and her children offer to Mr. Moreau and me a pair of deer hide slippers, elegantly embroidered with beads and porcupine quills of all colours."

A similar practice occurred in the Lièvre Valley, where Métis Marie-Louise Riel (File 12) produced a large quantity of moccasins during the 1840s.[11] The Riel/McGregor family was known for its expertise in tanning deer hide using traditional Indigenous methods. Furthermore, at the Grand Lac post, Élisabeth McPherson (File 13) was paid by the HBC to lace snowshoes,[12] while Métis Ambroise Beaulieu (File 2) is reported as having paid a debt to the HBC by building birchbark canoes.[13] The persistence and continued use of products and manufacturing techniques typical of First Nations communities is clearly illustrated by the Naud family (File 13). While the Naud/McPherson couple was living at the post at Grand Lac in 1835, François Naud bought a quarter pound of vermilion for his family's use.[14] This product, which was sold in the fur trade posts, generally had two uses. The first was tied to religious practices, as described by Catholic missionaries passing through this region in 1839:

> After advancing a few leagues, we arrived at the strait of the Cèdres [Opasatica Lake, Abitibi] where we found hanging from trees the heads of wild beasts coloured with vermilion and marked with many hieroglyphs which we did not understand. It seems that the *Sauvages* use these signs to share news with those of their nation who must pass by these locales where they are put in evidence. (Poiré 1840, 45; our translation)

Misunderstood by the priest Poiré, the suspended skulls also served a religious function. According to another priest, the Oblate Joseph-Étienne Guinard, the bones were suspended to prevent dogs from eating them, so as not to offend the spirits of the deceased animals and to ensure success in future hunts. Given the spiritual connotations, the practice was long criticized by Catholic priests in western Québec as mere superstition.[15]

Another ancient recorded use of vermilion among First Nations in North America was as body pigment (Laberge and Girard 1999, 82). In all likelihood, the Naud/McPherson family used the vermilion for one of these two practices, in spite of the Western education that Élisabeth received at Cornwall and François Naud's Canadien origins. The purchase suggests that distinctive Indigenous cultural practices were transmitted in one of the principal Métis families, which was later found at Lac-Sainte-Marie. The vermilion was evidently not purchased for trade with First Nations as Naud bought it with his voyageur salary, as an HBC employee.

These examples suggest that practising the "industries of the *Sauvages*" should be considered part of the distinctive cultural traits of the Métis of the greater Outaouais region in Québec, from Lake of Two Mountains north to Lake Abitibi. In situ observations from the first half of the nineteenth century demonstrate the existence of distinctive cultural practices and provide some intriguing insights into the Métis culture of this region, a culture postulated as present in all the fur trade posts following the testimony of the missionary Bellefeuille. Again, this evidence suggests that we are not in presence of Métis so named (and also referred to by contemporary observers as Half-breeds, Métifs, and Bois-Brulés) simply by virtue of mixed blood but because they had a distinctive and collective identity with a noticeable material culture.

### The Métis Cabin

As is the case with many ethnic groups of the past, the material culture of the Métis of the Outaouais region is not easy to document, being identified only in a scattering of historical data in diverse sources such as HBC accounting journals and correspondence. Nonetheless, the existing examples provide some insight into the richness of expertise and skill tied to trade and travel (maps, canoes, moccasins, snowshoes, sashes, and so on), as well as decorative arts and symbolism (carved pipes, use of vermilion, beadwork, embroidery using beads or porcupine quills). We also explore here one of the most visible examples of Métis material culture: the log cabin.

*Hunter with Gun and Pack across Back,* by Cornelius Krieghoff, c. 1856.
*Credit: Library and Archives Canada, 1989-479-32*

This distinctive habitation was first noted by the geologist William E. Logan in the surroundings of Fort Témiscamingue in 1845. On his way up the Ottawa River, this scientific explorer visited the HBC fort, a stop required of all travellers at the time. Fort Témiscamingue was the most significant hamlet between Fort Coulonge to the south and Moose Factory to the north at James Bay. In his journal, Logan provides a useful description of log cabins inhabited by Métis at the fort: "There are a few wooden houses in the vicinity [of Fort Témiscamingue] for servants or voyageurs of the Company all inhabited by half breeds" (Smith and Dyck 2007, 161). The fact that HBC employees at Fort Témiscamingue were not necessarily all Métis (Marcotte 2017) did not stop Logan from referring to the occupants of the cluster of cabins as such.

Logan is not the only one to associate Métis with log cabins. They are a recurring element in historical portraits of the majority of documented

Métis communities, and a common motif in descriptions of Métis residing in the Outaouais region. The reflections of the celebrated artist Arthur Heming, who visited the HBC trading post at Abitibi Lake a bit farther north, are a case in point. Almost fifty years later, Heming's (1902, 38) description echoes Logan's observations: "At the outer end, in a cluster of poplars, stood the 'House of Abitibi.' Behind it ranged the massive, weather-beaten store-houses, wherein the business of the post goes on. Next, a number of small log-cabins, where the half-breeds lived. Then, a village of tepees, in which the families of Indian hunters spend midsummer."

In Heming's description, Métis and Indians lived differently, even though both were highly mobile. The Métis travelled primarily within fur trade circuits, whereas First Nations of the larger Outaouais region practised a subsistence-based nomadism as families moved between various territories to hunt, fish, and gather needed resources for their families and communities. As travel via the water routes facilitated the movement of families and goods, Algonquins and other Indigenous populations in the greater Outaouais region would visit the fur trade posts in the summer to trade and, starting in the 1830s, congregate at neighbouring Catholic missions. Then, at the end of summer, they dispersed to their hunting territories. Métis families lived in log cabins the entire year, as the men often worked at the post. They occasionally travelled out in the winter to find Indigenous trading partners, a practice known as *la dérouine*. They also travelled both within and outside trade circuits. With rare exceptions, there was a marked difference between Métis and First Nations movement across the territory, which explains in part their different habitation preferences around fur trade forts. Freemen Métis, who were not employed by the fur trade companies, generally had cabins as well, some close to fur trade posts, others clustered elsewhere, as was the case at Lac-Sainte-Marie. The use of log cabins thus appears to be a revealing trait, defining a Métis way of life that contrasted with that of the surrounding First Nations. Métis established themselves in cabins around the fur trade outposts decades before Algonquins followed suit. With a fixed domicile, they exercised mobility principally within the network of trade posts; after all, mobility was related largely to their occupation in the fur trade.

Father Du Ranquet notes the presence of log cabins in his 1843 journal, but at Dumoine River he also refers to a Métis man who was cultivating the land, presumably a form of subsistence agriculture inherited from either Canadien or Scottish forebears:

> We saw there [at the mouth of the Dumoine River] a few log cabins; the clerk of Fort Will[i]am often places a sentinel there for trout [trade].[16] There is a Métis there who cultivates; he looks at us passing without bothering to get out of his house; we had a letter for him, a small boy comes out to retrieve it. We do not disembark on land; it was not in Mr. Moreau's nature to make advances for those with so little desire. The *Sauvages* call this man the bad Sauteux [Saulteaux]. (Du Ranquet [1843] 2000, 148–49; our translation)

The observation of cabins at the Dumoine River, where there was at least one Métis family, suggests that the practice of building cabins existed not only in northern Outaouais region but also to the south.

Offering additional clues about Métis habitation, the Surveyor General Joseph Bouchette (1832a, 190) explains that Métis generally built cabins without any prior authorization or deed: "A short distance east of Kinnell Lodge is the mouth of the Madawaska river; and nearly opposite, apparently a speck on the margin of the lake, is the miserable habitation of a bois-brulé, one of that class of people known under the denomination of Squatters." Bouchette directly associates the practice of squatting with the Bois-Brûlés; in fact, he goes so far as to identify them as a distinct class ("one of that class of people").[17]

Occasionally, documents from the nineteenth century allow us to identify the owners of log cabins with great probability. For example, in 1829, the Ingall expedition discussed in Chapter 3 mentions the following encounter: "At 32 minutes past 12 o'clock, we had the pleasure of entering Lac du Sable [des Sables], passing at the entrance a large low island, bearing elm and red maple. We saw some old log huts on our left hand, and near them a post belonging to a private individual" (Ingall, Nixon, and Adams 1830, 256). In this case, Ingall observes that the cabins adjoin a trading post, but not the HBC post that the expedition will visit a bit later. Its status as an independent post is signalled by his reference to "private" ownership, and the nearby cabins would undoubtedly have been occupied by the employees of the post. HBC documents inform us that two competing posts were located at Lac des Sables in 1829: one belonging to Day & McGillivray, and the other to J. Stanfield, or Stanfeld.[18]

*Joseph Bouchette,* by John Cox Dillman Engleheart, 1815. Surveyor General Joseph Bouchette offers rare testimony on the Bois-Brûlé "class" in his two-volume 1832 publication on the topography of Lower and Upper Canada.
*Credit: Library and Archives Canada, 1976-104-5*

Stanfield abandoned his post in the summer of 1829 after threatening two employees – André Lacroix (File 8) and Joseph Paquette (File 14)[19] – who then went to work for the HBC. The documents also identify Ambroise Beaulieu (File 2) as a former employee of Stanfield at Lac des Sables.[20] At this time, the voyageurs Beaulieu and Paquette were both the heads of Métis families: Beaulieu and his wife were Métis, while Paquette was married to an Indigenous woman and had at least one Métis child. HBC clerk John McLean also confirms that the two men had dependent families in 1828.[21] Thus, given the number of cabins observed and the families documented in the area, the post that Ingall noted would have been Stanfield's. The cabins were occupied over a number of years by these Métis families, attesting to the material culture of the region's Métis along the corridor leading to Culotte Lake, a location associated with the Bois-Brûlés in Ingall's account.

The caption of this engraving, published in *L'Opinion publique* newspaper in 1882, reads, "Winter house of Noui Icipaiatik, Algonquin Métis. Route followed by a missionary in the lumber yards." This association of log cabin and Métis offers an example of the continuity of cultural practices that were in evidence decades earlier in the same region.
*Credit:* L'Opinion publique, *March 16, 1882, 130–31*

Occasionally, documents from the era reveal more details about the cabins' Métis occupants and how they used them. For example, an engraving published in the newspaper *L'Opinion publique* in 1882 (130) is accompanied by a caption and short article specifying that the cabin it depicts belonged to the "Métis Algonquin" Noui Icipaiatik and was located on the shores of Porc-épic Lake (in all likelihood today's Lake Vennor), a couple of kilometres inland from the Coulonge River. This description places the cabin in the centre of the greater Outaouais region, some distance from the main canoe routes. The engraving literally illustrates a material practice that other documentary sources merely mention in passing. It also uses a local ethnonym, "Métis Algonquin," reflecting a patrilineal Canadien influence in the cabin owner's name. Icipaiatik is the Algonquin translation of Lacroix, and this patronym was inherited from Noui's father André Lacroix, a freeman who was active in the Rivière Désert/Lac des Sables region.[22]

The illustration of Noui Icipaiatik's cabin, along with the accounts of Logan, Heming, Du Ranquet, and Bouchette, establishes a cultural trait that we can consider distinctive for the Métis of the greater Outaouais region. Living in cabins often distinguishes Métis from their Indigenous kin. The use of cabins is also an indicator of a different way of life. Whether they worked for trading companies or as freemen, the Métis tended to be relatively settled; they would venture from their trading posts and cabins to the interior for trade but not as a subsistence strategy. Algonquins and other First Nations travelled much more over their hunting grounds, and consequently relied on tents as their primary habitation. This was true even in the relatively late period Heming describes, in the early years of the twentieth century.

The log cabins described above may have been owned by the fur companies that employed their occupants, or may have been built by and for the Métis at the margins of the trading posts. They probably housed Métis families when the men of the households were away on fur trade or hunting excursions. By piecing together evidence from multiple sources, it is possible to identify the likely inhabitants of some cabins, and thus to demonstrate how the dwellings formed part of Métis material culture. These Métis were identified in the same sources using a number of ethnonyms – Bois-Brûlés, Métifs, Métis, Half-breeds – defining a distinctive collective inhabiting the greater Outaouais region in what is now western Québec.

# 5

## *Algonquin Half-Breeds, Priests, and the Métis Collectivity*

VARIOUS LATE-NINETEENTH-CENTURY sources point to the existence of a Métis population in the greater Outaouais region. In addition to use of the term *Bois-Brûlé* and evidence of a distinctive material culture over many years, we also find the term *Algonquin Half-Breeds* in the correspondence of Father Nédélec between 1892 and 1896. Jean-Marie Nédélec (1834–96) was ordained as a Catholic priest in France in 1859. Wanting to serve as a missionary, he came to Canada to join fellow Oblates. He learned the Montagnais (Innu) language, which was closely related to Algonquin and Cree, and in 1867 began his missionary work, first heading to Abitibi and then to Témiscamingue and James Bay. In the winter of 1867–68 he ventured to the lumber camps of Maniwaki. Then, in 1869, he was stationed as the resident priest of Mattawa; in the summers, he would venture to the lumber and railway building work camps as well as to Indigenous communities. In 1892, he was assigned to the Témiscamingue region, where he would spend the final years of his life (Carrière 1990).

Most interestingly, Father Nédélec refers to a Métis social collective, a distinctive population. Though he would have employed the term *Métis* when communicating in French, the Catholic cleric uses *Half-breed* in his ongoing English-language correspondence with the Indian Department, and it in turn uses this term, as does Indian agent Angus McBride, who was stationed at the Témiscamingue Reserve. Nédélec was jousting by letter with government officials to have Métis integrated into the reserve. By the end of the nineteenth century, both forestry and the spread of settler colonialism had contributed to making the fur trade a marginal activity in the Témiscamingue region, as had occurred earlier in the southern region of the Outaouais territory. As forest was cleared by both foresters and incoming farmers, pressure on the Algonquin people intensified as their traditional subsistence territories quickly succumbed to the axe and plow, but they retained a small refuge on the reserve. The Métis,

*La Tête du Lac, or at the Head of the Lake,* by Bruno Charron, c. 1890. At the mouth of the Rivière des Quinze (a section of the Ottawa), to the north of Lake Témiscamingue, a reserve of the same name was created in 1853. Father Nédélec sought to relocate a number of Métis there, but they did not have the right to settle under Indian Affairs regulations and the 1876 Indian Act.
*Credit: Archive Deschâtelets-NDC, Richelieu*

in this context, faced the loss of their primary source of income – the fur trade – and now had to deal with the prejudices of the incoming settler population. As the descendants of First Nations women, Métis were also caught up in identity politics that centred on their rights, or lack of them, to reside on reserve. Father Nédélec enters into these debates in his correspondence with the Department of Indian Affairs.

Worried about their well-being, Father Nédélec hoped that the "Algonquin Métis" or "Algonquin Half-breeds," as he referred to them in his correspondence, would be integrated into the Témiscamingue Reserve. In a letter addressed to the superintendent of Indian Affairs and dated November 4, 1892, Nédélec suggests, "All the half breeds connected with the tribe either by blood or language" should have the right to settle on the reserve.[1] Interestingly, he does not specify blood alone. Furthermore, he declares, "Another raison [sic], it [is] the wise and just wish of the government to see the Indians settling on the Reserve and the half Breeds also. Better, than to settle at the tavern's door along the Ottawa or camps in the vicinity of the shanties."[2] Nédélec also proposes the construction of a school, though there was apparently already one on the reserve, and asks for Métis representation on the band council through a guaranteed two of six seats: "According to my humble opinion that council should be composed of six members: 2 indians, 2 half-breeds, the agent nominated by the indian department and besides another member nominated by the Indians to counterbalance the agent."[3]

In its response, the Department of Indian Affairs suggests that each case of admittance to the reserve should instead be studied individually based on merit:

> With regard to the land question, and the right of the Halfbreeds to occupy land upon the Reserve, I beg to state that the right of each Halfbreed family has to be considered on its own merits: consequently, the Department would require, before determining as to the rights of occupancy by any Halfbreed, to know through the Indian Agent from which side his Indian blood is derived; that is, whether from the fathers or the mothers side.[4]

Under existing legislation, those with only maternal Indian blood would be excluded, effectively ensuring that no Métis would merit inclusion.

As for including Métis on band councils, the government bureaucrat largely ignored the suggestion, simply stating that the creation of band councils has always been encouraged. Agent McBride entered into the dialogue as well, giving his own view on Nédélec's concerns in a letter to Indian Affairs in which he states that a band council already exists on the reserve and that under no condition should the Indian community of Témiscamingue accept people "from below":

> In regard of get[t]ing indians and half breeds from below in this Reserve, we can not agree to that, as we are living very peacefully here at present. But if we were to be mixt-up with indians and half breeds from below, we knew that we would not live so peaceful, Because they are habit of using intoxicated liquor ... though we have no Objection in taking in other indians whom that we knew such as Keepaway [Kipawa] indians, som of our relations are living ther, and they have no Reserve ther.[5]

The clarification McBride provides is intriguing as he confirms that those living on the reserve did not want to accept Métis (and Indians) from

Betsy Flora Polson, her husband, Angus McBride, and their daughter, by an
unknown photographer, c. 1869. Betsy was the daughter of Métis Flora Lévesque
and William Polson, a long-time employee at the HBC post at Lake Abitibi. Angus
McBride, son of Nor'Wester George McBride and an Indigenous woman, became
Indian agent at the Témiscamingue Reserve after a long career with the HBC.
*Credit: Bibliothèque et Archives nationales du Québec, Rouyn-Noranda, Fonds Groupe
perspectives jeunesse de Notre-Dame-du-Nord, 08-Y, P48, P3*

"below," or downstream from, Kipawa Lake, as they would not have considered them close relations. The geographical reference to "below" thus
includes Métis and Indians living at Mattawa, Fort Coulonge, and even
on the waterways flowing into the Ottawa: the Coulonge, Gatineau, and
Lièvre rivers.

Following the provocative letter from the Indian agent, Nédélec sent off another missive to the Department of Indian Affairs reaffirming the right of Métis to establish themselves on the reserve:

Concerning the right of algonquin half-Breeds for settling on the Reserve, there is something and even many things wrong. To have that question to the agent alone, is nothing but foolishness and rashness. The local council should decide such a right. We see it by a long experience on that matter. Therefore do not be surprised to see the indian Reserve diminishing instead of increasing ... The half-breeds are not allowed to settle on it, only by favours or connection with the agent [us?] here at Temiskamingue. Is it that fair? Not surely.

[I] was advised by the Indians or the half-Breeds to warn the indian department, [I] have done it without any view of my own.[6]

Father Nédélec concludes his letter by revisiting the question of favouritism: "The agent allows all his children to settle on the Reserve without asking and even his son in-law, a pure white man ... Why two balances for justice?"[7]

This correspondence sheds light not only on the Métis living in the Outaouais region but also on the conflict between the missionary priest Nédélec and the Indian agent McBride, who was himself Métis. A few years earlier, McBride had tried to influence the outcome of band elections at Témiscamingue by suggesting that Half-breeds were the only apt candidates for chief. In a letter dated September 4, 1890, he specifies that the then Algonquin leader does not wish to allow "any half Breed to vote" for fear of losing power.[8] The Algonquins opposed his efforts, refusing to allow the Métis to interfere in their electoral process. According to ethnohistorian Leila Inksetter (2017, 443–50), Métis lineage would not have been the genuine reason for Algonquins wanting to exclude certain individuals from the band, as members of the Stanger, McBride, and Polson families were elected in the years that followed. This argument does not take into account, however, that in the 1890s McBride apparently succeeded in having Métis from his kin network gain eligibility for Indian status. His manipulation of band membership to the advantage of some Métis from his immediate entourage, which gave them access to band membership in their own right, is particularly visible in correspondence between 1896 and 1900, archived in another file. This correspondence suggests that related members of the Métis King family first entered the reserve with a simple residence permit, only to find themselves full members a few years later without the consent of many Indians.[9] Thus, McBride probably also succeeded later in influencing band elections, ensuring that Métis would be elected despite the failure of his earlier efforts.

In revisiting the correspondence mentioned by Inksetter (2017, 445), we understand more fully why Nédélec wished not only to let all Métis who wanted to join the reserve do so but also to give them political weight on the band council. Although some of McBride's Métis kin were apparently included in the band, other Métis "from below" remained excluded and did not benefit from the support of either the Indian agent McBride or officials from Indian Affairs. Nédélec sought to have more Métis accepted into the reserve in the hope of increasing the number of farmers. In his letters, he emphasizes that he is representing the opinion of the Indians and the Métis of the region, not his own. Though it is difficult to judge whether this altruism is authentic, the correspondence highlights a desire to give some political weight to Métis on the band council by integrating families "from below" who had kinship (blood) ties to those on the reserve, as well as those who did not.

### Who Were the "Algonquin Half-breeds"?

Throughout the correspondence between Nédélec and McBride, "Algonquin Half-breeds" are consistently identified as a distinctive collective by all writers. Both Nédélec and McBride agreed that they were neither Euro-Canadians nor Indians. The bureaucrats seemed content to cite the legislation: only Métis who could trace their Indian blood through the paternal line were eligible for Indian status and thus to live on the reserve. Thus, as Ted Binnema (2014) argues, the law was successful in doing what it had been crafted to do in earlier pre-Confederation iterations: keep out plausible insiders such as the Métis. Not only was Nédélec seeking to undo decades of governmental policy, but he wanted to give these "plausible insiders" a collective political voice on band councils. Nédélec's letters reveal that the Métis had become a collectivity that was clearly distinguishable from both Indians and whites from the same region. The response to Nédélec's demands was articulated in an internal memo prepared by a bureaucrat named Sinclair. This memo is highly significant, and it would eventually bear serious consequences:

It does not appear that anything can be added to what has been already said to him on the subject of the land question, and the right of Half-breeds to occupy locations on the Reserve, or with respect to the laying out of a village and the survey of the same into streets. It appears to the undersigned that even if the Indians had money enough to spend in this way, and were willing to incur the expenditure, that it would be a measure of doubtful policy, and not in accord with the general policy of the Department, which aims at the segregation of the Indians when they are engaged in agricultural pursuits, and is opposed to assembling them together in communities, such as that at Caughnawaga, St. Regis, and elsewhere.[10]

Not surprisingly, Indian Affairs had a negative response to Nédélec's continued demands that Métis be allowed to settle on a reserve, or that a village or community be established. Such ideas were contrary to government policy to segregate Indians when they were farming on reserve. Additionally, Indian Affairs opposed the creation of communities such as those at Caughnawaga (now Kahnawake) and St. Régis. Although it's not clear why Sinclair singled out these communities, we hypothesize that they were well known for having a high level of conflict tied to the presence of individuals identified as "Métis." In Caughnawaga, for example, violence against Canadiens and "Métis" led to the death of Ozias Meloche, who was burned alive at his farm (*Montreal Daily Witness* 1878).

Father Nédélec responded to the first refusal by stating that those Indians who were the first to oppose the entry of Métis to the reserve were also the first to abandon the reserve; that is, they did not want to practise agriculture on the reserve. Nédélec also clarified his ideas concerning the foundation of a village using reserve lands: "It would be a good thing for the Indians to grant a part of the lower part of the Reserve to be divided in town's lots. It will give ten times more value to the rest of their land."[11] In its final letter, Indian Affairs gave its own interpretation of Nédélec's recommendation: "With respect to your proposition that a part of the lower portion of the Reserve be divided into twon [sic] lots for the purpose, it is presumed, of selling the Lots to white people, the Department is not prepared to act upon this suggestion."[12]

This typed letter also contains a sentence fragment reiterating that Indian Affairs was not amenable to the idea of settling whites in proximity to Indians, but it is struck through with a pencil. This leads us to note an important detail about the ethnonyms used in Indian Affairs correspondence. Oddly, Métis are sometimes presented as distinct, and at other times as equivalent to Euro-Canadians. To be more precise, in the language of the era they are sometimes referred to as "Half-breeds," but because they are not considered as Indians under the Indian Act, they are at other times classified as white. Even when Métis were living on reserve, the correspondence did not consider them to be indistinct from Indians. Rather, as Gerhard Ens and Joe Sawchuk (2016, 238) note, Métis identity was maintained in several locales, even if it was in an attenuated form within families. Of course, some Métis families on reserves came to adopt an Indian identity (or to shed one if they left), but this process was not instantaneous. It was a gradual transition that seems to have still been underway in the greater Outaouais region at the end of the nineteenth century.

In addition to misunderstandings surrounding ethnonyms, it's quite clear that the three parties in Nédélec–McBride–Indian Affairs correspondence did not always understand one another. The final Indian Affairs letter, for example, seems to equate the desire of Métis to settle on the reserve with Nédélec's suggestion that lots be established and sold on the reserve. It is therefore challenging to interpret the letters fully, but three important pieces of information emerge from the correspondence. First, the category of "Half-breeds" or "Algonquin Half-breeds" described a distinctive group in Témiscamingue and greater Outaouais region; the group was distinctive enough, according to Nédélec, to warrant a political voice within the reserve once they were settled there. Second, some Métis were excluded from the Témiscamingue Reserve either by Indian Affairs (in conformity with the Indian Act), or by the Indian agent McBride, who favoured the entry of his close Métis kin, or, most likely, by some Indians on the reserve. Third, Nédélec seemed preoccupied by the category of Métis (or Half-breed, in his English correspondence), which McBride in turn defined as existing below or downstream of Kipawa Lake. There is no question that Nédélec knew this population quite well. He was assigned to the region of Maniwaki in 1868 and then to Mattawa the following year, where he stayed until 1892. His life as a missionary priest obliged him to cover the forestry towns and Indian missions and thus to interact with the various populations in these places (Carrière 1990). Nédélec in fact provides one of the most significant firsthand accounts of the cultural and collective presence of Métis in the region.

Government officials' refusal to give Métis of the greater Outaouais region the option to settle on reserves reflects a desire to assimilate them into the white population. Clearly, the Métis were not being confused with Indians of mixed ancestry. They are described collectively as seeking land to form a community, with a distinct identity that needed to be preserved through political representation. The discrimination they endured is in keeping with the era's segregation policies, which also sought to instrumentalize farming as a means of "civilizing" the "Sa(u)vages." Historically, the wish to assimilate the Métis to the whites is not surprising. It must be understood as part of a chain of government decisions and policies dating back to the 1840s. Already by 1847, colonial officials had decided not to grant Métis the customary presents allotted to Indians, a new policy that was explicitly articulated in Appendix T of the Bagot Report. Such policies would force Métis to integrate fully into the tribe with which they had kin relations or see themselves excluded from the category of Indigenous, particularly if differences between Métis and neighbouring Indian bands were readily visible and hence attracted the attention of Indian agents: "That no half breeds, or descendants of half breeds, where the difference is clearly marked, receive Presents, unless they be adopted by the Tribe with which they are connected, and live as Indians among them" (Province of Canada 1847, T-14).

The pressure for assimilation increased following the refusal of William Robinson, who was negotiating with Ojibwe chiefs in Ontario, to grant a particular status to Métis petitioners from Sault Ste. Marie. His exclusion of the Métis from the Robinson Treaties of 1850 left their political fate to the discretion of the Indian chiefs (Leighton 1983, cited by McNab 1985, 63). Both the Bagot commissioners and Robinson thus delegated the decision to local officials, the Indian agent, and local Indian chiefs, as opposed to dealing directly with Métis themselves. Thus, the refusal of the authorities to give the Métis a distinct status in the 1890s, when Nédélec was writing to Indian Affairs, is comparable to the situation of the Métis of Sault Ste. Marie in 1850. This refusal is especially significant when one considers that Algonquins of the same region of the Outaouais also never had the opportunity to negotiate treaties. It is important to acknowledge that no known treaties were negotiated or ratified with the Indians who inhabited the southwestern territory of the province of Québec, including the Gatineau Valley. The Bagot Report confirms this scenario in stark terms: "Of these reserves, the several Tribes still retain possession, and there is only one section of the country, viz.: on the Ottawa, in which the Indians have been dispossessed of their ancient hunting grounds without compensation" (Province of Canada 1847, T-17).

It follows that Bois-Brûlés in the Outaouais region who did not wish to assimilate into local Algonquin bands, or who were rejected by the latter, found themselves in the most precarious of positions – a position that was rendered complete with the adoption of the 1876 Indian Act, which specifies in article 3 that Métis are to be excluded from any protection offered to Indians within the act. These circumstances left the Métis vulnerable, as they became defined as "squatters," without any rights or title to the territory they inhabited (Indigenous and Northern Affairs Canada 2010).

### Who Are the Métis of the Greater Outaouais?

The documentary evidence we have so far analyzed demonstrates the distinctive character of Métis culture in the greater Outaouais region. That character is visible in several ethnocultural markers due, in large part, to the influence of European and Indigenous parentage tied to the fur trade. On an individual level, such markers may appear banal or insignificant – to be common in every colonial context – but as Michael Billig (1995) argues, sometimes it is precisely the "banal" that provides the foundation for a sense of community, including nationhood. Nonetheless, the very act of *métissage* (mixing) and having mixed heritage does not always lead to the formation of a new identity (Thistle 2007, 74–75).

In the greater Outaouais region, the multitude of families who shared similar experiences tied to their mixed heritage and work in the fur trade clearly favoured the emergence of a common identity. Along with outsiders' descriptions of these people and the names they gave them (Métifs, Bois-Brûlés, Métis), the commonality of experience certainly suggests the emergence of a community with clear cultural contours. Moreover, this community is sufficiently distinctive from Europeans, Canadiens, and First Nations to merit its own ethnonym – Bois-Brûlé – which has been demonstrated to be found across the continent and used to describe the predominantly French-speaking Métis. Amplifying these observations is the noted presence of a lived Catholicism informing continental kinship and social ties among the Métis, as well as the existence of a distinctive material culture, notably cabins and *sauvage* industrial arts. The historical record thus demonstrates that the contours of a distinctive Métis population in the Outaouais region are evident from a cultural standpoint.

As the fur trade economy waned, Father Nédélec, as we've seen, lobbied government officials to settle "Half-breeds" on the Témiscamingue Reserve, even arguing that they should be guaranteed representation on the band council. Had they until this point been seen as indistinct from First Nations living on the reserve? Father Nédélec's failure to convince officials of his proposal is tied to a government policy shaped decades before, which in effect attempted to exclude those Métis who did not share the First Nations way of life and were thus seen as undeserving of either presents or rights. Binnema (2014) argues that the regulations stripping women and their children of Indian status if they married a man without status emerged precisely to keep out such "plausible insiders." Quite often such policies emerged because members of First Nations pushed the Department of Indian Affairs to exclude those who were not deemed legitimate members of their communities, as also seems to be the case on the Témiscamingue Reserve. Thus, as occurred in Sault Ste. Marie and elsewhere, many Métis were excluded from reserves and pushed to become white.

The passage below, penned by the priest Du Ranquet in 1843, summarizes the ethnocultural markers that appear to characterize the Métis of the greater Outaouais region. It is all the more noteworthy because it was written before the negotiation of the Robinson Treaties and the colonial push into what is now southwestern Québec. It also highlights the distribution of Métis families in this region:

> The chief of all the affairs of the [Hudson's Bay] Company in Canada is in Montréal; the bourgeois who resides in the village of Lachine, a bit above Montréal, oversees the communication line from Outaouais to Hudson's Bay; that of Moose [Factory] is the District Chief, and this district includes several posts of bourgeois. The time served, as well as merit I believe, conducts [HBC officers] from the lowest to the highest ranks; almost all these merchants are English or Scottish. They give the title of clerk to employees attached to the service of posts for specific tasks that do not belong to [the affairs of] the Company. Some are placed as sentinels on the locales most frequented by the *Sauvages.* At the two principal forts that we visited, the bourgeois do not deal directly with the *Sauvages,* they hire as clerks Métis that know very well French, English and some *Sauvage* [languages]; these clerks or businessmen dine ordinarily at the table of the bourgeois, but their families have a separate house [unlike the bourgeois, who are housed at the post]. The one [clerk]

at Témiscamingue and the one at Abitibi are Protestants as they are of Anglo-Algonquin origin, their wives are Catholic *Sauvagesses* as are their children. The guide also belongs to the administrative personnel of the posts; ordinarily it is a *Canadien* or a Métis, who conducts bands of voyageurs that the posts expedite with trade goods, supplies or pelts; he oversees the camping sites, distributes victuals, etc. (Du Ranquet [1843] 2000, 113–14; our translation)

Unlike higher-ranking company officials, *bourgeois,* as they were called by the *engagés,* or contract employees, did not own and were not given any shares in the company. Thus clerks were not shareholders. This passage is also a reminder that the territory over which the HBC had a trading monopoly was divided into different districts, and that in these districts employees who served as clerks and/or guides were hired on contract. These *engagés* were invariably Métis or Canadien and could converse in French, English, and Indigenous languages. The officers of the company, the *bourgeois,* were generally recruited from England or Scotland, and though they may have been posted as clerks, the expectation was that they would rise up the ranks if, as Du Ranquet suggests, they showed any merit. The Canadien and Métis, even the English-speaking Protestant Métis, did not have such career prospects.

This excerpt, like many others reviewed in Part 2 of this book, thus suggests the presence of a Métis population that was distributed across the greater Outaouais region, from Fort Coulonge to Abitibi, hundreds of kilometres to the north. This population was demarcated by various ethnocultural markers, including mixed parentage; speaking both European and Indigenous languages; roles as cultural intermediaries; presence in the region prior to the arrival of a colonial agricultural settler society; and an intimate knowledge of the territory. These markers also trace the contours of a way of life shaped by the fur trade and the occupations in which the Métis excelled, notably as interpreters, canoe men, guides, and other diverse employment connected to the trading posts. Du Ranquet also confirms in his journal the attachment of Métis families to a version of lived, or folk, Christianity, and he highlights their use of wood cabins in proximity to trade posts. Finally, Du Ranquet uses *Métis* to refer to a distinctive collective, reminiscent of the other ethnonyms used in the region, notably *Bois-Brûlé, Métif,* and *Half-breed.*

Part 3 examines in greater detail the geographic zone formed by Rivière Désert (Maniwaki), Lac-Sainte-Marie, and Lac des Sables. Our goal is to narrow the geographical focus to one smaller region within the greater Outaouais region in order to identify any ethnocultural markers among the Métis there. We investigate a community of squatters at Lac-Sainte-Marie, strategically placed in relation to Bytown, as well as the similarities of this community to that of Sault Ste. Marie in Upper Canada, to identify commonalities in culture and sociopolitical structures. That work reveals the existence of a sociopolitical structure composed of interconnected Métis family networks cross-cutting a number of trade posts in the region. To fully understand this history, we examine desertions from trading companies, as well as the contraband of furs and alcohol with which the Métis of the Gatineau region have been associated, both individually and collectively. We also discuss Violet Lalonde's oral historical account of how the region welcomed and gave refuge to the fugitive Louis Riel, as it effectively demonstrates how local Métis traditions preserved the past, and tied past and present together.

*Part 3*

# Métis of the Gatineau Valley

## Rivière Désert, Lac-Sainte-Marie, and Lac des Sables

# 6

## *Crowded Crossroads*

As WE HAVE SEEN, Métis were found historically throughout the greater Outaouais region. A closer look at Lac-Sainte-Marie, however, reveals a cluster of Métis squatters who appear to have established themselves as a community next to the lake, which flows into the Gatineau River. Retired fur trade company employees could use the locale as a convenient point of entry into more distant lands to the north. Practically speaking, this location allowed these free traders to circumvent the HBC, buying goods, including alcohol, from the rapidly growing lumber and commercial centre of Bytown, which they then traded with First Nations in the interior, all the while selling furs for cash. A network of families were engaged in contraband and trade, undermining the HBC trade monopoly. Unlike the two other settlements that emerged in the region, Rivière Désert (Maniwaki) and Lac des Sables, the Lac-Sainte-Marie community was not located near a HBC post. Keeping their distance, the freemen and petty traders of Lac-Sainte-Marie could seek to best their much larger and better organized rival, the HBC. These three Métis settlements form a case study of the emergence of a historical Métis community in the greater Outaouais region.

The Lac-Sainte-Marie community shares many parallels with the other Sainte-Marie, that of the Sault or Soo. It was also tied to the continental Métis, reputedly providing refuge to Louis Riel following the resistance that led to the creation of the province of Manitoba and caused him to flee the country before returning to lead a second uprising against Canadian colonial forces in 1885. This incipient Métis community – though it would be enveloped first by foresters and then by agricultural settlers – has come to have a distinct legacy that can be traced down to descendants who continue to live in the Gatineau Valley of Québec.

### Bytown and the Independent Traders

Strategically, the opening of a fur trade post at Lake of Two Mountains (1819–20) ensured that the Indigenous people who descended the Ottawa River with furs in the spring would be intercepted by company traders, rather than petty traders, as the HBC derisively referred to them. The Ottawa River flows into this lake before its waters enter Lac Saint-Louis and thus the St. Lawrence. By controlling access to the Ottawa, the HBC hoped to control access to more distant lands and to block the movement of small rival independent traders.

The HBC aggressively defended its trade interests with the Algonquins to the north, knowing full well that the fur trade would eventually collapse with the expansion of the pioneer front as the forestry industry and agricultural settlement pushed into these territories. This trend was evident, as colonization was already underway. Having visited the region around the Chaudière Falls in the 1790s, American farmer and entrepreneur Philemon Wright brought five settler families and some two dozen labourers there from Massachusetts in 1800. Known as Wright's Town, their settlement provided a focal point for the growing forestry industry, which was booming as Napoleon's embargo forced the British to look beyond Europe for suitable timber to build their naval ships. Great rafts of white pine were floated down the Ottawa to Québec City, from where they could be exported. Nonetheless, the HBC continued to have an interest in controlling Lake of Two Mountains, as it served as a base for independent traders peddling their wares on the Ottawa and in the Témiscamingue region since the 1780s (Mitchell 1977, 34).

Indeed, the HBC was preoccupied by the growth of independent trade, as well as with traders who had served with its former competitor, the NWC, in the Outaouais region (Stone Circle Consulting and Know History 2015, 60–61). The comings and goings of Métis and Canadien voyageurs, occasionally accompanied by their wives and families from the Indian Country, also worried the company, and HBC governor George Simpson's policies tried to stamp out this kind of mobility. In a letter sent to Montréal and dated May 16, 1841, Simpson writes, "I have further to request that no families, of whatever rank or standing they may be, be allowed to proceed to the Interior in the Canoes, unless specially authorized by the Governor & Committee ... Applications have been made to me from a variety of sources for passages for families from time to time, but uniformly objected to."[1] Writing from Sault Ste. Marie, Simpson refers here to the requests he has received since leaving Montréal, passing by the Ottawa River. Many Métis employees had retired to the Outaouais, adding to the ranks of Métis, or Bois-Brûlés, encountered by Ingall and Shirreff a decade earlier and of the independent traders that the company did not want to see setting up shop in the region (Stone Circle Consulting and Know History 2015, 63–69). The socioeconomic context of the region was propitious for the emergence of a class of free traders who would compete with the HBC, crimping its revenues while increasing costs.

This free trade was pivotal in the development of a Métis population in the Gatineau Valley. Independent traders effectively positioned themselves between two economic powers, one a century old and the other just emerging. While Philemon Wright attempted to build commercial hegemony in the forest trade and the HBC continued to seek control of the fur trade, Bytown, which emerged in 1826 after colonial authorities undertook the building of the Rideau Canal, quickly grew to become an important commercial centre. The canal, of course, facilitated the shipping of goods; thus, independent traders could now travel down the Gatineau River to freely buy trade goods, including alcohol, and sell their pelts for cash. The HBC always tried to trade furs for goods, usually at inflated prices, and thus make additional profit by keeping its cash in reserve. At Bytown, American merchants came up via Kingston (Newton 1991, 3) and, for the first time, independent traders had competitors in both selling trade goods and buying furs. The Rideau Canal was built following the War of 1812 to ensure that the territory would not fall into American hands. Construction was completed that same year, and the first steamboat paddled up the canal from Kingston in 1832, ensuring that large quantities of goods could be sent back and forth between not only Bytown and Montréal but also Bytown and Kingston at a reduced cost. With the canal, Bytown became a central transportation hub that linked Upper and Lower Canada and in turn tied both to larger international markets (Legget 1988; Newton 1991, 3).

The HBC, its managers, and employees began to feel the cumulative effects of the growth of Bytown. The commercial hold of Wright and other emerging forestry barons in the Outaouais region ran counter to the HBC's attempts to establish a fur trade monopoly in the upper reaches of the Ottawa River basin. The so-called petty traders pushed farther north up the Ottawa and its tributaries, extending the terrain they could profitably cover (Mitchell 1977, 154). Faced with this changing landscape in

*Entryway to the Rideau Canal, Bytown,* by Philip John Bainbrigge, c. 1838. The
Rideau Canal was completed in 1832, beginning a new era of free trade in the
Outaouais region.
*Credit: Library and Archives Canada, 1970-188-1989*

what the HBC referred to as its "frontier," the company focused on check-
ing the spread of petty traders into the richer and more profitable fur-
bearing regions, as opposed to gaining any real profit in this zone (Bond
1966, 8; Du Ranquet [1843] 2000, 132). The HBC's two main strategies
to counter the threat to its operations were to offer more generous tariffs
to hunters, which would reduce the flow of pelts to independent traders,
and to follow the petty traders by canoe or by snowshoe in order to control
their activities. Both strategies increased costs and cut profits in the frontier
zone, but they also protected more lucrative markets from competition.

In 1832, John McLean, an HBC clerk stationed at the Lac des Sables
post, stated unambiguously that Bytown was a "free" centre for the fur
trade, and in the same correspondence denounced the trapper Amable
Foubert, whom we consider tied to the Métis Joseph Foubert (File 6).
McLean writes, "I fear the Company will find it a difficult matter to secure
Foubert as he never remains more than a couple of Days with his Family
& then off to the Woods – I understand he is frequently seen about Bytown
(where he goes to dispose of his hunt)."[2] Because Foubert owed the HBC

for goods he had bought on credit, company officers and employees tried to confiscate his furs.

A group of traders under the leadership of the Fleury family make a frequent appearance in the HBC correspondence. In 1831, their zone of influence covered a significant portion of the greater Outaouais region:

> I learn from the Crew of the large Canoe that three of Fleury Men are on their way up & that he is only to join them himself (as they report) about the latter end of the month of september, when I dare say he'll take the Field with all his Forces. The younger Fleury actually started from Lachine about the time we were informed & is by all accounts gone in the direction of Fort Coulonge accompanied by Bill Hodgson & I fear his design may be to penetrate to the interior in that Quarter & afterwards come round to join his party at this Place [Lac des Sables].[3]

This letter demonstrates the apprehension of the HBC employees who tracked and reported the comings and goings of petty traders and other adventurers who circulated through the Outaouais region, many of whom were aided by or had ties to the local Métis. Though we do not know the ethnic origins of the Fleurys, we do know that they were associated with a Métis man in the region, Bill (William) Hodgson.[4] We also learn in the HBC correspondence that the Fleurys got their trading supplies in Bytown, and when they penetrated into the interior, at Lac des Sables, they used cash to trade with Indian hunters, thus short-circuiting the control that the HBC attempted to exert over its Indigenous trading partners.[5]

In addition to the Fleurys, numerous comments in the HBC records about the McConnell brothers attest to a growing suspicion about their activities in the territories that the company wanted to control. According to rumours circulating within the HBC, the McConnell brothers' forestry enterprise was being used as a cover for free trade in furs as far as Témiscamingue (Du Ranquet [1843] 2000, 144; Mitchell 1977, 162). The unravelling of HBC efforts to control the fur trade is evident in reports that even Indians from Lake of Two Mountains were trading directly with Bytown merchants (Newton 1991, 5–8).

It is apparent that the socioeconomic context of the frontier zone favoured the freemen and other independent fur traders in the Maniwaki region. The same context likewise provided a rich terrain for the emergence of a Métis population. The region was not under direct colonial authority and it had pronounced commercial competition, yet it was sufficiently remote and isolated to favour traders wintering out in the Indian Country. These practices led to a concentration of interethnic unions that, in turn, led to the emergence of a historical Métis population (Devine 2004; Foster 2001).

### Squatters and Free Traders of Lac-Sainte-Marie

A review of the HBC archival documents makes it clear that not only First Nations but also certain Métis families living at Rivière Désert, Lac-Sainte-Marie, and Lac des Sables capitalized on the competitive trade hub of Bytown. When the surveyor Alphonse Wells surveyed the lands at Lac des Sables in 1846, he identified three heads of families as squatting: Ambroise Beaulieu (File 2), Joseph Jussiaume (File 7), and Pierre Goulin (Goudreau 2014b, 56–57). Beaulieu was Métis, while Jussiaume had been married to a Métis woman and had a Métis son, who was living not far away. Goulin may also have been Métis. We do know that in all likelihood he worked for the HBC before this date and was engaged in the sale of Indigenous crafts in the 1840s.[6] Lac-Sainte-Marie was also ideally placed to facilitate the emergence of a small "squatter" community bringing together retired fur trade employees, free traders, and Métis couples and families. The community was strategically located, providing a direct route to Bytown via the Gatineau River, as well as access to the Saint-Maurice River watershed to the northeast by way of the Lièvre River and a few portages (Cormier 1978, 110).

The trading activities of this community worried certain HBC employees.[7] In his 1838 correspondence, Allan Cameron, a clerk at the Lac des Sables company post, openly complains about the behaviour of one of Lac-Sainte-Marie's most illustrious inhabitants, Marie Pinesi-okijikokwe, an Indian who was married to former HBC clerk Andrew McPherson (File 13). According to Cameron, Pinesi-okijikokwe was in the thick of the free fur trade economy that linked Grand Lac, Lac des Sables, Rivière Désert, Lac-Sainte-Marie, and Bytown.[8] Historian Elaine A. Mitchell (1977, 199) notes the presence in the Outaouais region of families of mixed heritage with ties to First Nations communities, and explains the impact their trading activities had on HBC profits there. The Métis of the Gatineau are reported as travelling and independently exploiting the chain of lakes lying between the Gatineau and the Lièvre rivers. This was an ancient canoe route, and their activities notably affected the expected revenues of the HBC post at Lac des Sables (Cormier 1978, 110; Newton 1991, 13).

The individuals and families who settled at Lac-Sainte-Marie preoccupied HBC officials, and Allan Cameron was intent on knowing their true intentions. In 1838, he writes,

> There have lately arrived in vicinity of Outpost [Rivière Désert] a Crew of 5 or 6 apparently old voyageurs who give out that they Came for the purpose of Trade. As far as I Can learn Mr McPherson's (lately of Grand Lac) son & son in law are of the number, when I will have learnt more particularly their intentions I shall write you more fully. In the meantime I do not feel apprehensive of their being able to do much.[9]

In a second letter Cameron notes that François Naud, who was Andrew McPherson's son-in-law and a former HBC guide, was effectively pursuing trade in furs, and that Naud hoped to cultivate some land that he had bought from another freeman.[10] Naud reportedly offered to sell his furs to the HBC, which would have made him an intermediary and ensured a profit margin to help support his Métis family. In 1839, the trading activities of the Lac-Sainte-Marie squatters were once again reported to HBC officials.[11] Naud, no doubt to the chagrin of the HBC, did not abandon his independent trading activities in subsequent years.

HBC clerk George Sharpe, writing at Lac des Sables in a letter dated March 2, 1841, specifies that this petty trade was still taking place at Lac-Sainte-Marie: "I entend going to Rivière Desert on the 4th and on my return to go down the Gatineaux as far as Jacques Naud's who gets a few furs by selling whisky and may probably be tempted to dispose of them for cash."[12] The error in Sharpe's sentence suggests that his English was influenced by French, as it carries a trace of the French expression "J'entends aller" (I intend to go). Such intermingling of languages would not have been unprecedented. The Irishman Ross Cox (1832, 218) complained that he was losing his English, and that "bad French and worse Indian began to usurp the place of English" as his "conversation [was] gradually becoming a barbarous compound of various dialects."

Regardless, the practice of trading spirits for furs finds an echo in Superintendent John Keating's description of Métis at Huron Lake as detailed in the Bagot Report, noting the intermediary role the Métis

The freeman François Naud and the Métis Élisabeth McPherson, photographer
and date unknown. After François retired from the HBC, the couple established
themselves at Lac-Sainte-Marie in 1838 with other families that were tied to the fur
trade. The McPherson family had been living at Grand Lac (today Kitcisakik), and
is now found across the continent. Élisabeth and her sister, Philomène, relocated
to the Gatineau Valley, while their brother, George, ventured out to the Red River
region of Manitoba, as well as living in the area around Lake of the Woods in
Ontario.
*Credit: Claude Hubert, Maniwaki, reproduced in Marcotte (2017, 302)*

played between company men and First Nations. Sharpe's 1841 description of the Naud/McPherson extended family likewise echoes the later
reports of James Martin (1895, 31), the Indian agent on the Maniwaki
Reserve. In a missive dating to 1894, Martin accuses the Métis of traffick-
ing in hard liquor: "The Indians can only obtain intoxicants through the
medium of whites or half-breeds, and, although drunkenness among them
has not ceased, it has greatly diminished." This illicit alcohol trade did
not disappear quickly in the Gatineau Valley. The Métis of the region were
once again explicitly identified as the principal culprits in selling contraband alcohol to Indians, and they were also described as a distinctive
collective, separate from their First Nations kin. An Indian Affairs report
authored by Martin Bensen in 1909 reads, "There are about ten licensed
hotels and liquor shops [at Maniwaki], and, though none are known to
sell liquor direct to the Indians, they have no difficulty in getting it through

their half-breed and French-Canadians relatives and friends."[13] Such descriptions confirm the geographical proximity of the social actors in question.

The Métis of the Gatineau thus share comparable ethnocultural markers and were often criticized for pursuing illicit activities as intermediaries, as was also the case for the Métis of the Great Lakes, the Illinois Country, and western Canada,[14] and similar to Keating's description for the Bagot Report. Through these historical descriptions and other documentary sources, it is possible to discern shared individual experiences fashioned by familial, social, and occupational structures that tied together individuals and Métis families participating in the illicit trade in contraband fur and alcohol as far as the 1830s in the Outaouais region. Through analysis of case studies such as the Nauds, McPhersons, and Hodgsons, it is indeed possible to identify the ethnocultural and experiential cement that binds a community and shapes Métis culture, the culture of a people who "own themselves" and their destiny,[15] operating in open networks that follow traditional fur trade circuits.

Two Métis brothers, Amable and Ignace (Angus) McDougall (File 11), were among the voyageurs who joined the community of Lac-Sainte-Marie, and they illustrate the composition of the ethnocultural glue that bound individuals and families together. Demonstrating the breadth of the historical network and the mobility that characterized the Métis way of life, the archival documents reveal connections between the brothers and Lake of Two Mountains, Kingston, and the Red River (in all likelihood Manitoba). Amable McDougall is described by a surveyor travelling on the Gens-de-Terre River, who portrays him as a celebrated Métis who had worked for the HBC for many years: "From the mouth up to seventy miles the Jean de Terre receives eight tributaries capable of carrying lumber. The only information I was able to gather about them was from Amable McDougall a well known halfbre[e]d who has been many years in the service of the Hudson Bay Company as a travelling trader" (Russell 1851, cited in Sabourin 2010, 72). The portrait of Amable corresponds to the typical Métis of Scottish origin who can be classified as French speaking.[16] We suspect he was also capable of speaking at least one First Nation language, as one of the Catholic missionary registries records him with the Algonquin name Kapimioewittang.[17] McDougall evolved over the course of his "professional" travels, residing at different trade posts and engaging in the sale of contraband alcohol. The surveyor Russell writes of McDougall with high esteem for the information he can provide about the terrain, a characteristic he shared with the Métis Jean-Baptiste Bernard (File 3) and Thomas Brown, both of whom work as guides in the same region. McDougall is also noted for his many years of service in the fur trade. Thus, his life mirrors the lived experiences of many individuals who were tied to the historical Métis culture.

Intriguingly, the McDougall brothers had familial ties through the marriage of Cécile, their probable sister, to the Lavigne and Riel families, recorded by the surveyor John Snow in 1848 as squatters residing in the community of Lac-Sainte-Marie (see File 11). The evidence indicates the presence of shared kinship ties as well as occupations that connect individuals who were (or later would be) clearly identified as Métis (or Half-breed, or part Indian, etc.) in the surroundings of Lac-Sainte-Marie.

### The Notebook of John Snow

The notebook of the surveyor John Allan Snow provides a trove of information about the presence of other former fur traders and Métis families at Lac-Sainte-Marie.[18] Snow was born in 1824 in Hull Township in Lower Canada, and he returned to Canada from New York after training as a surveyor (Bowsfield 1982). Between 1845 and 1865, as a deputy provincial surveyor, he set out many of the township lines, covering much of what is now eastern Ontario. While fulfilling these duties he recorded the presence of a number of families living at Lac-Sainte-Marie. His assignment in the Gatineau region was an extension of work he was conducting in the unified Province of Canada. He also oversaw the building of colonization roads that brought agricultural settlers to what was still the fur frontier.

Because of this expertise, he was later recruited by the Ministry of Public Works of the newly created Dominion of Canada in 1868 to oversee the building of a road between Lake of the Woods and Upper Fort Garry (Winnipeg) in the Red River. This road was "to provide employment 'to the distressed population' of the Red River Settlement and to 'alleviate their sufferings' brought on by an almost complete crop failure. The long-range goal was to satisfy the demands of Canadian expansionists for better communication with the west" (Bowsfield 1982). As is evident, the tasks of surveying and road building were invariably tied to colonization, and this activity would come to a boil in the Red River region. The men who were recruited to build the road refused to work solely for provisions, and in 1869 went on strike for better wages. They threatened to drown Snow because he had refused to pay them their wages for the day and a half they were on strike. Snow was embroiled in the Red River Resistance, as he and Dr. John Christian Schultz – a local physician, businessman, and political agitator with whom Snow came to be associated in his road-building venture – sought to buy some land from the "Indians," stoking fears of dispossession. All told, Snow certainly contributed to inflaming passions, which in part provoked the eventual armed uprising. This later led to the accusations that Snow had fomented the 1870 uprising (Bowsfield 1982; Clark 1990).

Returning to the Outaouais region, Snow recorded in his notes individuals living on the territory who did not have deeds or title to their property. At Lac-Sainte-Marie he enumerated twenty heads of families, or at the very least twenty men, who inhabited the area as "squatters" in 1848. His notebook attests to the existence of a social structure in situ as well as to the relative geographical proximity of the individuals and, by extension, their likely families. A close analysis of the notebook permits

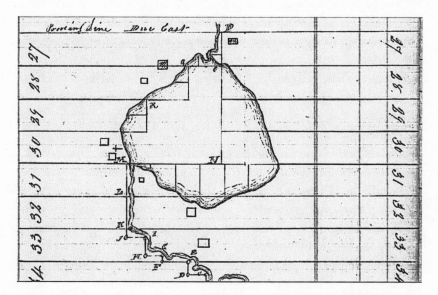

Excerpt from the notebook of surveyor John Allan Snow depicting Lac-Sainte-Marie, including the lots he recorded in 1848. The location of the community chapel is marked on the left with a cross. It was erected on a clearing belonging to François Naud and Élisabeth McPherson.
*Credit: Bibliothèque et Archives nationales du Québec, Québec, Carnet G-25, Cantons Aylwin et Hincks/John Allan Snow.—1848-05-08, Fonds Ministère des Terres et Forêts, Folio 36*

the identification of eleven families tied to the professional and familial networks of the fur trade. Of these eleven, only two do not include Métis. Thus, the majority of the inhabitants of Lac-Sainte-Marie were directly tied to the fur trade (eleven of twenty), and close to half were tied to families that were known to be Métis (nine of twenty). Given the mobility of fur trade employees and freemen, as well as the use of nicknames and naming variants, some of the remaining nine yet to be identified may also have been former fur trade employees, and they may have been Métis as well. Nonetheless, given the preponderance of evidence collected on the eleven identified, a credible argument can be made that Lac-Sainte-Marie was a historical Métis community concentrated in one locale. Snow's notebook was a fortuitous find. Colonial officials did not require or necessarily want him to devote time and energy to recording the names of "squatters," and these names could easily have disappeared without a trace had he not noted them almost by happenstance.

Below are the names he included on his list, using his own spelling[19] followed by an alternative name or names and a short description of the individual, if they are among the eleven we have positively identified based on either their work in the fur trade or other primary sources. Also given are the names of their wives when they are known to have been Indigenous:

- Andrew Sabourain (André Sabourin), a retired voyageur of the HBC and a free trader[20]
- Isaac Truchon
- Thomas McKay
- Francis Noe (François Naud), a former HBC guide and winterer who worked at the Grand Lac post and was then a free trader, married to Élisabeth McPherson (File 13), a Métis woman from the same region
- Louis Fournier, a former HBC winterer at the Rivière Désert post and free trader married to Philomène McPherson (File 13), a Métis woman from the region of Grand Lac
- Peter Barbear (Pierre Barbier), an HBC winterer and voyageur at Abitibi Lake who retired in 1837 (Bellefeuille 1840b, 64)[21]
- Jean Louis
- James Beads (File 1), a Métis from James Bay and former HBC winterer at Moose Factory
- Baptiste Laville

- Jacob Lavine (Jacques Lavigne), a former winterer for the Day & Murdoch Company and in all likelihood Métis (File 10)
- Antoine Biel
- Francois Renville
- Alexander Delange
- Jean B.C. Riel
- Melien Riel (Émilien Riel), a man of unknown occupation married to Métis Henriette McDougall (File 11)
- Francois Venois (François Vanasse), a former seasonal voyageur for the HBC married to Métis Louise Forcier, in all likelihood originally from the West (File 19)
- Amable McDougall (File 11), a retired Métis HBC winterer posted at Lac des Sables
- Joseph Laville (Joseph Lavallée), a former HBC guide and winterer stationed at the Grand Lac post and married to Marie Angélique Masanakomikokwe, an Indian woman of the region (File 9)
- Joseph Fournier, a man of unknown occupation married to Métis Marie Vallière and who possibly participated in free trade with his brother Louis Fournier (File 18)
- Joseph Jobin.

It is also notable that Snow uses the term *squatter* to describe the inhabitants of Lac-Sainte-Marie, a term that mirrors that of the surveyor Joseph Bouchette in 1832. Bouchette describes as squatters individuals in the same region whom he also labels as Bois-Brûlés (Métis). Thus, Snow's *squatter* is not coincidental in light of the larger sociopolitical factors, as discussed in the previous chapter. The Métis who inhabit the region, like the surrounding Algonquin population, do not have recognized title to the land, and no treaty is known to have been negotiated or ratified. In addition to the squatters who were formally associated with this settlement at Lac-Sainte-Marie, a few other Métis or former voyageurs have also been identified in other archival documents as having ties to the area. For example, retired voyageur François Vallière (File 18) is at Lac-Sainte-Marie in the 1840s,[22] as is the Métis Léon Paul (File 15), who is described in 1856 as a "farmer of St. Marie of the Gatineau River."[23] This locale thus serves, by all accounts, as a more or less permanent residence for a number of Métis or Canadiens who had ties to the fur trade.

## "Squatters" or "Bois-Brûlés"?

The majority of Métis living in this region were not accepted as Indians; nor were they able to integrate into reserves, such requests being largely denied by both the Indian agent and the Department of Indian Affairs, as the correspondence of Father Nédélec demonstrates. As was the case for Métis of Red River or those of Rainy Lake (Lac à la Pluie), Métis in the Gatineau region found themselves in the untenable position of having no legal collective rights to the lands they occupied, and thus being reduced to the status of individual squatters in their homes. They therefore had to navigate between two identities in the hope of securing some form of transferable title. Colonial and later government officials who negotiated with Métis in various regions across what became the Canadian Confederation invariably presented them with the choice of being white or Indian.

These people were not simply squatters, however, scattered and isolated here and there in the vicinity of Maniwaki. To see them as such is to brush aside their historical significance as a Métis community in its regional sense. Reducing them to merely wandering squatters conceals the process of ethnogenesis at play. Also by overlooking the larger historical community ties, this mislabelling of the Bois-Brûlés could be used to deny collective Indigenous rights to families that are thus labelled as the descendants of squatters, or as merely mixed. The evidence suggests that these so-called squatters were actually a community with a shared culture distinct from that of both First Nations and Euro-Canadians. A significant portion of the squatter population was in effect Métis – usually referred to as Bois-Brûlés, Half-breeds, Métifs, and so forth – and constituted a community. Outside observers note distinctive cultural markers, such as a preference for hunting and fishing as opposed to farming, expertise in Indigenous industrial arts, trade activities (whether as free traders or traffickers of contraband goods such as alcohol), Christianity (attested to by a Catholic chapel on land belonging to François Naud), and participation in the fur trade. They were often recruited for their expertise as guides and interpreters. Like Métis elsewhere, they were confronted with the challenge of the shifting fur frontier, as surveyors were often followed by large-scale agricultural settlement, which too often left the Métis alienated in lands where their families had lived for generations.

# 7

# *Comparing Lac-Sainte-Marie and Sault Ste. Marie*

THE PRECARIOUS STATUS OF the squatters at Lac-Sainte-Marie or, as we argued, the Bois-Brûlé (Métis) community there, becomes even more apparent when we compare historical descriptions of this locale in western Québec with the historical Métis community of Sault Ste. Marie, Ontario, located in the strait connecting Lakes Superior and Huron. These two communities share some striking ethnocultural similarities, and Father Du Ranquet's observations in his journals are again quite telling:

> Lake Sainte-Marie, also called Round Lake, is a league and a half from the river; arriving at the closest portage, Mr. Moreau and I, with a man and a Sauvagesse, we left our canoes to follow a trail through the forest, which leads to this mission. We arrived as dusk fell, at Mr. James Now's home, former winterer at La Truite Lake; his wife, his mother-in-law are Algonquin. There are a few other Sauvagesses married to Canadiens recently established on the shores of the little lake. Mr. Moreau received confessions long into the night.
>
> Brother Jennesseaux who had camped with our men on the Gatineau arrived the next day with a few of them, carrying all that was needed for mass. The inhabitants on the lakeside who were noticed the night before came eagerly. They were waiting for their missionary to arrive in a few days, and as such we had little work to do except for the Sauvages. (Du Ranquet [1843] 2000, 239–40; our translation)

Father Du Ranquet describes the population of Lac-Sainte-Marie as largely constituted of mixed unions between Canadiens (whom we know to be retired traders of the region) and *Sauvagesses* (largely Algonquin).[1] Father Du Ranquet reveals that not only do the "inhabitants" of Lac-Sainte-Marie attend mass but also some "Sauvages" take advantage of his presence to participate in religious service. This population of *Sauvages* does not seem to reside at the lake, as those who do live there are awaiting the arrival of "their missionary." Most of the *Sauvages* in all likelihood were those who came to trade with the inhabitants, already reputed to be independent traders.[2]

Even though exogamous unions were evident, the missionaries who visited the community of Lac-Sainte-Marie clearly discerned three ethnic groups within it. They distinctly identify Canadiens, Métis, and *Sauvages* (the majority of whom were Catholic) living alongside each other in the same mixed community in 1847. An anonymous and unpublished document in the Chronicles of the Oblate Missionaries recounts,

> In heading up the Gatineau, to 20 leagues from its mouth, we find two miles from the left bank, a small lake named Walliag Kang that is also given the name of Sainte-Marie, because of a small chapel elevated on its shore five years ago by care of Mr. Desautels and dedicated to the Saint Virgin. Sixteen Canadien, Métis and Sauvage families have fixed their domicile there. We have given them, two years ago, a short retreat.[3]

Further, the community of Lac-Sainte-Marie featured another characteristic associated with the Métis: subsistence agriculture was carried out sparingly, being largely neglected in favour of hunting and fishing. In a letter dated May 3, 1842, Father Joseph Desautels (1843, 61; our translation) reports that most of the families of Lac-Sainte-Marie "live off the hunting and fishing that they do in the neighbouring large lakes which are rich in fish." Surveyor John Snow confirms this in his notes, recorded some six years after the missionary penned his letter:

> As a general Remark it may be said that the Land on both sides of the River & Lake St Mary is of the best quality ... The inhabitants [illegible word] have subsisted chiefly by Hunting & Fishing of which the Lakes & Vicinity afford a super abundance. The[y] are Commencing however, to pay more attention, to the improvements of their farms.[4]

Here again we see that hunting and fishing are crucial to subsistence. Similar practices were observed in other Métis communities in the region, such as Lac des Sables. The McGregors (File 12), active in the area in the 1840s, are reported to have provided such a quantity of tanned deer hides to a merchant in Buckingham[5] that it seems the Métis family was hunting over much of the year. As for fishing, suffice it to say that Lac des Sables had already acquired a reputation by 1832 as an excellent locale for this activity (Bouchette 1832b, "Lac des Sables").

### Similarities with Sault Ste. Marie

The Métis community of Sault Ste. Marie, Ontario, provides a useful point of comparison with Lac-Sainte-Marie, particularly as it is now widely accepted as a historical Métis community among experts in Métis studies (Jones 1998; Ray 1998, 2011, 2016). The similarities between the communities are evident. The Catholic missionary Gaulin notes the same ethnocultural features at Sault Ste. Marie in a letter he titled "Mission chez les Sauvages du Haut-Canada," dated September 25, 1838:

> There are on the northern shore of the Sault Ste. Marie [River] fifty-seven families composed of French Canadians, Métis and a few *Sauvages,* all Catholic, and forming a population of some two hundred souls. I am not speaking of the winterers of the company [HBC] who are in the interior and whose tally I was not able to obtain. I do not add either the multitude of *Sauvages* who were recently baptized. (Gaulin 1841, 54; our translation)

Gaulin's description of Sault Ste. Marie is consistent with that of Gabriel Franchère, who passed through the region some two decades earlier:

> The inhabitants are for the most part old Canadien voyageurs married to women of the country. They live off fish during a large part of the year, and as long as they harvest enough potatoes to get through the rest, they are happy. It is regrettable that they are not more industrious and harder working as the land could not be more fertile especially on the north shore [of the River Sainte-Marie]: Mr. Ermantinger showed us some wheat which was ripening and the stalks measure three to four feet in height. The other grain [crops] were also equally nice. (Franchère 1820, 279; our translation)

Franchère's description parallels Snow's, but Franchère also highlights the importance of having a potato crop for periods of the year when resources run low.

Like the Métis of the Gatineau, therefore, Métis in Sault Ste. Marie were criticized for not doing much in the way of agriculture. In fact, Franchère's comments were echoed a generation later by Father Köhler in his discussion of the Métis community at Sault Ste. Marie in 1850:

This village [Gachkiwang, on Saint-Joseph Island, near Sault Ste. Marie] previously had given some hope of growing, but since the establishment of the Bruce Mines located some 12 miles hence, it seems to have been quickly reduced to nothing. Its inhabitants rely almost solely on fishing to live and are found, to say it thus, under the domination of a few village philosophers, descendants, probably, of the youngest sons of families who having lost everything in France or Lower Canada, had gone to seek fortune in the middle of the Sauvages in the service of a few fur companies. Most of inhabitants of Gachkiwang are Métifs and, as all that is sauvage, devote little thought to tomorrow. The lack of industry, like the shortage of perseverance, among people who go build on all the shores, establishing farms, and never finishing anything, is in part the cause of the loss of the village. The heads of families that comprised it are almost all former voyageurs, in the past employed by the Hudson's Bay Company to run the woods for trade [*courir la dérouine*] among the Sauvages, that is to say to watch when they leave for the hunt and when they return in order to obtain from them, often for a vile price, their furs. (Köhler [1850] 1973, 691–92; our translation)

Comparing the observations of Du Ranquet, Desautels, Gaulin, Franchère, and Snow, we see that the communities of Lac-Sainte-Marie and Sault Ste. Marie both feature a tripartite ethnic population of Métis, Canadiens, and *Sauvages*, in which a Métis identity is highlighted.

In both locales, the population was largely Catholic, spoke French, and comprised the descendants of voyageurs and fur trade employees, most of whom were *Canadien* and Scottish, or Métis. Most Métis men in these communities were married to Indigenous women. Both locales also shared experiences in common at the individual and community level. Both featured populations whose way of life was tied to the fur trade and associated with activities such as hunting and fishing, often to the detriment of agriculture as practised by settlers who came later and were said to be civilized or white. The agricultural practices of both communities were used largely to ensure survival at times of year when hunting, fishing, and, one assumes, gathering wild plant foods would not be sufficient to meet the needs of families.

Colonial authorities considered the practice of agriculture tied to sedentary life as the marker of superior civilization that must be instilled in *Sauvages* and Métis. This type of prejudice is evident in a letter dated

November 27, 1857, sent by the missionary Déléage, which describes a plan of action for the *Sauvages* of Maniwaki:

> Their progress this time, whether moral, religious or work habits, has not been very advanced; however, we have observed a betterment when they have not been impeded by the obstacles that I will discuss below. Thus, as concerns religion, they have become more enlightened, and religion has improved their mores, as we have seen them become more moral as the religious senti-ment and Christian truths have better penetrated in their spirit and their heart. As for industry, a certain number have begun to devote themselves to agriculture. (Déléage 1858, 169; our translation)

The Métis of both Sault Ste. Marie and Lac-Sainte-Marie, it is apparent, were not conforming to this ideal as they were not dedicated agricultural-ists. Rather, they had gardens and limited farming to supplement activities such as trading, hunting, fishing and gathering.

An 1886 text by Louis-Arthur Prud'homme exemplifies the colonial goal of supplanting the nomadic way of life practised by *Sauvages* with agriculture. A lawyer, Prud'homme was born in Saint-Urbain, south of Montréal, and settled in Saint-Boniface in 1880. He was appointed as a judge in 1885 and served for forty years. He wrote extensively on the fur trade, publishing works on the history of the French Canadian and Métis in the North-West. Prud'homme notes the mediocre results achieved ac-cording to this colonial criterion in the early decades of the nineteenth century, and proposes the assimilation of *Sauvage* – a term used pejoratively by colonial authorities – children via residential schools, said to be indus-trial schools:

> It is necessary to state that in the era of which speaks McKenzie, the mission-aries had neither the time nor the resources to do what he suggested. To teach agriculture to the Sauvages, but do we know that it is a secular work, and that in practice, has to the present time produced little in the way of satisfactory results? Here, close to 100 years after this author wrote what preceded, the civilization that has penetrated the West has not yet succeeded in having the Sauvages lose their habits [culture] and nomadic way of life. The only way of making a farmer out of the Sauvage, is it not to do what Mgr Grandin proposed: isolating the child from the rest of the tribe, removing

the influence of the family and training the child in industrial and useful arts as says McKenzie? (Prud'homme 1886, 9; our translation)

Such concerns echo those of the Bagot Commission discussed previously. The questionnaire sent to Indian agents by the Commission was meant, in part, to determine not only whether Indians were farming but whether they were farming effectively, based on what and how much they were producing. These agriculture-specific questions were followed by a series of questions on schools, attendance, and even one about what children were learning in schools located on reserves or in Indian settlements under the jurisdiction of the Indian Department.

It should come as no surprise that such prejudices were also evident in the greater Outaouais region, and always in terms that opposed cultural modes of life emanating from agricultural civilization and First Nations practices. This is evident in the 1889 annual report of the Department of Indian Affairs:

> Many of the Indians of this country remain, like a large number of those of the County of Ottawa, almost entirely in the woods; but when game and fur-bearing animals become so rare that they can no longer subsist by capturing them, they will likewise be compelled to settle upon their reserve on Lake Temiscamangue [sic], and to adopt civilized methods for obtaining a living, the principal of which must necessarily be agriculture. (Canada, Parliament 1890, xx–xi)

The documentary sources relating to both Lac-Sainte-Marie and Sault Ste. Marie thus reveal that outsiders recognized a distinctive culture among the Métis populations around these trading posts and religious missions, as well as the social and structural contours of a clustering of families in close proximity within each community.

### Linking Métis Communities through Family Ties

The emergence of Métis families originating from different trading posts demonstrates how those employed by the fur trade companies brought their families along after having been relocated to a new post, in spite of Governor George Simpson's attempts to eradicate such practices. Representing the Métis community as a village can be problematic, however, as this concept does not correspond to the historical sociocultural fabric of the Métis of the Gatineau Valley. Local hamlets such as Rivière Désert, Lac-Sainte-Marie, and Lac des Sables should be understood, rather, as situated within a much larger regional community, the existence of which is supported by the historical record. By applying the concept of *regional* community to the analysis of the Métis of the Gatineau and larger Outaouais region, it is possible to better understand the distinctive culture that was shared by Métis families. We use the concept of a regional community in spite of the geographical dispersion of its members, as they nonetheless remained connected through fur trade networks and a common culture.

The Cadotte family provides an example of how webs of Métis kinship were spun transregionally. Members of this family were found across the larger Outaouais region (Lac des Sables, Fort Coulonge, Lac des Allumettes) as well as in other regions (Sault Ste. Marie, Fond du Lac), demonstrating the inherent mobility of the Métis. Among the members of the Cadotte family, we find a Marguerite Cadotte and a Jean-Baptiste Cadotte in the registry of the missionaries at Lac des Allumettes (Fort William) in 1837; they are identified as "métisse" and "métif," respectively.[6] Other members of the Cadotte family were at Lac des Sables, where we find Mary Keith (File 17), daughter of James Keith and Marie Cadotte (see front cover). Marie was the daughter of the illustrious Jean-Baptiste Cadotte, known as *le fils* (the son) so he would not be confused with his Canadien father of the same name. Mary Keith thus had her roots in Sault Ste. Marie via her grandfather. She was married to the Métis Thomas Taylor.

Interestingly, an HBC clerk named McLean noticed the people of Lac des Sables in the 1820s for their distinctive "mixedness," as well as their surprising behaviour: "Being a Stranger in this Country & unaquainted with the Manners & Customs prevalent among its mixed inhabitants you will excuse my Curiosity if I enquire of you whether it be yankee or Canadian Hospitality to envite a Friend to sup or Dine with you & then make him pay."[7] Clearly, McLean considers the customs at Lac des Sables odd, to say the least. Even though he refers to both American ("yankee") and French Canadian (the norm at the time was to use "Canadian" to refer to French Canadians), he sees the "mixed" inhabitants as different and distinctive from the Canadiens with whom they would invariably have shared a common language, religion, and even kin ties.

McLean's trading post certainly had a Métis presence. Around the fort, we find the Beaulieu/Godin family (File 2) and the Paquette family (File 14). HBC employee Joseph Paquette and an unidentified Indigenous woman lived at the fort and had at least one child.[8] In addition to referring to the Beaulieu and Paquette families quite early in his correspondence, McLean also mentions John Knight, an interpreter and clerk working for the HBC at Lac des Sables. Knight was Métis and hailed from James Bay,[9] but he seemed to be quite familiar with the surrounding territory. Four families were living at the trading post in 1828, according to McLean, but other than the Beaulieus and the Paquettes he does not identify them by name.[10] Given the locale and the period, it is reasonable to assume that all four families were Métis or had Métis family members. The historical record indicates that the McGregor/Riel family (File 12) revisited this locale in the 1820s[11] and thus may have been one of the four living at the post. The other potential family is that of the Métis Jean-Baptiste Bernard (File 3), as he was married to Élisabeth Shaw, who is mentioned as living at Lac des Sables in 1829.[12] Jean-Baptiste was a winterer for the HBC at the time.[13] When McLean alludes to mixed inhabitants, he therefore in all likelihood means the Beaulieu/Godin, Paquette, McGregor/Riel, and Bernard Métis families, along with Knight. Regardless of the ethnicity of the individual who did not extend the hospitality McLean expected (whether "Yankee" or "Canadian"), he interprets the incident within an ethnic framework, emphasizing the "mixed" nature of the people in question. The families tied to the fur trade were certainly mixed and sufficiently present in McLean's entourage to provoke this cultural observation.

Returning to the familial history of the Keiths and Cadottes, we see how the fur trade was a structuring force for the multiple generations of those who worked within it, creating kin networks across the continent. Mary Keith's husband, Thomas Taylor, was a clerk originally from Rupert's Land, most likely from the Severn Post on Hudson Bay;[14] he worked at the Lac des Sables post in the 1840s. Governor Simpson describes Taylor in an 1832 note:

> Taylor Thomas. A half breed about 35 Years of Age. Was a Labouring apprentice for 7 Years, was my own body Servant for ten Years, and has for the 3 past years been one of the most effective Postmasters in the Country. Speaks several of the Native Languages, is a great favorite with Indians, is "a Jack of all Trades" and altogether a very useful man in his line. (Williams 1975, 233)

Thomas Taylor, 1850s or 1860s, by an unknown photographer. This Métis from Hudson Bay married Mary Keith in the Red River Colony and was a clerk for the HBC at Lac des Sables from 1843 to 1849. Taylor, described as a Half-breed, refers in his 1846 correspondence to the presence of other Half-breeds in the Outaouais region.
*Credit: Hudson's Bay Company Archives, 1995/43/1*

Taylor, a Métis from the North-West, presents the same ethnocultural traits as Amable McDougall, Thomas Brown, Jean-Baptiste Bernard, and John Knight. He too was identified as a "half breed" and valued for his multiple talents, which were tied to occupational niches in the fur trade. In addition to English (and in all likelihood French), Taylor spoke a number of Indigenous languages, a trait we find in descriptions of the historical Métis in the Outaouais region and elsewhere. The grandfather of Mary Keith, Jean-Baptiste Cadotte Jr., also belonged to an illustrious Métis family, as he followed his father's footsteps in the fur trade and eventually rose up the ranks to become a full partner of the NWC (Armour 1983; Goldring 1985). David Thompson, the famed explorer who crossed the Rockies and reached the Pacific via the Columbia River, reports that Cadotte Jr.

spoke fluent English, French, and Ojibwe as well as knowing Latin, which again highlights the linguistic erudition often found among the Métis (Tyrrell 1916, 252).

The intergenerational transfer of a way of life inherited from the fur trade is thus observed over the course of unions between Métis families of the greater Outaouais region. The marriage of Jean-Baptiste Cadotte's daughter to James Keith, and that of his granddaughter Mary Keith to Thomas Taylor, illustrate this reality. Additionally, two sons of the latter couple had careers with the HBC, starting with a clerkship for Thomas Jr. in the Outaouais region and the promise of a position in the North-West for James.[15] Their daughter, Rose Taylor, married retired HBC winterer Moyse Lavallée; she is also identified as "métisse" in the registry of a Témiscamingue mission (Martineau 1991, 40).[16] Although the Taylor/ Keith family was evidently becoming gentrified, it nonetheless appears that its Métis identity was maintained. Mary Keith was raised not by her parents but in the household of her uncle George Keith (Goldring 1985). Her father, James Keith, was the head of the Montreal Department of the HBC from 1827 to 1835 and then from 1837 to 1843 (Goldring 1985), while her uncle George was a chief factor, an important rank in the HBC hierarchy, and was posted to diverse districts of the West over his career (Brown 1985). George was married to a Métis woman (Nanette Sutherland) who moved with him to Scotland in the 1840s. There, she drew attention for her Indigenous craft (Van Kirk 1999, 126). Given the milieu in which she grew up and was educated, Mary Keith would have conserved a mix of European and Indigenous cultural influences. The pattern exhibited by this family is comparable to that documented across the continent: the second and third generations in the fur trade intermarried, while new employees and winterers began to marry into this kinship network. Such networks are fundamental to the Métis ethnogenesis in the continental fur trade, and once an identity had been forged, as is evident with respect to the Sault Ste. Marie Métis, it could persist even once exogamous marriages became the rule.

As observed among the Taylor-Keith-Cadotte kin, these unions reflected the numerous zones of geographical influence that tied East and West and facilitated alliances. For example, we see a network linking Montréal, Lac des Sables, Fort Coulonge, the Red River in Manitoba, Hudson Bay, and Sault Ste. Marie. Métis men invariably criss-crossed the continent in the fur trade. Jean-Baptiste Cadotte Jr., like his father, travelled across

Portrait assumed to be of Thomas Taylor Jr., 1850s or 1860s, by an unknown photographer. Son of two Métis parents active in the fur trade, Thomas began working for the HBC in 1847 as an apprentice clerk at Fort Coulonge, and ended his career with the company on the prairies at the end of the century.
*Credit: Hudson's Bay Company Archives, 1995/43/6*

Sault Ste. Marie, Lac Rouge (Minnesota), Michilimackinac (Michigan), and other regions before becoming an interpreter for the Department of Indian Affairs in Lower Canada (Schenck 1994, 194).

All these locales were important centres in the fur trade, and historical records attest to the existence of Métis there (Foxcurran, Bouchard, and Malette 2016). In fact, in the Outaouais region and across the continent, this great mobility was intrinsic to the lives of many Métis families. The Beaulieu family of the Outaouais region, for example, undertook a voyage west for reasons that have not yet been uncovered. A family friend who was working at Lac des Sables suggested in a letter that Marie Godin be left at Sault Ste. Marie, perhaps to wait for the arrival of her husband, Ambroise Beaulieu, who seems to have been delayed at Montréal.[17] Though the full story of the trip is not known, the letter highlights how families could call upon professional networks such as the NWC or HBC, as well as on kinship and cultural networks, to facilitate their travels as they moved across the continent.[18] We found numerous other examples of Métis of the greater Outaouais region heading west to make their lives there. For example, a missionary notes that the Métis James King (Roy), discussed earlier, had a daughter who married a "bourgeois" (high-ranking officer) of the HBC and moved to the Red River region.[19] Likewise, Josephte Siveright, a Métis born at Sault Ste. Marie from a Métis mother and Fort Coulonge trader John Siveright, married Alexis Goulet, thus integrating herself into a well-known Red River Métis family (Arthur 1985).

This kind of mobility also characterizes the McGregor family of the Gatineau (File 12). The McGregor family, originally from Sault Ste. Marie, travelled to Pointe-Claire, at the western end of Montréal island, to have one of their children baptized.[20] They were later married at the Lake of Two Mountains mission,[21] and one year later found themselves at Lac des Sables at the same time as the Beaulieu Métis family.[22] Mobility equally shapes the Jussiaume family (File 7), which was present on the Lièvre River in the 1830s and 1840s. The Jussiaume family also has its origins in the Sault Ste. Marie community, as Marguerite Alexandre, the mother of Joseph Jussiaume, was recorded as a "*Mitive* recently descended from the upper country,"[23] born, to be more precise, at Sault Ste. Marie.[24] She later married Joseph Jussiaume Sr., a voyageur working with the HBC at Lac des Sables.[25] Returning to the Outaouais region, the two Joseph Jussiaumes, father and son, find themselves "squatters" on the Lièvre River, along with other Bois-Brûlés mentioned by the surveyor Bouchette and explorer Ingall in the same general area.

From a continental perspective, the Cadotte family demonstrates how the Métis were at the core of networks and exerted political influence over wide territories, notably in the signing of treaties, including in the United States. Four uncles and/or aunts of Mary Keith of the Cadotte family received land grants from the American government under the first Fond du Lac Treaty, in 1826 (Morice 1908, 58), most likely because of their kinship ties with the Ojibwe (Chippewa). A Jean-Baptiste Cadotte who resided at Lake Superior – certainly another relative of Mary Keith – was probably a signatory to the second Fond du Lac Treaty on behalf of the Métis of La Pointe. The treaty was signed in 1847 in Duluth, Minnesota, between the United States and the Ojibwe (Minot 1862, 906). Finally, we find Charleau, Michel, Alexis, Louis, and Louison Cadotte among Mary

Keith's kin. They are mentioned among the Métis who were potentially to receive land grants along with the Ojibwe chiefs of Sault Ste. Marie under the Robinson-Huron Treaty being negotiated in 1850 (Holmes 1996, 32–35). Thus, it seems that several members of the Cadotte family, distributed across territory spanning both British and American political jurisdictions, sought to secure lands for themselves and on behalf of the Métis more generally during the negotiation of treaties, demonstrating kinship connections that spanned vast distances, including in the Outaouais region.

Even though it is difficult to capture the contours of Métis culture given its diffuse nature, lack of a defined centre, and rhizomatic structure, we believe the task is not insurmountable. A close reading of documentary sources reveals that the Métis culture in the Outaouais region was characterized in part by a combination of mixed endogamous and exogamous unions emerging out of a highly mobile way of life. These migrations followed professional networks that moulded the lives of the Canadien Métis who dominated the roles of voyageur, diplomat, interpreter, guide, and hunter in the fur trade. This mobility characterizes not only the Métis of the Illinois Country, the Great Lakes, and western Canada (St-Onge and Podruchny 2012, 61–62; Thorne 1996) but also that of the Métis of the Gatineau, who inhabited the greater Ottawa River basin and also drew on geographically extended kin networks.

### Clandestinity and Collective Markers

The mobility of the Métis of the Gatineau was also demonstrated within local, clandestine networks. Thomas Taylor, himself a western Métis, confirms illicit activities tied to Métis mobility in an 1846 letter, which he wrote while working as a clerk at Lac des Sables:

> The rumour that was about an opposition starting up from ByTown, I am glad has now turned out to nothing, it was true enough that a Person in B.Town whose name I do not now recol[l]ect had engaged a few men, some Halfbreeds & Indians and amongst them the man who deserted from [HBC employee Sévère] St. Denis of the Out Post of Grand Lac, they all have been discharged, the new Trader having thought better of it.[26]

This passage follows an accounting of how many barrels of flour Taylor had purchased in Bytown and at what cost. The letter indicates that the

*Portage,* by Cornelius Krieghoff, c. 1856. The Gatineau River was known during this era for its numerous and difficult rapids, notably on the interior lower course.
*Credit: Library and Archives Canada, 1989-479-24*

Métis of the Gatineau Valley were active in free trade. Taylor identifies them collectively as Half-breeds, and views them as distinctive enough that he specifies some Indians were also recruited. These distinctions between Indians and Métis persist for decades.

As previously mentioned, in 1894 and again in 1909, Indian agents James Martin and Martin Bensen accused Métis of bootlegging alcohol on the Maniwaki Reserve, and decades earlier, in 1841, George Sharpe observed that François Naud used whisky as a medium of exchange in his free fur trade. The archival sources suggest that the Lac-Sainte-Marie community was a hotbed of smuggling and free trade, as well as a refuge for HBC deserters in the 1830s and 1840s. A letter sent from Lac des Sables by Allan Cameron attests to this in 1839: "With reference to my letter of the 10th Inst. I beg to inform you that the Deserter Louis Sérurier is now staying with André Sabourin upon the Gatineau about 25 miles from this place and it is reported that they intend going inland immediately after the opening of the Navigation for the purpose of Trading with the Indians."[27] Cameron's observation tells us that the deserter Sérurier was residing at Lac-Sainte-Marie. As a matter of practice, HBC employees wintering in distant outposts signed a three-year contract obliging them to complete their full term. As was the case for military personnel, employees who abandoned their posts could be arrested and later tried in court. The fact that Lac-Sainte-Marie was a refuge for a known deserter, and that he was even recruited for a trade excursion by André Sabourin, a retired HBC employee and free trader, highlights the independence of the community from the HBC.

This was not an isolated case. Another deserter, André Brazeau (File 4), who in the winter of 1844 abandoned his post at Cawassieamica, between the Grand Lac and Rivière Désert posts, was reported as hiding in the company of an Indian vagabond, probably on the Gatineau River. The HBC bourgeois who discovered his whereabouts hastily wrote to the clerk of the Rivière Désert post to have Brazeau captured.[28] Brazeau is also indirectly described in Thomas Taylor's 1846 letter as part of a group of Half-breeds and Indians.[29] The free spirit of the Gatineau Métis is thus evident in the correspondence exchanged between HBC employees.

In the case of Sévère St-Denis (File 16), what draws our attention are the apparent ties between contraband networks operated by Métis of the region. This HBC employee, who worked successively in almost all the posts of the Outaouais region – Fort Coulonge, Lac des Allumettes, Mattawa, Grand Lac, and Cawassieamica – also deserted the company in 1838 (Marcotte 2017, 379–84).[30] Shortly afterwards, he married Élisabeth Frances McDonell, the Métis daughter of a trader and an Indian woman. After having been reintegrated into the ranks of the HBC, St-Denis was posted to Cawassieamica on Poulter Lake, between Grand Lac and Rivière Désert, circa 1840 (Marcotte 2015, 83). St-Denis's desire not to conform to the commercial politics of the company was evident even when he was in their employ in 1845, as he pursued a complex parallel fur-trading scheme that implicated certain HBC employees.

This internal competition was a serious scourge, denounced by the era's HBC agents (Mitchell 1977, 190). In a letter dated January 29, 1845, for example, James Cameron at Grand Lac complains that the clerk at Lac des Sables, Thomas Taylor, had sent one of his men to winter close to Sévère St-Denis at Cawassieamica with the express goal of stopping the latter from trading with François Naud and his entourage at Lac-Sainte-Marie. What irritates Cameron most is that to prevent St-Denis from doing business with the Lac-Sainte-Marie free traders, Taylor had sent a trade expedition under the leadership of the McDougalls (the "Christineaux," as discussed on page 261 in note 21) to Lac à la Truite to tap into a fur area normally tied to Grand Lac and thus under Cameron's own supervision:

> St Denis is behind his last year's trade at same date but he could not go much about as Mr Tom Taylor sent a [word cut off] to winter alongside of him so as to prevent his trading with Jacques [certainly Naud] etc. and at same time equiped the Christineaux to go after the Indians of Trout Lake etc. however with all their manouvering we succeeded in getting a fair share of the Furs.[31]

Using various strategies to work within and outside the HBC, Métis families of the region garnered some of the fur trade – to their advantage and the detriment of HBC profits. In this example of a system established to divert furs from some HBC posts to other ones, we find the McDougalls assuming the role of *gens de la dérouine* for the Métis Taylor family and making an expedition to the Indian winter hunting grounds. A parallel network involved Sévère St-Denis and the mixed community of Lac-Sainte-Marie ("Jacques" or François Naud, etc.).

The anecdote reveals the competing interests of two Métis families (St-Denis and Taylor) that were sparring over the share of the trade that each of their respective posts should be receiving, and this in spite of the directives coming from their employer, the HBC. We know that in 1848, St-Denis bought a small farm at Rivière Désert, and the HBC reported that he was using this locale to pursue illicit trade with lumberjacks and others.[32] This trade possibly extended to Indians, as a complaint was made against him (or his son) by certain Indians of Maniwaki in 1862 (Sabourin 2010, 110).

To summarize, Métis contraband networks irrefutably existed at the heart of the underground fur trade economy of the greater Outaouais region. All the sources suggest a certain social cohesion among Métis families of the Gatineau, as well as a likely need for shared discretion to ensure the successful operation of contraband activities. After all, they most often pursued these activities while employed by the very company they sought to foil. Such vigilance and secrecy help to explain an archival silence about the existence of this Métis community, which had no interest in attracting the attention of company or colonial officials.

# 8

## *Louis Riel and the McGregors of the Lièvre*

DEFIANCE OF RULES AND regulations, along with mobility, were useful traits that were in all likelihood valued most by those who sought anonymity to pursue contraband activities. According to a still vivid oral tradition among Métis families of the Outaouais, Louis Riel sought refuge in their region, exploiting these clandestine networks as he was dogged by bounty hunters hoping to collect the five-thousand-dollar price on his head declared by Ontario premier Edward Blake. Local tradition holds that Marie-Louise Riel protected her nephew Louis while he was hiding in the Lac-Sainte-Marie region between 1870 and 1878. Riel had to flee Red River and the newly created province of Manitoba for his own protection. Although he was elected to the House of Commons, he could not publicly take his seat given the bounty for his arrest.

Violet Lalonde, Marie-Louise Riel's great-great-granddaughter, wrote a fifty-six-page account of Riel's exile in the region. She signed the typescript, which she produced in English and which contains handwritten annotations. La Société de généalogie de l'Outaouais (a genealogical society established in 1978) obtained the typescript following the death of Ernest Blondin, who had kept it in his collection after being given it by Violet Lalonde while he was conducting a research project. It was then acquired by Québec's National Library and Archives. The typescript appears to date from 1980–82, as it refers to a historical dramatization of Louis Riel's life that was televised in 1980 but makes no mention of the 1982 repatriation of the Constitution, which would add Métis to Canada's foundational legal charter. Violet explains that information was gathered from family members who knew Marie-Louise Riel. Her account is thus a work of auto-ethnohistory: the retelling of historical events based on living family traditions passed from one generation to the next. It relates the events surrounding the welcoming and protection of Louis Riel, notably in relation to the ties with his alleged aunt Marie-Louise Riel McGregor, as well

Undated portrait assumed to be of Marie-Louise Riel, by an unknown photographer. According to oral tradition in the Gatineau Valley, Marie-Louise continued to serve as a healer there until a very advanced age, as did her daughter after her. Violet Lalonde gave a copy of this photograph to historian Pierre-Louis Lapointe.
*Credit: Stéphane Jobin*

as with several members of the McGregor family who were living in the Gatineau Valley.[1] The typescript also affirms that Marie-Louise Riel McGregor belonged to a Métis people, neither white nor Indian, yet she felt at home among both Métis and Indians.

Based on raw family histories, this is an authentic part of the oral history of the Gatineau Valley Métis. It reaffirms the mobility that characterized this community, as well as the clandestine networks that were called into play to protect Louis Riel as he was chased by bounty hunters. The typescript also details several anecdotes about the life of Marie-Louise, her culture, and her kinship ties. Violet Lalonde's account spans the history of a community centred on the fur trade to one pursuing its livelihood in a territory that was fully integrated into first the forestry frontier and then agricultural settlement. The events she describes occurred in the midst of that transition, highlighting how the community came out of the fur trade frontier and foreshadowing the challenges and history that we review in the chapters that follow. It is a parenthesis to our study but reminds us that the history being recounted belongs to what Gaudry

(2018) would call a "living Métis community," though of course in the East, not the West. An elderly descendant of one of the core families of the Outaouais Valley Métis community, Violet typed out her account at a time when identifying as Métis would have had no benefit to her or her family, and she is certainly not "race shifting," to borrow Gaudry's (2018) term. But her actions undoubtedly suggest she considered it important to ensure that her family's history was passed on to the next generations. Fortunately, by happenstance, her account was preserved as an archival document, but it could just as easily have ended up in a landfill. Thus, we consider it important to include her story as a reminder that it belongs to a community; it is a necessary entr'acte to underscore the importance such accounts play in the oral history of families and communities, enhancing conventional academic history grounded in archival records.

Though Marie-Louise's early years are difficult to trace in the historical record, Violet's account provides insights into Marie-Louise's adult life and the community's oral history of Louis Riel's sojourn in the Outaouais region. Violet's account thus calls upon the oral tradition of the Métis community of the Gatineau while presenting the main characteristics of the Métis way of life in this region.[2]

### Who Was Marie-Louise Riel?

In Violet Lalonde's account, Marie-Louise Riel (c. 1800–98) was the eldest child of Jean-Baptiste Riel and Métis Marguerite Boucher. She was followed by siblings Sophie and Louis, the latter being the father of Louis Riel who led the Métis resistance at Red River and then the North-West Territories. In Violet's account, Marie-Louise travelled as a child with her parents from Île-à-la-Crosse (Saskatchewan) to Lower Canada as Jean-Baptiste sought to escape the Pemmican War, which pitted the NWC against the HBC. After a brief stop in Mattawa (Ontario), the family eventually reached Sainte-Geneviève-de-Berthier, where the children were baptized. As recounted by Violet, Marie-Louise Riel married Scottish trader Robert McGregor when she was fifteen (see File 12). Her sister Lucie married John Lee, and settled in the Montréal region. Marie-Louise and the Riel/ Lee family helped their nephew, the fugitive Louis Riel.

The archival record, however, does not fit Violet's account precisely. Though Jean-Baptiste Riel's children Louis and Sophie were baptized in 1822, Marie-Louise was not;[3] and although she did marry Robert

McGregor, the church records (Newton 1991, 16)[4] her as Marie-Louise Chipakijikokwe, who was baptized a few months prior to the wedding. Her baptismal record does not provide the names of her parents but does note that she was of the Saulteaux Nation (the Saulteaux being an Anishinaabe First Nation now located on the prairies, but whose homeland was in the Sault Ste. Marie region). The Catholic church records confirm the marriage of a Lucie Riel, the daughter born after Sophie, to John Lee in Montréal.[5] It is only later, however, with the baptism of her children, that Marie-Louise Riel appears in baptismal records. Given that the children's father is recorded as Robert McGregor, this confirms that Marie-Louise Chipakijikokwe was the same woman as Marie-Louise Riel McGregor. The question then arises why Marie-Louise would have chosen to identify herself as a Riel[6] if she were Saulteaux and had neither been baptized nor married under that name.

There are two reasonable explanations. There is a good chance that as a Saulteaux, Marie-Louise would have been from Sault Ste. Marie, and the fact that she and Robert had one of their children baptized there seems to corroborate this theory.[7] The first possibility that would tie Marie-Louise to both Sault Ste. Marie and the Riel family is that she was the daughter of Jean-Baptiste Riel and a Saulteaux woman from Sault Ste. Marie, not Marguerite Boucher. She would thus have been raised in a community of retired fur trade employees and their families and Saulteaux families, and she could have joined her father's family at a later date. That would make her the half-sister of Louis Riel Sr. and still the legitimate aunt of Louis Riel Jr.[8] The second option is that Marie-Louise was not blood kin per se to the Riels but acquired the symbolic status of sister to Louis Riel Sr. This was a prevailing practice in the fur trade, a form of kinship that does not easily fit into the strict confines of European tradition (Podruchny 2006, 193). Either option would explain the kinship ties linking Marie-Louise with the Riel family, including Louis Jr.

Having the double Riel and McGregor surname and through them ties to a Métis way of life would have been sufficient for Marie-Louise to consider herself the aunt of Louis Riel Jr., and this memory would have perpetuated itself in the oral tradition of the family. One historical source does suggest that Marie-Louise was a relative of Louis Riel. In 1906, the husband of a great-granddaughter of Marie-Louise (also named Marie-Louise), Thomas Bélanger, was killed in Buckingham. The newspaper *La*

*Patrie* described Bélanger as the nephew of Louis Riel. But the next day, the Bélanger family asked for a correction, asserting that the Bélanger family was not tied to the Riel family. Even though the young Marie-Louise was not mentioned, the paper presumably confused his family's history with that of his wife (La Patrie 1906a, 14; La Patrie 1906b, 5; Lapointe 2006, 235).

Lalonde recounts that Marie-Louise Riel McGregor was not only the aunt of Louis but also an important humanitarian figure for the inhabitants of the Gatineau, whether Indian, Métis, or settlers. She had a quasi-mythical persona because of her therapeutic expertise, the memory of which the Elders of Val-des-Bois still recall. These accounts specify that she mastered five languages – French, English, Gaelic, Cree, and Chipewyan[9] – and that she applied her expertise in obstetrics to aid both the settlers of the region and her own people, the Métis.[10] Having lived a long and healthy life, Marie-Louise also had a reputation for being knowledgeable in medicinal plants, setting fractures, hunting, fishing, tracking in the forest, and archery with a bow and arrow, and for deftness in wielding a knife and axe as well as making birchbark canoes. Lalonde depicts Marie-Louise as wearing moccasins that she made herself and a traditional long dress complemented by a cedar wood rosary.

In addition to her Euro-Canadian and Indian ancestry, mastery of several languages, and Christian faith infused with Indigenous practices – a way of life resembling that of the freemen (such as her husband) – Marie-Louise was also known for her skill in the industries of the *Sauvages,* as her talent in making moccasins is attested to in the account book of a Buckingham merchant in 1844. The latter bought more than thirty pairs of moccasins from Marie-Louise in less than nine days,[11] and these sales multiplied over time. Marie-Louise Riel thus presents all the characteristics that define a Métis culture, including a way of life tied to hunting and fishing (as opposed to agriculture) and renowned cultural and geographical mobility.

Lalonde describes the territory known and travelled by her great-great-grandmother, conveying the mobility that was required to keep the fugitive Riel safe using a network of kin and community ties:

Let me tell you about the "hide-away" as told to me by my father Wilfred McGregor. Look at a map of Quebec and find the following places: Hull,

McGregor Lake, Buckingham, Notre Dame de la Salette, High Falls, Val des Bois and Maniwaki (Lake St. Marie).[12]

With a pencil connect these locations and you will see that they make a circular formation on the map. This was where my nomadic grand grand mere lived, fished, travelled the water-ways, worked amongst the people, and, of course, hid Louis – her fugitive nephew, from the clutches of the law ...

Grand grand mere McGregor realized that it was important to keep Louis on the move which well suited her nomadic existence, for she too – was constantly on the go. Relatives and friends took turns hiding him. Mary Louise's children – Robert, Elizabeth, and Maria, as well as her own sister Lucy and granddaughter Hermeline, all played a part in this adventure and were known as the "family pack." That's what my father called them when he referred to them in his stories.[13]

We see in this account the defiance of the Métis, the *family pack,* whose members do not hesitate to flout the law to protect one of their own. They succeeded in protecting Riel by mobilizing a defining cultural characteristic: their intimate knowledge of the territory and the ease with which they could travel over it.

This description of Marie-Louise McGregor's use of the territory not only confirms the mobility exhibited by Métis in numerous documentary sources but also supports the existence of a regional Métis community in the Gatineau Valley, including Lac-Sainte-Marie. Lalonde quite clearly identifies the members of this community as the Métis people Marie-Louise visits and assists: "It was not uncommon to find her delivering infants into the isolated homes of the pioneers and her people – the Métis. Upon the moment of birth, she would perform a Baptism and place the soul of the new born into the hands of its Creator."[14]

The notion of a Métis people also appears in a passage about Lalonde's father, Wilfred McGregor, and those he considered his people as he recalled past exploits:

As you may recall, Mary Louise was a nomad and did not remain in one location for too long. On her next move, to Val des Bois, she took with her Regis and young Wilfred. The sister remained at home with the grandparents. During his stay, Wilfred helped with the chores which must have seemed endless to a five year old. His favorite pastime was listening to the stories of their people the Métis and of Louis Riel, especially after the hanging.[15]

Similarly, the exploits of Louis Riel and his sojourn in the Gatineau region appears in the oral tradition of other Métis families of the region. In an interview, Métis Elders Benoît Guilbault and Liliane Cyr (herself a descendant of Marie-Louise Riel McGregor) agree that Louis Riel indeed sought refuge at Val-des-Bois and its surroundings, and to be more precise in the residence of a Mr. Latour. They explain that Riel moved between Trente et Un Milles and Poisson Blanc lakes, stopped at Lac-Sainte-Marie, and finally reached Maniwaki by canoe. Liliane Cyr also mentions that her mother knew Marie-Louise Riel as a midwife and healer (Malette 2016). In another interview, this one conducted by Guillaume Marcotte, Laurier Riel of Maniwaki declares that his grandfather's uncle – who was a member of the McGregor family and resident of Lac-Sainte-Marie – had told him Marie-Louise stored some of Louis Riel's personal belongings at Lac-Sainte-Marie. Laurier Riel adds that Marie-Louise, whom he considered to be the sister of Louis Riel, travelled constantly with him when sojourning in the region, during which time he was meant to be sitting as a member of Parliament.[16]

The testimony of these Métis Elders of the Gatineau region concerning the same oral history suggests a strong attachment to the emblematic figure of Louis Riel.[17] This feeling is characterized by pride in having protected Riel, as well as a strong sentiment of belonging to the Métis people. Lalonde's historical portrait also confirms their descriptions of the Métis families who inhabited the region. Many Métis in the Outaouais used their mobility, dispersal over the region, and extensive knowledge of the territory – still considered in many ways *sauvage* – to their advantage. This is evident in accounts not only of harbouring Louis Riel but also of hiding deserters from HBC officials or participating in clandestine activities.

### Oral Tradition Substantiated by Historical Sources

Historical records, including archival sources that would not have been accessible to her in 1980, confirm details in Violet Lalonde's account. Documentary sources suggest that Louis Riel did indeed visit Québec's Outaouais region between 1873 and 1875, and it appears that he stayed in Hull, at Pointe-Gatineau, and at Angers.[18] A letter sent by Louis Riel to his mother confirms his stay in the Outaouais region in May 1874 for roughly eight or nine months.[19] During one of Riel's visits to Québec, a man named LaRivière suggests to Riel in a letter dated October 17, 1873, that he use villages north of the Ottawa River to safely reach Hull: "When you will be in Montréal, if you want to go to Ottawa, I believe the best route would be to pass through the countryside to the north of Ottawa River and thus to Hull ... I do not have any other suggestion for you besides, as you know your business better than anybody else, by the Grace of God!"[20] LaRivière's description of the countryside accurately describes the Lièvre and Gatineau valleys, particularly if Riel's final destination was the region of Hull farther to the south.

A 1904 article in the newspaper *La Patrie* about "Mother Valiquette," the daughter of Marie-Louise Riel, confirms the kinship ties (real or fictive) between the McGregor family and Louis Riel. The article also highlights several traits associated with Marie-Louise Riel according to oral tradition, including her Métis identity:

> Mother Valiquette was born in the North-West around 1818: her mother was a Métis woman by the name of Riel, first cousin of Louis Riel, who played a certain role in the North-West. Her father, J. McGregor, was Scottish, at the service of the Hudson's Bay Company at this time. A few years after her birth, her parents came to live in Bytown and from there to the Lac des Deux Montagnes; they were baptized when passing through Sault Ste. Marie ... Mother Valiquette was well known and highly esteemed by all the settlers of the region, from Buckingham to Ferme Neuve. Her old mother, dead on the river a few years ago at the age of 113, had taught her the arts of being a midwife and doctor at the same time. – An art at which the mother and the daughter excelled ... For certain illnesses, we retained her services, eight, fifteen days, one month ahead of time, and at night, during the day, we came hurriedly to get this courageous old mother, in birch bark canoe, the only way to travel at that time during impossible weather conditions ... Mother [Valiquette] would place herself at the back or the front of the canoe, depending on the skill of her companion, a paddle in her hands, wielding it for five, ten, fifteen, twenty miles to their destination ... A great number of patients were treated and healed in her care. The mountains and swamps provided her all the medications necessary for her art: she understood the value of medicinal plants and always used them successfully. (La Patrie 1904, 7; our translation)

This passage is extremely significant, first, because it connects Marie-Louise Riel to a distinctive way of life that she then passed on to her daughter (Mother Valiquette), and, second, because it confirms many details also transmitted by oral tradition: the use of birchbark canoe, medicinal plants, and midwifery. Moreover, the article identifies Marie-Louise as Métis and comments on her kinship connection with Louis Riel, although it does not mention him hiding among Métis families in the Outaouais.

In light of contraband activities and desertions from the HBC, it is logical that many Métis families of the Gatineau would not have openly made grand political declarations such as those emanating from the Red River in Manitoba, and they would not have publicized the fact that they had broken the law to shelter Louis Riel. Rather, they lived in the shadows of a zone that remained a fur trade and lumber frontier for generations, where to loudly trumpet one's Métis identity would have drawn unwanted attention from authorities. Among the Métis of Québec's Outaouais region, discretion and collusion were the norm. Individuals survived in a context in which colonial systems of justice had little traction and in a region where majestic pines soared above the *dérouines,* or trading expeditions, as they met with First Nations in their hunting camps. Violet Lalonde's ethnohistorical account, like the testimony of the Elders, could not be any clearer. The Métis of the Gatineau Valley have inherited an oral tradition about their identity. They consider themselves indubitably Métis.

### Who Are the Métis of the Gatineau Valley?

According to the documentary sources analyzed thus far, the strategic importance of Bytown proved to be a determining factor in the emergence of a Métis historical community in the Gatineau Valley. The existence of the town and its merchants, and the prospect of buying cheap goods directly from them for cash, facilitated the emergence of freemen who could counter the monopoly of the HBC in the Gatineau region. And it is precisely this process of emerging free trade that the academic literature has often associated with the appearance of historical Métis communities in other regions of Canada (Devine 2004; Foster 2001). This context clearly played a determining role in the emergence of a community of "squatters" at Lac-Sainte-Marie, a community with ethnocultural particularities identical to the classic definitions of Métis communities elsewhere in the country.

As historians Norman Anick (1976, 186) and Michael Newton (1991, 13–16) suggest, the HBC was concerned about the activities of Métis in the region. The company was evidently preoccupied with the stratagems of the illicit free traders, the contraband of alcohol, and the fugitive deserters from the HBC ranks. The correspondence of the era reveals ethnocultural markers similar to those witnessed elsewhere in the greater Outaouais region, but in the Gatineau Valley they were magnified and more detailed. The cunning of Métis families is evident, as is their material culture and their histories. But perhaps most singular was the whispered object of their pride, having assisted the great Métis leader Louis Riel.[21]

In several locations, the characteristics of a Métis population provoked the application of collective and distinctive ethnonyms that went beyond kinship ties or isolated individuals. The descriptions of Martin, Bensen, and Thomas Taylor overlap with those of Ingall, Shirreff, Du Ranquet, Proulx, Bellefeuille, Cameron, Logan, Bouchette, Heming, and Nédélec on the subject of the "Métis" of the Outaouais region, as detailed in Part 2. The sum of these accounts gives great precision to the scale of ethnocultural markers found in the Gatineau region and neighbouring territories, testifying to the existence of a Métis community between 1830 and 1900 in an area comprising Lac des Sables, Lac-Sainte-Marie, and Rivière Désert (Maniwaki) and the surrounding countryside (see Map 3). What remains to be explored is how this identity was maintained and transmitted in the successive generations from the nineteenth to the twentieth century.

## Part 4

# Historical Continuity and Contemporary Concerns

# 9

# *A New Era*

## The Creation of the Maniwaki Reserve

THE DOCUMENTARY SOURCES present a regional Métis community firmly entrenched in the Gatineau Valley. Tightly tied to occupational niches embedded in the fur trade, the evidence suggests that a Métis community emerged over several generations. The question before us remains whether the Métis presence and culture survived rapid transformation from the fur trade to the lumber camps, and finally into an expanding settler agricultural landscape. Indeed, the countryside of the Gatineau was radically changed in the second half of the nineteenth century, from forested fur-trading frontier to farmland. Yet in spite of these massive alterations, it seems that Métis culture endured, finding new niches in the changing economic landscape.

Economic transformation occurred in overlapping stages. The fur trade persisted in the Gatineau Valley, as the historical records testify. Trapping continued but was increasingly marginalized in the local economy, and usually took place in the distant territories to the north and west. As settlers moved in, hunters and trappers were forced to retrench in more remote areas and trading posts. The fur trade eventually had to relocate farther inland, pushing traders to travel greater distances during their *dérouines* to First Nations camps while still capitalizing on the presence of growing urban centres in a not-too-distant south to maximize profits.

The forest industry in the Gatineau Valley was controlled in large part by one family, that of Philemon Wright, at the outset of the nineteenth century. Their absolute control waned in subsequent decades (Gaffield 1994, 165; Ouellet and Thériault 1988), but Wright's children were represented within a small group of families that were granted a monopoly over the forest industry in 1832. The other forestry families included the Hamiltons, Lows, Aylens, and McGoeys, and their stranglehold over a growing economy often blurred the line between private industry and power and public interest (Gaffield 1994, 163). In this economic context,

*Timber Slide on the Ottawa River, Chats Falls,* by John Philip Bainbrigge, 1840. The transition to an economy centred on timber was inevitable in the Outaouais at this time, as the 1840s marked a rapid decline in the fur trade, including in the hinterland. Timber slides allowed timber to pass through rapids on its way to market, and they were therefore established all along larger rivers. Métis were part of a workforce of raftsmen who ensured the movement of logs from forest lumber camps to market.
*Credit: Library and Archives Canada, 1983-47-8*

agricultural settlement was delayed (Hughson and Bond 1964), favouring a social and economic climate that can best be described as "frontier."[1] The monopoly over the Gatineau's lumber gradually came to an end, however, with the adoption of the Crown Timber Act in the now unified Canada in 1843. The new legislation allowed for the establishment of land concessions that encouraged and facilitated the more organized arrival of agricultural settlers. The decades between 1843 and 1873 saw spectacular growth in forestry, as well as a growing demand for labour. In addition to the stereotypical "lumberjack" and "log driver," forestry barons also needed forest guides who knew the territory intimately and could scout out new prime timber stands.

This period also featured exploration by government surveyors who progressively mapped out the region (Turgeon et al. 2005, 100–3). The interior of the Outaouais region was surveyed between 1846 and 1912, beginning with a primary survey of the Lièvre Valley in 1846 with the goal of establishing townships. The townships of Aylwin and Hincks were laid out in 1848, and Maniwaki and Egan followed in 1849.[2] As reviewed in previous chapters, some preliminary survey work had been conducted earlier in the Outaouais region, notably by Bouchette, and the records those surveyors left behind indicate that the hinterland of the Outaouais was inhabited principally by First Nations (the majority being Algonquin), Bois-Brûlés or Métis, (French) Canadian voyageurs, free traders, forestry entrepreneurs, and employees tied to the forestry industry and the fur trade. The demographic composition of the region then changed drastically in the second half of the nineteenth century. Though forestry was still the driving economic force, it began an inexorable decline from 1873 onward, and by 1926 only one forest concession was granted to a forest company (Turgeon et al. 2005, 44).

Tied to expanding colonization of the territory, the Oblates of Mary Immaculate founded a permanent mission at Rivière Désert (Maniwaki) in 1849 to better serve the various Indian missions in the area (Inksetter 2017, 247). This is the same missionary order of Catholic clerics that was active in the Red River and the North-West. A few years later, in 1853, the reserve of Maniwaki was established following the adoption of legislation in 1851 that at least theoretically set aside territory for the Algonquins, Nipissings, and Têtes-de-Boule (or Atikamekw) whose traditional territories occupied the lands between the Saint-Maurice and Ottawa rivers (Frenette 1993, 43). A number of Algonquin families that had been demanding a territorial concession seized the opportunity to relocate to the reserve, and they were joined by other families. Such migrations require some context. At the time, a Mohawk faction was seeking to commercially exploit a pine grove at Oka but was being opposed by the Sulpicians, a Catholic order that had been granted a mission for Iroquois and Algonquins at Lake of Two Mountains. A growing number of Mohawks had embraced Methodism, whereas the Algonquins had largely remained Catholic. With this growing conflict as a backdrop, Chief Pakinawatik, who represented the Algonquins of the Gatineau, left Oka to settle in the newly created reserve of Maniwaki. His people had been clearing the lands of the region for some time by this point (Philpot 2010, 159–65; Frenette 1993, 40–43; Scott 1883).

This new legal framework in the Gatineau quickly generated conflict. Those Métis who were not strictly associated with the Maniwaki Algonquins saw their identity marginalized starting in 1853. From this point on, archival sources make increasing references to Métis being labelled as "not real Indians" or simply as whites. Such traces, we suggest, testify to the sustained existence of the Métis in the region and hint at the contours of a Métis community. Some archival sources notably testify to an enduring Métis traditional economy centred on trapping and trade, while others demonstrate that the Métis continued to play a role as social intermediaries, as they had throughout their history. Documentary sources indicate that the Métis recycled their expertise, cultural aptitudes, and talents in the forestry industry. Various accounts highlight the continuity of the Métis cultural presence in the Gatineau Valley, as individuals and communities adapted to the shifting economic landscape.

### Continuity as Intermediaries: The Riel Family

The Riel family of the Outaouais region is a great example of continuity in the role of Métis as intermediaries. In 1880, the Riels come to the fore as a cultural intermediary with the First Nations community. Long relegated to the fur trade, their role as cultural go-betweens was noticed in the upper reaches of the Gatineau River at the end of the nineteenth century when a humanitarian crisis struck. During a smallpox epidemic, Indian agent Charles Logue at Maniwaki expedited a canoe crew under the direction of someone who seemed best suited to bring relief to the "Têtes-de-Boule Indians" of the region: a man named Paul Riel.[3] The son of Émilien Riel and Henriette McDougall (File 11), Paul Riel was a resident of Lac-Sainte-Marie in the 1840s. In a letter dated September 9, 1880, Logue describes Paul Riel as "part Indian," or Métis, following the ethnocultural markers defined and discussed in previous chapters.[4] To carry out the task assigned to him, which was to find families dispersed over the territory, Paul Riel would most likely have required fluency in the Algonquin language and perhaps even the Atikamekw language. Additionally, he would have needed a thorough knowledge of the territory and skill in canoeing to reach these families. Paul Riel was fluent in French, so at minimum he would have been bilingual, and possibly a polyglot. In a letter dated August 31, 1880, Logue writes, "The most important Consideration being to get them some provisions, I secured the services of Mr Paul Riel a very reliable and intelligent man and sent him up on the 27th accompanied with another man named Thomas Schocier."[5] The two Métis men, Paul Riel and Thomas Schocier, or Chaussé,[6] carried with them supplies, medication, and munitions to deliver to survivors of the epidemic. They were also tasked with helping the families, notably in burying numerous abandoned corpses. Upon their return to Maniwaki, Paul Riel provided a detailed account, and he took the opportunity to specify that it was "one of the 'hardest jobs' I had ever undertaken, or witnessed."[7]

Interestingly, the correspondence relating to this tragic episode also recounts that Paul Riel was considered a representative of the whites in the eyes of the Indians. Riel describes being greeted by an "Indian" family in the vicinity of Baskatong Lake:

> When I informed them of the object of my visit, they were delighted, and big Alexis a leading man amongst them, said to me that I was a Government man and that they must pay me respect, and respect the good white chiefs at Ottawa who had not forgotten them in their misfortunes. He opened out an old package, and drew forth a small flag: a union jack: which he attached to a long pole, and then planted the pole on the Edge of the lake. I gave them their share of provisions and ammunition.[8]

It is evident from Riel's testimony that he was perceived by the "Indians" of the region not as one of them but as an agent of the Canadian government, and they therefore received him with an old colonial protocol: raising the British flag in the presence of such officials. In this, they were following the much older conventions of the fur trade, also enacted when treaties were signed (Long 2010, 18, 337; Willmot and Brownlee 2010, 60). Notably, the Indian agent considered Riel's account credible: "From my personal knowledge of Mr Riel I believe his statement to be true and correct."[9] Logue specified, moreover, that Dr. Comeau, who had been tasked with treating the smallpox epidemic in the Maniwaki Reserve, did not recommend that pain medication be expedited to the Indians of the Upper Gatineau but that such medication was sent at the express request of Paul Riel. As Logue also remarked that Riel is part Indian, he seems to imply that the request stemmed from an affinity for the Indians of the region. Is it thus possible to tease out Riel's compassion for Indigenous families hard hit by the epidemic as an empathy that went beyond the task assigned to him? Logue finally yielded and provided Riel with several bottles of pain medication, writing, "I allowed Paul to have his way in the matter."[10] The correspondence also documents that Riel had to act as a go-between to alleviate the reluctance of the Indians to accept medications from the whites.[11]

As the preceding example demonstrates, as late as 1880 the Métis were still seen as having an intermediary role and identity: sometimes considered by Indians as belonging to the white world, and by whites as part of the Indigenous world. Another illustration of this intermediacy can be found in the 1881 Canadian census, in which Paul Riel is identified as a French-Canadian farmer,[12] whereas Charles Logue identified him the previous year as part Indian. The Riel family thus offers a useful illustration of how demographic data can at first glance support the idea that the Métis in the Gatineau were largely assimilated.[13] If that were the case, it would be quite easy to ignore the cultural context of Paul Riel's life and assume that he had assimilated to a strictly Euro-Canadian identity.[14] Yet when a broader sweep of historical documents is included in the analysis, the Riel family demonstrates Métis cultural continuity from the fur trade onwards, as evidenced in the knowledge of Indigenous languages and the territory and the ease with which the Riels served as intermediaries. The multiple ethnonyms attributed to them, moreover, highlights the need to analyze the much broader sociocultural context in order to fully understand the maintenance of a Métis culture in Québec's Outaouais region.

## Trade and Continuity: The Naud, St-Denis, and Chaussé Families

The growing forestry industry is often perceived as the spearhead of colonization, pushing back and assimilating Indigenous populations while destroying traditional economies and ways of life tied to the forest (hunting, trapping, fishing, gathering, and trade). This interpretation can certainly be applied to the Outaouais region, as the spread of forestry shattered the countryside. Trading activities nonetheless persisted among Métis families of the region until the eve of the twentieth century. As such, their continued role as free traders attests to the cultural continuity of individuals and the community under study.

The Naud family provides a great example. Daniel Naud, son of the voyageur François Naud and the Métis woman Élisabeth McPherson (File 13), appears in correspondence exchanged between bureaucrats starting in 1889. In a letter addressed to the director of Indian Affairs in Ottawa, Indian Agent James Martin at Maniwaki writes,

Sir, I have the honour to inform you that Daniel Nault of Maniwaki lately a
trader but at present of no occupation, has made application for the privilege
of renting lot No 111 Notre Dame Street Maniwaki[.] As he bears a very good
moral character I would recommend that he be allowed to lease the above
mentioned lot at the yearly rental of $11[00] which I consider sufficient.[15]

The letter makes use of the older term *trader*, highlighting that the fur
trade remained a significant occupation for at least one of the children
of the Naud/McPherson couple until the 1880s. The correspondence
offers some tantalizing details about the state of those who relied on the
fur trade and were left with "no occupation" as this economic activity
progressively disappeared. Though Naud succeeded in procuring the lot,
he fell behind in his payments. Nine years later, in 1898, another letter
from Indian Affairs in Ottawa notes that Naud has defaulted for the past
four years and abandoned the lot without having made any improvements to the property.[16] In the meantime, he had acquired two other
properties, one at Montcerf and another close to the Maniwaki Reserve.[17]
This letter is reminiscent of those describing Lac-Sainte-Marie or Sault
Ste. Marie, where colonial officials in the 1830s, '40s, and '50s indicated
that Métis establishments were "abandoned" and described the inhabitants as preoccupied above all with fishing, hunting, or trading, as opposed
to using parcels of land for agriculture.

The Nauds were not alone in having persisted in the fur trade until a
very late date. The St-Denis family (File 16) also continued trading in the
region into the 1860s. A number of archival documents highlight their
trading activities, often in partnership with the HBC, although the exact
nature of the partnership remains obscure. Such documents include a
contract concluded at Rivière Désert in 1866 with Sévère St-Denis (File
16) and Basile McDougall (File 11),[18] as well as account statements dating to 1866 tied to several "St Dennis Indians," referring in all probability
to the activities of the St-Denis family as the HBC subcontractor trading
in the back country.[19] Finally, lists of merchandise in the 1866 HBC accounting records are tied to "St Dennis Trader etc."[20] Clearly, the family
was still active in the fur trade, pursuing an economic activity that had
been prominent in Métis communities.

According to the memoir of the missionary Joseph-Étienne Guinard,
the Métis Chaussé family was also involved in the fur trade as late as 1899.
On his way north, Guinard reports stopping at a place called Michomis,

some hundred or so kilometres from Maniwaki (see Map 2). There, he went to "Mr Pierre Chaussé," whom he describes as a buyer of furs.[21] Chaussé would have been running his trading operations out of his home. Elsewhere in his memoir, Guinard specifies that a Métis (distinct from Indigenous people, whom he called "Têtes de boule") was trading furs in the same area, at a fork of the Gatineau River 30 kilometres from Michomis, during the same period: "There was also a métisse[22] [sic] who was trading in furs. I saw in his little store some ten Têtes de boule that I had known at Weymontaching, they had come this far because the HBC no longer gave them credit and this because the English were waging war on the valiant little people, the Boers."[23] This passage reveals economic activity by independent fur traders as late as 1899; the Métis here was, in all likelihood, Pierre Chaussé Jr. (File 19). Missionary correspondence from the 1890s also confirms the Métis presence in the fur trade of the Upper Gatineau. In a letter dated 1894, Father Guéguen reports that he met at Michomis "nine *Sauvages* or Métis Families who had fulfilled their religious duties."[24]

Father Guéguen recommended creating a new residence for missionaries at Michomis. In an April 1894 letter, Monseigneur N.Z. Lorrain remarks that the Upper Gatineau and Lièvre rivers are inhabited by "*Sauvages* and Métis" who could be better served at this new locale.[25] Asked for clarification, Lorrain described the population he was referring to: "The missionaries at Michomis would serve all the missions now under the direction of Father Guéguen in the vicariate, additionally, they would give their care to a few Whites, to Sauvages, and to the Métis who are quite numerous in the diocese of Ottawa on the Gatineau and Lièvre Rivers."[26] Once again, the correspondence describes a tripartite ethnic population on the Gatineau and the Lièvre – white, *Sauvages* (First Nations), and Métis – echoing historical accounts from other Métis communities, such as Sault Ste. Marie and Red River. Like others, Lorrain sees the three ethnic groups as distinctive, but specifies that the Métis are quite numerous. Thus, as late as 1894, the Métis are signalled as neither white nor First Nations and still tied to the fur trade, which emphasizes that this was a distinctive way of life.[27]

The continuity of fur trading ventures among some Métis families goes hand in hand with the trapping activities of other families. An article published in a local newspaper called *The Equity* (1913, 5) hints at this

*Hunters with Dead Moose,* by Cornelius Krieghoff, c. 1860. In the Outaouais in the middle of the nineteenth century, the winter dress of Métis men, much like that of Algonquins and Canadiens, was almost invariably composed of a wool coat and hood, reminiscent of the "capot," as well as moccasins and a sash, or *ceinture fléchée.* Credit: *Library and Archives Canada, 1950-14-1*

when recounting a drama involving two Métis trappers a bit west of the Gatineau Valley:

> Pilon, a half-breed trapper, was camped on Wolverine creek with his wife and two children, a boy of about three and a girl of nearly two years. He left camp about October 30, presumably to procure same [sic] provisions, went to Des Joachims, a small village on the Ottawa ... He was accompanied by another half-breed, and both appeared to be under the influence of liquor.

The article then narrates the tragic death of the trapper's family. Pilon's wife was found some seven miles from the camp, while the bodies of the two children were found a week later half a mile from their mother's corpse. While recounting the tale in macabre detail, the author surmises that the likely cause was alcohol. He goes so far as to add a commentary on the illegality of selling alcohol to the "Indians." But, as noted, the sale of alcohol to Métis seems to have been tolerated, as they were not considered "Indian." This episode sheds light on both the continued trapping and hunting traditions of Métis families and their access to alcohol as intermediaries facilitating a contraband trade to First Nations.

### Surviving after the Reserve: The Chaussé, Budge, Vanasse, and Brosseau Families

A series of other examples illustrates how cultural continuity surged forward following the creation of the Maniwaki Reserve in 1853. Access to the territory became regulated by government officials, and the movement of Indians, Métis, and whites became significantly more complex. New bureaucratic controls were imposed that led to a hardening of Métis and Indian identities, which had until then been somewhat more fluid and organic.

Documentary sources stating that "Indians" rented or wished to rent lots to Métis families exemplify this hardening of identities because of government policy. Métis Pierre Chaussé Jr. (File 19),[28] for instance, wanted to lease some land from the Indian Amable Watagon; Chaussé would have to clear the land before building a house for Watagon. In correspondence dating to 1888, the Department of Indian Affairs orders Indian agent Charles Logue to short-circuit the agreement reached between Watagon and Chaussé by refusing to recognize any "Indian" privilege associated with the latter's Métis identity. Indian Affairs reminds Logue that Chaussé does not belong to the Indian Band: "[Chaussé] whom you describe as a half breed married to an Indian woman. His marriage of course gives him no right to own or occupy land in the Res.[erve]."[29] If Chaussé wanted to rent a lot, he would have to do so as a white. Policies were in place to regulate land transfers, and the transfer would have to be carried out by the band, rather than by an individual. The alternative was for Watagon to hire Chaussé as a labourer, but Chaussé would still have no right to reside on the reserve. Métis and Indian identities were thus separated and regulated by government officials, with Métis having no rights or recourse with Indian Affairs because the Indian Act specified that Métis did not fall under the jurisdiction of the act.[30] This example echoes the experience and pressure that the Métis of Sault Ste. Marie faced, as they were given the choice of becoming either Indians or whites following the failure to negotiate a treaty.

The same type of discrimination is observed in the case of Métis Daniel Budge, according to correspondence from 1890 to 1892.[31] In these letters, we learn that in spite of an oral agreement between the former chief Pakinawatik and Daniel's father, William Budge,[32] permitting William to live on the Maniwaki reserve, the Department of Indian Affairs wanted to expel his son Daniel. William Budge had been living on the reserve for some twenty years, and his son was married to a member of the band, Elizabeth Commanda. Daniel was refused residence on the reserve and was considered merely a renter, as any white would have been, despite the band's wish for him to stay because of his family ties. In correspondence with his superiors, the Indian agent attempts to make a case for Daniel, highlighting the Budge family relations with the Maniwaki community and its difficult financial situation: "His [William's] son Daniel who also occupies the same land is married to Sabeth Comondo a member of this band[.] William Budge has died recently[.] His family as well as his son Daniel and family are very poor."[33] Indian Affairs refused to consider any right of the Budge family to live on the reserve, however, even if the Algonquin community was in favour. The only alternative the department would accept was to remove the parcel of land from the reserve in agreement with the Algonquins. In an act of generosity by the Algonquins, this is in fact what seems to have occurred in 1892. Clearly, Indian Affairs policies affected the Métis, even those who lived among the Algonquins on the reserve with their permission. Paradoxically, Métis identity was reinforced by a policy that by all accounts was intended to avoid the assimilation of the Métis in the Algonquin community. The legislation permitted Métis women to join the band and gain Indian status – but only if they married status-bearing Indian men.

Another example of discrimination, less harmonious with the Algonquins, is provided by the Vanasse Métis family. The children of François Vanasse and Louise Forcier (File 19), who grew up at Lac-Sainte-Marie, petitioned Indian Affairs in 1879 to uphold their use of a parcel of land at Bitobi Lake, then located within the Maniwaki Reserve.[34] By the time the petition was sent, their French-Canadian father and Métis mother had died and they had no direct family ties to the Algonquins living on the reserve. On behalf of all his brothers and sisters, Eustache Augustin

Water carrier and "chore man" Andrew Budge, carrying buckets of water at the
M. Kearney logging camp, by an unknown photographer, c. 1943. The Budge family
still lives in the Maniwaki region.
*Credit: Library and Archives Canada, Office national du Film Canada, Photo library,*
*1971-271 NPC*

Vanasse sent a request for the return to the family of the paternal cabin,
which had been erected on the reserve some thirty years earlier. At the
time of the petition, a member of the Algonquin Commanda family was
residing in the cabin following the absence of the Vanasse family for a
year, which explains the complaint lodged by the family "that the Chiefs
and the Indian Agt here have allowed one of them of the name of 'Antoine
Commandant' to take possession of the land and improvements in question in spite of our remonstrance and contrary to all principals of right
& justice."[35] The Vanasse family said they had asked the Algonquins for a
meeting to negotiate payment for the rental of the land on which the
cabin was located so that they could continue to live in it. The Algonquins
had refused to come to an agreement on the matter. The Indian agent,
at the request of the Algonquins, answered with a divergent version of the
affair. In his account, François Vanasse had abandoned his establishment
twice to live with his son Louis on the Ottawa River, thus neglecting the

farm. The Algonquins also contested the occupation date of the elder Vanasse, placing it after the creation of the reserve. The Indian agent finally ruled against the Vanasses, restating the arguments of the Algonquins about the date of occupation and the lack of significant improvement to the lot. Consequently, no compensation was deemed to be owed to the Vanasse family.[36]

In another matter, Marie (probably Marie-Agnès), one of the daughters of François Vanasse and Louise Forcier, asked for permission to obtain a parcel of land on the reserve on which to build a cabin. Her stated intention was to sell woven items along the road, which had a fair amount of traffic.[37] Once again, the Department of Indian Affairs refused the request, by default categorizing requests to rent or buy land on the reserve as tied to white identity: "In reply I have to inform you that the land in question is not for sale and that no white person can be allowed to settle or build on an Indian Reserve."[38]

The absence of any direct kinship tie with the Algonquins seems to have played against some members of the Vanasse family despite recognized Métis origins. Pierre Chaussé Jr., by contrast, claimed Indigenous ties via his mother, Julie Vanasse, the daughter of the Métis Louise Forcier with François Vanasse. Chaussé was identified as Métis ("half breed") by the Indian agent at Maniwaki, and possibly by Father Guinard. In short, Métis who hoped to live on the reserve seem either to have put forward their Indigenous origins, as Pierre Chaussé Jr. did, or to have left them aside. This suggests that many Métis families of the region had a very pragmatic understanding of the way the Indian Act defined Indian and Métis identities.[39]

With the gradual legalization of identities, which increasingly differentiated Indians and Métis, these categories were often used strategically. In a case involving orphaned children who were reputed to be "Indians," and at the instigation of some members of the Algonquin community, Suzanne Brosseau was required to answer the Indian Department about the guardianship of her nieces and nephews. The Indian agent presented the following version of events in his first letter: "[The children] are at present with a Mrs Brosseau Sister of their mother, but not Indian, nor belonging to any Band, who took the children against the will of the Indians. The Indians have decided to give the children to Mathias Techenne member of River Desert Band."[40] To shed light on this imbroglio, the Department of Indian Affairs demanded answers to nine questions, one of which was about the legal status of Mrs. Brosseau,[41] and specifically the extent of her Indigenous ancestry. Several signed declarations were sent to Indian Affairs, including Mrs. Brosseau's, who responded to the fourth question as follows: "(4) That Mrs Peter Buckshot was my full sister and our Father was a white man and our mother was an Indian woman."[42] She also identifies herself as the aunt of the children, and contends that neither she nor her husband are claiming exclusive guardianship. Indian Affairs, which asserted exclusive authority in the matter of such litigation, finally decided in favour of Mrs. Brosseau on the grounds that it was preferable for the children to live with a close family member rather than someone with no clear kin ties, even if that person were full Indian.

Mrs. Brosseau's formal declaration of self-identification underscores her dual ancestry. Although expressed within the framework of a legal requirement, it is interesting to note how mixed origins are instrumentalized by both the Algonquin band and Mrs. Brosseau. The band, using the Indian agent as an intermediary, refused to acknowledge any indigeneity in Mrs. Brosseau: she is "not Indian, nor belonging to any Band." In response, Mrs. Brosseau specifies that "our Father was a white man and our mother was an Indian woman," and in so doing anchors herself as having "Indian" ancestry, which then raises the question of whether legal guardianship of "Indian" children can be granted to someone living outside the reserve, or at the very least outside the legal framework of the Rivière Désert Band.

With a decision that was made outside the bounds of the legal and customary definitions of what it meant to be Indian, the case reveals an explicit intention by "Indian" complainants to deny Mrs. Brosseau any form of indigeneity because she was not status Indian. In spite of a certain permeability to the categories of Indian and Métis at the end of the nineteenth century, a number of legal shackles were imposed, whether by the regulations and policies of Indian Affairs or by customary practice and the desire of the Algonquins to influence the definition of indigeneity. Paradoxically, these exclusionary forces encouraged those with a Métis identity to remain conscious of being Indigenous yet not Indian – in short, of being Métis. In other words, social and legal forces that were external to the Métis contributed to the maintenance of a Métis or Half-breed social category in the region.

As has been illustrated, the existence of a collective and distinctive Métis or Half-breed identity is seen in the documents of the era. The continuity of that identity is exemplified through the documents and by the problems that faced the Métis when a reserve was established and legal orders excluded them from "Indian" status. Métis were simply not allowed to live on the reserve as Métis. They had to "become" Indians, or to rent lots as whites. The failure of a request put forward by Monseigneur Guigues – in 1850 he asked that whites married to Indians not lose their property rights through the creation of the reserve at Maniwaki – surely testifies to this (Carrière 1962, 92–93). This exclusion kept Métis families at the margins of the reserve, forcing them to become squatters in the vicinity of Maniwaki. It follows that Métis in the region became disadvantaged by not being able to secure any form of collective protection *as Indigenous peoples*. As the next chapter explores, the growing rigidity of both social and geographic barriers led to discontent, as evidenced in a series of petitions that challenged official policies and practices.

# 10

## *Petitions and Politics*
### The Maniwaki Reserve and the Forest Industry

THE CULTURAL CONTINUITY OF Métis in the Maniwaki region is illustrated in petitions presented by the inhabitants of the area to address tensions over identity and conflicts over access to lots on the reserve. These conflicts boiled over in the spring of 1874, provoked by the interference of Indian agent John White in the management of Indian lands on the reserve and the leasing of lots by Indians to Métis and Euro-Canadian families. Two petitions were sent to the Honourable R.H. Scott: the first from the Indians of the Maniwaki Reserve (here called Petition A); and the second from the inhabitants of Maniwaki and surroundings (here called Petition B).

Both petitions concerned John White's management of resources. In the first, the "undersigned Indians of the 'Indian Reserve of Maniwaki'" reproach White for having "shown great partiality in the distribution of our Semi-Annual Grant by giving money to parties who had no right to get any and refusing others who were justly entitled to a share." The petition enumerates how White unjustly distributed blankets, money for seed grain, and other resources. The signatories denounce him as "acting against many of us through malice, because we will not be subservient to his will."[1]

The second petition echoes the first in complaining of the capricious nature of White's administration. The petitioners write that "the officiating Agent of the River Desert Indians is incapacita[t]ed by age" and argue that he has used his authority in a "partial and unjust manner." The crux of the complaints centres on the rental of lots. The petitioners are incensed that some of the "inhabitants" rented lots from the "Indians" in "good faith"; one paid forty dollars and the other twenty-five dollars as rent. Then, "Mr. White afterwards rented the said lots to another party against the consent of the Indians, who had originally bargained for it, and in violation of every principle of justice." Here, too, White is accused of acting "through partiality and malice which he did not attempt to disguise."

The second paragraph repeats that White is "acting through sheer malice," and both petitions present him as using his authority to unjustly favour some to the detriment of others.[2] Both seek to have White replaced.

The language of Petition B reveals how the community defined itself. Notably, the petitioners, the "inhabitants of River Desert and Vicinity," never use the terms *white* or *settler* to identify themselves;[3] rather, they use the more inclusive *inhabitants* and refer to the community as *mixed*, specifying that this mixedness comprises "all classes":

> That owing to the partial and unjust manner [in which] he has discharged his duties he has lost the confidence of all classes of the community in this section ... Your petitioners therefore hope that M White will immediately be replaced by a man in whom the general public will have confidence, as we are certain his removal will avoid impending trouble and tend to cement the friendly relations which should exist in a mixed community like this.[4]

The 116 signatories to Petition B include known Métis families such as the St-Denis, Riel, Naud (via Jean-Baptiste Paquette), and Vanasse (via Pierre Chaussé Sr.) families.[5] Other signatories are Euro-Canadian and, through marriage (only men signed the petition), women said to be Indian or Métis. Through the use of the term *vicinity*, the petition reinforces the idea of a regional community, rather than just one settlement. It also highlights that the concerns are not limited to the reserve but include the territory surrounding Maniwaki.

This description echoes other documents that describe historical Métis communities as comprising (French) Canadians, Indians, and Métis. It depicts a community explicitly qualified as mixed, comparable, for example, to the Sault Ste. Marie and Red River communities. The use of the term *mixed community* permits the inclusion of different ethnocultural constituents, including Métis. It is indeed the presence of Métis that, we argue, motivated the choice of terminology in the second petition. The distinctive Métis population could not be simply conflated with Euro-Canadians in one undifferentiated community, on the one hand, or with the "Indians" of Maniwaki, who had their own petition, on the other.

### The Maniwaki Métis

The second petition suggests that the population of the region not only saw itself as a mixed community but also recognized distinctions between

*Indian Encampment on Desert and Gatineau Rivers,* by Alfred Worsley Holdstock, c. 1870. The Algonquin habitation style, suitable for a very nomadic way of life at this time, can be contrasted to that of the Métis, who were frequently described as living in log cabins as early as the 1830s.
*Credit: Library and Archives Canada, 1970-188-2346*

at least three constitutive elements. If it had been a matter of binary opposition between Indian and white, it would have been possible to specify two classes or both classes, rather than "all classes of the community." Given the historical composition of the community, logically, there were three "sub-communities," the Métis being one. This ethnic distinction is even more evident when one considers that the first petition refers to the "Indians of the Indian Reserve," and the term *mixed community* would not be applicable there.

The expression "all classes of the community" adds precision to its mixed composition. In its historical context, *class* refers to the ethnic or racial components of the population in question, as it was used in the nineteenth century to designate such differences (classes of the community and classes of peoples). It is also used locally by the surveyor Bouchette to designate the Métis ("Bois-Brûlés") who were located in what is now the land south of Gatineau Park. He uses the same vocabulary to define the Métis, moreover, as squatters: "a bois-brulé, one of that class of people known under the denomination of Squatters" (Bouchette 1832a, 190).[6]

Spanning more than a century from 1828 to 1946, the recurring historical references to "mixed" community reinforce this reading of the documentary record, which suggests that the population of Maniwaki and its surroundings formed a tripartite community composed of distinct umbrella groups that cut along ethnic lines: Indians, who were made up of various nations; Métis; and whites, comprising various ethnic elements.[7] Indeed, Father Joseph-Étienne Guinard describes a tripartite ethnocultural division of the community when he reports from Maniwaki as late as the 1940s. He refers not only to Indians and whites but also to Métis, describing the latter as a distinctive group in a discussion about the devotion of parishioners on the Maniwaki Reserve: "The Indians were without piety; not attending mass and few fulfilled their Easter duties. The population was 650 souls, including Indians, Métis and Whites, almost all Catholic."[8] We suggest that Guinard does not simply throw out the term *Métis* to mean mixed from a biological standpoint, as some critics might suggest. Rather, he discusses cultural and distinctive behaviours he associates with the Métis "race," here understood in its older signification of a people:

> The Indian blood mixed with that of the Whites forms a race that is very beautiful and resilient. Like the Indians, these Métis love to hunt the forest and have a very well-developed sense of orientation, even at night – our immense forests cannot lead them astray. They find what they need to live where the Whites would die of starvation. Like the Indian again, the Métis do not hold long at work, they love liberty, the open air and travelling, but they rarely emigrate; this Biblical reproach does not apply to them: "Like a bird that flees its nest is anyone who flees from home."[9]

Clearly, Father Guinard distinguishes Métis from Indians and whites in spite of observed similarities between them.[10]

The director of Indian Affairs also unambiguously identifies a tripartite division of the population, in a 1942 directive concerning hunting and trapping permits in the Maniwaki region. He uses the same classification as Guinard: "Indians, whites or halfbreeds." Here, too, the collective existence of the Métis ("halfbreeds") is identified with respect to regulations concerning a specific way of life that was traditional to many Métis families, hunting and trapping: "These licences may be issued to Indians only. They are not to be issued to either whites or halfbreeds. The presence of an applicant's name on the nominal roll of the Indians of your agency may be accepted by you as evidence of his eligibility for a licence."[11] This last example shows how the distinction between Indians, Métis, and whites was maintained by Indian Affairs bureaucrats into the mid-twentieth century, in spite of some difficulties expressed by Indian agents to dissociate

Métis and Indians and enforce a strict separation of the two, forcing the Métis to effectively become whites. The band list was the inevitable outcome of separating Métis from Indians, granting status to the latter while ensuring that the former were excluded.

The 1874 petition of the mixed community is thus a striking document, woven into a much larger documentary trail that reinforces our understanding of the ethnocultural composition of Maniwaki and the historical presence of Métis in this area. The evidence suggests that a number of Métis families in the region continued to occupy the middle ground between whites and Indians, while being categorized as a distinctive class of people, or race, by both clerics and government functionaries as late as the 1940s.

### Maniwaki Algonquin versus Métis

Company bureaucrats, government authorities and clerics were not the only ones to describe the collective and distinctive existence of the Métis in the Maniwaki region. The Algonquins also corroborated the presence of French and Scottish Métis in the region. As agent White's management continued to provoke tensions on the Maniwaki Reserve, correspondence attesting to the Métis presence surged following an election held after the death of the elderly Chief Pakinawatik. The event was followed by a third petition, this one by the Algonquins of Maniwaki dated December 29, 1874. Here too the agent White is accused of stealing money and giving seed to "Half Breeds," but the signatories are dissatisfied not only with his outdated policies (and those of his sons) but also with all those who are not "pure Algonquins," whom the petitioners accuse of attempting to become their chiefs: "We Algonquins affirm that when we asked this land of Maniwaki from the Government we did not say that the Iroquois or the half Ottawa Breed or those whose origin is from Red River[12] should come to be our chiefs here."[13] This is the crux of the first paragraph and the grievance of the petitioners, along with the contention that "it was only after we had received the grant of Maniwaki that they came to share our land." The petition reveals a power struggle between First Nations factions, including the "Iroquois" (presumably the Mohawks) and maybe Algonquins of paternal Odawa descent ("half Ottawa breed"), who are both presented as distinct from the Algonquins.

The petitioners then identify those they accuse of seeking to profit from the newly constituted reserve: "We therefore ask our Great Chief [the

Pakinawatik, first Indian chief of the Maniwaki Reserve, by an unknown photographer, c. 1854–74. The death of Pakinawatik opened the door to a conflict over his succession in which the Métis were involved.
*Credit: Alexandre Castonguay/Library and Archives Canada, PA-068278, 1933-024 NPC*

Crown] whether he prefers these Half Scotch or Half French Breed to us pure Algonquins."[14] The Algonquin Indians thus identify French and Scottish Métis in the surroundings of the reserve in 1874, both collectively and distinctively. In turn, the Algonquins present themselves as "pure" and thus opposed to admitting Métis to the reserve, in conformity with the policies of Indian Affairs. But their rationale is perhaps different from that of Indian Affairs. Later in the petition, the Indian agent is rebuked for giving the presents – annuities – reserved for the Algonquins to "pure French," here distinct from "French" Métis: "When our money was distributed John White gave some of it to pure French and thereby wronged us of our money."[15]

Another letter in the same correspondence dossier in the archives is also quite significant, as it lists electors who should not have voted in the band election: namely, Métis and other outsiders to the band. Reinforcing this notion of distinct identities in the area, the list of dubious electors came from the Algonquins and specifies whether the individuals are French-speaking Métis, English-speaking Métis, or have another affiliation that is not recognized by the Algonquins.[16] Each elector is identified solely by a number, and these numbers seem to correspond to another list of electors provided to Indian Affairs a few days before and probably supplied by Métis and/or other excluded voters. The latter list is constituted almost exclusively of Indigenous names, which makes identification of Métis much more difficult, but it could be assumed that the use of Indian as opposed to European names for Métis individuals (who often had both) was a way of legitimating their participation in the election.[17]

These conflicts are corroborated by the Oblate archives. The Oblate priests of Maniwaki were well aware of the tensions, as the Oblate historian Gaston Carrière testifies:

It consisted of a family feud between the Indians and Father Déléage explained the whole problem to [Monseigneur] Duhamel, February 20, 1875. He affirmed that the Indians were divided into two camps: the pure Algonquins, the most numerous, the most moral, the purest, and the very best. The other group was formed by a hodgepodge of all sorts of Indian tribes and various Métis: the latter forming the majority and were principally Scottish Métis. They were the most wicked, drunkards, immoral, etc. They were elected as chiefs in October because the pure Algonquins were almost all off hunting. The pure Algonquins were extremely irritated and would often come and share their grievances with the father [priest]. (Carrière 1968, 137; our translation)

Even though Carrière seems to consider the Métis and Algonquins as members of one large family, the indigeneity expressed by Déléage is relevant to issue of Indigenous identity in general. He distinguishes these two groups in terms of moral and cultural characteristics: the Algonquins are for him more moral and more pure, though this does not necessarily mean that their heritage was entirely unmixed. The Métis are judged as immoral drunkards (a reminder of their role in bootlegging alcohol), and implicitly as not having adopted the nomadic way of life tied to winter hunting grounds. Additionally, in a letter sent to Indian Affairs during the same period, Father Déléage refines his perspective by explaining that certain Indians of Maniwaki are not, in his opinion, "real" Indians,[18] which is yet another way of identifying the Métis.

The Algonquins considered the question of Métis and Indians who were "strangers" living on the Maniwaki Reserve serious enough to send an official delegation to Ottawa to transmit their petitions, as newspapers of the time reported. Indeed, a short news report from 1875 mentions the "Indians and Métis who reside on Algonquin territory" (*Le Journal de Québec* 1875; our translation). The Métis denounced in this petition certainly did not constitute all Métis in the region; rather, they represented the faction that sought to join the Algonquin Rivière Désert community. Such political manoeuvres were frequent among the Métis in Ontario and the North-West, for example, with the signing of treaties (Ens and Sawchuk 2016, 161–64). Individuals made a strategic decision to seek Indian status and the protection afforded by life on a reserve, as opposed to the life of a white citizen, at a time when the changing political context and economic climate offered fewer and fewer benefits to those who openly declared themselves Métis (Ens 2001, 174).

Taken together, the documentary sources suggest that the population of Maniwaki was not only ethnically tripartite but also culturally tripartite. Evidence supports the interpretation that the Métis formed a collectivity ("Half Scotch or Half French Breed"), which the "Indians" recognized as distinct from themselves and did not want to have on the reserve.[19]

Even after agent White was replaced, relations with his successor remained tense. Again, identity seems to have been at the centre of these conflicts. Tensions were reported, for example, between the new Indian agent, Baudin, and the Métis McDougall family. Baudin's correspondence reports that he was in fact expelled from the cabin of Jean-Baptiste McDougall *manu militari* – by the force of arms – when he was conducting a census of the reserve and its inhabitants. Writing to his superiors, Baudin lodges a complaint about his forceful expulsion in 1874: "The second day we arrived at a little house where lives a certain John Baptiste McDougall, who has been treated as an Algonquin, though his father was a half breed from the Christinos of Red-River."[20] As we can see, the agent contests the Algonquin identity and thus the Indian status of McDougall, who seems to have been a descendant of Red River Métis in Manitoba.[21] Here we see how the new agent treated the two identities as distinct, providing him with a supplemental argument to discredit Jean-Baptiste McDougall.

McDougall's Métis origin also served as an ethnic marker when Métis and other Indigenous populations were accused of seizing lands and power (elected as chiefs) on the reserve. It must be remembered that this nebulous Red River origin was at the heart of the ethnic debate formulated in the Rivière Désert petition. Whatever the true origin of the McDougall family may be, it is clear that both the Algonquins who signed the petition and the Indian agent Baudin associated it with the Red River region and Métis identity.

### Toward a New Economy: Métis Raftsmen and Foresters

The presence and cultural continuity of the Métis in the region is observed not only in the conflicts that affected the Maniwaki Reserve but also in documents related to the nascent forestry industry. Though historically the fur trade was closely tied to Métis ethnogenesis, evidence demonstrates that the Métis also worked in forestry, where they were able to repurpose their aptitudes in a growing industry as it eclipsed the fur trade in the second half of the nineteenth century.

The following anecdote, which again implicates the McDougall Métis family, illustrates this trend. The incident in question involves the rescue of the crew of an American hot air balloon in 1859. The crew had to carry out an emergency landing in the Gatineau Valley forest. With great difficulty, the travellers managed to reach a cabin in the vicinity of Baskatong Lake. An individual described as a "half-breed Indian" opened the door. Amable McDougall stood in the doorway, speaking French and English. Accompanied by his son, forestry agent Angus Cameron,[22] and Cameron's assistant at the Gilmour Company, Amable then guided the lost crew members to Maniwaki. From there, the crew found other guides to take them to Ottawa (Haddock 1894, 354–55). It should be added that Amable McDougall's ability to orient new arrivals in the forest territory had already been noted in 1851, as had his interest in forestry work, which he carried out for the Hamilton & Low Company as early as 1842, apparently with his brother Ignace (Angus) and the Métis Naud family.[23] As the McDougall family illustrates, the transition to an economy dominated by the forestry industry did not entirely erase signs of a Métis presence in the Gatineau Valley. The incident with the hot air balloon demonstrates Métis ability not only to serve as forest guides but also to speak many languages, which was certainly useful to navigate a region inhabited by Algonquins and

Lumber camp north of Ottawa River at Rouge River, Québec, 1865.
*Credit: Alexander Henderson, Library and Archives Canada, PA-135033 1983-069 NPC*

freshly colonized by French-Canadian personnel and a significant Irish population.[24]

A work titled *The Lumber Trade of the Ottawa Valley* (1872) contains a direct allusion to Métis ("half-breeds") who, along with the Indians, worked as scouts (a term used also for guides) for foresters:

> Having secured the limit the next step is to dispatch a party of experienced scouts, generally Indians or half-breeds, to examine the land and seek out groves of valuable timber. The skill of these self-taught surveyors is sometimes very remarkable, they will explore the length and breadth of the unknown territory and report upon the value of its timber, the situation and capabilities of its streams for floating out timber and the facilities for hauling and transportation. (Anonymous 1872, 16)

This description echoes the case of the crashed hot air balloon crew, confirming the reputation of the Métis for deep knowledge of the countryside. Notably, Métis – as did Indians and a few experienced lumberjacks –

produced maps of the Ottawa River watershed and its various waterways that were used by fur traders as well as other professionals such as geologists. Some Métis also produced geographical sketches of the forestry potential of different sectors,[25] and the ethnographer J.G. Kohl (1861, 285) notes that these various cartographic representations were valued:

> The maps drawn by Indians, half-breeds, and hunters of the Hudson's Bay Company are, however, not altogether to be despised. Mr Logan [geologist] had the goodness to show me a map of this kind of a portion of a river, which he had received before the survey, and when he afterwards compared it with the results he had obtained by a more scientific method, it appeared that the narrowing of the channel, its angles and windings, the form and position of its islands, its lake-like expansions, &c., were laid down with wonderful fidelity.[26]

The passage quoted earlier from Moses Foster Sweetser's *The Middle States: A Handbook for Travellers* (1876) adds another element to the description of the Métis ("half-breeds") who were employed on the Ottawa River: "Long lines of lumber-booms are found on this reach; and the steamer passes timber-rafts bearing low square sails and numerous huts, and great islands of logs drifting down to the Ottawa saw-mills. These rafts are managed by French Canadians and Indian half-breeds, – hardy, powerful, and semi-civilized men, who still chant the old Norman boat-songs amid these wild forests" (Sweetser 1876, 132). The "old Norman" in this passage refers to the language spoken by some of the French ancestors of the Métis, who were in large part originally from Normandy. Interestingly, this mention of Norman heritage echoes the observation of Alexis de Tocqueville that the "Bois-Brûlé" or Métis man he encountered on the shores of the Saginaw River spoke with a "Normand" accent. Similarly, a brochure dating to 1873 suggests the possibility that a tourist seeking the exotic can cruise down the rivers of the Outaouais region on a steamboat and observe "French Canadians, a few Indians and half-breeds among them" (Union Forwarding & Railway Co'y. 1873, 14).

A text published in 1880 by Frederic G. Mather attests to earlier travels up the Ottawa River by the Métis. Mather reports a conversation between the foreman of a lumber camp and the group accompanying the author. The foreman was asked to recount the ancient history of the region and replied, "Before the present century [before 1800] this valley was the home of Indians, half-breeds and French" (Mather 1880, 144). Oral tradition thus affirms the presence of a Métis population in the Outaouais region a few decades before the earliest documentary evidence we can find. Even if such oral accounts are occasionally distorted over time, their key elements conform to the general tenor of the historical record reviewed up to this point.

In fact, the presence of the Métis of the Gatineau Valley in the forestry industry, notably on the log drive, was sufficiently significant to inspire the literature of the era. In her poem "Gatineau Point," S. Frances Harrison (1891, 33) describes the raftsmen in these terms:

> A half-breed, slim, and sallow of face,
> Alphonse lies full length on his raft,
> The hardy son of a hybrid race.
>
> ...
>
> That upon this sun-bak'd blister'd place
> He sleeps, with his hand on the burning haft,
> A Metis – slim, and sallow of face,
> The hardy son of a hybrid race!

These two stanzas use "half-breed" and "Metis" interchangeably – as personified in a raftsman at the mouth of the Gatineau River – to describe not only a single individual but a distinct population, a race, characterized by its hybridity.

The theme of Métis as forest workers was taken up in the novel *Risques d'hommes* by Rolland Legault (1950). The action takes place on the Coulonge and Gatineau rivers, and the Métis character central to the storyline is Bisson, nicknamed Le Diable, or the Devil. Bisson is the antithesis of the good French-Canadian log drivers. His Métis character is also emphasized vis-à-vis other ethnic identities: "A bit apart, in a larger group of older men, we remarked the cook, Jos. Bisaillon, the Sauvage Henry, the Englishman Barnes and most of all the Métis Thomas Bisson, who caught the attention of the young Cabana for much longer" (Legault 1950, 112; our translation). In sum, Legault juxtaposes Métis, Indian *(Sauvage)*, English, and French-Canadian identities (the latter via many characters not mentioned in this passage but present throughout the novel).

These two examples drawn from works of fiction, along with the more conventional historical sources, are good indicators of the ethnic composition of the nineteenth-century forestry industry in the Outaouais region, which was clearly known for its Métis element. The evidence suggests the continuity of a distinctive Métis population in the region from the first recorded observations we examined, from the 1830s. Two petitions from 1874, including one from a community that self-identified as "mixed," also support this idea. And a third petition, this one advanced by "pure Algonquins," identifies French Métis and Scott Métis as distinctive groups. Moreover, other historical documents illustrate that Métis culture endured in the Upper Gatineau region despite the shift toward a lumber industry, or more precisely, that the skills associated with Métis culture were also used in lumber industries, and that the presence of the Métis was significant enough to influence the literature of this later period. We can thus develop a clearer picture of the contours of the historical Métis population of the Maniwaki region. The next chapter turns to more contemporary evidence to explore whether such historical continuity extends into the twentieth and twenty-first centuries.

# 11

# *The Great Awakening*
## Outaouais Métis Voices, 1969–2017

THE PRESENCE OF MÉTIS in the Gatineau Valley passes largely unnoticed in the archival records for some thirty years, from the 1940s to the 1970s. Documents mentioning the Métis of the Outaouais in this period are difficult to find, but the Gatineau Métis returned to the local and national stage in the 1970s. From that point onward, a new generation of activists has sought media coverage and political change as they advance their concerns and claims. Their activism has not occurred in a vacuum; it is part of a much larger pan-Indigenous movement that has seen individuals and communities push to gain greater rights and recognition for Métis and non-status Indians. These political endeavours led to the Métis being included under section 35 of the 1982 Constitution as Aboriginal peoples, along with First Nations and Inuit. Their inclusion was in large part achieved by Métis and non-status Indians working together under the leadership of Harry Daniels. This grassroots political movement involved Métis from across the country, among them individuals who identify as Métis in Québec, and specifically in the Outaouais region (Gendron, Laforest, and Léveillé 1981, 153).

The contribution of Métis of the Gatineau and larger Outaouais region to national recognition for Métis people has gone mostly unnoticed by historians, but local and regional newspapers and other primary sources reveal the contours of a Métis movement in the Gatineau that precedes the constitutional reforms of 1982. Our reading of the primary sources provides a balanced account of the contemporary history of this Métis community and efforts over the past half-century to have its rights recognized.

It seems that a Métis identity in the Outaouais region is not the fruit of recent instrumentalization or of a recent wave of self-indigenization following constitutional recognition, as some scholars and activists suggest (O'Toole 2017a, 2017b; see also Leroux 2017; Vowel and Leroux 2016).

Historical documents instead indicate that the first association to represent Maniwaki Métis was founded in 1969 and incorporated in 1976 as a local branch of the Alliance laurentienne des Métis et Indiens sans statut (Michaux 2014, 149). Local branch 18 of what became known later as the Alliance Autochtone then broke away from this larger Indigenous alliance in 2005 to become the Communauté Métis Autochtone de Maniwaki (REQ 2005), and this organization continues to exist.

The newspaper *L'Alliance, la voix des Métis et Indiens sans statut du Québec* provides insights into the rationale behind the creation of the local chapter of the larger alliance, as well as the activities and positions taken by the Métis of the Outaouais region, or more specifically Maniwaki. As reported by Rhéal Boudrias, in the 1970s the Maniwaki community (followed by the Kipawa region of northwestern Québec) was actively engaged in bringing together Métis and non-status Indians in provincial associations such as the Alliance laurentienne des Métis et Indiens sans statut. Referring to Kermot Moore, one of the founders of the Alliance laurentienne, Boudrias remarks, "He recruited people over a yearlong period, in Maniwaki at first, then in Kipawa and in the North-west. The movement finally spread throughout Quebec" (*L'Alliance* 1980, 7). We can assume that Moore chose to recruit first in regions where there was a greater concentration of Métis individuals and families. In fact, this passage suggests that the Maniwaki community was among the first to organize itself and join a larger provincial movement to defend the interests of the Métis and non-status Indian collective across Québec.

The Métis of the Outaouais region thus spearheaded a movement to promote Métis claims in Québec. It is important to note, however, that because this association brought together a broader coalition of interests, the definition of *Métis* was long debated. Some saw Métis identity as largely tied to the eventual recovery of Indian status, which would garner more immediate rights vis-à-vis federal authorities; some even limited the identity to a specific blood quantum, although that idea was eventually rejected; and others perceived Métis as an identity independent of Indian identity.[1]

Being Métis in Québec was not seen solely as a question of being mixed, as opposed to culturally Métis. In fact, testimony in *L'Alliance* delineates Métis identity from a cultural standpoint, in clear continuity with the evidence from archival sources that we have discussed. Articles published in the 1980s, years after the creation of the local chapter of the provincial association – such as "Élections en avril, à Maniwaki" (Elections in April at Maniwaki) (Veilleux 1984, 3) and "Local de Maniwaki" (The Maniwaki Local) (Robertson 1986, 11) – attest to its continued cultural and political participation in the Maniwaki community. Continuity is also evident in the fact that annual general assemblies and elections, as well as cultural activities to bring the community together, were still being organized. Articles mention the "Métis Games" being organized in Region 02 (which includes Maniwaki); a membership census was taken; and several articles note a conflict over the exclusion of the local "Métis" hockey club from participating in a league apparently reserved for status Indians (*L'Alliance* 1985a, 17; 1985b, 17; 1985c, 17).

Among the political demands espoused by provincial organizations, as articulated by the Métis of the Outaouais (including Maniwaki), is an insistence on the right to hunt, trap, and fish. Even prior to the Constitution Act, 1982 – while efforts were underway to have the Métis recognized in the constitution – Métis in Québec lobbied the provincial government for recognition of their hunting, trapping, and fishing rights. In 1979, a general policy was put forward to this end (ALMISSI 1979, 9). In fact, the Métis of Maniwaki participated in constitutional delegations with the express aim of having these rights enshrined in the Constitution. The Métis of the Outaouais, in other words, were politically active, as an article published in the journal *Recherches amérindiennes au Québec* also attests. The article describes a delegation from the Outaouais in the audience at the Commission de Révision constitutionnelle des Métis et Indiens non inscrits du Canada (Commission on constitutional amendments regarding Métis and non-status Indians in Canada) held on March 7, 1981, in Québec City: "Thus, the representatives of the Outaouais Region were capable of exposing the administrative constraints tied to the exercise of their traditional activities of hunting, fishing and trapping" (Gendron, Laforest, and Léveillé 1981, 153; our translation).

### Squatters on Their Own Lands

Both the cultural dimensions of Métis identity and indicators of historical continuity are perhaps best exemplified by the arguments of Nelson Amos, the representative of the Outaouais Métis, who denounced the loss of their trapping territories in 1981. As Amos puts it, the loss of their permits obliged the Métis to become squatters on their traplines, on their traditional lands, thus depriving them of an essential subsistence activity. A long passage from this denunciation is warranted:

> Mister Commissioner,
> Members of the Commission,
>
> Ladies and Gentlemen,
>
> The Métis of the region of Pontiac-Labelle [Outaouais] met to discuss together the rights that they want to see enshrined in the Canadian Constitution. These rights, they are both numerous and specific. As the Government of Canada has accepted to recognize us as aboriginals, the Métis of this country, we expect that this commission will exert the necessary pressure so that the rights that they are preparing to grant us with regard to our aboriginal status are defined with precision in the Constitution ...
>
> The lands where our ancestors trapped and hunted are the property of companies often foreign ... For us, Mister Commissioner, this situation is unacceptable and demonstrates clearly our situation as "squatters" on our own lands ...
>
> Today, in our region, those activities which were fundamental to our ancestral economy are forbidden to us. Day after day, the Métis of our region lose their trapping territories; traplines they were forced to obtain by resigning themselves to apply for them along with all the non-aboriginal citizens of Québec ... Economically our region is quite depressed, and these practices allow us to gain some additional revenue for our families, as well as being a right that we consider fundamental given that our ancestors used them as the basis of their economy for millennia. (Amos 1981, 14; our translation)

Amos's comment about "squatters" echoes the 1847 Oblate chronicles of squatters at Lac-Sainte-Marie, where sixteen Métis, French-Canadian, and First Nations families lived. The use of the term also hearkens back to the remarks of that era's surveyor Bouchette, who associated the Bois-Brûlés (that is to say, Métis) with squatters living on the shores of the rivers. Furthermore, in the historical North-West, Métis and French Canadians who took possession of a long lot of land without legal title, following the customs of the land, were described as squatters (Payment 1990, 265).

Here, however, squatting does not refer to principal habitations but to locales where flora and fauna are harvested – that is, traplines and hunting grounds. It should also be noted that squatters in the past (Métis or not) sometimes welcomed surveyors, hoping to have their title to territory or their occupation recorded. The relationship between squatters and surveyors was thus not necessarily antagonistic. But Amos refers to "squatters" to emphasize the inherent dispossession of the Métis, and the injustices they faced with respect to a territory that they had historically occupied.

Also notable in Amos's discourse is the implicit suggestion that there is a collective and distinctive Métis community in the region of Pontiac-Labelle, a geographical area that includes Maniwaki. Although the association he represents includes non-status Indians, Amos refers to a Métis identity that can be distinguished from them. He elaborates on this topic in an interview granted to Rhéal Boudrias and published in *L'Alliance* (1981, 13). Amos notes that it was "the Métis" of the region of Pontiac-Labelle (thus of the Outaouais) who controlled the trapping zones until 1945, before the forestry and paper industries caused vast perturbations of the territory:

MR. BOUDRIAS: You were speaking of the paper companies who razed the ground, who cut the trees and leave nothing in the wake. In this agreement that you are discussing would you want to take over the land? Would you want to have the right to repossess the lands?

MR. AMOS: We would also like to have something to say about what is being touched. If they continue to do what they are doing nothing will be left. Some day we will have no land even if we want to take them back. There will be nothing left to take back.

MR. BOUDRIAS: If the land has been wasted there will be nothing left to take back. As far as the trapping lands are concerned, has it been many years – you said you had to get trapping and fishing grounds since when[?]

MR. AMOS: I really don't know the exact date. 1945.

MR. BOUDRIAS: Since 1945? Before that it was the Métis who controlled the region?

MR. AMOS: At least they controlled hunting and trapping. As I said in my presentation, since [then] we have [had] to apply for a licence, anyone Native.

The discussion reveals continuity in the problems affecting the Outaouais Métis, as we've seen in previous chapters. Amos highlights the devastating effect of the forest industry on the ancestral practices of the Outaouais Métis, particular those tied to subsistence trapping, hunting, and fishing on traditional territories. The conversation also confirms the desire of the Métis to maintain these practices in spite of socioeconomic disturbances resulting from forestry. Amos furthermore affirms that the Métis of the Outaouais continue to pursue the traditional activities of hunting, trapping, and fishing, and emphasizes their commitment to continuing these practices, as demonstrated by their political mobilization.

Métis claims in Québec did not recede when the Constitution was repatriated in 1982 and Métis rights were enshrined. In fact, many feared the position of the provincial government, as it tended to deny the existence of Métis in Québec. Echoing divergences over the definition of *Métis,* the president of the Native Council of Canada testified that in 1983 many members of his Québec organization, the Alliance laurentienne, considered themselves to be Métis, even though their Indigenous origins were criticized as too distant or diluted. Louis "Smokey" Bruyère made this idea explicit in a speech in Québec City on November 24, 1983, in which he eloquently referred to Métis roots:

> It may well be that, at the time of confederation many Quebecers chose to identify with their French ancestors rather than with their Indian heritage. Certainly that is their right, and we support them in their choice. But we cannot extend that support to include the deliberate and unilateral exclusion of those aboriginal people in Quebec who do honour their aboriginal heritage and identify themselves as Metis.
>
> We can serve notice here, that if the Quebec delegation insists on maintaining its current position that there are no Metis in the province of Quebec at the constitutional conference, we will have no choice but to consider the current Government of Quebec a major obstacle to the just aspirations of our constituents in Quebec. (Bruyère 1983, 6)

In concluding his speech, Bruyère presented three recommendations to the government of Québec. The second is particularly noteworthy, as it concerns Métis identity: "Contrary to present Quebec policy, there are significant numbers of aboriginal people in Quebec who identify themselves as Metis people and who must be accommodated in any policy this committee might propose for aboriginal people in Quebec" (6).

In the early 1980s, the situation of the Métis in Québec, both in general and in the Gatineau Valley, was far from enviable, in spite of the fact that the Métis of the Outaouais had contributed to the political process that helped Métis gain recognition in the constitution. The government of Québec simply denied any formal recognition of Métis within the province. Yet various published testimonies affirm the presence of a distinctive Métis identity in Québec. For example Aubé Brière, from the Mont-Laurier local of the Alliance laurentienne – in his 1979 article "Quelle est notre identité?" (What is our identity?) – asserts the existence of a strong but oppressed "people" that proudly remembers its roots: "We Métis must be proud of our blood, 'proof' of the Alliance of peoples who built the new world. All the continent of North America will hear the voice of the awakening of its children" (Brière 1979, 10; our translation). In "C'est quoi la justice?" Raymond Lafond and Charles Beaudoin go further, highlighting the very difficult context in which the Métis found themselves while underscoring what makes the Métis identity unique:

> We are now considered as landless, as vagabonds.
>
> Why would not a law recognize us, the Métis, the disinherited ... We are not asking for the impossible, we demand that the white part of our blood recognize that it [Métis] exists. We demand justice.
>
> Justice, first, in recognizing our existence. Justice later in recognizing rights to our Indian ancestors, which would allow us to choose a way of life we desire. Only then will we have the right to exist, because we will have access to all that our ancestors gave us. We will be able to unite the two cultures within our reach, reconciling in us the White and the Indian and become whole beings, worthy of all our ancestors. (Lafond and Beaudoin 1979, 10; our translation)

### The Dream of Louis Riel

The continuity and cultural aspects of contemporary Outaouais Métis are also visible in a strong and persistent attachment to the figure of Louis Riel, the leader of the 1870 and 1885 resistances in Manitoba and the North-West. Such attachment can be found, for example, in an article written by the president of the Alliance laurentienne, Fernand Chalifoux.

In a 1981 article entitled "Let Us Remember the Broken Treaties of the Past," Chalifoux uses the term *people* to identify Métis and non-status Indians of Québec. Chalifoux even suggests a kinship between the memory of the Métis in the West and those in Québec, while affirming the collective existence of Québec Métis. Louis Riel is portrayed as a rallying figure, "one of *our* great leaders" (Chalifoux 1981, 2).

This cultural memory of Louis Riel is significant for other Métis of the Outaouais, as it was for Violet Lalonde (see Chapter 8). In her 1985 article "Mon frère Louis Riel," for instance, Marie-Joseph Riel describes the difficulty of living with the name Riel when one is Métis:

> I am called Marie-Joseph Riel, Marie Jo for those who are close to me.
>
> Riel for me was a character who lived in the history of Canada, first as a traitor then as a hero. He is also my brother, my father, my ancestor.
>
> He is someone who made me cry, someone I detested, then that I loved.
>
> To live one's childhood in a little village close to Ottawa in 1947 when one is called Riel, it is not a lot of fun most days. At school, when I was in the first grade, the oldest children, that is to say those who were in grades 3 and 4, treated me as a traitor, pushed me around and I did not know why. I would return home crying. I would have really wanted to be called something else at that moment. (Riel 1985, 3; our translation)

While remembering the political events surrounding the life of Louis Riel, Marie-Joseph formulates a definition of being Métis. She presents an identity both distinctive and collective when she rhetorically asks, "But those who carry the name Riel in reality and in our heart, we mixed-bloods, we Métis[,] will we remain at the bottom of the hole while there are things going on around us?" (5; our translation).

A similar attachment to Louis Riel vis-à-vis the Métis culture is also observed in an anonymous open letter to Riel written in 1985 and partially reproduced below. In all likelihood, the author is referring either to oral tradition concerning Marie-Louise Riel (see Chapter 8) or to Louis Riel's aunt Lucie, who lived in the Montréal region:

> Louis Riel, you were one of our sons, but your kin, it is us, your people. This year because of you, we are celebrating the centenary of a part of the history of a people, but a people is composed of great-great-grand-mothers, great-great-grandfathers, grandmothers, grandfathers, mothers, fathers, sisters,

brothers, sons, daughters, grandsons, granddaughters, cousins, uncles and aunts, neighbours. Why do you forget this on this historic day? ...

Louis Riel, you knew best one day to hide at your aunt's when you were an outlaw, you came back to your people, why do you forget it? ...

Speak to them of your people of Prince Edward Island, of Nova Scotia, of New Brunswick, of Ontario, of Québec, of Manitoba, of Saskatchewan, of Alberta, of British Columbia, of the Northwest Territories or of the Yukon, as your story Louis, denies us an existence as a distinct people. The Métis people, your people, it is all of us, the Métis from one ocean to the other.

In the name of the Métis people,

A member of the people to whom you belong (Anonymous 1985, 17, our translation)

The notion of Métis peoplehood is central in this text, which contains an inclusive affirmation that the Métis people extends from one ocean to the other. As we can see, as part of that continuum, Outaouais Métis identity can hardly be reduced to a racial construct artificially imposed by outside forces. It is shaped by cultural traditions and shared historical memories that define the community. Maniwaki Métis are not confused about their indigeneity. (See Andersen 2014 for such accusations.) Rather, Métis identity in the Outaouais region is based on a cohesive culture with a significant degree of historical continuity.

In addition to these personal testimonies, some newspaper articles articulate a Métis collective consciousness of a highly political nature. An open letter sent by the executive of L'Alliance to Federal Minister Otto Lang in 1979 recalls an intriguing moment in the history of the Métis in Québec. After elaborating their stance on a posthumous pardon for Louis Riel, the authors add the following declaration: "One hundred years ago, the spokespeople of the Métis in Québec asked for the clemency of Upper Canada in favour of Louis Riel, one of its courageous sons, proud of his Métis heritage" (L'Exécutif de L'Alliance 1979, 6; our translation). Barring a fortuitous discovery in the archives, this political intervention by the "spokespeople of the Métis of Québec" in 1885 remains impossible to prove, yet the mere mention of it is still symbolically significant in 1979.

In the same year, the same description of belonging to a Métis collectivity that is not limited to the borders of Québec is also expressed in an article announcing a joint annual general meeting of the Native Council of Canada and the Alliance laurentienne des Métis et Indiens sans statut in Manitoba:

> For many Québécois, this will be their first visit to the land which burnt into history the reality of the Métis nation in the history of this continent ... The Provisional Government of Riel of 1869–70 legitimately governed the vast territory of Rupert's Land, stretching from the Rockies and crossing Saskatchewan, Manitoba, the north of Ontario and Québec (including Val d'Or and all of Abitibi!). This immense region had been given by the King Charles II (without having seen it) to the adventurers and merchants that were named the Hudson's Bay Company. Many Métis are direct descendants of employees of this company who were sent here to trade with our ancestors ... The rights of these individuals are not taken seriously by a provincial administration who gave us Bill 101 and a cultural ethic and who governs illegitimately along the shores of the St. Lawrence ... Riel governed all these lands claimed in the name of the Aboriginal people and their descendants, those who peopled the interior of these frontiers. And he governed from Fort Garry situated some twenty miles from Bird's Hill Park where we will be meeting all as the Métis nation once again, from August 20 to 25, 1979, at Manitoba's Grand National Assembly. We WILL RELIVE the past! (*L'Alliance* 1979, 6; our translation)

This not only affirms a collective identification of the Métis Nation as tied to the political project of Louis Riel but also explains the origins of many Métis who were directly linked to former HBC employees and diverse Indigenous peoples – a fact to which our previous chapters unequivocally attest. The indicators noted by *L'Alliance* furthermore testify to an important political and social mobilization that occurred between 1970 and 1985 among the Métis of Québec, including the Métis of the Outaouais, who united to demand recognition of their Indigenous rights by the various levels of government. The various articles discussed above illustrate the participation of the Métis of Maniwaki in the political process; they were, for example, the first to join the Québécois organization of the Alliance laurentienne, and their participation in that organization and its successors seems to have been maintained over decades, as is evident in the archival documents.

### Métis Elders of the Gatineau Speak

The testimony of Elders from the vicinity of Maniwaki corroborates a host of details that we found in the archives.[2] Certain excerpts from these interviews drew our attention, as they directly touched upon the themes identified in our research and presented throughout this book. The Elders' memories of events tied to Maniwaki and the continuity of certain cultural practices relating to the Métis of this region are striking.

In the first excerpt, Paul-Émile Nault, a descendant of Élisabeth McPherson (File 13), indicates the presence of the Métis as a collective in the region of Maniwaki ("des Métis" or "some Métis") while emphasizing the predominance of the French-speaking Métis. His point is reminiscent of the writings of Father Bellefeuille in 1838, and of the Algonquin petition of 1874 denouncing the presence of the "Half French Breed" in the region of Maniwaki (see Chapter 10). Nault explains:

> My grandfather, his mother was a pure Indian. In those times there was a lot of that. That's the reason why there are many Métis, that it came to be like this, even on the reserve here ... In my opinion, I heard it said, that there were more Frenchmen who were in liaisons with Indian women than the English gang at Maniwaki, it seems. (CRCIM 2008c, our translation)

In the second interview, featuring Liliane Cyr, a descendant of Marie-Louise Riel (File 12), the term *Métis* is also used to refer to a collective whose exact number, she states, is not known. Cyr describes an existence that she associates with life in the forest and certain traditional practices and self-reliance based on hunting, fishing, and tanning. Her testimony recalls that of the surveyor John Snow on the hunting and fishing practices that characterized the way of life of the Métis of the region:

> Yes, a girl ... she did leather work. She lives all alone at Edja Lake. She lives on the land. There hunts a bit, fishes, I don't think she goes out to fish. She does leatherworking, woodworking, she does it all, she gets herself organized alone. She lives alone in this house there on the shores of the lake. Yes, she is Métis. There are others also, I don't know them all ...
>
> Here in Maniwaki, it is quite common that people will live all alone in the forest, the Métis. (CRCIM 2008e, our translation)

Laurier Riel, a descendant of the Riels of Lac-Sainte-Marie (File 11), similarly evokes the preponderance of activities such as hunting and fishing among the Métis of the Gatineau Valley. He also alludes to the proximity of Métis and Algonquin families, some with kin ties, as mentioned in previous chapters:

INTERVIEWER: Do the other members of your family identify themselves as being Métis?

RIEL: Yes, definitely. We have all been close to the Métis and the Indians, as our family always crossed with Indians and Métis. Being crossed like that, there are always those somewhere ... You see, my mother, she was the first cousin of the wife of the Grand Chief, of Mr. William Commanda who is ninety-five years old now. His wife was the first cousin of my mother. Thus, there are always some lines. I hunted, I trapped with Mr. Commanda. The trapline of Mr. Commanda was just next to that of my family. We had familial hunting grounds. In those days, the clans were divided by family. My family comes from Baskatong, Baskatong Island, that is now a lake, Baskatong Lake, which is the hydroelectric reservoir that flooded the reserve in fact. My grandparents had a trapline to the north of Lake Baskatong ...

INTERVIEWER: More personal, it is your grandfather and your great-uncle who familiarized you [with your Métis identity]?

RIEL: Yes, and for the men it was normal too, I would not have stayed at home and skinned the animals with the women. I am capable of doing it, but traditionally, it is the man who is the hunter and provider. It is the men who gave me their knowledge. That's usual. It has not changed. Do you understand my point of view on this? It is not because the women did not have anything to bring to us as well. Not because we are macho either. It was the specific role of men to do this. It is us who left the morning, who went up the mountain, two kilometres, there, and who set the snares for the hares. We brought it back to the house, and it is the women who skinned it. Then we gutted it, and then the women cooked it. The cycle was set up like that. It is us who got up at four in the morning, in the light of dawn, to go set the traps at the other end. We got used to it. It was fun.

(CRCIM 2008b; our translation)

In another interview, Norman Henrie, a descendant of Philomène McPherson (File 13) mentions the Métis family Knight,[3] who lived at Lac-Sainte-Marie. Henrie describes a way of life tied to furs and trapping, but he also mentions the practice of bootlegging. In so doing, his testimony echoes the charges levied by Indian agents Martin and Bensen against Half-breeds who were involved in contraband at the end of the nineteenth century (Chapter 6):

> HENRIE: Yes. I don't remember his name. We called him Ti-Vieux [little old man], Ti-Vieux ... Ti-Vieux Knight, but ...
>
> INTERVIEWER: From Lac-Sainte-Marie?
>
> HENRIE: Yes, yes! Yes! It was ... He did not have any children, he was not married. He was single. All his life. And he trapped. And ... He had ... my father, that interested him, I know that well. And he had shown my father how to prepare the furs, and how to set the traps, and all that.
>
> INTERVIEWER: That was in the years, maybe '30 [or] '40, or I don't know?
>
> HENRIE: No, no. In the years '50 [or] '60.
>
> INTERVIEWER: Okay, and this Mr. Knight, was he considered an Indian at Lac-Sainte-Marie or was he like you?
>
> HENRIE: He ... No, more than us.
>
> INTERVIEWER: Okay, ah yes?
>
> HENRIE: The Knights they were more ... They themselves were closer to the Indians. As the ... you see the mother ... the mother of Ti-Vieux Knight there, it was the generation of my father. Their mother, or at least their grandmother, was an Indian, her. It is her who was making moonshine there ... She was making ... booze for contraband. She was a widow I think and she had a gang of kids, and ... she made ends meet at the end of the month with that. They lived in the bush, them, on the other side of Lake Sainte-Marie. (SMC 2017; our translation)

Adding to these testimonies, Mario Carpentier, descended from Métis Moïse Ouellette of Manitoba, describes his own identity as he underlines the historical ties between the Métis of Manitoba and Maniwaki traced through his family. He also reveals the Algonquin heritage within his family, echoing Father Nédélec's description of "Algonquin Half-breeds" (Chapter 5). His account confirms one of the particularities of the oral tradition concerning Marie-Louise Riel, as it highlights the connections between Métis families at Maniwaki and those of the historical North-West, for example, the Beaulieus (File 2), Davids (File 5), Taylors (File 17), Pauls (File 15), and possibly the McDougalls (File 11):

As for the Métis identity, I always knew it. My Métis branches on my mother's side, they are Algonquin. It is all mixed. And there is a branch which goes up on the side of Moïse Ouellette, Manitoba. We even have the photo of Moïse Ouellette ...

I know as a Métis that in Manitoba they say, they aren't Métis [in Québec]. I even saw a reporting of a woman who said: *you can call them the way you want they are not Métis* [italicized English in original]. Well. There is here in Manitoba where there are Métis. Note that I have origins in Manitoba, Moïse Ouellette. I try to see the logic of what that person said. It was one of the leaders in Manitoba. They will call themselves whatever they want, in Québec, they are not Métis. What? *Halfbreed? What the fuck are you gonna call them?* [italicized English in original] How will we call ourselves if we are not Métis? (CRCIM 2008f; our translation)

In another interview, Benoît Guilbault, a descendant of Gabriel Guilbault, discusses the difficulties tied to Métis identity. His testimony illustrates the often pejorative connotation of the term *mixed-blood,* which he notes was used in the 1940s and often masked the Métis identity of families of the region. This racial discrimination is reminiscent of the uncomplimentary descriptions of Bois-Brûlés in the nineteenth century:

*Mixed-blood,* [italicized English in original] that was what they said to us in the years '40, '42, '43, when I was small, I was often told this. Oh, it is true nonetheless, but it is not nice to use it to hurt someone. Even, I heard my father say it. At the time, I did not understand it that way, I thought it was my mother who had jumped the fence. There are others who told me. Mixed-blood, they said it in French, in English, in both. Already, English was common here. Boots, overcoats, overshoes, it was all in English these terms. You spoke in French, but 50 per cent of the words were in English. We all lost that.

[When asked about the use of the terms *Métis* or *Michif*]: No, not that, but mixed-blood. When I was small, seven, eight years, ten years [old]. We did not know at all, at all, at all that time. I thought that I was not the child of my father. This is the first time that I speak of this. (CRCIM 2008d; our translation)

Finally, Serge Lafrenière, a descendant of Joseph David (File 5), testifies to the historical presence of two groups that he qualifies as Métis communities that were mistreated when the dams were built, among other times. This recognition recalls the historical importance not only of Lac-Sainte-Marie but also of Baskatong Lake, a later community that we have not explored in detail:

> But we had Métis communities that did not have limits, and we acted according to our order of goods, that is to say to acquire goods, but we lived in Métis communities nonetheless. And that ... that they succeeded ... in ridding us of that. Either in building dams or other things. You know there were no ... There were maybe some [communities] out there close to the rock cliffs. There wasn't maybe much at Lac-Sainte-Marie, where they are in the rocks over there. And there was one [community] ... at Baskatong. And both have ... a village, it was closed, and flooded hard. (CRCIM 2008a; our translation)

Running through the interviews is a series of themes about the Métis of the Gatineau Valley: ties to indigeneity (without Indian status); a lifestyle tied to Métis identity (living alone in the forest); connections between Métis families in the East (Québec) and West (Manitoba); ties to the Algonquins; hardships endured following the stigmatization of the Métis identity (or "mixed-bloods"); the presence of ancestral Métis practices (trapping, hunting, fishing, dressing of furs and hides); the presence of contraband alcohol in the oral history linked to the Métis; and, finally, memories of historical collectivities associated with the Métis (Lac-Sainte-Marie and Baskatong). While not exhaustive, these interview excerpts illustrate a significant degree of cultural continuity among the Métis of the Outaouais. They corroborate a living oral history tradition, augmenting and supporting the archival documents that we've analyzed and thus revealing the contours of a regional community in the Gatineau Valley.

### The Continuity of the Outaouais Métis

The documents and oral accounts presented in the final part of this book offer a detailed portrait of the cultural continuity evident among the Outaouais Métis, demonstrating that a community emerged and persisted in the Gatineau Valley from the mid-nineteenth century to at least the late twentieth century. Various documentary and literary sources from the forestry era indicate that the Outaouais Métis provided a specialized labour force to the ever-growing industry, while remaining distinct from the French Canadians and Indians with whom they often worked. They are identified as Métis or Half-breeds by outsiders. While some families were actively working in forestry, others continued to participate in the fur trade even as it waned, such as the St-Denis and Chaussé families. These traders, working alone or under contract with the HBC, pushed north up the Gatineau and Lièvre rivers as forestry was followed by agricultural settlement that expanded into the southern and middle zones of these river regions. In northern zones such as Michomis, it was still possible for some families to generate revenue in the fur trade.

Not only did families adapt to the new economic landscape but, in the second half of the nineteenth century, communities began to organize and advance their concerns. A case in point is the 1874 petition by signatories who represent a self-identified mixed community. This is not to say that all the petitioners were Métis or, to use the terminology of the Algonquin petition of the same year, Half French Breed and Half Scotch, but the use of the term *mixed* certainly suggests that the community was not simply divided into white and Indian. It had at least three different components, including the Métis. The petitions centred on the newly created Maniwaki Reserve: access to its resources (notably through renting lots), and the role of the Indian agent in managing the affairs of the reserve. In a petition by those who defined themselves as "pure Algonquins," the signatories do not see the Métis as part of their community, but they do not view them as Euro-Canadian whites, either. Some Algonquins wished to exclude Métis from the reserve and the political structure established by the Indian Act and enforced by various Indian agents.

The example of the Chaussé, Brosseau, and Vanasse Métis families, moreover, highlights the challenges of dealing with the Indian agent and the management of reserve affairs. Whether it was a question of claims on cabins and other capital that had come to be located on the reserve, or guardianship of orphaned children by their Métis kin, the lines had been drawn, and, as is evident in the historical record, a process was underway that kept most Métis out of the Maniwaki Reserve. The liminal Métis were further marginalized, excluded from both Indian society on reserves and the larger colonial society. When the Témiscamingue Reserve was established, Métis "from below" were actively excluded in spite of the efforts of Father Nédélec, who advocated in a four-year correspondence with Indian Affairs (1892–96) to have them incorporated into the reserve and given a political voice on the band council.

Having been refused inclusion, the Outaouais Métis were often labelled "squatters" as they sought some way to maintain their homes and traplines.

Decades later, in the 1960s and 1970s, they were still struggling. With the election of the Parti Québécois in 1976 on the crest of a promise to hold a referendum on the independence of Québec, talk of political and constitutional reform came to the fore. That led to the failed referendum of 1980 and eventually the Constitution Act of 1982, which saw the Métis officially included as one of Canada's Aboriginal peoples.

During this time of political upheaval, political mobilization was evident in the newspaper *L'Alliance*. In the 1970s and 1980s, the Métis in Québec organized and sought to have their rights recognized, which would allow them to pursue traditional activities. Recurring themes in *L'Alliance* articles of this period include Métis identity, the loss of the ancestral right to pursue subsistence activities, and the desire to obtain some form of title that would protect access to the land. As the community became increasingly organized, a number of articles also formulated an identity tied to Riel and a larger Métis community. The Outaouais Métis claimed Riel as their own, and positioned themselves as rightfully Métis even if the province of Québec denied the existence of any Métis on its territory. These concerns and themes also emerge in interviews with Métis Elders from the Gatineau Valley. The contours of the community appear again as they tell their stories, as well as their memories of the stigma associated with being Métis or mixed-blood.

# Conclusion
## Toward Recognition?

PAST AND PRESENT, THERE are numerous examples across the country of an evolution of Indigenous identities that led Métis families and individuals to adopt cultural expressions of their indigeneity, in the process challenging the myth that "Métis" and "Indian" identities must follow separate and unbroken historical trajectories to qualify as authentic. The lack of recognition that continues to beset the Métis of western Québec can be explained in part by the historical judicialization and ostracization of Métis identity. As explored in the first part of this text, Indian status as a legal category emerged as colonial authorities sought to lighten the load on the public treasury. The Bagot Report mentions this preoccupation explicitly and presents a solution that was already being considered in the 1840s: curtailing the distribution of presents to the Métis, including those in Lower Canada (which would become Québec). As part of the Bagot Commission's (1842–44) fact-finding endeavours, a detailed list of questions was sent out to Indian agents; the commission asked the Indian agents, among other things, how many Half-breeds were present in the community. Invariably, Indian agents in Lower Canada answered that almost all were Half-breeds, so the category had to be refined. As Ted Binnema (2014) notes, the challenge in Lower Canada was to sort out those who were truly "Indian" (insiders) from those who had Indian ancestry but were considered "outsiders." To this end, culture was operationalized to exclude the Métis or Half-breeds: having Indian ancestry was not sufficient; it was necessary to have a way of life deemed *sauvage*. Hence, the Bagot Commission recommended that presents not be paid to Half-breeds unless they lived as and among Indians. Indian agents were also required to draw up lists of those who qualified to receive presents and thus have a recognized Indian status. As our research demonstrates, this was not a straightforward process. It was often left to the discretion of the Indian agent, and, as the Algonquin petitioners of Maniwaki highlight, agents sometimes identified people who were not considered "pure Algonquins" by the Algonquins themselves.

The effects of the Bagot Commission were nonetheless significant. In the negotiation of the Robinson Treaties of 1850, the Métis were consciously excluded by representatives of the Crown. In Lower Canada, and later Québec, true members of Indian "bands," whether or not they had European ancestry, were distinguished from the Scottish and French Métis. The former were generally given Indian status later, under the Indian Act of 1876, while the latter were generally excluded both from status and from the reserves created for status Indians, as was the case of Maniwaki and Témiscamingue. Another lasting legacy of the Bagot Commission and efforts to sort the "pure" from the Half-breed was the stripping of status from women who married non-status men. Their children were also denied status. Not surprisingly, then, the Alliance laurentienne, the association that represented Métis and non-status Indians of Québec a century later, strove to establish criteria to distinguish Métis from non-status Indians, and to define both in relation to the administrative category of status Indians. This situation, we suggest, is the inevitable outcome of colonization and the judicialization of the Métis identity, under which still – to this day – courts are the final arbiters of who is included or excluded from legal recognition. This has often had terrible and lasting consequences for Métis plaintiffs and defendants.

The exclusion of the Métis was also a political process, leading to resistance in various forms. Before they were left out of the treaties negotiated by William Benjamin Robinson in 1850, the Métis mounted an armed resistance, seizing the Mica Bay copper mines with the full support of the Ojibwe chiefs. Their action followed a petition seeking redress from colonial officials, but these efforts eventually failed. The colonial officials then created mutually exclusive identitarian categories with no place for the Métis: they had to become either "Indians," if the Ojibwe wanted them, or "White," effectively stripping them of any Indigenous rights. It wasn't until the 2003 *Powley* decision, some 150 years after the Robinson treaties, that the Sault Ste. Marie Métis were finally recognized in their own right. *Powley* sent a shockwave across Canada to other Métis communities as a positive, public affirmation of their identity. In the Northwest Territories, a similar sorting of Métis from Indians occurred. Following armed resistance and the creation of the province of Manitoba, the Métis were granted scrip, with the express intent of extinguishing their Indigenous rights. As

Lieutenant Governor Alexander Morris stated, scrip made the Métis white, while treaties defined who Indians were. The Métis were thus enfranchised in the eyes of government officials through scrip, which could be exchanged for title to land and individual property. Sadly, however, many Métis ended up landless, pejoratively known as "road allowance people" because they were squatting on lands that had been set aside for future roads, and these were not given out as 160-acre homesteads to settlers (Campbell 2012).[1] The situation parallels what happened in Québec, where some Métis were forced to become "squatters," whether on their home lots or later on their traplines. The details vary but the Métis faced similar challenges across the continent and in various jurisdictions, nation-states, and provinces.

The acts of Métis defiance that have been recorded in history invariably involve armed resistance. The resistance of Louis Riel and the Métis of the Red River Colony against the encroaching surveyor led to the creation of Manitoba and its inclusion as a province in the new Canadian Confederation. Some guarantees were granted to the Métis in terms of land and language; the new province would be officially bilingual, with guaranteed French-language schools. In reality, Riel was exiled from his home province with a price on his head, and land granted in the form of scrip to families in financial difficulty too often enriched speculators, who bought the scrip for cash. Finally, the province ignored its language guarantees for more than a century, gradually abolishing the legal status of French and eliminating schooling in the French language. Six years after the creation of Manitoba, Canada enacted the Indian Act and surveyors pushed into Rupert's Land. The Indian Act specifically excluded the Métis from its provisions and effectively resolved the "Indian problem" by making status Indians wards of the state, under the supervision of Indian agents and the Department of Indian Affairs. The Canadian state then imposed regulations prohibiting cultural practices such as the potlatch on the West Coast, and established residential schools, which Chief Justice of the Supreme Court Beverley McLachlin has unequivocally called a "cultural genocide" (Lehmann 2015; Truth and Reconciliation Commission of Canada 2015).

With the creation of the Maniwaki Reserve in 1853, the logic of winnowing out Half-breeds continued; Métis families and women who were reputedly Indian but married to non-Indians – and therefore "enfranchised" and stripped of status – were removed from the reserve. Little by little, a cultural genocide occurred as Métis indigeneity, including in the

Outaouais region, was reduced to silence, crushed by government measures that were preoccupied with defining "true" indigeneity. Métis families were torn apart by this sorting out of "races," as some opted for an Indian identity when possible. Other families were pushed to live on the margins of the reserve, where they turned to a variety of activities, including petty trading and participating in the sale of contraband alcohol. Those who gained Indian status fell under the regulations of the Indian Act, and they, like all Indian families, became confined to reserves as their legal status was regulated by outside bureaucratic forces. Children were silenced as the government established a system of residential schools to assimilate and "civilize" them at great human, social, and cultural cost. Métis who were expelled from reserves and not granted status were exempt from some of the policies of the Indian Department, but they were forced into a liminality of identity, pressed to become white and gradually stripped of their right to engage in traditional activities such as trapping, fishing, and hunting as they competed with Euro-Canadians for permits.

Métis of western Québec nonetheless endure. With a distinctive way of life shaped by their status as cultural and social intermediaries, being the cultural fruit of unions between Indians and Europeans, they continued to express themselves, as is evident in the lives of Métis such as Paul and Marie-Louise Riel. Paul embraced his role of providing relief to the Atikamekw as they suffered from a smallpox epidemic, while Marie-Louise served as a midwife and healer to all, and hid Louis Riel in the Outaouais. These more mundane stories are not any less grand than the armed battles of the Métis bison hunters, in our opinion. Accounts in both archival records and oral histories reveal much about the historical Métis culture that has been dispersed over the four corners of North America, including in Québec. Historically, the Bois-Brûlés – that is the French or, perhaps more accurately, Canadien Métis – took root in two soils. A noted attachment to the French language and pride in Indigenous heritage and languages forged a Métis identity regardless of the degree of blood proximity, as Louis Riel emphasized in his 1885 writing. Expedition leader Frederick Ingall, HBC clerk John Lorn McDougall, and geologist William Logan also noted the persistence of these cultural traits and of Bois-Brûlés acting as cultural intermediaries. The squatter status attributed to Métis did not escape the attention of the surveyor Joseph Bouchette, who noted the presence of Bois-Brûlés near what is now Gatineau Park, on the outskirts of Canada's current capital city. Forester Alexander Shirreff described

La Passe, not far distant from Fort Coulonge, as a nest of Bois-Brûlés. Furthermore, in 1838 Father Bellefeuille described all the fur trade posts of the Outaouais region as inhabited by "Métif" descendants of Canadiens, Scots, and "Sauvages."

One of the main vectors for determining the cultural identity of the historical Métis, as we've seen, is language. Monseigneur Alexandre-Antonin Taché categorized Métis into two groups, either French Métis or English "Half breeds," explaining that the Canadien Métis also included descendants of the French-speaking and Catholic Iroquois who had moved west to work in the fur trade and married Indigenous women from other nations (David 1882, 72–73).[2] As the evidence has shown, these subgroups of Métis culture can also be found in the Outaouais region, with a noticeable presence of Scottish Métis in the Témiscamingue area and inter-marriages between these families. An aggregate of other cultural markers, including the presence of two ethnic heritages (one being Indigenous), characterize the formation of a historical Métis identity and are found in the Outaouais region. Archival documents and oral histories reveal a number of these markers, which together help to define a distinctive collective identity. The markers were in fact sufficiently noteworthy to have captured the attention of numerous observers over two centuries. Even the Algonquins of the Maniwaki Reserve complain of "Half French Breeds" in an 1874 petition, signalling that this Métis population ought not to be confounded with either the Indians or the whites. The Métis of the Outaouais are also noted for their trade activities, whether as freemen hunters, petty traders, or even contraband traders, a role played by the Métis across the continent and in various regions of Canada (see Giraud 1945; Macdougall 2010; St-Onge 2004). This preference for trading and traditional activities (trapping, hunting, and gathering) over farming is another marker that sets the Métis of the Outaouais apart from agricultural settlers.

A close examination of archival documentation reveals numerous familial and kin ties between Sault Ste. Marie in Ontario and the Gatineau Valley in Québec's Outaouais region. The two communities were described in similar terms in the nineteenth century, and the markers that defined Métis in the Outaouais were shared by Métis communities across the continent. Given that the fur trade and continental reach of the fur trade companies encouraged individuals and occasionally families to move from post to post, often from one side of the continent to the other, it should not be surprising that individuals had widely dispersed family members and friends. It was a rhizomatic network that united the Bois-Brûlés in a continental community with a set of ethnosymbolic touchpoints and cultural references in common (Foxcurran, Bouchard, and Malette 2016).

All these findings therefore raise a key question: why the silence in Québec about the existence of the Métis? One of the most powerful explanations is found in the correspondence of Father Nédélec, who tried in vain from 1892 to 1896 to have the Témiscamingue Reserve accept those he described as Algonquin Métis (Algonquin Half-breeds). In a string of correspondence between Nédélec, the Indian agent Angus McBride, and the Department of Indian Affairs, McBride consistently refused Nédélec's appeals, as sanctioned by his departmental superiors. McBride wanted only Métis from his core group to be admitted to the reserve, and they became status Indians by various stratagems. McBride's selective admittance was probably an attempt to seize the reserve from the political control of the "Algonquins." As some of these Algonquins were also of mixed ancestry, their rationale for describing themselves as "Indians" rather than "Half-breeds" should not be seen solely as biological. The distinction between Algonquins and Métis was not just a matter of mixedness but of political and cultural background, a fact exemplified by the proposition of Nédélec that Half-breeds "from below" have their own political representation on the reserve. In the end, neither the Indian agent nor Indian Affairs had any interest in accepting each and every Métis – with or without Algonquin roots – onto the reserve to form a distinct community. Ultimately, Indian Affairs hoped that the Half-breed population would disappear. Its policies called for the Métis of the East to make themselves either Indian or white, forcing them to adopt an identity that was never theirs. Evidently, with the passage of time, some Métis who were incorporated into reserves would become fully Algonquin, in the same way that in the North-West many Métis were incorporated into First Nations communities when treaties were signed and then relocated in turn to reserves (Ens and Sawchuk 2016). But even then, some individuals returned to a Métis identity, notably prior to 1985, when women had to leave the reserve following marriage to non-status Indians. This was the case with the Powley family in Sault Ste. Marie.

This work, with its many examples of Métis presence, has sought to counter the ongoing cultural genocide of the Outaouais Métis. We attempted this crucial task by providing nuanced analysis of complex historical realities based on archival findings, uncovering the will of government authorities who effectively blocked the formation of a Métis community in western Québec. In spite of the difficulties of such a project, the documentary sources shed light on the cultural continuity of the Outaouais Métis. Clues are found in references to the raftsmen and forest workers of the Outaouais, where the skills and knowledge of the Métis were valued and put to use in the growing forestry industry. Continuity was also apparent in 1969, when the Métis organized themselves politically in Maniwaki and surroundings. Moreover, it is evident in the recorded voices of the Métis, whether in print or in oral interviews, who see Louis Riel either as their spiritual and political leader or as a continuous source of inspiration. Continuity is also seen in the complaints of Métis trappers who see their traplines stripped by forestry, as they are denied ancestral rights and treated as squatters.

The continuity of the Outaouais Métis is unambiguous when we consider the sum of the evidence. Claims of a Métis presence in the Outaouais region cannot be simply brushed aside as unfounded gossip by Québécois cynically seeking either to assuage colonial guilt or to gain some pecuniary benefit. Rather, we suggest that the intersections of indigeneity and the identity of French speakers in Québec are perhaps more complex than is often acknowledged. To be clear, this is not to say that all Québécois should identify as Métis, or even that all who claim to be Métis could gain legal recognition, but neither does it mean that any and all French speakers in Québec who claim Métis heritage are automatically a tool of colonialism under some false pretense or mere opportunism. A nuanced historical analysis should not fall victim to an overtly aggressive analysis or an angelic reading of the historical record to document the "original innocence" of the Métis; that did not exist in either East or West, as some previous work illustrates (see Malette and Marcotte 2017).

At the dawn of the drive to constitutional reform, the Métis of the Outaouais region joined the larger pan-Canadian organization, the Native Council of Canada, under the leadership of Harry Daniels. Joining forces, community organizations that brought together Métis and non-status Indians emerged across Canada, including in the Outaouais. Following arduous negotiations spearheaded by Daniels, the Métis people were included in section 35 of the Constitution Act, 1982. Paradoxically, this victory ruptured the pan-Canadian political unity of the Métis movement with the emergence of the Métis National Council in 1983. The MNC represents the Métis in the West and defines the Métis people in strictly western terms. This organization still holds that the only true Métis are those who emerged from the armed resistance at Red River, and thus only they should benefit from the 1982 recognition of Métis. In this view, the descendants of this "true" Métis Nation are those who can trace their ancestry back to the Red River or to the confines of territory and communities accepted by the MNC. That currently excludes almost all of Ontario (including recently Sault Ste. Marie, after years of inclusion), the entirety of Québec (including the Outaouais region), and the Maritimes, as these areas fall outside the newly defined Métis Nation Homeland. Eastern Métis are still largely deprived of government recognition and the funding enjoyed by western Métis.[3]

This ideological stance, which has grown in popularity in certain academic circles since 1983, butts up against a major obstacle – namely, the archival record and the unpublished history of the Outaouais. Striving to avoid the tautology imposed by such nationalist narratives, our work has sought to tease out evidence of Métis ethnogenesis in the Outaouais region, an ethnogenesis connected to a continental rhizomatic cultural entity (see Foxcurran, Bouchard, and Malette 2016). We analyzed the archival documents to see what evidence there was of culture, and identity, in order to trace the meaning of *Bois-Brûlé, Métif,* and *Métis* in the region as part of a larger Métis "frontier" at the margins of colonial power (British North American and American) and attested to by nineteenth-century witnesses such as Alexis de Tocqueville and Valery Havard.

We sought to disrupt at least three different historical readings that we see as incomplete. Our first correction calls into question models of ethnogenesis that favour a village or atomic model of a nation, a position that has been embraced by some proponents of a Red River ethnogenesis of Métis nationhood. The documentary sources we reviewed reveal a much more fluid landscape, in which the Métis did not inhabit a sole village, valley, or even geographic zone (the prairies). Instead, they were located within a much larger network of trading forts and outposts, and individuals continually moved within this network, both regionally and continentally. For this reason, the Métis community of the Outaouais integrated individuals with origins tied to Sault Ste. Marie, the Red River region, and the Far North. What they shared was the predominant use of the French language as well as Indigenous languages, often Catholicism as "lived" religion, pride in Indigenous heritage, and a healthy dose of resistance against colonial authorities. On that note, it should be added that the political is not simply the outcome of national expressions and grand battles; sometimes it is quite local and parochial, expressed in smaller actions such as giving refuge to HBC deserters or challenging the HBC trading monopoly.

In other words, the Métis identity cannot be constrained by romantic concepts of a neatly homogeneous and tightly defined territorial entity – namely, the West exclusively. This identity cannot be contained in primordialist political imaginings whereby armed battles generate nations. That notion shoehorns the Métis Nation into a nineteenth-century model of nationhood as comprising a single people, speaking a single common language, occupying a single common territory with defined borders, having a shared psychological character, and striving for statehood. Rather, the documentary record analyzed here reveals an open-ended diaspora culture that is fluid and resistant; its participants worked in the fur trade economy but found other niches in the decades that followed, whether as raftsmen or as bootleggers. The Métis of the Outaouais shaped and lived a culture that they then passed on to successive generations, in spite of the stigma attached to being mixed-blood. They faced political, judicial, and sociological barriers in their path toward recognition. The Métis exist today, as yesterday, regardless of what governments, scholars, and ideologues may say, and their voices, though muted, still resonate.

Our second correction challenges the historiography that simply seeks to eradicate the terms *Bois-Brûlés* and *Métifs* from Québec's history. That approach ignores the documented history of individuals and communities identified as Bois-Brûlé or Métif in the Outaouais region. Even if the majority French-speaking population can make it challenging to discern the contours of a French-speaking Métis community in the province, it does not mean that such a community did not or does not exist. Researchers must diligently read the archival record to determine an accurate picture of what was, as opposed to what they expect should have been. Moreover, the fact that the Métis were capable of participating in the cultural universe of both Euro-Canadians and Indians does not mean that they were assimilated to either community.

As Louis Riel himself articulated, it is more accurate to conceptualize French-Canadian and Métis identities not as mutually exclusive but as at times overlapped: identities between which individuals can navigate, identities that can be reclaimed, and combinations thereof. Rather than reducing reality to a Manichean world view that opposes identities such as white versus Indian, or white versus Métis, or lastly Québécois versus Métis, it is necessary to analyze a cultural and historical landscape in which identities are ever shifting and evolving as living entities, in which individuals and communities can call upon elements of their ethnic and symbolic heritage to define and redefine themselves.

Finally, our third correction challenges the current understanding of the Indigenous peoples in Québec. Québec's historiography has largely erased even the possibility of a historical Métis population in Québec, and in doing so it has contributed to suffocating any discussion on this important subject. To correct this lack of recognition, we focused not solely on the archival documents of the nineteenth century but also on those dating to the 1960s. From an anthropological and historical standpoint, it became clear that there was and still is a Métis community in western Québec. The evidence indicates continuity between a contemporary Métis regional community in the Outaouais and a historical community of mixed heritage, described since at least the 1830s as Métis, mixed, Half-breed, Métif, and Bois-Brûlé. Were government authorities to recognize the Métis officially as one of the Indigenous peoples that currently exist in the province of Québec, it would thus be a significant gesture toward reconciliation. Algonquin Elder William Commanda had already traced a path to a better future for Québec when he co-wrote a letter that was published in 1973. He specifies that a bridgehead is necessary to bring the various ethnic groups of the province together, and more precisely that the Indian people and Métis people desire to stand shoulder to shoulder with the Québécois to build their foundations. His words still echo as he calls upon all – newcomers, white, anglophone, francophone, First Nations, Inuit, and Métis – to join forces and wits to ensure a healthier future for all (Commanda, Plourde, and Bourgeois 1973, 4).

# *Appendix*
## Principal Métis Families of the Gatineau

THESE FILES DOCUMENT THE large Métis families that inhabited the Gatineau Valley in the middle of the nineteenth century. The names of founding couples of the families appear in bold, as do those of their children, although the use of bold is limited to the first appearance of the individual's name within the file for that person's family. The names of individuals who are not known to have been Métis, or for whom no clear evidence of Métis origin has been found, are italicized. Thus the name of a non-Métis founder of a Métis line is shown in italic, and also in bold on first mention. The italicized names include spouses, family members, and individuals who were allied to Métis families. Further research may demonstrate that they were in fact Métis as well, or confirm that they were Euro-Canadian or Indian.

The files refer to the key families mentioned regularly throughout the text, but they do not represent an exhaustive inventory of all individuals and families in the Gatineau Valley that could be classified as Métis. Additional research would be necessary to provide a more complete list of the Métis population, both past and present. Because of the connections between Métis, Indian, and Euro-Canadian identities, certain individuals listed in this appendix – or even their descendants – probably experienced various identity trajectories. Similarly, as individuals migrated from one region to another in the nineteenth century, the Métis community of the Gatineau developed the diasporic nature that invariably defines such communities throughout North America.

At the end of each file is a summary of ties between families. These proposed links should be considered a sample of a potentially much larger network, and they reflect not only actual kinship (brother-in-law, cousins, and so forth) but also religious ties (godparents, witnesses at marriage ceremonies). The sample nonetheless permits us to observe ties between families as follows:

- Beads and McDougall
- Beaulieu and Vanasse
- David and St-Denis
- Foubert and McPherson
- Lacroix and Vanasse
- Lavallée with McPherson and Vanasse
- Lavigne with McPherson, Vallière, and McDougall
- McDougall with McPherson, Lavigne, Vallière, and Beads
- McPherson with Foubert, Lavigne, Vallière, Lavallée, and McDougall
- St-Denis with Vanasse and David
- Vanasse with Beaulieu, Lavallée, St-Denis, and Lacroix
- Vallière with McPherson, Lavigne, and McDougall.

## FILE 1: BEADS

The Beads family is represented in the Gatineau Valley solely by **James Beads**. He is Métis, originally from Moose Factory, James Bay, born circa 1810. In 1834, he is in the service of the HBC as a winterer at Moose Factory, where his family is well represented[1] and where at this time the missionary priest Father Dominique Du Ranquet mentions a Métis village (Du Ranquet [1843] 2000, 213). James Beads quits the HBC in 1836, leaving for Lower Canada.[2] According to the surveyor John Snow, he was one of the squatters at Lac-Sainte-Marie circa 1842.[3] Later, James Beads is once again employed by the HBC, this time at Lac des Sables.[4] He has no known children.

### *Ties between Families*

James Beads is godfather to a son of Henriette McDougall (**File 11**), where he is recorded under the name of Jacques Bills.[5]

## FILE 2: BEAULIEU

The founding couple of the Beaulieu family is **Ambroise Beaulieu** and **Marie Minoé8é/Godin**. Ambroise is Métis and in all likelihood from the Great Slave Lake region,[6] or at the very least from the "Indian Country" (Beaulieu 2013, 62–66).[7] Marie probably comes from Fort Coulonge or Lake of Two Mountains. She is the daughter of Joseph Godin,[8] who seems to be a clerk at Fort Coulonge at the beginning of the nineteenth century (McLean 1849, 67). Marie is said to be "Algonquine ou métive."[9] Ambroise Beaulieu and Marie Godin are married at Montebello in 1832 but live at

Lac des Sables for many years.[10] Ambroise is employed by various trading companies ( J. Stanfield, Day & McGillivray, HBC) at least from 1822 to 1831,[11] while Marie is the assigned seamstress at the J. Stanfield trading post at Lac des Sables in 1827–28.[12] Once he leaves the employ of the fur trade companies, Ambroise remains at Lac des Sables and produces, among other things, birchbark canoes for the HBC.[13] The couple's known children are **Marie Anne Beaulieu**, born circa 1828;[14] **Jean-Baptiste Beaulieu**, born in 1830;[15] **Ambroise Beaulieu Jr.**, born and baptized in 1833;[16] **André Antoine Beaulieu**, baptized in 1841;[17] **Angélique Beaulieu**, married to Moïse Lemery in 1854;[18] **Suzanne Beaulieu**, married to Pierre Filiatrault in 1858.[19]

### Ties between Families

A daughter of André Antoine Beaulieu and *Henriette Sawanakwatokwe* marries *Joseph Minens* (or *Okimawinensi?*).[20] They have a son named Jacques Minens, whose godfather is Jacques Chaussé (**File 19**).[21] Jacques Minens then marries a daughter of Élisabeth Vanasse (**File 19**).[22]

### FILE 3: BERNARD

The Bernard family was founded by **Jean-Baptiste Bernard** and *Élisabeth Shaw*. Jean-Baptiste is born circa 1793 in the Pays d'en Haut, either in the western region of the territory or north of Montréal, child of "Jean Baptiste Bernard et d'une Sauvagesse." He is brought to Sainte-Geneviève-de-Berthier by another voyageur, Pierre Mailloux, at the request of his father, who hoped to have his eleven-year-old "mitif" baptized (Smith and Dyck 2007, 97).[23] Bernard becomes a very respected HBC guide on a semi-continental scale. In 1831, he establishes a tavern in the vicinity of Fort Coulonge but continues to work for the HBC sporadically until at least 1847 (Watson 2010, 196). In the 1820s, he is a winterer for the HBC at Lac des Sables, where *Élisabeth* is evidently also present in 1829.[24] They have at least two children. **Catherine Bernard** is born circa 1818 and marries at La Passe in 1836.[25] Given her date of birth, she in all likelihood lives at the post of Lac des Sables in the 1820s with her parents. The second child, **a son**, dies as an adult at Fort Coulonge in 1843.[26] In the 1830s, Bernard is clearing land in the vicinity of Fort Coulonge (Smith and Dyck 2007, 97). As for *Élisabeth*, she could be the Métis daughter of NWC trader *Angus Shaw*, but her origins are unclear.

## FILE 4: BRAZEAU

This family is represented in the Gatineau Valley solely by **André Brazeau**, a wintering voyageur serving the HBC in the sector of Grand Lac in the 1840s.[27] He deserts the post of Cawassieamica in 1844, where it is learned that he probably fled in the direction of the Gatineau River.[28] A letter penned by Thomas Taylor and dated 1846 classes Brazeau among a group of "Halfbreeds & Indians" participating in free trade in the region.[29]

## FILE 5: DAVID

The David family is formed by **Joseph David** and *Rose Robert*, who marry at Buckingham in 1840.[30] The marriage certificate specifies that Joseph is Métis. He is the son of *Basile David* and Thérèse Dufault, a Métis woman from the North-West, probably the Red River region in Manitoba. When Joseph's sister, Madeleine David, files for scrip in 1875 in Manitoba she specifies her Métis origins.[31] After squatting on the Lièvre River since at least 1841, the family moves to the township of Cameron on the Gatineau River (Goudreau 2014b, 54). In 1881, the Canadian census appears to show three of the couple's children living within the same census division: **Alexandre David**, born circa 1849; **Benonie David**, born circa 1854; and **Basile David Jr.**, born circa 1863. Seven grandchildren are associated with these three men, as are their three wives.[32] It should be noted that the ages of Joseph and *Rose* as recorded by the census takers are evidently wrong, but Joseph's "Red River" origin is duly indicated. Father Joseph-Étienne Guinard's manuscript mentions the Herculean strength of Joseph David, as well as his remarkable ability in portaging canoes and his proverbial kindness toward the entire population of the Gatineau. Joseph leaves a parcel of land to the Baskatong Mission for the building of a church.[33]

### Ties between Families

Alexandre David is a witness at the marriage of Sévère St-Denis Jr. (**File 16**).[34]

## FILE 6: FOUBERT

**Joseph Foubert** is married to *Caroline Rocbrune* (or *Larocque*). He is the son of *Amable Foubert* and a "Sauvagesse inconnue."[35] Joseph is listed among the squatters on the Lièvre River circa 1842.[36] He is also mentioned as an independent fur trader in 1845 on the same river.[37] He then moves to the Gatineau circa 1881(Goudreau 2014b, 60–61). The known children of Joseph and *Caroline* are **Joseph Foubert Jr.**, **Amable Foubert Jr.**, **Alfred Foubert**, **Alexandre Foubert**, and **Isidor Foubert**, born respectively circa 1850, 1853, 1857, 1859, and 1860.[38]

### Ties between Families

The father of Joseph Foubert, *Amable Foubert,* is perhaps the free trapper frequently mentioned in connection with the Lièvre River in the 1830s.[39] If this is not the same man, he is certainly a close family member of the trapper. A *Marie Foubert* who is listed as godmother to one of the daughters of Philomène McPherson (**File 13**)[40] is likely to be a relative of Joseph Foubert.

## FILE 7: JUSSIAUME

**Joseph Jussiaume** (or Dussiaume) marries *Anastasie Ozawikijikokwe*[41] and/or *Marie Josephte Kotcane.*[42] Joseph is the son of voyageur *Joseph Jussiaume Sr.* and Marguerite Alexandre,[43] who is described on her 1812 marriage certificate as a "Mitive nouvellement descendue des pays d'en haut": a Mitive (an older term to designate a Métis woman) newly arrived from the upper country.[44] At her baptism the previous day, she is noted as having been born at Sault Ste. Marie.[45] The younger Joseph Jussiaume works for the HBC at Lac des Sables from 1829 to 1835, perhaps with some interruptions, and then from 1836 to 1838. He is a seasonal voyageur in the same sector in 1840,[46] and is counted among the squatters to the north of Lac des Sables in 1843.[47] The known children of the couple are **Pierre Dussiaume**, baptized at five years old in 1841 at Mitcikanabikong, east of Grand Lac;[48] and **two children** baptized in 1840 and 1842 at Oka (Goudreau 2014b, 56).

## FILE 8: LACROIX

The Lacroix family began with *André Lacroix* and the "Indian" *Véronique Mactini* (or *Tcipadjiwanokwe*).[49] *André,* after working for the petty trader J. Stanfield, is hired by the HBC at Lac des Sables.[50] He and *Véronique* have the following children: **William Lacroix**, baptized in 1835;[51] **Louis Lacroix**, baptized in 1837;[52] **Sophie Lacroix**, baptized in 1839;[53] **Marie Angélique Lacroix**, baptized in 1841 at Lac des Sables;[54] **Marguerite Lacroix**, married in Maniwaki in 1857.[55] *André* himself describes his daughter Sophie as a "half breed."[56]

### Ties between Families

Marie Angélique Lacroix marries Eustache Augustin Vanasse (**File 19**).[57] Louis Vanasse and Pierre Chaussé Sr. (**File 19**) are witnesses at the marriage of Marguerite Lacroix.[58] Marguerite's daughter marries a son of Julie Vanasse (**File 19**).[59] Élisabeth Boutin,[60] a granddaughter of the *Lacroix/ Mactini* couple, marries Pierre Robillard (**File 19**), a grandson of the *Vanasse/*Forcier couple. Another granddaughter of the *Lacroix/Mactini* couple, Marie Lacroix, marries another grandson of the *Vanasse/*Forcier couple, Pierre Chaussé Jr. (**File 19**).[61]

## FILE 9: LAVALLÉE

The Lavallée family originates with *Joseph Lavallée* and *Marie Angélique Masanakomikokwe.*[62] *Joseph* is an HBC voyageur serving largely in the Grand Lac sector and its outposts from 1827 and 1843, working as a labourer and canoe steersman as well as a guide.[63] It is possible to follow this family from their departure from the fur trade post to their establishment at Lac-Sainte-Marie. A rumour circulated that Joseph was attempting to undertake free trade.[64] A number of children are born from this union: **Louise Lavallée**, born circa 1830 at either the Lac à la Truite post or that of Grand Lac and baptized at the latter in 1838;[65] **Angélique Lavallée**, born circa 1832, and **Marguerite Lavallée**, born 1838, both baptized at Grand Lac;[66] and **Julienne Lavallée**, born in 1841 and baptized the same year at the Mitcikanabikong mission, between Grand Lac and Lac à la Truite (Marcotte 2014, 65).[67]

### Ties between Families

*Joseph Lavallée* is godfather to a daughter of Louise Forcier and *François Vanasse* (**File 19**).[68] *François Naud* (**File 13**) witnesses the marriage of *Joseph Lavallée.*[69]

## FILE 10: LAVIGNE

The founding couple of the Lavigne family is not known, although two adult family members are found in the Gatineau Valley in the mid-nineteenth century: Jacques and Marie-Josephte.

**Jacques Lavigne** is in a union with **Cécile McDougall** (**File 11**).[70] Jacques lives in the parish of Hull in 1825, working as a voyageur trader for Day & Murdoch in the Outaouais.[71] We then find him as a squatter at Lac-Sainte-Marie, at least from 1842 to 1848.[72] He dies in 1864 at Sainte-Anne du Grand-Calumet, close to Fort Coulonge (Goudreau 2014a, 288).[73] As he spends his final years at Île-du-Grand-Calumet, we can assume that Jacques is the brother or close relative of Marie Lavigne, wife of the former voyageur *Louis Brizard,* who also lived at this location (Du Ranquet [1843] 2000, 102).[74] Marie Lavigne is described by a missionary as an "algonquine mais [qui] vit à la canadienne," an Algonquin living as a French Canadian (105). The French first and last names of Marie and Jacques Lavigne – and this before the missionary push, at least as concerns Jacques – along with his employment as a voyageur winterer in the fur trade suggest that they are likely to have been from a Métis family. The known children of the Lavigne/McDougall couple are **François Lavigne**, born circa 1827 (Goudreau 2014a, 288); Marie-Josephte Lavigne (see below); **Madeleine Lavigne**, born in 1842;[75] and **Joseph Lavigne**, born in 1844.[76]

**Marie-Josephte Lavigne** is present at Lac-Sainte-Marie in the 1840s, as are her parents. She is married to *Norbert Beaudoin* in 1848 at that location.[77]

### Ties between Families

Jacques Lavigne is godfather to the daughter of Marie-Josephte McDougall (**File 11**).[78] His daughter and son, Madeleine Lavigne and Joseph Lavigne, have *Émilien Riel* and Henriette McDougall (**File 11**) of Lac-Sainte-Marie as their godfather and godmother.[79] Marie-Josephte Lavigne is the half-sister of Marie Vallière (**File 18**). She is also the godmother of Basile McDougall and Marie-Josephte McDougall, the son and daughter of Amable McDougall (**File 11**).[80] Marie-Josephte Lavigne has as potential uncles and aunts all the adult McDougalls mentioned in **File 11** (the exception being of course her mother, Cécile McDougall). One of the sons of Marie-Josephte Lavigne has as godfather *Louis Fournier* (**File 13**).[81]

### FILE 11: McDOUGALL

The original McDougall couple is not known, and the family origins are quite complex in terms of both geography and ethnicity. Some documents allude to the Red River region as the original home of this family. As the Métis heritage of Amable McDougall is confirmed by a surveyor (Russell) and an adventurer (Haddock) – and as his brother Ignace (Angus) McDougall is active in the fur trade at the same period and in the same locales[82] – it is likely that the other adult McDougalls in the same hamlet of Lac-Sainte-Marie are also Métis, probably brothers and sisters or at least very close relatives. We enumerate seven adults sharing the McDougall family name at this location: Amable, Ignace, Joseph, Henriette, Marie-Josephte, Marie-Anne, and Cécile.

**Amable McDougall**, also known as Amable Christineau (or Kapimioe-wittang), is born circa 1812. The HBC identifies his birthplace as Kingston.[83] Amable has a union with *Marguerite Kwekidjiwanokwe*.[84] He is a wintering voyageur for the HBC at Lac des Sables from 1832 to 1838;[85] a canoeman for forestry companies in 1838;[86] and an independent trader (possibly with his brother Ignace) in 1841.[87] He lives at Lac-Sainte-Marie at least from 1842 to 1848.[88] We find him as a contraband trader in the vicinity of Lac à la Truite in 1844–45.[89] He is a hunter and free trader in 1853 in the Grand Lac sector.[90] He dies in 1873 at Maniwaki.[91] Amable and *Marguerite* have at least three children: **Marguerite McDougall**, born in 1842;[92] **Basile McDougall**, born in 1845;[93] and **Marie-Josephte McDougall**, who is born in 1847[94] and should not be confused with the woman of the same name mentioned below in this file. The latter is likely to be her aunt or a close relative.

**Ignace** (or **Angus**) **McDougall** is also occasionally named Christineau, or Perillard or Saiâkanwêgomote. He is born in 1809 or 1811, and the HBC gives his birthplace as Kingston.[95] HBC correspondence identifies him as the brother of Amable McDougall.[96] Ignace enters into a union with *Anne Outastedjouan*, or *Makademikokwe* or *Makkatemikokwe*, of the Têtes-de-Boule (Atikamekw) Nation.[97] He is a wintering voyageur for the HBC at Lac des Sables from 1832 to 1838;[98] a canoeman for forestry companies in 1838;[99] and an independent trader, probably with Amable, in 1841.[100] Two of his children are baptized at Lac-Sainte-Marie.[101] Ignace's marriage certificate mentions that he is the son of voyageur *Joseph Perillard* and *Marie Catherine Tetipapakokwe*,[102] providing a clue about the Métis origins of the McDougall family. Two other sources mention Kingston and the Red River, respectively, as the original homeland of the two McDougall brothers,[103] but the reference to Ignace's father is difficult to reconcile with this because *Joseph Perillard* worked on the Lièvre River from 1808 to 1811 for the NWC, probably at the Lac des Sables post.[104] It is possible, however, that Kingston and/or the Red River region were where *Perillard* lived at the start of the nineteenth century. If *Perillard* is, as seems likely, father of all the McDougalls, his life would explain not only their knowledge of the territory of the Lièvre and Gatineau valleys but also an origin in Red River. Ignace's marriage certificate, which is found in the Catholic registry at Oka, also indicates that he is known as "Kristino" *(dit Kristino),* making it possible to identify him conclusively as the Angus McDougall noted in HBC registries as being also known as Christineau. The known children of Ignace and *Anne* are **Pierre McDougall**, born circa 1837;[105] **Marie McDougall**, born in 1838;[106] **Jean-Baptiste McDougall**, born in 1841;[107] and **Paul McDougall**, born in 1843.[108]

**Joseph McDougall** is mentioned as a witness for the marriage of *Joseph Fournier* and Marie Vallière (**File 18**) at Lac-Sainte-Marie in 1844.[109] As this is the sole mention of Joseph, it is possible that he is in fact either Amable or Ignace.

**Henriette McDougall** is born around 1819 in Upper Canada, according to the 1861 census.[110] She marries *Émilien Riel* in 1838 in Ottawa,[111] and the couple establish themselves at Lac-Sainte-Marie circa 1845[112] or possibly 1841.[113] Thereafter, they are found close to Maniwaki.[114] She is described as Indian by the census taker in 1861.[115] The known children of the *Riel*/McDougall couple are **Thomas Riel**, born circa 1840;[116] **Joseph Riel**, born circa 1841;[117] **Maxime-Émilien Riel**, born in 1842;[118] **Pierre-Romuald Riel**, born in 1844;[119] **Marie Riel**, born circa 1847;[120] **Paul Riel**, born circa 1849;[121] **Véronique Riel**, born circa 1857;[122] **Gilbert Riel**, born circa 1859;[123] and **Henriette Riel**, born circa 1860.[124]

**Marie-Josephte McDougall** marries *Pierre Kitchikanaguoët*.[125] Though appearing only once, in the 1845 Catholic registry at Lac-Sainte-Marie for the baptism of their daughter, this couple seems to have stayed in the region long enough for the father to have been qualified as a "cultivateur du lac S^te Marie."[126] Their only known child is **Cécile Kitchikanaguoët**, born in 1844.[127]

**Marie-Anne McDougall** marries *Antoine Tomosko*.[128] Their only known child, **Ignace Tomosko**, is born in 1844[129] and baptized in 1845.

**Cécile McDougall** is in a union with *François Vallière* (**File 18**), and then with **Jacques Lavigne** (**File 10**).

### Ties between Families

The godmother of two of the children of Amable McDougall is Marie-Josephte Lavigne (**File 10**).[130] Among the witnesses of the burial of Ignace

McDougall, at Maniwaki in 1858, are his brother-in-law *Émilien Riel* and his nephew by marriage *Joseph Fournier* (**File 18**), both former residents of Lac-Sainte-Marie.[131] Joseph McDougall is mentioned as a witness at the marriage of *Joseph Fournier* and Marie Vallière (**File 18**).[132] Henriette McDougall is the godmother of a daughter of Élisabeth McPherson and *François Naud* (**File 13**),[133] of two children of Jacques Lavigne (**File 10**),[134] and of a daughter of Marie Vallière (**File 18**).[135] Cécile Kitchikanaguoët's godfather is Jacques Lavigne (**File 10**).[136] Ignace Tomosko's godmother is Marie Vallière (**File 18**).[137] One of the sons of Henriette McDougall has as his godfather James Beads (**File 1**), who is listed as Jacques Bills.[138]

## FILE 12: McGREGOR

The McGregor family was founded by *Robert McGregor* and **Marie-Louise Riel**, also known by the name **Chipakijikokwe**.[139] Marie-Louise is described as a Métis woman in a document relating to the family's oral tradition,[140] as well as in a newspaper article published shortly after her death (La Patrie 1904, 7). The couple arrive in Lower Canada in the 1820s from Sault Ste. Marie or perhaps somewhere farther northwest (La Patrie 1904, 7).[141] In 1827, the couple has a child at Lac des Sables,[142] suggesting that they must have been in this sector often. The *McGregor*/Riel couple have the following children: **Marie-Louise McGregor**, baptized in Sault Ste. Marie;[143] **Marie-Anne McGregor**, baptized in 1825;[144] **Marie-Madeleine McGregor**, born at Lac des Sables and baptized in 1827;[145] **Richard Robert McGregor**, baptized in 1829;[146] **Élisabeth McGregor** and **Charlotte Marguerite McGregor**, both baptized in 1835;[147] **François Toussaint McGregor**, baptized in 1838;[148] **Philomène McGregor**, baptized in 1840;[149] **Léocadie McGregor**, baptized in 1842;[150] and **Julia McGregor**, baptized in 1844.[151] The McGregor family is discussed in detail in Chapter 8, and is also well represented among the citizens of the Métis Nation of Ontario.

### Ties between Families

Marie-Louise Riel seems to have a kin tie to Louis Riel though its precise nature is somewhat vague.

## FILE 13: McPHERSON

The McPherson family was founded by an HBC clerk of Grand Lac, *Andrew McPherson,* and an Indian woman named *Ikwesens* or *Marie Pinesi-okijikokwe*.[152] At least three of their children are to be found in the

Gatineau Valley thereafter: Élisabeth, George, and Philomène. This Métis family is also well represented among the citizens of the Métis Nation of Ontario.

**Élisabeth McPherson** enters into a union with retired HBC guide *François Naud* in 1838,[153] who is mentioned among the squatters of Lac-Sainte-Marie by surveyor Snow in 1848. Father Bellefeuille, in his 1838 journal, describes Élisabeth as a "métisse."[154] After a stay in Montréal, where their union is recognized in marriage, Élisabeth and *François* establish themselves at Lac-Sainte-Marie in the company of other retired voyageurs, with the goal of cultivating some land and being free traders.[155] This branch gives rise to the Métis Naud family. The couple has at least fourteen children: **Marie Marguerite Naud**, born circa 1833 at Grand Lac; **François Xavier Naud**, born circa 1836 at Grand Lac; **Marie Célina**, born in 1838 at Témiscamingue while the family is travelling;[156] **Brigitte Naud**, born circa 1839;[157] **Sophie Naud**, born in 1841;[158] **Marie Naud**, baptized in 1843;[159] **Joseph Naud**, born circa 1846;[160] **André Naud**, born in 1848;[161] **Baptiste Naud**, born circa 1852;[162] **George Naud**, born circa 1855;[163] **Daniel Naud**, born circa 1857;[164] **Isaïe Naud**, born circa 1859;[165] **François Naud Jr.**, born circa 1859[166] and **Alexandre Naud**, born circa 1860.[167]

**George McPherson** enters a union with **Isabella Okwikimighiwa**, a Métis woman born circa 1810 (Lefebvre 2006, 22), in all likelihood after having left Lac-Sainte-Marie. George begins his career in the fur trade around 1830. At the end of autumn 1830, he is dispatched by the HBC with two other men to the post of Migiskan, in Abitibi, to trade.[168] In June 1837, George McPherson is still at Grand Lac, where he is making purchases.[169] A McPherson is then mentioned as belonging to a group of retired voyageurs who founded the settlement of Lac-Sainte-Marie in 1838.[170] This can be assumed to be George or one of his brothers. After that, he works at the posts of Albany (James Bay), Osnaburgh, and Rat Portage, and is found at the last of these in 1871. He lives in the Red River settlement between 1856 and 1858 (Lefebvre 2006, 22).

**Philomène McPherson** is probably born at the post of Grand Lac, circa 1825. She is baptized in Buckingham in 1840,[171] and the following year marries the voyageur *Louis Fournier* at Lac-Sainte-Marie. *Louis* is found serving the HBC at the post of Rivière Désert (Maniwaki) from 1835 to 1837,[172] then at Lac des Sables from 1837 to 1839,[173] when he leaves on a free trade expedition in the direction of Grand Lac and Lac à la Truite.[174] The McPherson/*Fournier* family is living in the same township in 1861 and 1871 (Goudreau 2014a, 287).[175] The known children of Philomène and *Louis* are **Philomène Fournier**, born in 1842;[176] **Louis Fournier**, born in 1843;[177] **Élisabeth Fournier**, born in 1844;[178] **Hilaire Fournier**, born in 1848;[179] **Margaret Fournier**, born circa 1851; **Joseph Fournier**, born circa 1853;[180] **Vincent Fournier**, born circa 1855;[181] **Charles Fournier**, born circa 1859;[182] **Elzéar Fournier**, born circa 1861; **Jeanne Fournier**, born circa 1863; **Gilbert Fournier**, born circa 1865; **Théophile Fournier**, born circa 1866; and **Julienne Fournier**, born circa 1869.[183]

### Ties between Families

*François Naud* is the godfather of a daughter of Henriette McDougall (**File 11**),[184] and his daughter Sophie Naud has Henriette as her godmother.[185] *François Naud* is also a witness at the marriage of *Joseph Lavallée* (**File 9**),[186] the marriage of Marie-Josephte Lavigne (**File 10**),[187] and the marriage of Amable McDougall (**File 11**).[188] Philomène McPherson and *Louis Fournier* have Marie Vallière (**File 18**) as their sister-in-law. One of their daughters has as her godmother *Marie Foubert*,[189] who is likely to be related to Joseph Foubert (**File 6**).

### FILE 14: PAQUETTE

This family comprises the voyageur *Joseph Paquette* (originally from Sainte-Geneviève-de-Berthier) and an **Indian or Métis woman** whose name is unknown. This family had at least one child in 1828. *Joseph Paquette* was then employed by the HBC at Lac des Sables,[190] and by the independent trader J. Stanfield before deserting his service.[191]

### FILE 15: PAUL

This family is represented in the Gatineau by **Pierre Paul** and *Marie Antoinette Richer*. Pierre Paul is born circa 1794 in the North-West. He is baptized at the age of six at Sorel under the first name Joseph, as the natural child of Joseph Hus Paul and a "Sauvagesse de Nation Siouse."[192] As an adult, Pierre becomes a voyageur like his father, who was known as the strongest man in the North-West. In 1819, father and son are captured to the north of Lake Winnipeg by HBC men during the conflict raging between the HBC and the NWC (Morice 1908, 222–23). Returning to Lower Canada, Pierre marries *Marie* at Saint-Ours in 1820. The marriage certificate specifies that he is a "voyageur dans les pays hauts."[193] Later, the Paul family installs itself between Maniwaki and Lac-Sainte-Marie.[194] A long-time employee of the fur trade companies, Pierre Paul works for the HBC on the Lièvre in 1841.[195] The censuses of 1861 and 1871 affirm his birthplace as somewhere in the territories of "Hudson's Bay."[196] In 1861, he lives in proximity to the Métis Joseph David (**File 5**). In 1871, his son **Léon Paul** lives next to him, along with his wife and their seven children. Previously, Léon was a "cultivateur de St. Marie de la Rivière Gatineau" and thus one of the Métis squatters of Lac-Sainte-Marie.[197]

### FILE 16: ST-DENIS

The St-Denis family is founded by *Sévère St-Denis* and **Élisabeth Frances McDonell**. Élisabeth is the daughter of fur trader *John McDonell* and an Indian woman named *Mackuteikwe*.[198] The exact origins of Élisabeth and her family are unclear. John McDonell apparently died before 1844, and his name does not match that of any traders known in western Québec. It is also possible that the name is an error on the part of the priest who recorded it. Élisabeth (either the wife of *Sévère St-Denis* or possibly a child of his by another woman) appears to have been boarding temporarily at the post of Lac des Sables in 1842 or 1843.[199] She and *Sévère* marry at Lake Abitibi in 1844,[200] while the family is undertaking a voyage for the HBC (Marcotte 2017, 379–84). The St-Denis family occasionally accompanies *Sévère* on his trading trips, as attested by his marriage certificate and by the baptism of his daughter Lucie at Abitibi in 1847. At the time of her baptism, *Sévère* is stationed at Grand Lac, in the district of Témiscamingue, and he is therefore likely to have brought the family with him to Abitibi on his way to deliver furs to James Bay.[201] In 1848, the family buys a small farm at Rivière Désert, where it is suspected of conducting clandestine trade.[202] The St-Denis family still seems to be present in the Maniwaki sector in 1862, where Sévère father or son is the object of a complaint lodged by the Algonquin concerning his sale of alcohol (Sabourin 2010, 110). The known children of the *St-Denis*/McDonell couple are **Lucie St-Denis**, born in 1846;[203] **Antoine St-Denis** and **Marie Flora St-Denis**, twins born in 1849;[204] **Sévère St-Denis Jr.**, married in Maniwaki in 1879;[205] and **Jean St-Denis**, born in 1851.[206]

### *Ties between Families*

The godmother of Lucie St-Denis is the Métis Betsy Flora Polson of the Abitibi post.[207] Marie Flora St-Denis is the godmother of one of the daughters of Julie Vanasse (**File 19**).[208] Alexandre David (**File 5**) is a witness at the marriage of Sévère St-Denis Jr.[209]

## FILE 17: TAYLOR

This family is founded by **Thomas Taylor** and **Mary Keith**. Thomas is described by HBC Governor George Simpson as a "half breed" (Williams 1975, 233.). He is originally from Rupert's Land, probably the northern coastal post of Severn.[210] Mary's father is James Keith of the HBC and her mother is the Métis daughter of Jean-Baptiste Cadotte of Sault Ste. Marie (Goldring 1985). Thomas and Mary marry in the Red River Colony in 1831.[211] Thomas is posted as an HBC clerk at Lac des Sables from 1843 to 1849, then elsewhere in the Outaouais until 1855.[212] The couple has the following children: **James Taylor** and **Thomas Taylor**, baptized in 1833; **George Taylor**, born in 1838; **William Taylor**; **Florence Taylor**, died in 1882; **John Swanston Taylor**, born in 1839 and died in 1841; **Albert Taylor**, died in 1844;[213] and **Rose Taylor**, married to the freeman Moyse Lavallée (Marcotte 2017, 247; Martineau 1991, 40). This family is also well represented among the citizens of the Métis Nation of Ontario.

## FILE 18: VALLIÈRE

The Vallière family is formed by *François Vallière,* a former HBC wintering voyageur in the Lake of Two Mountains district at the start of the 1820s,[214] and **Cécile McDougall** (**File 11**).[215] Even though Cécile has a child with another man (Jacques Lavigne, **File 10**), we know that *François Vallière* is also living at Lac-Sainte-Marie in the 1840s.[216] We know of at least one child of this couple, Marie Vallière, before her mother enters into a union with Lavigne.

**Marie Vallière** enters into a union with *Joseph Fournier,*[217] one of the squatters at Lac-Sainte-Marie.[218] He may have participated in free trade activities led by his brother *Louis Fournier* at the end of the 1830s,[219] as both would have been living at Lac-Sainte-Marie at the time. Marie Vallière is at Lac-Sainte-Marie at least between 1844 and 1848. She and *Joseph* marry there in 1844[220] and have at least two children: **Marie Fournier**, born in 1845;[221] and **François Fournier**, born in 1848.[222] Marie Vallière dies before 1870 (Goudreau 2014a, 289).

### Ties between Families

Marie Vallière is the half-sister of Marie-Josephte Lavigne (**File 10**). She is also the godmother of a son of *Émilien Riel* and Henriette McDougall (**File 11**),[223] and of the son of *Antoine Tomosko* and Marie-Anne McDougall (**File 11**).[224] Marie Vallière is also the sister-in-law of Philomène McPherson

(**File 13**). Finally, she has as potential uncles and aunts all the adult McDougalls mentioned in **File 11** (excluding, of course, her mother, Cécile McDougall). Marie Fournier's godmother is Henriette McDougall (**File 11**).[225] *François Vallière* is godfather to a son of Amable McDougall.[226]

## FILE 19: VANASSE

The Vanasse family can be traced back to *François Vanasse* and **Louise Forcier**, who marry at Maskinongé in 1834.[227] Louise Forcier is Métis, as baptized on the day of her marriage, born of an unknown mother and with a father living in the Pays d'en Haut. The Métis heritage of Louise is later confirmed when her grandson, Pierre Chaussé Jr., is described as a Half-breed by an Indian agent. The only Métis link he has is via his grandmother Louise Forcier. As for *François Vanasse,* the fact that he is associated with the squatters of Lac-Sainte-Marie, the majority of whom had ties to the fur trade, permits us to identify him as one of the seasonal voyageurs employed by the HBC and sent westward, at least for 1837 and 1838.[228] The known children of *François* and Louise are **Julie Vanasse**, who is married to wintering HBC employee *Pierre Chaussé Sr.;*[229] **Eustache Augustin Vanasse;**[230] **Marie-Agnès Vanasse**, married to *François Brouillard;*[231] **Olive Vanasse**, baptized at Lac-Sainte-Marie in 1848;[232] **Louis Vanasse;**[233] **France Vanasse**, married to *Marie Rivard;*[234] **Élisabeth Vanasse**, baptized at Maniwaki;[235] and **Madeleine Vanasse**, baptized at Maniwaki.[236]

### *Ties between Families*

Eustache Augustin Vanasse marries Marie Angélique Lacroix in 1855 (**File 8**).[237] A grandson of the *Vanasse/*Forcier couple (Pierre Robillard) marries a granddaughter of the *Lacroix/Mactini* couple, Élisabeth Boutin (**File 8**).[238] Another *Vanasse/*Forcier grandson, Pierre Chaussé Jr., marries another *Lacroix/Mactini* granddaughter, Marie Lacroix (**File 8**).[239] A *Vanasse/*Forcier great-grandson, Philippe Chaussé, marries Sara Deschesnes, a Métis granddaughter of HBC voyageur Jérôme Godchère, all of whom are described as from Michomis (Marcotte 2017, 182).[240] A daughter of André Antoine Beaulieu and *Henriette Sawanakwatokwe* marries *Joseph Minens* (or *Okimawinensi?*).[241] They have a son named Jacques Minens, whose godfather is Jacques Chaussé.[242] Jacques Minens marries a daughter of Élisabeth Vanasse.[243] *Joseph Lavallée* (**File 9**) is the godfather of one of the daughters of Louise Forcier and *François Vanasse.*[244] Marie Flora St-Denis (**File 16**) is the godmother of a daughter of Julie Vanasse.[245]

# Notes

### Introduction

1 This work follows the precedent set by Gélinas (2011) and Dawson (2011) in that it neither affirms nor denies the existence of a juridical Métis community in line with section 35 of the Constitution Act, 1982, as this question is currently before the courts. Rather, this is a work solely of anthropological and historical scholarship in conformity with the expectations of an academic and evidence-based publication.

### Chapter 1: Studying Métis Identities

1 *R. v. Powley*, [2003] 2 S.C.R. 207, 2003 SCC 43.

2 To HBC officers, "Indian Country" denoted land where First Nations were still the dominant social and political force on the territory. In these areas, the collaboration of the First Nations was essential to the success of fur trading companies, which influenced but certainly did not control the Indigenous populations with which they traded.

3 Lettre de Beauharnois au ministre, October 9, 1739, Archives nationales d'Outre-Mer (ANOM), COL C11A 71, folios 49–50 (our translation).

4 In the October 2011 MNC newsletter, President Clément Chartier highlights the overarching aim of the Council: "In anticipation of a major victory in the Supreme Court of Canada, we must continue on our road to self-determination which we have always said would be through the exercise of self-government and the establishment of a land base for our people. This requires a clear statement of who we are as a people, where our traditional homeland is, and a political document which sets out the institutions, jurisdictions and attributes of our government" (Chartier 2011, 3). In the October 2012 newsletter, Chartier specifies precisely the contours of the Métis Nation: "We are a people, a Métis people, a Nation. We have a distinct place in the Aboriginal world. A new Nation which evolved in the North West of what is now known as Canada and the United States. We have customs, traditions and practices which define who we are. We have a group consciousness. We have a unique language, Michif. We have the Métis Nation flag which will be 200 years old in 1815 [sic], and first flew in defence of Métis rights at the Battle of Seven Oaks in 1816 under the leadership of Cuthbert Grant" (Chartier 2012, 3). This definition dovetails with that of Andersen (2014) and is largely the rationale that Peterson gives in her later work (notably 2012) for distinguishing Métis with a capital M. She argues that the Métis are a distinct, self-conscious nation and thus distinct from those with lowercase m mixed but not Métis origin. Chartier continues: "It is our responsibility and duty to safeguard our Nationhood and the right to exist as a people."

5 Similarly, whether the ancestry of those residing in 1763 New France was 0.4 per cent or 1 per cent or any other percentage is a moot point, as the ethnogenesis occurred

after the Conquest and the communities existed concurrently with those of the Red River. The families investigated in researching this book would have had Indigenous ancestry comparable to that of Louis Riel himself, as he had one First Nations great-grandparent on his father's side and none on his mother's side. Thus, Riel had one Indigenous ancestor out of eight great-grandparents, and she was born in the 1760s. Disqualifying the authenticity of ethnic identity by alluding to a dissimulated logic of blood quantum – that is to say, insinuating that the Indigenous ancestors are too distant to qualify the descendant as authentically Métis – would make the emergence and transmission of a Métis cultural identity impossible. This simply does not fit the available evidence concerning the heritage of many Métis across the continent, including in the Gatineau Valley of western Québec.

6  Attestation Paper of Patrick Riel (1295), 1914, Library and Archives Canada (LAC), Canadian Expeditionary Force (CEF), RG 150, 1992-93/166, box 8274-11.

7  The battle is often presented as a landmark in the emergence of Métis nationhood. Researchers should be wary of giving too much credence to that interpretation, however, as a few years later Red River inhabitants who were petitioning Bishop Plessis to send priests out to their community disavowed the violent events. Interestingly, the petitioners themselves describe their families as including Métifs or Bois-Brûlés. Correspondence, 1817, Société historique de Saint-Boniface (SHSB), Fonds Corporation archiépiscopale catholique romaine de Saint-Boniface, 0075, Joseph-Norbert Provencher, correspondance, 1540–44, copie MMS, cahier D, folios 14–18.

8  In reviewing selected documents pertaining to the Canadian Indian and the law, Derek Smith highlights a long-established tradition of giving "presents" in colonial North America. These generally consisted of annual payments of cash and/or goods and were also called quit rents, or gifts. As Smith (1975, xxvii) writes, "These derive historically, at least in part, from the practice of making annual gifts of 'grace and favour' or 'bounty and benevolence,' a prominent feature of Indian/non-Indian relations in early contact times in North America." The Selkirk Treaty, for example, specified, "Provided always, and these presents are under the express condition that the said Earl, his heirs and successors, or their agents, shall annually pay to the Chiefs and warriors of the Chippeway or Saulteaux Nation, the present or quit rent consisting of one hundred pounds weight of good and merchantable tobacco, to be delivered on or before the tenth day of October at the forks of Ossiniboyne River – and to the Chiefs and warriors of the Killistine or Cree Nation, a like present or quit rent of one hundred pounds of tobacco, to be delivered to them on or before the said tenth day of October, at Portage de la Prairie, on the banks of Ossiniboyne River" (Morris 1880, 299).

9  As Jones's (2013, 112) research highlights, Anderson promised Métis of the region that "when the Government should extinguish the Indian title, they would have a pre-emption right and their claim be confirmed by the Government."

10  The following negotiations and demands put forward by the Métis of the North-West led nowhere. Gabriel Dumont and other emissaries then sought out Louis Riel in the United States to recruit him as their leader. After the 1885 Indian and Métis resistance was tragically crushed at Batoche by a military force sent by Ottawa, Louis Riel was tried and hanged that same year (Howard 1994).

11  Chatelain is a mysterious character: his father was from Lower Canada, while his mother was Saulteaux (part of the Anishinaabe but living on the prairies). Little is known of his early history. He was reputedly a veteran of the War of 1812, but the first known documents, dating to 1823, have him employed by the HBC as an interpreter (McNab

1990). David McNab details how Métis had asked to be added to the negotiations underway with the Ojibwe but government negotiator Alexander Morris refused.

12 Much farther east, the Métis of Paspébiac, on the southern shores of the Gaspé Peninsula, experienced their own uprising in 1886. This population is described in newspapers of the time as distinctive, the Métis descendants of Acadians and Mi'kmaq (*Le Canadien* 1886, 3). The *New York Times* (1886, 5) does not hesitate to compare these Acadian Métis to those of the North-West, and demands that the same treatment be applied to their uprising. All the documentary sources clearly demonstrate that the terms *Métis, Bois-Brûlé,* and *Métif* were used across the continent without any geographic distinction. The case study presented in subsequent chapters examines one community in this larger historical context.

13 Lettre de Louis Riel à Paul Proulx, May 10, 1877, SHSB, Fonds Corporation archié-piscopale catholique romaine de Saint-Boniface, 0075, Série Alexandre Taché, Correspondance, 52987–52990, 3 (our translation).

## Chapter 2: Métis Identities and Ethnonyms

1 Michel Bouchard (2001, 2004; Bouchard and Bogdan 2014) has argued that religion is a catalyst for the emergence of a national consciousness. Both French and Scots arriving in the Americas would certainly have conceived of populations in national terms, and would have seen an emerging Métis identity as a "new nation," with or without armed insurrection or the modern statehood institutions many deem essential to the rise of such "national" phenomena.

2 The term "lived Catholicism," from Pigeon's (2017, 6–7) dissertation, refers to practices that are linked to Catholic beliefs but occur outside the institutional control of the Church. We agree with Pigeon that by preserving the contours of Métis identity and culture, "lived Catholicism" played a significant role for Métis populations across North America in terms of identity formation, political action, and, paradoxically, resistance to colonialism. The construction of a small chapel on land offered by François Naud in the little community of Lac-Sainte-Marie, and the godmothering practices of Élisabeth McPherson, his Métis wife – which highlight the role of Métis women in keeping the tenets of lived Catholicism in the region of Maniwaki as well – are good examples. We therefore employ this concept beyond the geographical boundaries that Pigeon ascribes to it, namely, the central plains and portions of the Great Lakes. We should add that lived Catholicism and other Métis cultural practices have sometimes opposed the strict rules of the Catholic Church, yet we should be careful in extra-polating from this. It would be problematic, for example, to infer a clear manifestation of Métis sovereignty solely from such matters as the refusal of Métis women to accept the advice of their priest not to sleep with their children (Pigeon 2017, 100). We concur that this is an example of political agency articulated in daily practices, but the term *sovereignty* carries a very specific historical significance that would not normally apply to the given example. Many of the examples of institutions that Pigeon discusses do not illustrate an overall political cohesion, which is not to say that the expression of Métis political will never came to be. The most famous expression came under Louis Riel.

3 Some of the terms used to identify Métis are *Indians, Half-Savages, Bois-Brûlés, Métifs, Métis,* and *Chicot.* The existence of multiple names and the porous contours of Métis cultures make it particularly challenging to pin down specific identification in any given era.

4  The French title is *Esquisse sur le Nord-Ouest de l'Amérique* (Taché 1869).

5  Census, Library and Archives Canada (LAC), 1871 and 1881. Though the name James King does not suggest a Canadien ancestry, HBC records indicate that he was born in the Hudson Bay Territories region, and there was a Jacques Roy in Moose Factory who could certainly have been his father. Given the tendency of sons to take the names of their fathers, along with the anglicization of Jacques to James and Roy to King, it would not be a stretch to consider that James King was the son of Jacques Roy (Marcotte 2017). Even his claim of being born in Montréal is not entirely unfeasible. We have documented cases of voyageurs returning with their wives and children to the St. Lawrence Valley. He could have been born in James Bay and brought to Montréal to be baptized as a baby. Also, the fact that he was Métis would not preclude his being Canadien, as across the continent one could be both Métis and Canadien (Foxcurran et al. 2016).

6  Journal d'une Mission faite dans l'Été de 1838, au lac Témiskaming, au lac d'Abittibi, au Grand Lac et au Fort des Allumettes [copy], 1838, Bibliothèque et Archives nationales du Québec, Rouyn-Noranda (BAnQ-RN), Fonds Donat Martineau, P10,S3,SS3, D4,P29, folio 6.

7  Nécrologie de la mission du Lac Témiscaming, 1863–1885 [copy], 1863–85, BAnQ-RN, Fonds Donat Martineau, P10,S3,SS3,D4,P19,11.

8  Census, LAC, 1871.

9  Census, LAC, 1901.

10  Tenth Census of the United States, 1880, Michigan State, Chippewa County, Sugar Island, 1880, folio 17 [C-146].

11  References to File 1, File 2, and so on refer to family histories presented in the Appendix: Principal Métis Families of the Gatineau. The files summarize archival documentation gathered on key Métis families that appear in this work and their movements over time and space.

12  Journal d'une Mission faite dans l'Été de 1838, au lac Témiskaming, au lac d'Abittibi, au Grand Lac et au Fort des Allumettes [copy], 1838, BAnQ-RN, Fonds Donat Martineau, P10,S3,SS3,D4,P29, folio 9.

13  BMS of Saint-François-de-Sales-de-Templeton, Pointe-Gatineau, Québec, August 25, 1847.

14  Census, LAC, 1861.

15  John Swanston recorded eighty-four heads of Métis families for all the fur trade posts of Lake Superior in 1850, a relatively modest number (Morrison 1993, 169). Accounts after 1850 report that a number of Métis families left the region to take up residence in the Batchewana and Garden River reserves, so that they could receive the annuities promised when the Robinson-Huron and Pennefather Treaties were signed in 1850 and 1859 (Jones 1998, 5–7, 13, 30–32; Morrison 1993, 201).

16  These gifts were initially intended to ensure peace and good relations with First Nations, as was necessary to occupy the territory, but they also included military pensions and occasionally humanitarian aid (Borrows and Rotman 2012).

17  There are no page numbers in the original published primary source. For the sake of clarity, we are following the numbering system used by Early Canadiana Online: 1845 Bagot Report, http://www.canadiana.ca/view/oocihm.9_00955_4_2/5?r=0&s=1; 1847 Bagot Report: http://www.canadiana.ca/view/oocihm.9_00955_6_1/3?r=0&s=1.

18  Such cultural markers are applied within a framework elaborated by the *Review of Reports and Cartographic Representation Pertaining to Historic Métis in Ontario* (Reimer

and Chartrand 2002, 4–5), which develops seven analytical criteria for expert witnesses and other scholars to determine if the historical and archival data truly documents the ethnogenesis of a Métis historical community. Our review of historical data from a very precise regional historical community in the Gatineau Valley in the Outaouais region builds on precedent from the prairie provinces, Ontario, and the far North in the case of the Métis of the Great Slave Lake region (Holmes 1996; Jones, n.d.; Ray 1998; 2005, 12–19).

### Chapter 3: The Outaouais Fur Trade of the Nineteenth Century

1 Barrière is not to be confused with "La Barrière," located in the vicinity of the source of the Ottawa River between Grand Lac and Lac à la Truite.

2 PAM (n.d.), *Hudson's Bay Company: Grand Lac* and *Hudson's Bay Company: Desert Post,* http://pam.minisisinc.com.

3 Montreal inward correspondence, 1822–26, Hudson's Bay Company Archives (HBCA), B.134/c/1, folio 100b.

4 Ingall's expertise in geology was essential to identifying soil types, but to complete the team a surveyor was required. The first one to be hired was Joseph Bouchette Jr. A surveyor like his father, he took over Bouchette Sr.'s affairs when the latter took leave to go to England in the fall of 1829. Within days of being hired, Bouchette came in conflict with Nixon and abandoned the expedition in a huff. John Adams was hired to replace him in short order. The question arises why Bouchette Jr. gave up his position, particularly as he was later forced to reimburse the advance that he had been given. The commissioners allude to "knowing that private circumstances rendered the employment peculiarly desirable to Mr. Bouchette" (Ingall, Nixon, and Adams 1830, 40). Though the report does not give the reason for the "trivial altercation" between Nixon and Bouchette, the commissioners hint that it was a question of the assigned hierarchy: "During the stay at Three-Rivers the Deputy Surveyor General evinced a pettishness of manner, even towards the Commissioners, which indicated a dissatisfied mind, and further took upon himself to interfere individually in the preparations for equipment, finding unfounded fault with the size, manning of the canoes, by remarks which tended to create discontent among the canoe men" (44). The report certainly implies that Bouchette's outrage is due to the fact that Nixon, a mere ensign, had greater rank in the team than Bouchette himself, as the latter sought to "change in the arrangement of the party" (44).

5 In their biography of the father, Boudreau and Lépine (1988) highlight that the elder Joseph had done much to ingratiate himself with the British and sought in many ways to join their ranks. This would alienate him from all the other Canadiens in the Parliament of Lower Canada, while his "desire to be identified with the English-speaking community created other difficulties for him. Being an office holder, he paid great attention to his public image. He lived beyond his means, which caused him many financial troubles." Thus he paid the price but gained few of the rewards. As he had believed in the need for a union of the two Canadas decades before Lord Durham, he was seen as "man who had sold out to the English" (Boudreau and Lépine 1988). (His youngest son, Robert Shore-Milnes, joined the Patriotes and fought against the British, then was exiled to Bermuda.) Both Joseph Sr. and Joseph Jr. strived to be accepted by English-speaking elites of the colony and the British elite more generally, but never quite succeeded. However, the importance of the father's work should not be underestimated as it demonstrates artistic and scientific talent.

6  The windigo (also wendigo or weendigo) was present in precolonial Cree and Ojibwe culture. As Shawn Smallman (2010, 572) explains, "The windigo ... is the spirit of winter that transforms a human into an asocial being whose heart turns to ice and who becomes consumed by cannibal desires." For Ojibwe author Basil Johnston, the windigo embodies selfishness. Though the term is not specifically used in the primary document, the report is clearly referring to a well-known phenomenon. Johnston (1995, 223) notes that those who lived "in harmony and balance" have nothing to fear from the terrifying creature: "At root is selfishness, regarded by the Anishinaubae peoples as the worst human shortcoming." With the rise of the fur trade, the HBC had to transact with the belief in windigos, and as Smallman (2010, 575) notes, the folk belief of the Canadien voyageurs in the *loup-garou,* or werewolf, became conflated with the windigo. Though the spirit of winter can transform any individual into a windigo – man, woman, or even baby – the eating of human flesh even during a period of starvation would be harshly condemned, often by killing the person who did so (Smallman 2010, 573–74). However, as Smallman recounts, there has been great debate in academia over whether belief in the windigo existed before the colonial period, and whether there were any true cases of individuals succumbing to the windigo condition.

7  Montreal inward correspondence, 1831, HBCA, B.134/c/11, folio 215.

8  Montreal Department abstracts of servants' accounts, 1827–28, HBCA, B.134/g/6, folio 14.

9  Montreal inward correspondence, 1831, HBCA, B.134/c/12, folio 26.

10  Montreal inward correspondence, 1835, HBCA, B.134/c/26, folio 99b.

11  Montreal inward correspondence, 1837, HBCA, B.134/c/36, folio 80, and 1838, B.134/c/37, folio 91.

12  It is necessary to point out that Têtes-de-Boule are not necessarily related to those present in the Upper Saint-Maurice at this time, as Inksetter (2017, 27–28) documents.

### Chapter 4: Shared Cultural Traits of the Bois-Brûlés

1  In this passage, Logan seems to use the expression "Algonquin" to signify that Bernard speaks the Algonquin language.

2  Montreal inward correspondence, 1834, Hudson's Bay Company Archives (HBCA), B.134/c/21, folios 98b–99.

3  To make the historical point that Bois-Brulés spoke predominantly French (or regional dialects of French) does not mean we endorse a French version of "manifest destiny" or some chauvinist validation of French colonialism, or romanticism of French–Indigenous relations. We are simply confirming a historical fact built on historical evidence and primary records. George Lang (1991) rightfully argues that no true continental pidgin emerged in the North American fur trade, as voyageur French served as a *lingua franca* between distant forts and as a central language of translation (Fox-curran, Bouchard, and Malette 2016). In fact, what could be interpreted as an anti-French reaction that exaggerates the geographical importance of Michif as the national language of all Métis should raise concern for the part it plays in creating a narrative that distorts the historical and lived reality of many Métis across North America.

4  Montreal inward correspondence, 1830, HBCA, B.134/c/8, folios 140b, underlined in original.

5  James Robertson, a Métis, was born at Eastmain (James Bay), circa 1785; see Southern Department abstracts of servants' accounts book, 1833–34, HBCA, B.135/g/17. He

was at this time in charge of the Migiskan post, located north of the Grand Lac post. The trading zones of the two posts bordered each other.

6 Correspondence, 1817, Société historique de Saint-Boniface (SHSB), Fonds Corporation archiépiscopale catholique romaine de Saint-Boniface, 0075, Joseph-Norbert Provencher, correspondance, 1540–44, copie MMS, cahier D, folios 14–18.

7 GSU, BMS of Sainte-Geneviève-de-Berthier, Québec, September 23, 1822.

8 GSU, BMS of Sainte-Geneviève-de-Berthier, Québec, July 19, 1791 (our translation).

9 Joseph-Étienne Guinard, Mémoires d'un père oblat, 1944–46, Archives Deschâtelets-NDC (AD), Fonds Deschâtelets, HEB 6964.E83C 1, folio 69.

10 Journal d'une Mission faite dans l'Été de 1838, au lac Témiskaming, au lac d'Abittibi, au Grand Lac et au Fort des Allumettes [copy], 1838, Bibliothèque et Archives nationales du Québec, Rouyn-Noranda (BAnQ-RN), Fonds Donat Martineau, P10, S3, SS3, D4,P29, folio 6 (our translation).

11 William Dunning Buckingham 1844, 1844–60, Bibliothèque et Archives nationales du Québec, Gatineau (BAnQ-G), Fonds William H. Dunning, P142, folio 152.

12 Grand Lac blotter, 1836–38, HBCA, B.82/d/3, April 28, 1837.

13 Montreal inward correspondence, 1838, HBCA, B.134/c/40, folio 48.

14 Grand Lac book debts, 1834–41, HBCA, B.82/d/6, folio 10.

15 Joseph-Étienne Guinard, Mémoires d'un père oblat, 1944–46, AD, Fonds Deschâtelets, HEB 6964.E83C 1, folio 101.

16 Though the word is "truite" (trout), it is certainly a transcription error for "traite" (trade).

17 In a report examining the history of the Métis of Mattawa in Ontario, these passages are interpreted to mean that Bois-Brûlés were coming to be "associated with another social pariah, squatters, in the minds of government officials" (Stone Circle Consulting, and Know History 2015). We agree that they were being associated, but not in the sense of joining other, non-Métis, squatters living on the territory; in other words, not all squatters were Métis, but almost all Métis were squatters. Here, we believe that the class of people referred to are the Bois-Brûlés and not the squatters. Let us note that Bouchette, the general surveyor, had an excellent reputation in his field and was well versed in the occupation of the lands of Lower Canada. His use of the term *Bois-Brûlé*, and the collective overtone he gives it, is thus highly significant. The association of the terms *squatter* and *Métis* is examined in greater detail in Chapter 6.

18 Montreal inward correspondence, 1829, HBCA, B.134/c/6, folio 229b.

19 Ibid.

20 Contracts of Ambroise Beaulieu, July 11, 1827, Centre du patrimoine, Voyageurs Contracts Database, http://shsb.mb.ca/en/Voyageurs_database.

21 Montreal inward correspondence, 1828, HBCA, B.134/c/4, folio 177b.

22 Montreal inward correspondence, 1836, HBCA, B.134/c/31, folio 109b. The fact that Noui Icipaiatik is identified as Métis suggests he in all likelihood described himself as such, which the accounts of likely family members from this period also suggest. Precise genealogies are sometimes difficult to trace before the installation of state structures, which in Québec include extensions of Catholic institutions, but all the evidence from other sources indicates that Noui was the son of André Lacroix, who recognized his children as Métis when writing to Indian Affairs in 1879 concerning his daughter Sophia: "She was a half breed, being my daughter." See Maniwaki Reserve – Andre Lacroix writes stating that one Xear Boutin is depriving his Indian granddaughter

from her land and annuity moneys, 1879a, Library and Archives Canada (LAC), RG 10, vol. 2084, file 12,930, folio 1.

## Chapter 5: Algonquin Half-Breeds, Priests, and the Métis Collectivity

1 North Temiscamingue Agency – Correspondence regarding the land occupied by half breeds, the hospital, the schools on the Temiscamingue Reserve, 1892–96, Library and Archives Canada (LAC), RG 10, vol. 2654, file 132, 413, folio 4.
2 Ibid.
3 Ibid., folio 5.
4 Ibid., folios 16–17.
5 Ibid., folio 24.
6 Ibid., folio 27.
7 Ibid., folio 28.
8 Timiskaming Agency – Correspondence regarding chiefs for the Temiscamingue Indians. 1884–94, LAC, RG 10, vol. 2262, file 53,304, folio 16.
9 Temiscamingue Agency – Band membership, 1896–1900, LAC, RG 10, vol. 2838, file 171,945, folios 2–3 and 12–13.
10 North Temiscamingue Agency – Correspondence regarding the land occupied by half breeds, the hospital, the schools on the Temiscamingue Reserve, 1892–96, LAC, RG 10, vol. 2654, file 132,413, folio 30.
11 Ibid., folio 38.
12 Ibid., folio 41.

## Chapter 6: Crowded Crossroads

1 Montreal inward correspondence, 1841, Hudson's Bay Company Archives (HBCA), B.134/c/48, folio 104b.
2 Montreal inward correspondence, 1832, HBCA, B.134/c/16, folios 52–52b.
3 Montreal inward correspondence, 1831, HBCA, B.134/c/11, folio 108.
4 William Hodgson was a Métis voyageur, born at James Bay or in its hinterland, whose family established itself on the Ottawa River at the dawn of the nineteenth century. Around 1837, he lived close to Mattawa with an Indian woman from Lake of Two Mountains (BMS Missions Diocese of Pembroke, 1836–42, Diocese of Pembroke Archives [DPA], June 21, 1837; Brown 1987; Cormier 1978, 133, 137).
5 Montreal inward correspondence, 1834, HBCA, B.134/c/21, folio 67.
6 William Dunning Buckingham 1844, 1844–60, Bibliothèque et Archives nationales du Québec, Gatineau (BAnQ-G), Fonds William H. Dunning, P142, p. 113; Montreal inward correspondence, 1832, HBCA, B.134/c/16, folio 40.
7 The accounting practices of the HBC following reforms initiated in the early decades of the nineteenth century included detailed accounts of the profitability of each and every post and operation. This allowed for very efficient management of the individual posts' affairs, including revenues and expenses as well as expected revenues and expenses. Andrew Wedderburn, who became a shareholder in 1808 and a member of the governing committee, spearheaded a change in management style. His pamphlet "Instructions for Conducting the Trade in Hudson's Bay," dated May 31, 1810, set the stage for a radically different approach to running the company's affairs (Spraakman and Margret 2005, 280–81). Wedderburn's analysis revealed that the inland posts were actually more cost-effective than the coastal posts, the inverse of what was expected (281). The company concluded that the "bayside posts had excess employees for the

required work" (282). The transition to management accounting began in the 1810s, but it was George Simpson who successfully imposed this radical change, starting in the 1820s (Spraakman and Wilkie 2000, 81). As Edith Burley (1993, 63), writes, "The energetic and ruthless George Simpson provided the necessary hardheaded leadership that had been absent in 1810." With such precise accounting methods, it is generally possible for historians to analyze the financial operations of individual posts in great detail. Even when the post account books did not survive, as was the case for Lac des Sables, the company correspondence demonstrates the constant worry of the officers to optimize savings.

8  Montreal inward correspondence, 1838, HBCA, B.134/c/37, folio 25.

9  Montreal inward correspondence, 1838, HBCA, B.134/c/40, folio 48.

10  Ibid., folio 59.

11  Montreal inward correspondence, 1839, HBCA, B.134/c/43, folio 175.

12  Montreal inward correspondence, 1841, HBCA, B.134/c/47, folio 173.

13  River Desert Agency – Maniwaki – Reports of inspector J.A. MacRae and Martin Bensen respecting schools in the agency, condition of the band members and valuation of lands, 1901–9, Library and Archives Canada (LAC), RG 10, vol. 3048, file 237,660, folios 15–16.

14  For a thorough description of contraband activities involving Métis kinship networks in the Illinois Country, see the excellent work of Tanis C. Thorne (1996, 86–91). As she explains, "The efforts of the English and Spanish authorities in the 1770s to retain the trade of their respective districts were frustrated by the mobile French Canadians and French-Indians. Ambitious merchants operating on both sides of the Mississippi abetted middlemen in their illicit activities" (88).

15  Our description of the Métis from the Outaouais region as a people who own their destiny, sometimes through the free trade of fur and contraband schemes, echoes descriptions of western Métis as owning themselves (i.e., being an independent and free people). Heather Devine (2004, xvii), for example, called her book *People Who Own Themselves: Aboriginal Ethnogenesis in a Canadian Family, 1660–1900*, explaining that Métis were described by the Cree term *Otipemisewak*, meaning "their own boss." From an eastern regional perspective, we find the Algonquin term *Abitawis,i* to describe those who were "half White and Indian" (hence Métis), according to Jean Andre Cuoq's (1886, 8) lexicon of the Algonquin language.

16  Though his last name is clearly Scottish, his given name "Amable" suggests that he is a French speaker. He thus fits the ethnocultural markers identified in the first part of this book and, like Métis such as Thomas Brown and others of Scottish, Irish, or other British ancestry, he could express himself in French, among other languages.

17  BMS Missions Diocese of Pembroke, 1836–42, Diocese of Pembroke Archives (DPA), August 11, 1842.

18  Carnet G-25, Cantons Aylwin et Hincks/John Allan Snow, May 8, 1848, Bibliothèque et Archives nationales du Québec, Québec (BAnQ-Q), Fonds Ministère des Terres et Forêts, E21,S60,SS3,PG25, folios 73–76.

19  Ibid.

20  Lake of Two Mountains inward correspondence, 1821–60, HBCA, B.110/c/1, folio 16; Montreal inward correspondence, 1839, HBCA, B.134/c/41, folio 238; Montreal Department abstracts of servants' accounts, 1827–28, HBCA, B.134/g/6.

21  Southern Department abstracts of servants' accounts book, 1836–37, HBCA, B.135/g/20; 1837–38, HBCA, B.135/g/21.

22  GSU, BMS of Saint-Paul-d'Aylmer, Québec, January 20, 1844; BMS of Saint-François-de-Sales-de-Templeton, Pointe-Gatineau, Québec, January 26, 1848.

23  GSU, BMS of Nativité-de-Notre-Dame-de-Bécancour, Québec, July 7, 1856 (our translation).

### Chapter 7: Comparing Lac-Sainte-Marie and Sault Ste. Marie

1  In spite of the existence of endogamous unions between Métis at Lac-Sainte-Marie, it must be noted that exogamous marriages were not rare. Two of Amable McDougall's presumed sisters (File 11), for example, married Indigenous men from the region: Marie-Anne with Antoine Tomosko (see GSU, BMS of Saint-Paul-d'Aylmer, Québec, June 18, 1845); and Marie-Josephte with Pierre Kitchikanaguoët (see GSU, BMS of Saint-Paul-d'Aylmer, Québec, January 26, 1845). These marriages illustrate the ties between "Métis" and "Indian" families in the region. Exogamous unions also brought together Métis and French-Canadien families in the same region. Joseph Foubert, a Métis man born in the region of Rigaud, married Caroline Rocbrune (Larocque), apparently a Canadienne, whose family could have had ties to the fur trade (see GSU, BMS of Saint-Grégoire-de-Nazianze, Buckingham, Québec, February 7, 1842).

2  Father Du Ranquet also specifies that he reached the settlement of Lac-Sainte-Marie by a trail, which confirms that the community is located some way from the Gatineau River. We can speculate that this may well constitute a discreet and strategic location, preferred by those engaging in clandestine activities such as contraband fur trade or sale of alcohol. Indeed, evidence shows that Métis from that community were involved in contraband activities.

3  Chronique de la Congrégation des missionnaires Oblats de Marie Immaculée de 1841 à 1893 ["Chronique des Oblats"], 1949, Archives Deschâtelets-NDC (AD), Fonds Notre-Dame du Cap, BM 2056-01-A, folio 74 (our translation). We reviewed the 1949 transcription of the original document, filed under BM 2056-01, as access to the original is restricted given its fragility.

4  Carnet G-25, Cantons Aylwin et Hincks/John Allan Snow, May 8, 1848, Bibliothèque et Archives nationales du Québec, Québec (BAnQ-Q), Fonds Ministère des Terres et Forêts, E21,S60,SS3,PG25, folio 76.

5  The accounting records of the merchant William Dunning contain numerous references to hides tanned by the McGregor family. They are paid either for "dressing" or for "smoking" hides. The former refers to softening the hides, while the latter refers to the final stage of tanning using Indigenous techniques (Richards 2004, 7, 20–21). Even if the McGregor family did not hunt all the animals whose hides they dressed or smoked (given the astronomical quantities of hides involved), their expertise in tanning without doubt attests to their hunting skills. Regarding the deer, moose, and caribou hides traded by the McGregors, see William Dunning Buckingham 1844, 1844–60, Bibliothèque et Archives nationales du Québec, Gatineau (BAnQ-G), Fonds William H. Dunning, P142, August 6 to October 30, 1846.

6  BMS Missions Diocese of Pembroke, 1836–42, Diocese of Pembroke Archives (DPA), August 8, 10, and 11, 1837. This Jean-Baptiste Cadotte is also found, probably as a voyageur hired by the missionaries, in the registry of Catholic missions in the interior of the Outaouais region. See BMS Missions Diocese of Pembroke, 1836–42, Diocese of Pembroke Archives (DPA), August 1, 1842.

7  Lake of Two Mountains inward correspondence, 1821–60, Hudson's Bay Company Archives (HBCA), B.110/c/1, folio 22.

8 Montreal inward correspondence, 1828, HBCA, B.134/c/4, folio 177b.

9 HBCA (n.d.), KNIGHT, Thomas, http://www.gov.mb.ca/chc/archives/hbca/
biographical/k/knight_thomas.pdf; Montreal inward correspondence, 1827, HBCA,
B.134/c/2, folio 162. One of John Knight's brothers, Thomas, also worked in the
Outaouais region as an interpreter for the HBC. He was stationed at Kiminisikeg.
See Montreal Department abstracts of servants' accounts, 1829–30, HBCA, B.134/g/7.

10 Montreal inward correspondence, 1828, HBCA, B.134/c/4, folio 148.

11 GSU, BMS of Saint-Joachim-de-la-Pointe-Claire, Québec, August 12, 1827.

12 Montreal inward correspondence, 1829, HBCA, B.134/c/5, folio 86b.

13 Montreal Department abstracts of servants' accounts, 1827–28, HBCA, B.134/g/6.

14 HBCA (n.d.), TAYLOR, George, https://www.gov.mb.ca/chc/archives/hbca/
biographical/t/taylor_george_1787-1818.pdf; HBCA (n.d.), TAYLOR, Thomas Sr,
https://www.gov.mb.ca/chc/archives/hbca/biographical/t/taylor_thomas-sr.pdf.

15 HBCA (n.d.), TAYLOR, Thomas Jr., http://www.gov.mb.ca/chc/archives/hbca/
biographical/t/taylor_thomas-jr.pdf; Montreal inward correspondence, 1858, HBCA,
B.134/c/77, folio 241b.

16 Père Mourier: "Coup d'œil général 1863–1895" et diverses biographies [copy], 1863–95,
Bibliothèque et Archives nationales du Québec, Rouyn-Noranda (BAnQ-RN), Fonds
Donat Martineau, P10,S3,SS3,D4,P5, folio 68b [copy from a document kept at Archives
Deschâtelets-NDC, filed under JH 401. C21R 12].

17 Montreal inward correspondence, 1827, HBCA, B.134/c/2, folios 25–25b.

18 This social cohesion, nourished by professional networks, can also be observed in an
account of the resistance at Red River, as recounted by Métis Angus McBride and his
colleague, Anderson, when they arrived on snowshoes at the post of Grand Lac from
Témiscamingue in February 1870. See Grand Lac post journal, 1869–70, HBCA,
B.82/a/4, folio 17b.

19 Nécrologie de la mission du Lac Témiscaming, 1863–1885 [copy], 1863–85, BAnQ-RN,
Fonds Donat Martineau, P10,S3,SS3,D4,P19, folio 11.

20 GSU, BMS of Saint-Joachim-de-la-Pointe-Claire, Québec, August 12, 1825.

21 GSU, BMS of L'Annonciation, Oka, Québec, August 14, 1826.

22 GSU, BMS of Saint-Joachim-de-la-Pointe-Claire, Québec, August 12, 1827.

23 GSU, BMS of Sainte-Madeleine-de-Rigaud, Québec, September 28, 1812.

24 Ibid., September 27, 1812.

25 Ibid., July 13, 1813; Montreal Department abstracts of servants' accounts, 1829–30,
HBCA, B.134/g/7. The upper country was the Pays d'en Haut, and the term *Mitive* is
derived from *Métive*, the feminine of *Métif*, which was the French standard before *Métis*
supplanted it. As the initial *é* of Métif was pronounced as an *i*, the word was pronounced
*Mitif* (feminine *Mitive*) and would then become *Michif*, a popular self-designation of
Métis on the prairies.

26 Montreal inward correspondence, 1846, HBCA, B.134/c/62, folio 411.

27 Montreal inward correspondence, 1839, HBCA, B.134/c/41, folio 238.

28 Temiscamingue inward correspondence, 1844–50, HBCA, B.218/c/1, folio 1.

29 Montreal inward correspondence, 1846, HBCA, B.134/c/62, folio 411.

30 Montreal inward correspondence, 1838, HBCA, B.134/c/38, folio 246.

31 Aeneas and Angus Cameron fonds, Angus Cameron – inward correspondence – private,
1843–50, HBCA, E.41/10, folio 11b.

32 Aeneas and Angus Cameron fonds, Angus Cameron – inward correspondence – Charles
Stuart, 1851–68, HBCA, E.41/14, folio 2.

## Chapter 8: Louis Riel and the McGregors of the Lièvre

1  Louis Riel et sa famille/Madame Violet Lalonde [copy], 1980, Bibliothèque et Archives nationales du Québec, Gatineau (BAnQ-G), Fonds Centre de l'Outaouais de Bibliothèque et Archives nationales du Québec, P1000, D65. For an analysis focused on the Lalonde manuscript and how Métis identity is articulated in the academic milieu, see Malette and Marcotte (2017).

2  As with any oral account, it is impossible to confirm every fact presented, but there is sufficient overlap between Violet's typescript and the historical record to be certain that she provided a relatively accurate account of the region's history. Some points it contains seem to belong to local legend and cannot be confirmed in the archival record.

3  GSU, BMS of Sainte-Geneviève-de-Berthier, Québec, September 23, 1822.

4  GSU, BMS of L'Annonciation, Oka, Québec, August 14, 1826.

5  GSU, BMS of Notre-Dame, Montréal, Québec, October 23, 1849.

6  Despite a number of minor historical discrepancies in Violet Lalonde's account, notably in the names and ages of Louis Riel's siblings, examination of the church registries in fact validates her information. A case in point is Sophie. The Berthier registry records her as fourteen months old when she was baptized in 1822. In Violet's account, however, we find what appears to be contradictory information: "When the third child (the Sr. Louis Riel) was born, in 1817, Mary Louise was a young girl of 8 years and five months, she loved her new brother and assisted her parents in caring for him as well as her four year old sister Sophie" (Louis Riel et sa famille/Madame Violet Lalonde, 3). Yet there is the record of the death of a Sophie Riel in 1830 in Mont-Saint-Hilaire, in which her parents are listed as Jean Bte Riel and Marguerite Boucher. The priest notes that the young woman of seventeen was the legitimate child of her parents (GSU, BMS of Mont-Saint-Hilaire, Québec, May 29, 1830). This would place her birth in 1813 and thus her age in 1817 as four, as Violet's account indicates. Still, the question arises why this Sophie was not baptized at Berthier in 1822 as well, and why the Riels would have named two daughters Sophie. Nonetheless, it does highlight that Violet is quite precise in telling a nebulous family history.

7  GSU, BMS of Saint-Joachim-de-la-Pointe-Claire, Québec, August 12, 1825; BMS of L'Annonciation, Oka, Québec, August 14, 1826.

8  As Marie-Louise Riel was many years older than Louis, Jean-Baptiste Riel could have met her mother in Sault Ste. Marie before heading west to Île-à-la-Crosse. It is also likely that the Riel family stopped at Sault Ste. Marie on their way to Lower Canada. Violet Lalonde writes, "The family made many stops along the way visiting with their people the Metis and the Indians" (Louis Riel et sa famille/Madame Violet Lalonde, 4). Thus, Jean-Baptiste could have certainly had the opportunity to see his daughter Marie-Louise while the family was making its way to Berthier.

9  Following the terminology used by Lalonde, it is difficult to know what Chipewyan signifies here, as the term *Chippewa* was used to refer to a nation, the Ojibwe, Saulteaux, or Anishinaabe, while *Chipewyan* was used for a Dene people of far northwestern Canada. Marguerite Boucher's ancestors were reputedly Chipewyan. She was the Métis wife of Jean-Baptiste Riel, the grandfather of Louis Riel. Thus, the language Marie-Louise spoke would have depended on whether Marguerite Boucher was her mother.

10  Louis Riel et sa famille/Madame Violet Lalonde, 17.

11  William Dunning Buckingham 1844, 1844–60, BAnQ-G, Fonds William H. Dunning, P142, folio 152.

12  Curiously, Lalonde associates Maniwaki with Lac-Sainte-Marie although they are separated by over 30 kilometres. This association may be tied to familial memories that confound the two regions for reasons we cannot explain, but, given the documentary evidence collected, it was probably due to the importance of both locales in the history of the region's Métis.

13  *Louis Riel et sa famille*/Madame Violet Lalonde, 38.

14  Ibid., 17.

15  Ibid., 52.

16  Interview transcript:

> *Laurier Riel (LR):* And him [McGregor] he told me that he lived at Lac-Sainte-Marie and that other McGregors lived there. And ... that they had goods that belonged to Louis Riel too. Because Marie, ahhh ... Marie-Louise she had brought those things with her, she had the ... the things she had brought to leave there, the ... the ... dishes, things like that.
>
> *Guillaume Marcotte (GM):* Marie-Louise who?
>
> *LR:* Marie-Louise Ri... Marie-Louise Riel. She brought stuff there to Lac-Sainte-Marie.
>
> *GM:* But who was that, Marie-Louise Riel, she was ...?
>
> *LR:* She would have been the sister of Louis. And she left stuff there at Lac-Sainte-Marie. Some ... some ... Sheets, dishes, things like that ... that she had brought.
>
> *GM:* During, like, the exile of Louis Riel?
>
> *LR:* During the time she travelled, there. She travelled with him. Because she came ... came with him ... to sit in Parliament. (SMC 2016; our translation)

17  We revisit this idea in Part 4 when discussing the testimony of contemporary Elders, which demonstrates a similar attachment to Louis Riel.

18  An oral tradition also existed in the area of Noëlville, Ontario, that Riel hid at Angers, and these accounts are found until at least the 1950s (Villemaire 1953).

19  Louis Riel à Julie Riel, Saint Paul, May 22, 1874, Société historique de Saint-Boniface (SHSB), Collection Louis Riel 0003, 1092-503, PAM MG 3 D 1, 503.

20  A.A.C. LaRivière à Louis Riel, Saint-Boniface, October 17, 1873, SHSB, Collection Louis Riel 0003, 1091-221, PAM MG 3 D 1, 221 (our translation).

21  The welcome given to Louis Riel by Métis in the Outaouais, as told by Violet Lalonde, perhaps explains a declaration in his 1885 correspondence about eastern Métis.

### Chapter 9: A New Era

1  We use the term *frontier* to refer to both a geographical zone and a space of interaction between two or more cultures from an ethnohistorical perspective (Axtell 1979, 2–3). *Frontier* can describe a buffer zone between the northern territories, where the HBC maintained a commercial monopoly, and the settled southern zones, where free commerce reigned. This frontier is thus more "free" and "*sauvage*," as colonial authorities quite often maintained only indirect control over these territories.

2  Carnet 29 Rivière du Lièvre/Alphonse Wells, January 13, 1847, Bibliothèque et Archives nationales du Québec, Québec (BAnQ-Q), Fonds Ministère des Terres et Forêts, E21,S60,SS2,P29; Carnet G-25, Cantons Aylwin et Hincks/John Allan Snow, May 8, 1848, BAnQ-Q, Fonds Ministère des Terres et Forêts, E21,S60,SS3,PG25; Carnet M27,

Cantons de Maniwaki et Egan/John Newman, January 1, 1849, BAnQ-Q, Fonds Ministère des Terres et Forêts, E21,S60,SS3,PM27.

3  Maniwaki Reserve – Outbreak of smallpox, 1880–85, Library and Archives Canada (LAC), RG 10, vol. 2119, file 22,639, folio 11.

4  Ibid., folio 22.

5  Ibid., folio 11.

6  Archival documents allow us to categorically affirm that the man named Thomas Schocier is in fact the Métis Thomas Chaussé, in all likelihood the son of the voyageur Pierre Chaussé (see Montreal inward correspondence, 1836, Hudson's Bay Company Archives [HBCA], B.134/c/31, folio 109b) and the Métis Julie Vanasse (File 19). A file of correspondence at Indian Affairs concerning the Chaussé family at this time names him "Schocier," while correspondence from the individual concerned gives "Chaussé" (Maniwaki Reserve – Application by Pierre Schocier to lease lot 6, Desert front, 1880–83, LAC, RG 10, vol. 2111, file 20,478, folios 2, 9).

7  Maniwaki Reserve – Outbreak of smallpox, 1880–85, LAC, RG 10, vol. 2119, file 22,639, folio 19.

8  Ibid., folio 18.

9  Ibid., folios 19–20.

10  Ibid., folio 22.

11  Ibid., folio 48.

12  Census, LAC, 1881.

13  This tendency is evident in the works of certain authors, notably genealogical studies of the Outaouais region by Serge Goudreau (2014a, 291; 2014b, 65–66).

14  Paul Riel is also among a list of names emanating from a resolution passed at a "meeting of the white settlers" held in June 1874, concerning the relocation of the Maniwaki cemetery (Maniwaki Reserve – Proposal by Father R. Deleage to move the burial ground from one site to another on the land of James O'Hagan, 1873–74, LAC, RG 10, vol. 1914, file 2646, folios 2, 4). No doubt organized by the mayor, whose name was first on the list, the meeting was probably called at the demand of white settlers but apparently did not exclude the participation of other "Non-Indians" (in which the Métis could be included).

15  River Desert Agency – Application of Daniel Nault to lease lot 111, Notre Dame street in Maniwaki, 1889–98, LAC, RG 10, vol. 2464, file 95,890, folio 2.

16  Ibid., folio 17.

17  Ibid., folio 16.

18  Four unidentified documents, n.d., n.p., Société d'Histoire du Témiscamingue (SHT), Fonds P49, Hudson Bay Company.

19  Ibid.

20  Ibid.

21  Joseph-Étienne Guinard, Mémoires d'un père oblat, 1944–46, Archives Deschâtelets-NDC (AD), Fonds Deschâtelets, HEB 6964.E83C 1, folio 41.

22  In French, *Métis* is masculine, *Métisse* is feminine, and *Métis* is the plural. Here, the masculine article *un* is used with the feminine *métisse*, which was certainly a spelling error as the trader was in all likelihood a man. Father Guinard makes this mistake on a few occasions.

23  Joseph-Étienne Guinard, Mémoires d'un père oblat, 1944–46, AD, Fonds Deschâtelets, HEB 6964.E83C 1, folio 58 (our translation).

24  Lettre du père J.P. Guéguen à Mgr. Duhamel, Maniwaki, February 26, 1894, AD, Fonds Notre-Dame du Cap. 2D9-3-66, folio 2 (our translation).

25  Lettre de N.Z. Lorrain à Mgr. Duhamel, Pembroke, April 24, 1894, AD, Fonds Notre-Dame du Cap, 2D9-3-70, folio 2.

26  Lettre de N.Z. Lorrain à Mgr. Duhamel, Pembroke, April 26, 1894, AD, Fonds Notre-Dame du Cap, 2D9-3-72, folio 1 (our translation).

27  With respect to Métis in the Michomis region, a 1905 marriage certificate sheds some light on their presence. The descendants of the Vanasse family are mentioned (File 19) as well as the Godchères, a family that originated from the post of Grand Lac and in which the father was a Canadien guide for the HBC and the mother an Algonquin (GSU, BMS of L'Assomption, Maniwaki, Québec, October 5, 1905; Marcotte 2017, 181–82).

28  Pierre Chaussé, the son, is named in the correspondence as "Pierre Socière." See note 6 above for an explanation of the equivalence of Socière/Schocier and Chaussé. Also, Chaussé is identified as a "half breed who is married to an Indian woman" (Maniwaki Agency – Correspondence regarding the renting by Amable Watagon to Pierre Socière of lot 17, Desert front range, Maniwaki, 1888, LAC, RG 10, vol. 2403, file 83,906, folio 2). In all likelihood, this is the same individual mentioned by Father Guinard as owning a small private trading post in the sector of Michomis.

29  Maniwaki Agency – Correspondence regarding the renting by Amable Watagon to Pierre Sociere of lot 17, Desert front range, Maniwaki, 1888, LAC, RG 10, vol. 2403, file 83,906, folio 8.

30  In spite of having one Indigenous great-grandparent to seven white, Pierre Chaussé Jr. (File 19) is nonetheless attributed a Métis identity by the Maniwaki Indian agent Logue. This was probably not based on distinctive physical characteristics but on self-identification with Métis origins going back two or three generations, as can be ascertained from many sources, including Pierre Chaussé himself in 1888.

31  Maniwaki Agency – Correspondence regarding arrears on leased lots, 1888–1929, LAC, RG 10, vol. 2421, file 86,853, folios 30, 43–57.

32  William Budge was a former HBC employee who worked in the Témiscamingue administrative district, most likely at the post of Grand Lac in the 1850s (Southern Department abstracts of servants' accounts book, 1854–55, HBCA, B.135/g/38). According to the correspondence, he was married to a woman of another tribe, not the Algonquins of Maniwaki (Maniwaki Agency – Correspondence regarding arrears on leased lots, 1888–1929, LAC, RG 10, vol. 2421, file 86,853, folio 30).

33  Maniwaki Agency – Correspondence regarding arrears on leased lots, 1888–1929, LAC, RG 10, vol. 2421, file 86,853, folio 30.

34  River Desert Agency – Maniwaki Reserve – Complaint by Augustus Vanose that he has been dispossessed of land at lake Betobi by Antoine Commandant, 1879, LAC, RG 10, vol. 2082, file 12,264.

35  Ibid., folio 5.

36  It is reasonable to conclude that the Vanasse family was prohibited from living in this locale, even if the correspondence ends without providing any additional details.

37  Maniwaki Reserve – River Desert Agency – Request by Mary Vance to build on Eagle River and to purchase fifty acres near the same place, 1875, LAC, RG 10, vol. 1968, file 5274.

38  Ibid., folio 4.

39  Knowing that its Métis identity provided no Indian right, the Vanasse family in all like-lihood opted for the procedures usually reserved for settlers, for strategic or pragmatic reasons.

40  River Desert (Maniwaki) Agency – Correspondence regarding the six children of the late "Widow P. Buckshot" of the River Desert Band who are living with an aunt Mrs Brosseau. The band wishes to place the children under the care of Mathias Techenne, 1899, LAC, RG 10, vol. 2991, file 216,500, folio 2.

41  Although the letter asks "whether Mr. Buckshot was an Indian by blood," this is clearly a typo for "Mrs." Buckshot (the mother). In fact, the late Mr. Buckshot would have appeared in the band registry, and Indian Affairs wanted to ascertain the status of the father of the two sisters involved in the affair: Mrs. Buckshot (recently deceased) and Mrs. Brosseau (who was the actual guardian of the children). See River Desert (Maniwaki) Agency – Correspondence regarding the six children of the late "Widow P. Buckshot," folio 4.

42  Ibid., folio 7.

### Chapter 10: Petitions and Politics

1  Maniwaki Reserve – Correspondence regarding 49 persons not paid by the Indian Department and four affidavits concerning irregular distribution of money by agent White, 1873, Library and Archives Canada (LAC), RG 10, vol. 1906, file 2284, folio 77.

2  Ibid., folio 78.

3  Although other documents from the same correspondence file refer to white complain-ants, it is important to remember that it was common for some observers, including Indian Affairs officials, to classify Métis as white, as they lacked Indian status. As for the French *colon* or English *settler*, it is also worth remembering that some Métis com-munities in many regions used to refer to themselves as such, one case being in Labrador (Kennedy 2014).

4  Maniwaki Reserve – Correspondence regarding 49 persons, folio 78.

5  Jean-Baptiste Paquette married Marie Marguerite Naud, one of the daughters of Élisabeth McPherson (File 13). Even though the couple was married at Pointe-Gatineau, they were at Lac-Sainte-Marie in 1848 (Goudreau 2014a, 284; GSU, BMS of Saint-François-de-Sales-de-Templeton, Pointe-Gatineau, Québec, August 8, 1847). Pierre Chaussé Sr. was the husband of Julie Vanasse (File 19) (GSU, BMS of L'Assomption, Maniwaki, Québec, February 21, 1849). For the St-Denis and Riel families, see Files 16 and 12, respectively. Many other names on the petition suggest Métis or mixed families (white husband and Indian wife), but this has not been investigated in depth. Let us simply cite the Logue, Bodin, Moreau, Malboeuf, Brousseau (sic), Brazeau, Caroll, Moore, Morin, and Portelance families.

6  In the same period, another passage drawn from a similar context but in another region of the world – namely, Brazil – refers to a mixed population and evidences the same usages and distinctions: "Since 1889, census-takers have been forbidden to take any notice of race. But even before that the idea was ridiculed. Codman said in 1872, 'Some years ago, when a census was to be taken, it was proposed to divide *the classes of the community* and to enumerate separately the *white, black and mixed*'" (Rogers 2012, 48).

7  One must keep in mind that in 1847 the Chronicles of the Oblate Missionaries report a distinctive tripartite population at Lac-Sainte-Marie: "Sixteen families, [French] Cana-diens, Métis and Sauvages, have fixed their domicile" (Chronique de la Congrégation des missionnaires Oblats de Marie Immaculée de 1841 à 1893 ["Chronique des

Oblats"], 1949, Archives Deschâtelets-NDC (AD), Fonds Notre-Dame du Cap, BM 2056-01-A, folio 74 [reviewed 1949 transcription of the original document, filed under BM 2056-01, as access to the original is restricted]). In 1828, let us recall, John McLean described the population of Lac des Sables thus: "Being a Stranger in this Country & unaquainted with the Manners & Customs prevalent among its mixed inhabitants you will [illegible] my Curiosity if I enquire of you whether it be yankee or Canadian Hospitality to envite a Friend to sup or Dine with you & then make him pay." See Lake of Two Mountains inward correspondence, 1821–60, Hudson's Bay Company Archives (HBCA), B.110/c/1, folio 22. In 1893, Indian agent James Martin made a series of remarks that also identify the tripartite character of the population of Maniwaki as Indians and non-Indians, the latter group being subdivided into white and Métis: "White or Half breed women who by their marriage to Indians were entitled to be placed on the pay list" (River Desert Agency – Paylists for distribution of the interest money to the River Desert band for the half year ending September the 30th, 1892, 1892–93, LAC, RG 10, vol. 2651, file 131,648, folio 14).

8   Joseph-Étienne Guinard, Mémoires d'un père oblat, 1944–46, AD, Fonds Deschâtelets, HEB 6964.E83C 1, folio 256 (our translation).

9   Ibid., folios 290–91 (our translation).

10  With respect to the rarity of Métis emigration, it is necessary to keep in mind that Guinard is meeting Métis at the turn of the twentieth century, when the great movements tied to the fur trade have long ago come to a close. Yet he describes Métis as continuing to like "to travel" in a fashion that one could describe as regional. It should be noted that this description of an ethnocultural trait goes beyond the biological reductionism that some perceive in it.

11  Quebec Fur Conservation – Correspondence and accounts regarding hunting and trapping licences, 1942–43, LAC, RG 10, vol. 6752, file 420-10-2, June 2, 1942.

12  "Red River" here may refer to the Red River (Rouge River) located in the Outaouais region, where a separate group of Algonquins are reputed to live, or to the Red River region in Manitoba. The evidence points to the latter, which suggests that the Métis McDougall family living in Maniwaki originated in the Manitoba Red River, but we cannot confirm it conclusively.

13  Maniwaki Reserve – Agent John White requesting authority for the River Desert Indians to hold an election of chiefs, 1874, LAC, RG 10, vol. 1934, file 3567, folio 2.

14  Ibid.

15  Ibid.

16  Ibid., folios 9–10.

17  Ibid., folios 14–15.

18  Maniwaki Reserve – Complaints by the chiefs against Mr. Baudin, the present Indian agent, 1874–75, LAC, RG 10, vol. 1940, file 3987, folio 16.

19  This parallels the creation of the Témiscamingue Reserve some twenty years later, when the Indians of that reserve objected to recognizing the Métis *from below* as part of their people. There, too, Father Nédélec hoped Métis would be given land on the reserve, and even political representation, but such projects were then opposed by the "Indians" and the Indian agent.

20  Maniwaki Reserve – Complaints by the chiefs against Mr. Baudin, folios 24–25.

21  "Christinos," and occasionally "Christineau," refers to Indians of the western Cree Nation, whose historical territory included the Red River. Donald Gunn (1860), a long-time resident of the Red River Colony, writes in an article published in the

*Nor'Wester* that Cree surrounded Lake Winnipeg and moved onto the prairies as the French traders advanced. He notes that the Cree had been decimated by the 1780 smallpox epidemic, and that the Ojibwe (Saulteaux) pushed westward, leaving the forests of Red Lake. They encountered Cree and Assiniboines at Pembina Mountain, where, Gunn writes, "they were received in the most friendly manner, and after smoking and feasting for two or three days, the children of the forest [the Ojibwe or Saulteaux] were formally invited to dwell on the plains – to eat out of the same dish, to warm themselves at the same fire, and to make common cause against their enemies the Sioux" (4). Gunn's account is substantiated by other primary historical sources. Alexander Henry (the elder), who in 1760 became the first Englishman to head west into French territory after the Conquest, reached Lake Winnipeg. At the entrance, he found "a large village of Christinaux," noting that the term was also written as "Cristinaux, Kinistineaux, Killistinoes and Killistinaux" (Henry 1809, 246–47). He adds that "Lake Winipegon is sometimes called the Lake of the Killistinons, or Cristinaux." Henry's nephew, Alexander Henry the younger (Gough 2013, 19), refers in 1800 to a locale on the edges of the prairie to the south of Lake Winnipeg, close to the juncture of the Red and Assiniboine Rivers. At this place, "formerly the Crees and the Assineboines were accustomed to assemble in large camp to wait the arrival of the Traders, and it is here where we may say the Meadow Country [i.e., prairie] commences in this direction." In 1806, he writes, "At Nine Oclock we passed the old Fort de Tremble where formerly there was an old Establishment which was attacked by the Crees in the Year 1781 when several of them were killed by the Canadians" (196). This fort was located on the banks of the Assiniboine River, some five miles from Portage La Prairie. The historical evidence thus supports Gunn's account, and the Cree would certainly have inhabited the Upper Red River in the 1780s. Thus, there is a strong likelihood that the name "Christineau," which is often attributed to the McDougall family, is tied to origins in the Red River. It is also possible, however, that the McDougalls originated from the other Red River, the one in the Laurentians in Québec, where one finds a historical Algonquin presence. Those Algonquins' attempt to join the Maniwaki Reserve could have occasioned some tensions, similar to those following the arrival of the Lièvre River Algonquins in the Maniwaki Reserve (Frenette 1993, 44–45). We do know that one of the Métis McDougalls frequented the Laurentian Red River in 1832 (see Montreal inward correspondence, 1832, HBCA, B.134/c/15, folio 64). That said, the family name Christineau applied to the McDougalls does not suggest Algonquin origins, but rather a Cree influence from the West. Additionally, we know that the Maniwaki Reserve was created for all Algonquins, Nipissings, and Têtes-de-Boule (Atikamekw), whose hunting territory covered the land between the Saint-Maurice and Gatineau rivers, thus including those of Québec's Red River (Maniwaki Agency – Correspondence stemming from a letter from Alonzo Wright suggesting that the Maniwaki Reserve be sold, 1882–88, LAC, RG 10, vol. 2170, file 35,600, folio 7). For this reason, excluding this McDougall from the reserve because he might have had origins in the Outaouais Red River area seems nonsensical.

22  This Angus Cameron appears to have no ties to the man of the same name who was an officer of the HBC in the nineteenth century in the greater Outaouais region.

23  Montreal inward correspondence, 1842, HBCA, B.134/c/53, folio 216.

24  This transition is also apparent among upper-class Métis families. A case in point: a former clerk at the Lac des Sables fur trade post, Thomas Taylor (File 17), affirms in

a letter dated 1855 that he has launched a forest enterprise in the region of Fort Coulonge (Montreal inward correspondence, 1855, HBCA, B.134/c/72, folio 673).

25 See mentions of forestry drawings and maps produced by the Métis John McKay at Lake Témiscamingue at the request of the HBC: Montreal inward correspondence, 1840, HBCA, B.134/c/45b, folio 22; 1844, HBCA, B.134/c/58, folio 263.

26 The map in question is likely to be one that Logan collected at Fort Témiscamingue. According to Guillaume Marcotte, the principal cartographer, a Métis interpreter at the post named John McKay, "by his belonging to a double sociocultural reality, integrated cartographic conventions originating from two distinct groups ... He knew how to integrate the 'genius of *Sauvage* industries,' of which he was himself heir to the requirements of merchant capitalism and the colonial social order" (Marcotte 2015, 89; our translation).

### Chapter 11: The Great Awakening

1 For a detailed discussion of continuing internal tensions concerning the use of the term *Métis*, see Tremblay 2009.

2 A series of interviews with Métis Elders living in the Gatineau Valley was conducted under the auspices of the Canada Research Chair on Métis Identity (Chaire de recherche du Canada sur l'identité métisse), as well as through a research project on the Status of the Métis in Canada: Agency and Social Issues (Le statut de Métis au Canada: Agencéité et enjeux sociaux), both under the direction of Professor Denis Gagnon of the Université de Saint-Boniface. The first project lasted a decade, starting from 2004; the latter was a five-year SSHRC-funded project that began in 2013. Both projects collected interviews from individuals who identify as Métis from across the country, using semi-structured interviews with verbatim transcriptions.

3 It appears that this family has ties to the Métis interpreter John Knight mentioned in Chapter 7.

### Conclusion: Toward Recognition?

1 Library and Archives Canada (LAC) defines a road allowance as follows: "A tract of land left between sections for road construction. Originally, road allowances measured 1.5 track links (99 feet) in width and extended along the four sides of each section. Subsequently, their width was reduced to 1 track link (66 feet) and two of the tracts of east-west land were no longer set aside for road construction" (LAC, 2012, "Road Allowance," Glossary – Métis Scrip Records, https://www.collectionscanada.gc.ca/metis-scrip/005005-5000-e.html#r).

2 In the words of Taché, "A small colony of Iroquois came from Canada [meaning Québec] to the Rocky Mountains; there they allied themselves with women from the Indigenous tribes, and oddly enough the children born of these unions are classified among our Métis. Not a drop of white blood flows in their veins and the descendants of these fierce warriors who used to make our ancestors tremble in the first settlement of Canada are today considered as Canadien-Métis" (David 1882, 72–73; our translation).

3 An academic version of this argument can be find in the work of Chris Andersen (2014), who posits that Métis achieved true nationhood as they achieved the prerequisite national consciousness in the strife leading up to the creation of Manitoba and the 1885 North-West Resistance, thus becoming fully Métis as opposed to simply mixed and thus truly Indigenous. This political maturity, and attendant national consciousness, would

be lacking among other mixed-bloods, who are considered either assimilated (thus white) or simply biologically mixed (lowercase métis), not truly Métis.

## Appendix: Principal Métis Families of the Gatineau

1  Southern Department abstracts of servants' accounts book, 1833–34, Hudson's Bay Company Archives (HBCA), B.135/g/17.

2  Southern Department abstracts of servants' accounts book, 1835–36, HBCA, B.135/g/19.

3  Carnet G-25, Cantons Aylwin et Hincks/John Allan Snow, May 8, 1848, Bibliothèque et Archives nationales du Québec, Québec (BAnQ-Q), Fonds Ministère des Terres et Forêts, E21,S60,SS3,PG25, folio 74.

4  Montreal inward correspondence, 1845, HBCA, B.134/c/60, folio 246; Montreal Department abstracts of servants' accounts, 1844–45, HBCA, B.134/g/19.

5  GSU, BMS of Saint-François-de-Sales-de-Templeton, Pointe-Gatineau, Québec, February 16, 1849.

6  See Fort Resolution on Map 1.

7  Montreal Department abstracts of servants' accounts, 1827–28, HBCA, B.134/g/6; 1829–30, HBCA, B.134/g/7; and 1830–31, HBCA, B.134/g/8.

8  GSU, BMS of Notre-Dame-de-Bon-Secours, Montebello, July 6, 1832.

9  Ibid.

10  Ibid.

11  Contracts of Ambroise Beaulieu, July 27, 1822, July 4, 1826, and July 11, 1827, Société historique de Saint-Boniface, Voyageur Contracts Database (SHSB-VC), 2010, http://shsb.mb.ca/en/Voyageurs_database; Montreal Department abstracts of servants' accounts, 1827–28, HBCA, B.134/g/6; 1829–30, HBCA, B.134/g/7; and 1830–31, HBCA, B.134/g/8.

12  Contracts of Ambroise Beaulieu, July 11, 1827, Centre du patrimoine, Voyageurs Contracts Database, http://shsb.mb.ca/en/Voyageurs_database.

13  Montreal inward correspondence, 1838, HBCA, B.134/c/40, folio 48.

14  GSU, BMS of Notre-Dame-de-Bon-Secours, Montebello, July 6, 1832.

15  Ibid.

16  GSU, BMS of Notre-Dame-de-Bon-Secours, Montebello, August 8, 1833.

17  BMS Missions Diocese of Pembroke, 1836–42, Diocese of Pembroke Archives (DPA), Lac des Sables, June 2, 1841.

18  GSU, BMS of L'Assomption, Maniwaki, Québec, February 6, 1854.

19  GSU, BMS of Saint-Grégoire-de-Nazianze, Buckingham, Québec, October 16, 1858.

20  GSU, BMS of L'Assomption, Maniwaki, Québec, July 24, 1877.

21  GSU, BMS of L'Assomption, Maniwaki, Québec, July 9, 1878.

22  GSU, BMS of L'Assomption, Maniwaki, Québec, February 15, 1915.

23  GSU, BMS of Sainte-Geneviève-de-Berthier, Québec, March 6, 1802.

24  Montreal inward correspondence, 1829, HBCA, B.134/c/5, folio 86b; Montreal Department abstracts of servants' accounts, 1827–28, HBCA, B.134/g/6.

25  BMS Missions Diocese of Pembroke, 1836–42, DPA, August 7, 1836.

26  Montreal inward correspondence, 1843, HBCA, B.134/c/55, folio 3.

27  Southern Department abstracts of servants' accounts book, 1843–44, HBCA, B.135/g/27.

28  Temiscamingue inward correspondence, 1844–50, HBCA, B.218/c/1, folios 1–2.

29  Montreal inward correspondence, 1846, HBCA, B.134/c/62, folio 411.

30 GSU, BMS of Saint-Grégoire-de-Nazianze, Buckingham, Québec, August 17, 1840.

31 Scrip affidavit for Gaudry, Madeleine, wife of André Gaudry [...], 1876, Library and Archives Canada (LAC), RG 15-D-II-8-a. vol./box 1321, container C-14928.

32 Census, LAC, 1881.

33 Joseph-Étienne Guinard, Mémoires d'un père oblat, 1944–46, Archives Deschâtelets-NDC (AD), Fonds Deschâtelets, HEB 6964.E83C 1, folio 69.

34 GSU, BMS of L'Assomption, Maniwaki, Québec, April 28, 1879.

35 GSU, BMS of Saint-Grégoire-de-Nazianze, Buckingham, Québec, February 7, 1842.

36 Carnet 29 Rivière du Lièvre/Alphonse Wells, January 13, 1847, BAnQ-Q, Fonds Ministère des Terres et Forêts. E21,S60,SS2,P29, folio 138.

37 Montreal inward correspondence, 1845, HBCA, B.134/c/59, folios 9–9b.

38 Census, LAC, 1871.

39 As a case in point, see his account as "trapper." Montreal Department abstracts of servants' accounts, 1836–37, HBCA, B.134/g/11.

40 BMS Missions Diocese of Pembroke, 1836–42, DPA, August 11, 1842.

41 GSU, BMS of L'Annonciation, Oka, Québec, July 10, 1837.

42 BMS Missions Diocese of Pembroke, 1836–42, DPA, Mitcikanabikong, June 19, 1841.

43 GSU, BMS of Sainte-Madeleine-de-Rigaud, Québec, July 13, 1813.

44 GSU, BMS of Sainte-Madeleine-de-Rigaud, Québec, September 28, 1812.

45 GSU, BMS of Sainte-Madeleine-de-Rigaud, Québec, September 27, 1812.

46 Montreal Department abstracts of servants' accounts, 1829–30, HBCA, B.134/g/7; 1830–31, HBCA, B.134/g/8; 1834–35, HBCA, B.134/g/9; 1835–36, HBCA, B.134/g/10; 1836–37, HBCA, B.134/g/11; 1837–38, HBCA, B.134/g/12; 1838–39, HBCA, B.134/g/13; 1839–40, HBCA, B.134/g/14; and 1840–41, HBCA, B.134/g/15.

47 Carnet 29 Rivière du Lièvre/Alphonse Wells, January 13, 1847, BAnQ-Q, Fonds Ministère des Terres et Forêts. E21,S60,SS2,P29, folio 137.

48 BMS Missions Diocese of Pembroke, 1836–42, DPA, Mitcikanabikong, June 19, 1841.

49 BMS Missions Diocese of Pembroke, 1836–42, DPA, June 2, 1841; GSU, BMS of Notre-Dame, Ottawa, Ontario, August 25, 1834.

50 Montreal inward correspondence, 1829, HBCA, B.134/c/6, folio 229b; Montreal Department abstracts of servants' accounts, 1830–31, HBCA, B.134/g/8.

51 GSU, BMS of L'Annonciation, Oka, Québec, September 2, 1835.

52 GSU, BMS of L'Annonciation, Oka, Québec, June 22, 1837.

53 GSU, BMS of Notre-Dame-de-Bon-Secours, Montebello, August 13, 1839.

54 BMS Missions Diocese of Pembroke, 1836–42, DPA, June 2, 1841.

55 GSU, BMS of L'Assomption, Maniwaki, Québec, March 10, 1857.

56 Maniwaki Reserve – André Lacroix writes stating that one Xear Boutin is depriving his Indian granddaughter of her land and an annuity, 1879a, LAC, RG 10, vol. 2084, file 12,930, folio 2.

57 GSU, BMS of L'Assomption, Maniwaki, Québec, April 17, 1855.

58 GSU, BMS of L'Assomption, Maniwaki, Québec, March 10, 1857.

59 GSU, BMS of L'Assomption, Maniwaki, Québec, July 14, 1873.

60 GSU, BMS of L'Assomption, Maniwaki, Québec, July 16, 1895.

61 GSU, BMS of L'Assomption, Maniwaki, Québec, January 8, 1872.

62 GSU, BMS of Saint-Paul-d'Aylmer, Québec, January 19, 1844.

63 Southern Department abstracts of servants' accounts book, 1829–30, HBCA, B.135/g/11; 1830–31, HBCA, B.135/g/13; 1831–32, HBCA, B.135/g/14; 1832–33, HBCA, B.135/g/15; 1833–34, HBCA, B.135/g/17; 1834–35, HBCA, B.135/g/18;

1835–36, HBCA, B.135/g/19; 1836–37, HBCA, B.135/g/20; 1837–38, HBCA, B.135/g/21; 1838–39, HBCA, B.135/g/22; 1839–40, HBCA, B.135/g/23; 1840–41, HBCA, B.135/g/24; 1841–42, HBCA, B.135/g/25; 1842–43, HBCA, B.135/g/26; and 1843–44, HBCA, B.135/g/27.

64   Aeneas and Angus Cameron fonds, Angus Cameron – inward correspondence – private, 1843–50, HBCA, E.41/10, folio 3.

65   BMS Missions Diocese of Pembroke, DPA, Grand Lac, August 6, 1838.

66   BMS Missions Diocese of Pembroke, DPA, Grand Lac, August 3, 1838.

67   BMS Missions Diocese of Pembroke, DPA, Mitcikanabikong, June 19, 1841.

68   GSU, BMS of Saint-François-de-Sales-de-Templeton, Pointe-Gatineau, Québec, January 26, 1848.

69   GSU, BMS of Saint-Paul-d'Aylmer, Québec, January 19, 1844.

70   GSU, BMS of Saint-Paul-d'Aylmer, Québec, June 28, 1844.

71   Contracts of Jacques Lavigne, August 3, 1825, Centre du patrimoine, Voyageurs Contracts Database, http://shsb.mb.ca/en/Voyageurs_database.

72   Carnet G-25, Cantons Aylwin et Hincks/John Allan Snow, May 8, 1848, BAnQ-Q, Fonds Ministère des Terres et Forêts, E21,S60,SS3,PG25, folio 74.

73   BMS of Sainte-Anne, Île-du-Grand-Calumet, Québec, May 18, 1864.

74   Montreal Department abstracts of servants' accounts, 1823–24, HBCA, B.134/g/4; GSU, BMS of Notre-Dame, Ottawa, Ontario, February 4, 1836.

75   BMS Missions Diocese of Pembroke, DPA, Lac-Sainte-Marie, August 11, 1842.

76   GSU, BMS of Saint-Paul-d'Aylmer, Québec, June 28, 1844.

77   GSU, BMS of Saint-François-de-Sales-de-Templeton, Pointe-Gatineau, Québec, August 17, 1848.

78   GSU, BMS of Saint-Paul-d'Aylmer, Québec, January 26, 1845.

79   BMS Missions Diocese of Pembroke, DPA, Lac-Sainte-Marie, August 11, 1842; GSU, BMS of Saint-Paul-d'Aylmer, Québec, June 28, 1844.

80   GSU, BMS of Saint-Paul-d'Aylmer, Québec, June 18, 1845; GSU, BMS of Saint-François-de-Sales-de-Templeton, Pointe-Gatineau, Québec, January 26, 1848.

81   GSU, BMS of Saint-François-de-Sales-de-Templeton, Pointe-Gatineau, Québec, February 16, 1849.

82   Montreal inward correspondence, 1832, HBCA, B.134/c/15, folio 180.

83   Montreal Department abstracts of servants' accounts, 1834–35, HBCA, B.134/g/9; 1835–36, HBCA, B.134/g/10; 1836–37, HBCA, B.134/g/11; and 1837–38, HBCA, B.134/g/12.

84   BMS Missions Diocese of Pembroke, DPA, 1842-08-11; Montreal Department abstracts of servants' accounts, 1834–35, HBCA, B.134/g/9; 1835–36, HBCA, B.134/g/10; 1836–37, HBCA, B.134/g/11; and 1837–38, HBCA, B.134/g/12.

85   Montreal Department abstracts of servants' accounts, 1834–35, HBCA, B.134/g/9; 1835–36, HBCA, B.134/g/10; 1836–37, HBCA, B.134/g/11; and 1837–38, HBCA, B.134/g/12.

86   Montreal inward correspondence, 1838, HBCA, B.134/c/39, folio 132.

87   Montreal inward correspondence, 1841, HBCA, B.134/c/50, folios 9–9b.

88   Carnet G-25, Cantons Aylwin et Hincks/John Allan Snow, May 8, 1848, BAnQ-Q, Fonds Ministère des Terres et Forêts, E21,S60,SS3,PG25, folio 75.

89   Aeneas and Angus Cameron fonds, Angus Cameron – inward correspondence – private, 1843–50, HBCA, E.41/10, folio 11b.

90   Grand Lac post journal, 1852–53, HBCA, B.82/a/3, April 3, 1853.

91  GSU, BMS of L'Assomption, Maniwaki, Québec, February 14, 1873.
92  BMS Missions Diocese of Pembroke, DPA, August 11, 1842.
93  GSU, BMS of Saint-Paul-d'Aylmer, Québec, June 18, 1845.
94  GSU, BMS of Saint-François-de-Sales-de-Templeton, Pointe-Gatineau, Québec, January 26, 1848.
95  Montreal Department abstracts of servants' accounts, 1834–35, HBCA, B.134/g/9; 1835–36, HBCA, B.134/g/10; 1836–37, HBCA, B.134/g/11; and 1837–38, HBCA, B.134/g/12.
96  Montreal inward correspondence, 1832, HBCA, B.134/c/15, folio 180.
97  GSU, BMS of L'Annonciation, Oka, Québec, August 16, 1840; GSU, BMS of L'Annonciation, Oka, Québec, August 18, 1840.
98  Montreal Department abstracts of servants' accounts, 1834–35, HBCA, B.134/g/9; 1835–36, HBCA, B.134/g/10; 1836–37, HBCA, B.134/g/11; and 1837–38, HBCA, B.134/g/12.
99  Montreal inward correspondence, 1838, HBCA, B.134/c/39, folio 132.
100  Montreal inward correspondence, 1841, HBCA, B.134/c/50, folios 9–9b.
101  GSU, BMS of Saint-Paul-d'Aylmer, Québec, April 13, 1841; GSU, BMS of Saint-Paul-d'Aylmer, Québec, March 24, 1843.
102  GSU, BMS of L'Annonciation, Oka, Québec, August 18, 1840.
103  Montreal Department abstracts of servants' accounts, 1834–35, HBCA, B.134/g/9; 1835–36, HBCA, B.134/g/10; 1836–37, HBCA, B.134/g/11; and 1837–38, HBCA, B.134/g/12; Maniwaki Reserve – Complaints by the chiefs against Mr. Baudin, the present Indian agent, 1874–75, LAC, RG 10, vol. 1940, file 3987, folios 24–25.
104  Contract of Joseph Perriard, July 20, 1808, Centre du patrimoine, Voyageurs Contracts Database, http://shsb.mb.ca/en/Voyageurs_database.
105  GSU, BMS of L'Annonciation, Oka, Québec, August 18, 1840.
106  Ibid.
107  GSU, BMS of Saint-Paul-d'Aylmer, Québec, April 13, 1841.
108  GSU, BMS of Saint-Paul-d'Aylmer, Québec, March 24, 1843.
109  GSU, BMS of Saint-Paul-d'Aylmer, Québec, January 20, 1844.
110  Census, LAC, 1861.
111  GSU, BMS of Notre-Dame, Ottawa, Ontario, October 21, 1838.
112  Carnet G-25, Cantons Aylwin et Hincks/John Allan Snow, May 8, 1848, BAnQ-Q, Fonds Ministère des Terres et Forêts, E21,S60,SS3,PG25, folio 75.
113  GSU, BMS of Saint-Paul-d'Aylmer, Québec, April 13, 1841.
114  Census, LAC, 1861.
115  Ibid.
116  Ibid.
117  GSU, BMS of Saint-Paul-d'Aylmer, Québec, April 13, 1841.
118  GSU, BMS of Saint-Paul-d'Aylmer, Québec, October 12, 1842.
119  GSU, BMS of Saint-Paul-d'Aylmer, Québec, January 26, 1845.
120  Census, LAC, 1861.
121  Ibid.
122  Ibid.
123  Ibid.
124  Ibid.
125  GSU, BMS of Saint-Paul-d'Aylmer, Québec, January 26, 1845.
126  Ibid.

127  Ibid.
128  GSU, BMS of Saint-Paul-d'Aylmer, Québec, June 18, 1845.
129  Ibid.
130  Ibid.; GSU, BMS of Saint-François-de-Sales-de-Templeton, Pointe-Gatineau, Québec, January 26, 1848.
131  GSU, BMS of L'Assomption, Maniwaki, Québec, November 26, 1858.
132  GSU, BMS of Saint-Paul-d'Aylmer, Québec, January 20, 1844.
133  GSU, BMS of Saint-Paul-d'Aylmer, Québec, April 13, 1841.
134  BMS Missions Diocese of Pembroke, DPA, Lac-Sainte-Marie, August 11, 1842; GSU, BMS of Saint-Paul-d'Aylmer, Québec, June 28, 1844.
135  GSU, BMS of Saint-Paul-d'Aylmer, Québec, January 26, 1845.
136  Ibid.
137  GSU, BMS of Saint-Paul-d'Aylmer, Québec, June 18, 1845.
138  GSU, BMS of Saint-François-de-Sales-de-Templeton, Pointe-Gatineau, Québec, February 16, 1849.
139  GSU, BMS of L'Annonciation, Oka, Québec, August 14, 1826.
140  Louis Riel et sa famille/Madame Violet Lalonde [copy], 1980, Bibliothèque et Archives nationales du Québec, Gatineau (BAnQ-G), Fonds Centre de l'Outaouais de Bibliothèque et Archives nationales du Québec, P1000, D65, 17.
141  GSU, BMS of L'Annonciation, Oka, Québec, August 14, 1826.
142  GSU, BMS of Saint-Joachim-de-la-Pointe-Claire, Québec, August 12, 1827.
143  GSU, BMS of L'Annonciation, Oka, Québec, August 14, 1826.
144  GSU, BMS of Saint-Joachim-de-la-Pointe-Claire, Québec, August 12, 1825.
145  GSU, BMS of Saint-Joachim-de-la-Pointe-Claire, Québec, August 12, 1827.
146  GSU, BMS of Notre-Dame-de-Bon-Secours, Montebello, August 15, 1829.
147  GSU, BMS of L'Annonciation, Oka, Québec, August 7, 1835.
148  GSU, BMS of L'Annonciation, Oka, Québec, August 1, 1838.
149  GSU, BMS of L'Annonciation, Oka, Québec, June 13, 1840.
150  GSU, BMS of Saint-Grégoire-de-Nazianze, Buckingham, Québec, April 10, 1842.
151  GSU, BMS of Saint-Grégoire-de-Nazianze, Buckingham, Québec, October 13, 1844.
152  GSU, BMS of Notre-Dame, Montréal, Québec, September 15, 1838; GSU, BMS of Saint-Paul-d'Aylmer, Québec, January 18, 1844.
153  GSU, BMS of Notre-Dame, Montréal, Québec, September 15, 1838; Southern Department abstracts of servants' accounts book, 1838–39, HBCA, B.135/g/22.
154  Journal d'une Mission faite dans l'Été de 1838, au lac Témiskaming, au lac d'Abittibi, au Grand Lac et au Fort des Allumettes [copy], 1838, Bibliothèque et Archives nationales du Québec, Rouyn-Noranda (BAnQ-RN), Fonds Donat Martineau, P10,S3,SS3,D4,P29, folio 9.
155  Montreal inward correspondence, 1838, HBCA, B.134/c/40, folio 48.
156  GSU, BMS of Notre-Dame, Montréal, Québec, September 15, 1838.
157  Census, LAC, 1861
158  GSU, BMS of Saint-Paul-d'Aylmer, Québec, April 13, 1841.
159  GSU, BMS of Saint-Paul-d'Aylmer, Québec, August 22, 1843.
160  Census, LAC, 1861.
161  GSU, BMS of Saint-François-de-Sales-de-Templeton, Pointe-Gatineau, Québec, August 18, 1848.
162  Census, LAC, 1861.
163  Ibid.

164 Ibid.
165 Ibid.
166 Ibid.
167 Ibid.
168 Montreal inward correspondence, 1830, HBCA, B.134/c/8, folios 140–40b.
169 Grand Lac blotter, 1836–38, HBCA, B.82/d/3, June 3, 1837.
170 Montreal inward correspondence, 1838, HBCA, B.134/c/40, folio 48.
171 GSU, BMS of Saint-Grégoire-de-Nazianze, Buckingham, Québec, September 13, 1840.
172 Montreal Department abstracts of servants' accounts, 1835–36, HBCA, B.134/g/10; and 1836–37, HBCA, B.134/g/11.
173 Montreal Department abstracts of servants' accounts, 1837–38, HBCA, B.134/g/12; and 1838–39, HBCA, B.134/g/13.
174 Montreal inward correspondence, 1839, HBCA, B.134/c/43, folio 175.
175 Census, LAC, 1861; Census, LAC, 1871.
176 BMS Missions Diocese of Pembroke, DPA, August 11, 1842.
177 GSU, BMS of Saint-Paul-d'Aylmer, Québec, August 22, 1843.
178 GSU, BMS of Saint-Paul-d'Aylmer, Québec, June 28, 1844.
179 GSU, BMS of Saint-François-de-Sales-de-Templeton, Pointe-Gatineau, Québec, August 15, 1848.
180 Census, LAC, 1861.
181 Census, LAC, 1871.
182 Census, LAC, 1861; Census, LAC, 1871.
183 Census, LAC, 1871.
184 GSU, BMS of Saint-Paul-d'Aylmer, Québec, April 13, 1841.
185 Ibid.
186 GSU, BMS of Saint-Paul-d'Aylmer, Québec, January 19, 1844.
187 GSU, BMS of Saint-François-de-Sales-de-Templeton, Pointe-Gatineau, Québec, August 17, 1848.
188 BMS Missions Diocese of Pembroke, DPA, Lac-Sainte-Marie, August 11, 1842.
189 Ibid.
190 Montreal inward correspondence, 1828, HBCA, B.134/c/4, folio 177b; Montreal Department abstracts of servants' accounts, 1827–28, HBCA, B.134/g/6.
191 Montreal inward correspondence, 1829, HBCA, B.134/c/6, folio 229b.
192 GSU, BMS of Saint-Pierre-de-Sorel, Québec, November 11, 1800.
193 GSU, BMS of Saint-Ours, Québec, April 24, 1820.
194 Census, LAC, 1861.
195 Montreal Department abstracts of servants' accounts, 1841–42, HBCA, B.134/g/16.
196 Census, LAC, 1861; Census, LAC, 1871.
197 Census, LAC, 1871; GSU, BMS of Nativité-de-Notre-Dame-de-Bécancour, Québec, July 7, 1856.
198 GSU, BMS of L'Assomption, Maniwaki, Québec, July 13, 1844.
199 Montreal inward correspondence, 1845, HBCA, B.134/c/59, folio 105c.
200 GSU, BMS of L'Assomption, Maniwaki, Québec, July 13, 1844.
201 Southern Department abstracts of servants' accounts book, 1844–45, HBCA, B.135/g/28; and 1847–48, HBCA, B.135/g/31; HBCA, B.135/a/151, June 17, 1846.
202 Aeneas and Angus Cameron fonds, Angus Cameron – inward correspondence – Charles Stuart, 1851–68, HBCA, E.41/14, folio 2.
203 GSU, BMS of L'Assomption, Maniwaki, Québec, June 11, 1847.

204   GSU, BMS of L'Assomption, Maniwaki, Québec, July 28, 1849.

205   GSU, BMS of L'Assomption, Maniwaki, Québec, April 28, 1879.

206   GSU, BMS of L'Assomption, Maniwaki, Québec, June 6, 1852.

207   GSU, BMS of L'Assomption, Maniwaki, Québec, June 11, 1847.

208   GSU, BMS of L'Assomption, Maniwaki, Québec, October 20, 1865.

209   GSU, BMS of L'Assomption, Maniwaki, Québec, April 28, 1879.

210   HBCA (n.d), TAYLOR, George, https://www.gov.mb.ca/chc/archives/hbca/biographical/t/taylor_george1787-1818.pdf; HBCA (n.d.), TAYLOR, Thomas Sr, https://www.gov.mb.ca/chc/archives/hbca/biographical/t/taylor_thomas-sr.pdf.

211   HBCA (n.d.), TAYLOR, Thomas Sr, https://www.gov.mb.ca/chc/archives/hbca/biographical/t/taylor_thomas-sr.pdf.

212   Ibid.

213   Ibid.

214   Montreal Department abstracts of servants' accounts, 1822–23, HBCA, B.134/g/2 and B.134/g/3; 1823–24, HBCA, B.134/g/4.

215   GSU, BMS of Saint-Paul-d'Aylmer, Québec, January 20, 1844.

216   Ibid.; GSU, BMS of Saint-François-de-Sales-de-Templeton, Pointe-Gatineau, Québec, January 26, 1848.

217   GSU, BMS of Saint-Paul-d'Aylmer, Québec, January 20, 1844.

218   Carnet G-25, Cantons Aylwin et Hincks/John Allan Snow, May 28, 1848, BAnQ-Q, Fonds Ministère des Terres et Forêts, E21,S60,SS3,PG25, folio 75.

219   Montreal inward correspondence, 1839, HBCA, B.134/c/43, folio 175.

220   GSU, BMS of Saint-Paul-d'Aylmer, Québec, January 20, 1844.

221   GSU, BMS of Saint-Paul-d'Aylmer, Québec, January 26, 1845.

222   GSU, BMS of Saint-François-de-Sales-de-Templeton, Pointe-Gatineau, Québec, August 16, 1848.

223   GSU, BMS of Saint-Paul-d'Aylmer, Québec, January 26, 1845.

224   GSU, BMS of Saint-Paul-d'Aylmer, Québec, June 18, 1845.

225   GSU, BMS of Saint-Paul-d'Aylmer, Québec, January 26, 1845.

226   GSU, BMS of Saint-François-de-Sales-de-Templeton, Pointe-Gatineau, Québec, January 26, 1848.

227   GSU, BMS of Saint-Joseph-de-Maskinongé, Québec, December 26, 1834.

228   Northern Department abstracts of servants' accounts, 1837-38, HBCA, B.239/g/17; 1838-39, HBCA, B.239/g/18.

229   Montreal inward correspondence, 1836, HBCA, B.134/c/31, folio 109b; GSU, BMS of L'Assomption, Maniwaki, Québec, February 21, 1849.

230   River Desert Agency – Maniwaki Reserve – Complaint by Augustus Vanose that he has been dispossessed of land at lake Betobi by Antoine Commandant, 1879, LAC, RG 10, vol. 2082, file 12,264; GSU, BMS of L'Assomption, Maniwaki, Québec, 1855-04-17; GSU, BMS of L'Assomption, Maniwaki, Québec, September 7, 1856.

231   GSU, BMS of L'Assomption, Maniwaki, Québec, May 28, 1855.

232   GSU, BMS of Saint-François-de-Sales-de-Templeton, Pointe-Gatineau, Québec, January 26, 1848.

233   River Desert Agency – Maniwaki Reserve – Complaint by Augustus Vanose that he has been dispossessed of land at lake Betobi by Antoine Commandant, 1879, LAC, RG 10, vol. 2082, file 12,264.

234   GSU, BMS of L'Assomption, Maniwaki, Québec, February 8, 1864.

235   GSU, BMS of L'Assomption, Maniwaki, Québec, January 2, 1854.

236　GSU, BMS of L'Assomption, Maniwaki, Québec, July 17, 1856.

237　GSU, BMS of L'Assomption, Maniwaki, Québec, April 17, 1855.

238　GSU, BMS of L'Assomption, Maniwaki, Québec, July 16, 1895.

239　GSU, BMS of L'Assomption, Maniwaki, Québec, January 8, 1872.

240　GSU, BMS of L'Assomption, Maniwaki, Québec, October 5, 1905.

241　GSU, BMS of L'Assomption, Maniwaki, Québec, July 24, 1877.

242　GSU, BMS of L'Assomption, Maniwaki, Québec, July 9, 1878.

243　GSU, BMS of L'Assomption, Maniwaki, Québec, February 15, 1915.

244　GSU, BMS of Saint-François-de-Sales-de-Templeton, Pointe-Gatineau, Québec, January 26, 1848.

245　GSU, BMS of L'Assomption, Maniwaki, Québec, October 20, 1865.

# Works Cited

## Archival Documents

*Archives Deschâtelets-NDC, Richelieu, Québec (AD)*
Fonds Deschâtelets
Fonds Notre-Dame du Cap

*Archives nationales d'Outre-Mer, Aix-en-Provence, France (ANOM)*
Fonds ministériels, Premier empire colonial, Correspondance à l'arrivée, Canada et
    colonies du Nord de l'Amérique, Canada, série principale, COL C11A

*Archives of Ontario, Toronto (AO)*
Eustache Lesage Death Certificate, 1922, Algoma District, Indian Reserve Division,
    Garden River

*Bibliothèque et Archives nationales du Québec, Gatineau (BAnQ-G)*
Fonds Centre de l'Outaouais de Bibliothèque et Archives nationales du Québec,
    P1000
Fonds William H. Dunning, P142

*Bibliothèque et Archives nationales du Québec, Québec (BAnQ-Q)*
Fonds Ministère des Terres et Forêts, E21

*Bibliothèque et Archives nationales du Québec, Rouyn-Noranda (BAnQ-RN)*
Fonds Donat Martineau, P10

*Bibliothèque et Archives nationales du Québec, Vieux-Montréal (BAnQ-VM)*
Fonds Cour des plaidoyers communs du district de Montréal, TL16

*Diocese of Pembroke Archives, Pembroke, Ontario (DPA)*
BMS Missions Diocese of Pembroke

*Genealogical Society of Utah, Salt Lake City (GSU), Baptism, Marriage,
Sepulture (BMS)*
BMS of L'Annonciation, Oka, Québec
BMS of L'Assomption, Maniwaki, Québec
BMS of Mont-Saint-Hilaire, Québec

BMS of Nativité-de-Notre-Dame-de-Bécancour, Québec
BMS of Notre-Dame, Montréal, Québec
BMS of Notre-Dame, Ottawa, Ontario
BMS of Notre-Dame-de-Bon-Secours, Montebello, Québec
BMS of Saint-François-de-Sales-de-Templeton, Pointe-Gatineau, Québec
BMS of Saint-Grégoire-de-Nazianze, Buckingham, Québec
BMS of Saint-Joachim-de-la-Pointe-Claire, Québec
BMS of Saint-Joseph-de-Maskinongé, Québec
BMS of Saint-Ours, Québec
BMS of Saint-Paul-d'Aylmer, Québec
BMS of Saint-Pierre-de-Sorel, Québec
BMS of Sainte-Anne, Île-du-Grand-Calumet, Québec
BMS of Sainte-Geneviève-de-Berthier, Québec
BMS of Sainte-Madeleine-de-Rigaud, Québec

*Hudson's Bay Company Archives, Winnipeg, Manitoba (HBCA)*
Cameron Papers, E.41
Grand Lac account books, B.82/d
Grand Lac post journals, B.82/a
Lake of Two Mountains inward correspondence, B.110/c
Montreal inward correspondence, B.134/c
Montreal Department abstracts of servants' accounts, B.134/g
Moose Factory post journals, B.135/a
Northern Department abstracts of servants' accounts, B.239/g
Southern Department abstracts of servants' accounts, B.135/g
Temiscamingue inward correspondence, B.218/c

*Library and Archives Canada, Ottawa, Ontario (LAC)*
Department of the Interior Fonds, RG 15
Files of the Canadian Expeditionary Force (CEF): Soldiers, nurses, and
    chaplains, RG 150
Indian Affairs Records, RG 10

*National Archives, Washington, DC, United States (NA)*
Fifteenth Census of the United States, 1930
Tenth Census of the United States, 1880

*Société d'Histoire du Témiscamingue, Ville-Marie, Québec (SHT)*
Fonds Hudson Bay Company, P49

*Société historique de Saint-Boniface, Winnipeg, Manitoba (SHSB)*
Fonds 0075, Corporation archiépiscopale catholique romaine de Saint-Boniface
Fonds 0003, Louis Riel

**Primary Published Sources**
Adams, John. 1831. "Sketches of the Tête de Boule Indians, River St. Maurice."
    *Transactions of the Literary and Historical Society of Quebec* 2: 25–39.

*L'Alliance*. 1979. "Le NCC et L'Alliance tiennent leurs assemblées ensemble: Manitoba site confirmé – 20–24 août." *Le Journal Alliance* 6, 1 (January): 6.

–. 1980. "Metis and Non-Status Indians: An Interview with Rhéal Boudrias." *Le Journal Alliance* 7, 2 (June): 7.

–. 1981. "The Lands We Used for Trapping and Fishing Are Now in the Hands of Strangers." *Le Journal Alliance* 8, 1 (June): 13.

–. 1985a. "Jeux Métis: Une première du genre au Québec." *Alliance* 12, 2 (April): 17.

–. 1985b. "La région 02 recense ses membres." *Alliance* 12, 2 (April): 17.

–. 1985c. "Discriminations entre Autochtones: Un club de hockey métis forcé de se retirer d'une compétition." *Alliance* 12, 2 (April): 17.

ALMISSI (Alliance laurentienne des Métis et Indiens sans statut). 1979. "Réflexions pour déterminer une politique cohérente sur le piégeage, la chasse, et la pêche pour les Métis et les Indiens sans statut." *Le Journal Alliance* 6, 3 (June): 9.

Amos, Nelson. 1981. "Nous devons nous prendre en main pour aller à contre-courant de la dépossession." *Le Journal Alliance* 8, 1 (June): 14.

Anonymous. 1872. *The Lumber Trade of the Ottawa Valley, with a Description of Some of the Principal Manufacturing Establishments.* 3rd ed. Ottawa: Times Steam Printing and Publishing.

–. 1886. *The Queen vs. Louis Riel, Accused and Convicted of the Crime of High Treason.* Ottawa: Queen's Printer.

–. 1985. "Lettre ouverte à Louis Riel." *Alliance* 12, 4 (July): 17.

Armstrong, H. 2003. Evidence of Ms Armstrong, transcripts vol. 4. *R. v. Powley*, [2003] 2 S.C.R. 207, 2003 SCC 43.

Arthur, Elizabeth, ed. 1973. *Thunder Bay District, 1821–1892: A Collection of Documents.* Toronto: Champlain Society.

Barbezieux, Alexis de. 1897. *Histoire de la province ecclésiastique d'Ottawa et de la colonisation dans la vallée de l'Ottawa.* Vol. 1. Ottawa: Compagnie d'Imprimerie d'Ottawa.

Bellefeuille, Louis Charles Lefebvre de. 1840a. "Précis de la relation de la troisième mission de Mr. Bellefeuille à Témiskaming, Abbitibbi et Grand Lac." *Rapport de l'Association de la propagation de la foi, établie à Montréal* 2:73–88.

–. 1840b. "Relation d'une mission faite en l'été de 1837, le long de la rivière de l'Outawa jusqu'au lac de Témiskaming, et au-delà jusqu'au lac d'Abbitibbi dans le district de Monseigneur de Juliopolis." *Rapport de l'Association de la propagation de la foi, établie à Montréal* 2:17–72.

Bonnycastle, Richard H. 1846. *Canada and the Canadians in 1846.* Vol. 1. London: Henry Colburn, Publisher.

Bouchette, Joseph. 1832a. *The British Dominions in North America; or a Topographical and Statistical Description of the Provinces of Lower and Upper Canada, New Brunswick, Nova Scotia, the Islands of Newfoundland, Prince Edward, and Cape Breton* [...]. Vol. 1. London: Longman, Rees, Orme, Brown, Green, and Longman.

–. 1832b. *A Topographical Dictionary of Lower Canada.* London: Thomas Davison, Whitefriars.

Brière, Aubé. 1979. "Quelle est notre identité?" *Le Journal Alliance* 6, 4 (August): 10.

Bruyère, Louis. 1983. "Presentation of the Native Council of Canada to the Special Parliamentary Commission on Aboriginal Affairs." *Le Journal Alliance* 10, 6 (December): 6.

Bryce, George. 1885. *The Old Settlers of Red River.* Winnipeg: Manitoba Daily Free Press.

Canada, Parliament. 1886. Sessional Paper no. 43, "Copy of a Letter to English and French Half-Breeds at Lake Qu'appelle." In *Sessional Papers, 1886.* Vol. 19, 13–14. Ottawa: MacLean, Roger & Co.

–. 1890. Sessional Paper no. 22, "Annual Report of the Department of Indian Affairs for the Year Ended 31st December 1889." In *Sessional Papers, 1890.* Vol. 10. Ottawa: Brown Chamberlain.

*Le Canadien.* 1886. "Nouvelles de Paspébiac." *Le Canadien,* February 19.

Chalifoux, Fernand. 1981. "Let Us Remember the Broken Treaties of the Past." *Le Journal Alliance* 8, 1 (June): 2.

Chartier, Clément. 2011. "Message from the President." *Métis National Council Newsletter* (October): 3. http://www.metisnation.ca/wp-content/uploads/2011/10/October-2011.pdf.

–. 2012. "President's Message." *President's Newsletter* (October): 3. http://www.metisnation.ca/wp-content/uploads/2012/10/PDF-Final-Newsletter-October-2012.pdf.

Chazelle, Pierre. [1844] 1973. "Le R.P. Chazelle, supérieur des missions de la Compagnie de Jésus au Canada, à son supérieur en France – Sandwich, 10 août 1844." In *Lettres des nouvelles missions du Canada, 1843–1852,* edited by Lorenzo Cadieux, 188–96. Montréal: Les Éditions Bellarmin.

Clapin, Sylva. 1894. *Dictionnaire canadien-français.* Montréal: C.O. Beauchemin et fils.

Commanda, William, Rhéal Plourde, and Michel B. Bourgeois. 1973. "Lettres au devoir: Rapprochant Indiens, Métis, et Québécois." *Le Devoir,* May 24.

Cormier, Louis-P. 1978. *Jean-Baptiste Perrault, marchand voyageur parti de Montréal le 28e de mai 1783.* Montréal: Boréal.

Cox, Ross. 1832. *Adventures on the Columbia River, Including the Narrative of a Residence of Six Years on the Western Side of the Rocky Mountains, among Various Tribes of Indians Hitherto Unknown, together with a Journey across the American Continent.* New York: J. and J. Harper.

Cuoq, J.A. 1886. *Lexique de la langue algonquine.* Montréal: J. Chapleau et fils.

David, Laurent-Olivier. 1882. *Monseigneur Alexandre-Antonin Taché, archevêque de Saint-Boniface.* Montréal: Librairie Saint-Joseph, Cadieux et Derome.

–. 1883. *Monseigneur Alexandre-Antonin Taché, archevêque de Saint-Boniface.* 2nd ed., rev., corr., and considerably augmented. Montréal: Librairie Saint-Joseph, Cadieux et Derome.

Déléage, R. 1858. Appendice no. 5. In *Rapport des commissaires spéciaux, nommés le 8 de septembre, 1856, pour s'enquérir des affaires des Sauvages en Canada,* 169–71. Toronto: Stewart Derbyshire and George Desbarats.

Derouet, Camille. 1896. "Les Métis canadien-français." *La Revue canadienne: Religioni, Patriae, Artibus* 32:611–20.

Desautels, J. 1843. "Mission d'Aylmer, Lettre de M. Desautels, à Mgr de Montréal." *Rapport de l'Association de la propagation de la foi, établie à Montréal* 4:55–63.

Driver, John. 1893. "John Driver to E. B. Borron, March 4, 1893." Document 53 of the Jones Report. *R. v. Powley,* [2003] 2 S.C.R. 207, 2003 SCC 43.

Dupuy, Jean-Baptiste. 1839. "Journal d'un voyage fait à Temiskaming en 1836." *Rapport de l'Association de la propagation de la foi, établie à Montréal* 1:24–53.

Du Ranquet, Dominique. [1843] 2000. "Journal du père Dominique du Ranquet, S.J., de la mission qu'il fit en 1843 avec le frère Joseph Jennesseaux, S.J., sous la direction de l'abbé Hippolyte Moreau dans l'Outaouais supérieur." In *Journal du père Dominique du Ranquet, missionnaire jésuite en Ontario de 1843 à 1900, de la mission qu'il fit en 1843 dans l'Outaouais supérieur sous la direction de l'abbé Hippolyte Moreau: Tensions socio-culturelles en dehors des peuplements majoritaires blancs au milieu du XIXᵉ siècle*, edited by Fernand Ouellet and René Dionne, 61–242. Ottawa: Les Éditions du Vermillon.

*The Equity.* 1913. "Tragedy in Upper Pontiac." *The Equity,* December 4: 5.

L'Exécutif de L'Alliance. 1979. "Lettre expédiée à Otta [sic] Lang." *Le Journal Alliance* 6, 1 (January): 6.

Franchère, Gabriel. 1820. *Relation d'un voyage à la côte du Nord-Ouest de l'Amérique Septentrionale dans les années 1810, 11, 12, 13, et 14.* Montréal: C.B. Pasteur.

Gaulin, R. 1841. "Mission chez les sauvages du Haut-Canada." *Rapport de l'Association de la propagation de la foi, établie à Montréal* 3:53–58.

Godley, John R. 1844. *Letters from America.* Vol. 1. London: John Murray.

Gough, Barry M., ed. 2013. *Red River and the Journey to the Missouri, 1799–1808.* Vol. 1 of *The Journal of Alexander Henry the Younger, 1799–1814.* The Publications of the Champlain Society vol. 56, edited by Robert Craig Brown. Toronto: Champlain Society.

Gunn, David. 1860. "Peguis Revisited." *The Nor'Wester,* April 28.

Haddock, John A. 1894. *The Growth of a Century: As Illustrated in the History of Jefferson County, New York, from 1793 to 1894.* Philadelphia: Sherman.

Harrison, S. Frances. 1891. *Pine, Rose, and Fleur de Lis.* Toronto: Hart.

Havard, V. 1880. "The French Half-Breeds of the Northwest." In *Annual Report of the Board of Regents of the Smithsonian Institution, Showing the Operations, Expenditures, and Condition of the Institution for the Year 1879,* 309–27. Washington, DC: Government Printing Office.

Heming, Arthur. 1902. "The Abitibi Fur Brigade." *Scribners* 32, 1 (July): 36–49.

Henry, Alexander (the Elder). 1809. *Travels and Adventures in Canada and the Indian Territories between the Years 1760 and 1776, in Two Parts.* New York: I. Riley.

Indigenous and Northern Affairs Canada. 2010. Ch. 18. An Act to Amend and Consolidate the Laws Respecting Indians. Assented to April 12, 1876. https://www.aadnc-aandc.gc.ca/DAM/DAM-INTER-HQ/STAGING/texte-text/1876c18_1100100010253_eng.pdf.

Ingall, Frederick L., Henry Nixon, and John Adams. 1830. *Report of the Commissioners Appointed under the Act 9th George IVth. Chap. 29, for Exploring that Part of the Province Which Lies between the Rivers Saint Maurice & Ottawa, and Which Still Remains Waste and Uncultivated.* Québec: Neilson and Cowen.

*Le Journal de Québec.* 1875. "Nouvelles générales." *Le Journal de Québec,* January 11.

Kohl, J.G. 1861. *Travels in Canada, and through the States of New York and Pennsylvania.* Vol. 1. London: George Manwaring.

Köhler, Auguste. [1850] 1973. "Le père Köhler, missionnaire de la Compagnie de Jésus dans l'Amérique du Nord, à son supérieur – Sault-Sainte-Marie, le 21 décembre 1850." In *Lettres des nouvelles missions du Canada 1843–1852,* edited by Lorenzo Cadieux, 682–96. Montréal: Les Éditions Bellarmin.

Lafond, Raymond, and Charles Beaudoin. 1979. "C'est quoi la justice?" *Le Journal Alliance* 6, 4 (August): 10.

LaRue, François-Alexandre-Hubert. 1863. "Chansons populaires et historiques." In *Le Foyer canadien: Recueil littéraire et historique.* Québec: Bureaux du "Foyer canadien."

Legault, Rolland. 1950. *Risques d'hommes.* Montréal: Fides.

Martin, James. 1895. "River Desert Agency, Maniwaki, Ottawa Co., Que., 11th Aug., 1894." In *Dominion of Canada Annual Report of the Department of Indian Affairs for the Year Ended 30th June 1894*, 31–32. Ottawa: S.E. Dawson.

Mather, Frederic G. 1880. "A Day with the Ottawa Chantier-Men." *Lippincott's Magazine of Popular Literature and Science* 25:137–47.

McLean, John. 1849. *Notes of a Twenty-Five Years' Service in the Hudson's Bay Company Territory*. Vol. 1. London: Richard Bentley.

Minot, George, ed. 1862. *The Statutes at Large and Treaties of the United States of America*. Vol. 9, *From December 1, 1845, to March 3, 1851*. Boston: Little, Brown.

*Montreal Daily Witness*. 1878. "The Caughnawaga Troubles." *Montreal Daily Witness*, May 22.

Moreau, S.A. 1889. *Précis de l'histoire de la seigneurie, de la paroisse, et du comté de Berthier, P.Q., (Canada)*. Berthier, QC: Cie. d'Imp. de Berthier.

Morris, Alexander. 1880. *The Treaties of Canada with the Indians of Manitoba and the North-West Territories, Including the Negotiations on Which They Were Based, and Other Information Relating Thereto*. Toronto: Belfords, Clarke.

*New York Times*. 1886. "The Destitute Fishermen: More Trouble Anticipated, Projects to Relieve the Poor Families." *New York Times*, February 17.

*L'Opinion publique*. 1882. "Maison d'hiver de Noui Icipaiatik, Métis Algonquin." *L'Opinion publique* 13, 11 (March): 130–31.

Payment, E. 1842. "Mission du St. Maurice." *Rapport sur les missions du diocèse de Québec, qui sont secourues par l'Association de la Propagation de la Foi* 4:86–97.

*La Patrie*. 1904. "La mère Valiquette, décédée à St-Gérard de Montarville – intéressantes notes biographiques." *La Patrie*, September 29.

*La Patrie*. 1906a. "L'affaire de Buckingham." *La Patrie*, December 13.

*La Patrie*. 1906b. "Feu Th. Bélanger, il n'était pas le neveu de Louis Riel." *La Patrie*, December 14.

Poiré, Charles. 1840. "Extrait du journal d'une mission faite en 1839, aux lacs Témiscaming et Abbitibbi, au Grand-Lac et au lac La Truite, &c. par Messrs. Poiré et Moreau." *Rapport sur les missions du Diocèse de Québec, qui sont secourues par l'Association de la propagation de la foi* 2:42–62.

Proulx, J.B. 1885. *Au lac Abbitibi: Visite pastorale de Mgr. J. Thomas Duhamel dans le Haut de l'Ottawa*. Montréal: Librairie Saint-Joseph, Cadieux et Derome.

Province of Canada. 1845. *Journals of the Legislative Assembly*. Sessional Papers, Appendix EEE, "Report on the Affairs of the Indians in Canada, Laid before the Legislative Assembly, 20th March 1845." (Bagot Report). Montréal: Rollo Campbell.

–. 1847. *Journals of the Legislative Assembly*. Sessional Papers, Appendix T, "Report on the Affairs of the Indians in Canada, Submitted to the Honourable the Legislative Assembly, for Their Information. Section III." Montréal: Rollo Campbell.

Prud'homme, L.A. 1886. "Joseph La France: Les trappeurs – Séduction de l'Ouest." *Revue canadienne*, n.s., 6 (January): 6–14. http://eco.canadiana.ca/view/oocihm.8_06483_244.

REQ (Registraire des entreprises du Québec). 2005. *Lettres patentes supplémentaires: Alliance Autochtone local 18 Maniwaki inc. changeant sa dénomination sociale en celle de Communauté Métis Autochtone de Maniwaki inc.* Québec: Registraire des entreprises du Québec.

*Revue britannique*. 1834. "Statistique – Du Commerce et de l'usage des pelleteries chez les anciens et les modernes." In *Revue britannique, ou Choix d'articles traduits des meilleurs écrits périodiques de la Grande-Bretagne*, 3rd series, vol. 1, 364–71. Brussels: Chez J.P. Meline.

Rich, E.E., ed. 1938. *George Simpson's Journal of Occurrences in the Athabaska Department and Report 1820–1821*. Toronto: Champlain Society.

Riel, Louis. 1985a. "3–072 Lettre à R.B. Deanne, à Edgar Dewdney, et à John A. Macdonald. Régina. 85/07/06." In *5 June 1884–16 November* 1885, edited by Gilles Martel, 117–29. Vol 3 of *The Collected Writings of Louis Riel/Les écrits complets de Louis Riel*, edited by George Stanley. Edmonton: University of Alberta Press.

–. 1985b. "3–154 Les Métis du Nord-Ouest. Régina. 85/10–11/?" In *5 June 1884–16 November* 1885, edited by Gilles Martel, 272–76. Vol. 3 of *The Collected Writings of Louis Riel/Les écrits complets de Louis Riel*, edited by George Stanley. Edmonton: University of Alberta Press.

–. 1985c. "3–156 Les Métis du Nord-Ouest. Régina. 85/10–11/?" In *5 June 1884–16 November* 1885, edited by Gilles Martel, 278–94. Vol. 3 of *The Collected Writings of Louis Riel / Les écrits complets de Louis Riel*, edited by George Stanley. Edmonton: The University of Alberta Press.

Riel, Marie-Joseph. 1985. "Mon frère Louis Riel." *Alliance* (November 16): 3–5.

Roberts, Theodore G. 1917. The War Spirit of Canada. *Windsor Magazine* 45:108–17.

Robertson, Gaétane. 1986. "Local de Maniwaki." *Alliance* 13, 3 (May): 11.

St. John, Percy B. 1867. *The Snow Ship: The Adventures of Canadian Emigrants*. London: David Bryce.

Scott, William. 1883. *Report Relating to the Affairs of the Oka Indians, Made to the Superintendent General of Indian Affairs*. Ottawa: MacLean, Roger.

Shirreff, Alexander. 1831. "Topographical Notices of the Country Lying between the Mouth of the Rideau and Penetanguishene, on Lake Huron, by Alexander Sherriff [sic], Esquire." *Transactions of the Literary and Historical Society of Quebec* 2:243–309.

Smith, Charles H., and Ian Dyck, eds. 2007. *William E. Logan's 1845 Survey of the Upper Ottawa Valley*. Gatineau, QC: Canadian Museum of Civilization.

Snelling, William J. 1830. *Tales of the Northwest, or Sketches of Indian Life and Character by a Resident beyond the Frontier*. Boston: Hilliard, Gray, Little, and Wilkins.

Sweetser, Moses Foster. 1876. *The Middle States: A Handbook for Travellers*. Boston: James R. Osgood.

Taché, Alexandre A. 1869. *Esquisse sur le Nord-Ouest de l'Amérique*. Montréal: Typographie du Nouveau Monde.

–. 1870. *Sketch of the North-West of America*. Translated by Donald Roderick Cameron. Montréal: John Lovell.

Taché, Joseph-Charles. [1863] 2002. *Forestiers et voyageurs: Mœurs et légendes canadiennes*. With an afterword, chronology, and bibliography by Michel Biron. Montréal: Boréal.

Tocqueville, Alexis de. 1860. "Quinze jours au désert: Souvenirs d'un voyage en Amérique." *Revue des deux mondes: Recueil de la politique, de l'administration, et des mœurs* 30:565–606.

Tyrrell, J.B., ed. 1916. *David Thompson's Narrative of His Explorations in Western America 1784–1812*. Toronto: Champlain Society.

Union Forwarding & Railway Company. 1873. *Union Forwarding & Railway Company's Traveller's Guide to the Upper Ottawa*. Ottawa: Free Press Steam Print.

Veilleux, Jean-Paul. 1984. "Élections en avril, à Maniwaki." *Le Journal Alliance* 11, 2 (March–April): 3.

Villemaire, Don. 1953. "Mark 70 Years of Marriage at Noëlville." *Daily Nugget*, October 8.

Williams, Glyndwr, ed. 1975. *Hudson's Bay Miscellany 1670–1870*. Winnipeg: Hudson's Bay Record Society.

**Interviews**

CRCIM (Chaire de recherche du Canada sur l'identité métisse). 2008a. Interview no. 6 with Serge Lafrenière, by Fabien Tremblay, Bouchette, Québec, June 13.

—. 2008b. Interview no. 9 with Laurier Riel, by Fabien Tremblay, Maniwaki, Québec, June 16.

—. 2008c. Interview no. 14 with Paul-Émile Nault, by Fabien Tremblay, Egan-Sud, Québec, June 19.

—. 2008d. Interview no. 16 with Benoît Guilbault, by Fabien Tremblay, Aumond, Québec, June 23.

—. 2008e. Interview no. 17 with Liliane Cyr, by Fabien Tremblay, Aumond, Québec, June 23.

—. 2008f. Interview no. 20 with Mario Carpentier, by Fabien Tremblay, Messines, Québec, June 27.

Malette, Sébastien. 2016. Interview with Benoît Guilbault and Liliane Cyr, by Dr. Sébastien Malette, Val-des-Bois, Québec, August 19.

SMC (Le Statut de Métis au Canada: Agencéité et enjeux sociaux). 2016. Interview no. 9 with Laurier Riel, by Guillaume Marcotte, Maniwaki, Québec, June 30.

—. 2017. Interview no. 12 with Norman Henrie, by Guillaume Marcotte, Gatineau, Québec, May 5.

**Secondary Sources**

Aboriginal Affairs and Northern Development Canada. 2012. "Les guerriers métis pendant la guerre de 1812/Métis fighters in the War of 1812." *La guerre de 1812/ The War of 1812*. http://publications.gc.ca/site/archivee-archived.html?url= http://publications.gc.ca/collections/collection_2017/aanc-inac/R44-3-2012-3. pdf.

Allen, William. 2011. "The Nesswabic (Petawawa) River Watershed: Zone of Political Tension over the Centuries." *Ontario Archaeological Society Arch Notes* 16 (2): 5–15. https://www.ontarioarchaeology.on.ca/Resources/ArchNotes/anns16-2.pdf.

Andersen, Chris. 2008. "From Nation to Population: The Racialisation of 'Métis' in the Canadian Census." *Nations and Nationalism* 14 (2): 347–68. https://doi.org/ 10.1111/j.1469-8129.2008.00331.x.

Andersen, Chris. 2014. *Métis: Race, Recognition, and the Struggle for Indigenous Peoplehood.* Vancouver: UBC Press.

Anick, Norman. 1976. *The Fur Trade in Eastern Canada until 1870*. Manuscript Report Number 207. Vol. 1. Ottawa: Parks Canada, Department of Indian and Northern Affairs. http://parkscanadahistory.com/series/mrs/207-1.pdf.

Armour, David A. 1983. "Cadot, Jean-Baptiste." In *Dictionary of Canadian Biography*, vol. 5. Université Laval/University of Toronto, 2003–. http://www.biographi.ca/en/bio/ cadot_jean_baptiste_5E.html.

Arthur, Elizabeth. 1985. "Siveright, John." In *Dictionary of Canadian Biography*, vol. 8. Université Laval/University of Toronto, 2003–. http://www.biographi.ca/en/bio/siveright_john_8F.html.

Axtell, James. 1979. "Ethnohistory: An Historian's Viewpoint." *Ethnohistory* 26 (1): 1–13. https://doi.org/10.2307/481465.

Azarya, Victor. 2003. "Community." In *The Social Science Encyclopedia*, 2nd ed., edited by Adam Kuper and Jessica Kuper. London: Routledge.

Bakker, Peter. 1997. *A Language of Our Own: The Genesis of Michif, the Mixed Cree–French Language of the Canadian Métis*. New York and Oxford: Oxford University Press.

Barbeau, Marius. 1942. "Voyageur Songs." *The Beaver* (June): 15–19.

Barkwell, Lawrence. 2012. *Métis Soldiers in the War of 1812*. Winnipeg: Louis Riel Institute.

Barman, Jean. 2014. *French Canadians, Furs, and Indigenous Women in the Making of the Pacific Northwest*. Vancouver: UBC Press.

–. 2016. *Abenaki Daring: The Life and Writings of Noel Annance, 1792–1869*. Montréal and Kingston: McGill-Queen's University Press.

Barth, Fredrik. 1969. "Introduction." In *Ethnic Groups and Boundaries: The Social Organization of Culture Difference*, edited by Fredrik Barth, 9–38. Boston: Little, Brown.

Beaulieu, George Z. 2013. "Les origines de François 'Old Man' Beaulieu, un père de la nation Métis de l'Ouest du Canada: Entre la réalité, les contradictions, et la légende." *L'Estuaire généalogique* 127 (1): 62–75.

Benkler, Yochai. 2006. *The Wealth of Networks: How Social Production Transforms Markets and Freedom*. New Haven, CT: Yale University Press.

Billig, Michael. 1995. *Banal Nationalism*. London/Thousand Oaks, CA: Sage Publications.

Binnema, Ted. 2014. "Protecting Indian Lands by Defining Indian: 1850–76." *Journal of Canadian Studies* 48 (2): 5–39. https://doi.org/10.3138/jcs.48.2.5.

Boas, Franz. 1911. *The Mind of Primitive Man*. New York: Macmillan.

Bond, C.C.J. 1966. "The Hudson's Bay Company in the Ottawa Valley." *The Beaver* 296 (Spring): 4–21.

Borrows, John J., and Leonard I. Rotman. 2012. *Aboriginal Legal Issues: Cases, Materials, and Commentary*. 4th ed. Markham, ON: LexisNexis.

Bouchard, Michel. 2001. "The Medieval Nation of Rus': The Religious Underpinnings of the Russian Nation." *Ab Imperio* 3:139–48. https://doi.org/10.1353/imp.2001.0040.

–. 2004. "A Critical Reappraisal of the Concept of the Imagined Community and the Presumed Sacred Languages of the Medieval Period." *National Identities* 6 (1): 3–24. https://doi.org/10.1080/1460894042000216481.

Bouchard, Michel, and Gheorghe Bogdan. 2014. "From Barbarian Other to Chosen People: The Etymology, Ideology, and Evolution of 'Nation' at the Shifting Edge of Medieval Western Christendom." *National Identities* 17 (1): 1–23. https://doi.org/10.1080/14608944.2014.920805.

Boudreau, Claude, and Pierre Lépine. 1988. "Bouchette, Joseph." In *Dictionary of Canadian Biography*, vol. 7. Université Laval/University of Toronto, 2003–. http://www.biographi.ca/en/bio/bouchette_joseph_7F.html.

Bowsfield, Hartwell. 1982. "Snow, John Allan." In *Dictionary of Canadian Biography*, vol. 11. Université Laval/University of Toronto, 2003–. http://www.biographi.ca/en/bio/snow_john_allan_11E.html.

Brown, Jennifer S.H. 1980. *Strangers in Blood: Fur Trade Company Families in Indian Country*. Vancouver: UBC Press.

–. 1985. "Keith, George." In *Dictionary of Canadian Biography*, vol. 8. Université Laval/ University of Toronto, 2003–. http://www.biographi.ca/fr/bio/keith_george_8F. html.

–. 1987. "Hodgson, John." In *Dictionary of Canadian Biography*, vol. 6. Université Laval/ University of Toronto, 2003–. http://www.biographi.ca/fr/bio/hodgson_john_6F. html.

Burley, Edith. 1993. "Work, Discipline, and Conflict in the Hudson's Bay Company, 1770 to 1870." PhD diss., University of Manitoba.

Calhoun, Craig. 2002. "Culture." In *Dictionary of the Social Sciences*, edited by Craig Calhoun. New York: Oxford University Press.

Calloway, Colin G. 2006. *The Scratch of a Pen: 1763 and the Transformation of North America*. Oxford: Oxford University Press.

Campbell, Maria. 2012. "Foreword: Charting the Way." In *Contours of a People: Metis Family, Mobility, and History*, edited by Nicole St-Onge, Carolyn Podruchny, and Brenda Macdougall, xiii–xxvi. Norman: University of Oklahoma Press.

Carrière, Gaston. 1962. *Histoire documentaire de la Congrégation des Missionnaires Oblats de Marie-Immaculée dans l'Est du Canada*. Part 1, *De l'arrivée au Canada à la mort du fondateur (1841–1861)*. Vol. 4. Ottawa: Éditions de l'Université d'Ottawa.

–. 1968. *Histoire documentaire de la Congrégation des Missionnaires Oblats de Marie-Immaculée dans l'Est du Canada*. Part 2, *Dans la seconde moitié du XIX^e siècle (1861–1900)*. Vol. 7. Ottawa: Éditions de l'Université d'Ottawa.

–. 1990. "Nédélec, Jean-Marie." In *Dictionary of Canadian Biography*, vol. 12. Université Laval/University of Toronto, 2003–. http://www.biographi.ca/fr/bio/nedelec_jean_ marie_12F.html.

Champagne, Juliette, Bob Beal, and Elmer Ghostkeeper. 2005. *A Historical Profile of the Upper North Saskatchewan River Area's Mixed European–Indian Ancestry Community*. Report for Department of Justice Canada. n.p.: Fort des Prairies Associates/Associés and Commonwealth Historic Resource Management.

Chrétien, Annette. 2005. "'Fresh Tracks in Dead Air': Mediating Contemporary Métis Identities through Music and Storytelling." PhD diss., York University.

Chute, Janet Elizabeth. 1998. *The Legacy of Shingwaukonse: A Century of Native Leadership*. Toronto: University of Toronto Press.

Clark, Lovell. 1990. "Schultz, Sir John Christian." In *Dictionary of Canadian Biography*, vol. 12. Université Laval/University of Toronto, 2003–. http://www.biographi.ca/ en/bio/schultz_john_christian_12E.html.

Cottrell, Michael, Elizabeth Mooney, John Lagimodiere, and Terrance Pelletier. 2005a. *Historical Profile of the Cumberland Lake Area's Mixed European–Indian Ancestry Community*. Discussion draft of report for Department of Justice Canada. [Ottawa]: Donna Cona.

–. 2005b. *Historical Profile of Western Mackenzie Valley Drainage Basin Area's Mixed European–Indian Ancestry Settlement*. Discussion draft of report for Department of Justice Canada. [Ottawa]: Donna Cona.

D'Andrade, Roy. 2003. "Culture." In *The Social Science Encyclopedia*, 2nd ed., edited by Adam Kuper and Jessica Kuper. London: Routledge.

Dawson, Nelson-Martin. 2011. *Fourrures et forêts métissèrent les Montagnais: Regard sur les sang-mêlés au Royaume du Saguenay*. Québec: Septentrion.

Delâge, Denis. 2011. "La peur de 'passer pour des Sauvages.'" *Les Cahiers des dix* 65:1–45. https://doi.org/10.7202/1007771ar.

Deleuze, Gilles., and Félix Guattari. 1987. *A Thousand Plateaus: Capitalism and Schizophrenia.* Duluth: University of Minnesota Press.

Descola, Philippe. 2005. *Par-delà nature et culture.* Paris: NRF Éditions Gallimard.

Desjardins, Bertrand. 2008. "La contribution différentielle des immigrants français à la souche canadienne-française." *Annales de Normandie* 58 (3–4): 69–79. https://doi.org/10.3406/annor.2008.6206.

Devine, Heather. 2004. *The People Who Own Themselves: Aboriginal Ethnogenesis in a Canadian Family, 1660–1900.* Calgary: University of Calgary Press.

Donna Cona. 2005. *Final Report for Historical Profile of the Lake of the Woods Area's Mixed European–Indian or Mixed European–Inuit Ancestry Community: Report to Justice Canada.* Ottawa: Donna Cona. http://www.metisnation.org/registry/citizenship/historicresources.

Eidheim, Harald. 1969. "When Ethnic Identity Is a Social Stigma." In *Ethnic Groups and Boundaries: The Social Organization of Culture Difference,* edited by Fredrik Barth, 39–57. Boston: Little, Brown.

Ens, Gerhard. 2001. "Metis Ethnicity, Personal Identity, and the Development of Capitalism in the Western Interior: The Case of Johnny Grant." In *From Rupert's Land to Canada,* edited by Theodore Binnema, Gerhard Ens, and R.C. MacLeod, 160–77. Edmonton: University of Alberta Press.

–. 2012. "The Battle of Seven Oaks and the Articulation of a Metis National Tradition, 1811–1849." In *Contours of a People: Metis Family, Mobility, and History,* edited by Nicole St-Onge, Carolyn Podruchny, and Brenda Macdougall, 93–119. Norman: University of Oklahoma Press.

Ens, Gerhard, and Joe Sawchuk. 2016. *From New Peoples to New Nations: Aspects of Métis History and Identity from the Eighteenth to Twenty-First Centuries.* Toronto: University of Toronto Press.

Evans, Mike, Marcelle Gareau, Leona Neilson, Lisa Krebs, and Heidi Standeven. 2007. *What It Is to Be a Métis: The Stories and Recollections of the Elders of the Prince George Métis Elders Society.* Prince George: UNBC Press.

Fischer, David H. 2009. *Champlain's Dream.* Toronto: Simon and Schuster.

Flanagan, Tom, and Glen Campbell. 2013. "Newly Discovered Writings of Louis Riel." In *Métis in Canada: History, Identity, Law, and Politics,* edited by Christopher Adams, Ian Peach, and Gregg Dahl, 249–76. Edmonton: University of Alberta Press.

Foster, John E. 2001. "Wintering, the Outsider Adult Male, and the Ethnogenesis of the Western Plains Métis." In *From Rupert's Land to Canada,* edited by Theodore Binnema, Gerhard Ens, and R.C. MacLeod, 179–92. Edmonton: University of Alberta Press.

Foster, Martha H. 2006. *We Know Who We Are: Metis Identity in a Montana Community.* Norman, OK: University of Oklahoma Press.

Foxcurran, Robert, Michel Bouchard, and Sébastien Malette. 2016. *Songs upon the Rivers: The Buried History of the French-Speaking Canadiens and Métis from the Great Lakes and the Mississippi across to the Pacific.* Montréal: Baraka Books.

Frenette, Jacques. 1993. "Kitigan Zibi Anishinabeg: Le territoire et les activités économiques des Algonquins de la Rivière Désert (Maniwaki), 1850–1950." *Recherches amérindiennes au Québec* 23 (2–3): 39–51.

Gaffield, Chad, ed. 1994. *Histoire de l'Outaouais.* Québec: Institut québécois de recherche sur la culture.

Gagnon, Denis. 2009. "La création des 'vrais Métis': Définition identitaire, assujettissement, et résistances." *Port Acadie: Revue interdisciplinaire en études acadiennes/Port Acadie: An Interdisciplinary Review in Acadian Studies* 2008–09:295–306.

Gaudry, Adam. 2018. "Communing with the Dead: The "New Métis," Métis Identity Appropriation, and the Displacement of Living Métis Culture." *American Indian Quarterly* 42, 2 (Spring): 162–90. https://doi.org/10.5250/amerindiquar.42.2.0162.

Gaudry, Adam, and Darryl Leroux. 2017. "White Settler Revisionism and Making Metis Everywhere: The Evocation of Métissage in Quebec and Nova Scotia." *Critical Ethnic Studies* 3, 1 (Spring): 116–42. https://doi.org/10.5749/jcritethnstud.3.1.0116.

Geertz, Clifford. 1973. *The Interpretation of Cultures: Selected Essays.* New York: Basic Books.

Gélinas, Claude. 2000. *La gestion de l'étranger: Les Atikamekw et la présence eurocanadienne en Haute-Mauricie, 1760–1870.* Sillery, QC: Septentrion.

–. 2011. *Indiens, Eurocanadiens, et le cadre social du métissage au Saguenay–Lac-Saint-Jean, XVII<sup>e</sup>–XX<sup>e</sup> siècles.* Québec: Septentrion.

Gendron, Gaétan, Richard Laforest, and Danielle Léveillé. 1981. "Compte-rendu commenté sur la révision constitutionnelle des Métis et Indiens sans statut." *Recherches amérindiennes au Québec* 11 (2): 153–54.

Giraud, Marcel. 1945. *Le Métis canadien: Son rôle dans l'histoire des provinces de l'Ouest.* Paris: Institut d'Ethnologie.

Goldring, Philip. 1985. "Keith, James." In *Dictionary of Canadian Biography,* vol. 8. Université Laval/University of Toronto, 2003–. http://www.biographi.ca/fr/bio/keith_james_8F.html.

Goudreau, Serge. 2014a. "Les pionniers du lac Sainte-Marie dans la vallée de la Gatineau (1837–1848)." *Mémoires de la Société généalogique canadienne-française* 65, 4 (282, Winter): 277–91.

–. 2014b. "Les pionniers de la Lièvre en 1846." *Mémoires de la Société généalogique canadienne-française* 65, 1 (279, Spring): 47–66.

Grammond, Sébastien. 2013. *Terms of Coexistence: Indigenous Peoples and Canadian Law.* Toronto: Carswell.

Havard, Gilles. 2003. *Empire et métissages: Indiens et Français dans le Pays d'en Haut, 1660–1715.* Québec: Septentrion.

–. 2016. *Histoire des coureurs de bois: Amérique du Nord, 1600–1840.* Paris: Les Indes savantes.

Hillery, George A. 1955. "Definition of Community." *Rural Sociology* 20 (2): 111–23.

Holmes, Joan. 1996. *Sault-Ste.-Marie Métis Historical Report.* Report for the Ontario Ministry of Natural Resources. [Ottawa]: Joan Holmes and Associates. http://www.metisnation.org/registry/citizenship/historicresources/

Howard, Joseph K. 1994. *Strange Empire: Descendants of Fur Traders and Indians, the Métis Mounted Insurrections against the Canadian Government in 1869–70 and 1885 Led by the Messianic Louis Riel.* St. Paul: Minnesota Historical Society Press.

Hughson, John W., and Courtney C.J. Bond. 1964. *Hurling Down the Pine: The Story of the Wright, Gilmour and Hughson Families, Timber and Lumber Manufacturers in the Hull and Ottawa Region and on the Gatineau River, 1800–1920.* Old Chelsea, QC: Historical Society of Gatineau.

Inksetter, Leila. 2017. *Initiatives et adaptations algonquines au XIX<sup>e</sup> siècle.* Québec: Septentrion.

Johnston, Basil. 1995. *The Manitous: The Spiritual World of the Ojibway*. Toronto: Key Porter Books.

Jones, Gwynneth. n.d. *Historical Profile of the Great Slave Lake Area's Mixed European–Indian Ancestry Community*. Report for Department of Justice Canada. [Ottawa]: Research and Statistics Division and Aboriginal Law and Strategic Policy Group. https://nsma.net/wordpress/wp-content/uploads/2016/08/DoJ-GSL-Jones-Report-1105.pdf.

–. 1998. *Characteristics of pre-1850 and Metis Families in the Vicinity of Sault Ste Marie, 1860–1925*. Report. Ottawa: Public History.

–. 2013. *The Historical Roots of Métis Communities North of Lake Superior*. Report for the Métis Nation of Ontario. Vancouver: Gwynneth Jones.

Karahasan, Devrim. 2006. "Métissage in New France: Frenchification, Mixed Marriages, and Métis as Shaped by Social and Political Agents and Institutions 1508–1886." PhD diss., European University Institute.

Kennedy, John C., ed. 2014. *History and Renewal of Labrador's Inuit-Métis*. St. John's, NL: Iser Books.

Kroeber, Alfred Louis, and Clyde Kluckhohn. 1952. *Culture: A Critical Review of Concepts and Definitions*. Papers of the Peabody Museum, Harvard University, vol. 47, no. 1. Cambridge, MA: Harvard University.

Kuper, Adam. 1999. *Culture: The Anthropologists' Account*. Cambridge, MA: Harvard University Press.

Laberge, Marc, and François Girard. 1999. *Affiquets, matachias, et vermillon: Ethnographie illustrée des Algonquiens du nord-est de l'Amérique aux XVIe, XVIIe et XVIIIe siècles*. Montréal: Recherches amérindiennes au Québec.

Lang, George. 1991. "Voyageur Discourse and the Absence of Fur Trade Pidgin." *Canadian Literature* 131 (Winter): 51–63.

Lapointe, Pierre Louis. 2006. *La vallée assiégée: Buckingham et la Basse-Lièvre sous les MacLaren, 1895–1945*. Gatineau, QC: Vents d'Ouest.

Laskaris, Sam. 2017. "Terry Fox Family Embraces Indigenous Ancestry." *Wind Speaker*, July 27, 2017. http://www.windspeaker.com/news/sports/terry-fox-family-embraces-indigenous-ancestry.

Lefebvre, Pierre. 2006. "From the Highlands to the Fur Trade: The Journey of the McPherson Family." *Métis Voyageur* (Fall–Winter): 21–22.

Legget, Robert F. 1988. "By, John." In *Dictionary of Canadian Biography*, vol. 7. Université Laval/University of Toronto, 2003–. http://www.biographi.ca/fr/bio/by_john_7E.html.

Lehmann, John. 2015. "Chief Justice Says Canada Attempted 'Cultural Genocide' on Aboriginals." *Globe and Mail*, May 28, 2015. https://www.theglobeandmail.com/news/national/chief-justice-says-canada-attempted-cultural-genocide-on-aboriginals/article24688854.

Leroux, Darryl. 2017. "Le révisionnisme historique et l'autochtonisation: La création des 'Métis de l'est.'" Paper presented at the DESS en récits et medias autochtones, Université de Montréal, Montréal, QC, September 27.

Long, John S. 2010. *Treaty No. 9: Making the Agreement to Share the Land in Far Northern Ontario in 1905*. Montréal and Kingston: McGill-Queen's University Press.

Lytwyn, Victor P. 1998. *Historical Report on the Métis Community at Sault Ste. Marie*. Report. Acton, ON: V.P. Lytwyn. http://www.metisnation.org/registry/citizenship/historicresources.

–. 2012. "In the Shadows of the Company: Nicolas Chatelain and the Métis of Fort Frances." In *Contours of a People: Metis Family, Mobility, and History*, edited by Nicole St-Onge, Carolyn Podruchny, and Brenda Macdougall, 194–229. Norman: University of Oklahoma Press.

Macdougall, Brenda. 2010. *One of the Family: Metis Culture in Nineteenth-Century Northwestern Saskatchewan.* Vancouver: UBC Press.

Malette, Sébastien, and Guillaume Marcotte. 2017. "Marie-Louise: Protector of Louis Riel in Québec." *Media Tropes* 7 (1): 26–74.

Marcotte, Guillaume. 2014. "Intempérance et piété chrétienne: Les *voyageurs* canadiens et l'implantation des missions catholiques chez les Autochtones d'Abitibi-Témiscamingue 1836–1863." *Rabaska: Revue d'ethnologie de l'Amérique française* 12: 57–87. https://doi.org/10.7202/1026784ar.

–. 2015. "Un 'tracé d'une grande valeur': La carte indienne de Cameron et son potentiel ethnohistorique associé à l'Outaouais supérieure, 1760–1870." *Recherches amérindiennes au Québec* 45 (2–3): 77–91. https://doi.org/10.7202/1038043ar.

–. 2017. *Les francophones et la traite des fourrures du Grand Témiscamingue: Un dictionnaire biographique, 1760–1870.* Québec: Éditions GID.

Martineau, Donat. 1991. *La vie témiscamienne en 1886.* Historical document no. 3. n.p.: La Société du patrimoine – Abitibi-Témiscamingue.

McLean, Donald. 1987. *Fifty Historical Vignettes: View of the Common People.* Regina: Gabriel Dumont Institute of Native Studies and Applied Research.

McNab, David. 1985. "Metis Participation in the Treaty-Making Process in Ontario: A Reconnaissance." *Native Studies Review* 1 (2): 57–79.

–. 1990. "Chatelain, Nicolas." In *Dictionary of Canadian Biography*, vol. 12. Université Laval/University of Toronto, 2003–. http://www.biographi.ca/en/bio/chatelain_nicolas_12F.html.

Métis National Council. 2018. "General Assembly Acts on Métis Nationalist Agenda." Métis National Council, News, November 29, 2018, http://www.metisnation.ca/index.php/news.

Métis Nation of Ontario. 2017. "Ontario and the MNO Announce Identification of Historic Métis Communities." Métis National Council, News, August 21, 2017. http://www.metisnation.org/news-media/news.

Michaux, Emmanuel. 2014. "Ni Amérindiens ni Eurocanadiens: Une approche néo-moderne du culturalisme métis au Canada." PhD diss., Université Laval.

Mitchell, Elaine A. 1977. *Fort Timiskaming and the Fur Trade.* Toronto: University of Toronto Press.

Morice, A.-G. 1908. *Dictionnaire historique des Canadiens et des Métis français de l'Ouest.* Kamloops, BC: A.-G. Morice.

Morrison, James. 1993. *The Robinson Treaties of 1850: A Case Study.* Report for the Royal Commission on Aboriginal Peoples. Haileybury, ON: James Morrison, Legal and Historical Research.

Newton, Michael. 1991. *Some Notes on Bytown and the Fur Trade.* Ottawa: Historical Society of Ottawa.

O'Toole, Darren. 2012. "The Red River Jig around the Convention of 'Indian' Title: The Métis and Half-Breed Dos-à-Dos." *Manitoba History* 69:17–30.

–. 2017a. "A Legal Look at the Métis of Chibougamau." *The Nation*, March 3, 2017. http://www.nationnews.ca/legal-look-metis-chibougamau.

–. 2017b. "Y a-t-il des communautés métisses au Québec? Une perspective juridique." *Nouveaux cahiers du socialisme* 18 (Fall): 29–36.

Ouellet, Fernand, and Benoît Thériault. 1988. "Wright, Philemon." In *Dictionary of Canadian Biography*, vol. 7. Université Laval/University of Toronto, 2003–. http://www.biographi.ca/fr/bio/wright_philemon_7E.html.

Papen, Robert. 1984. "Quelques remarques sur un parler français méconnu de l'Ouest canadien: Le Métis." *Revue québécoise de linguistique* 14 (1): 113–39. https://doi.org/10.7202/602530ar.

–. 2009. "La question des langues des Mitchifs: Un dédale sans issue?" In *Histoires et identités métisses: Hommage à Gabriel Dumont/Métis Histories and Identities: A Tribute to Gabriel Dumont*, edited by Denis Gagnon, Denis Combet, and Lise Gaboury-Diallo, 253–76. Winnipeg: Presses universitaires de Saint-Boniface.

Parsons, Talcott, and Leon H. Mayhew. 1982. *Talcott Parsons on Institutions and Social Evolution: Selected Writings*. Chicago: University of Chicago Press.

Payment, Diane P. 1990. *"Les gens libres – Otipemisiwak": Batoche, Saskatchewan, 1870–1930*. Ottawa: Environnement Canada, Service des parcs.

Peterson, Jacqueline. 1981. "The People In Between: Indian-White Marriage and the Genesis of a Métis Society and Culture in the Great Lakes Region, 1680–1830." PhD diss., University of Illinois.

–. 2012. "Red River Redux: Métis Ethnogenesis and the Great Lakes Region." In *Contours of a People: Metis Family, Mobility, and History*, edited by Nicole St-Onge, Carolyn Podruchny, and Brenda Macdougall, 22–58. Norman: University of Oklahoma Press.

Phalen, James M. 1939. "Valery Havard: Colonel, Medical Corps, U.S. Army." *Army Medical Bulletin* 50:126–29.

Philpot, Robin. 2010. *Oka: Dernier alibi du Canada anglais*. Québec: Les Intouchables.

Pigeon, Émilie. 2017. "Au nom du Bon Dieu et du Buffalo: Metis Lived Religion on the Northern Plains." PhD diss., York University.

Plouffe, Hélène. 2013. "Un Canadien errant." *Historica Canada*. Last modified December 16, 2013. https://thecanadianencyclopedia.ca/en/article/un-canadien-errant-emc.

Podruchny, Carolyn. 2006. *Making the Voyageur World: Travelers and Traders in the North American Fur Trade*. Lincoln: University of Nebraska Press.

Ray, Arthur J. 1998. *An Economic History of the Robinson Treaties Area before 1860*. Report for Ontario Court of Justice (Provincial Division), Sault Ste. Marie, with respect to *Regina v. Powley*. http://www.metisnation.org/registry/citizenship/historicresources.

–. 2005. *Métis Economic Communities and Settlements in the 19th Century*. Report for Pape, Salter Teillet LLP. Vancouver: Arthur J. Ray, History Department, University of British Columbia.

–. 2011. *Telling It to the Judge: Taking Native History to Court*. Montréal and Toronto: McGill-Queen's University Press.

–. 2016. *Aboriginal Rights Claims and the Making and Remaking of History*. Montréal and Kingston: McGill-Queen's University Press.

RCAP (Royal Commission on Aboriginal Peoples). 1996. *Report of the Royal Commission on Aboriginal Peoples*. Vol. 4, *Perspectives and Realities*. Ottawa: Indian and Northern Affairs Canada.

Reimer, Gwen, and J.-P. Chartrand. 2002. *Review of Reports and Cartographic Representation Pertaining to Historic Métis in Ontario*. Orleans, ON: Praxis Research Associates.

Rich, Edwin Ernest. 1983. "Longmoor, Robert." In *Dictionary of Canadian Biography*, vol. 5. Université Laval/University of Toronto, 2003–. http://www.biographi.ca/fr/bio/longmoor_robert_5F.html.

Richards, Matt. 2004. *Deerskins into Buckskins: How to Tan with Brains, Soap, or Eggs*. 2nd ed. Cave Junction, OR: Backcountry Publishing.

Rivard, Étienne. 2004. "Prairie and Québec Métis Territoriality: *Interstices territoriales* and the Cartography of In-Between Identity." PhD diss., University of British Columbia.

–. 2017. "The Indefensible In-Betweenness or the Spatio-Legal Arbitrariness of the Métis Fact in Québec." *Justice spatiale/Spatial Justice* 11 (March): 1–16. https://www.jssj.org/article/lindefendable-entre-deux-ou-larbitraire-spatiolegal-du-fait-metis-au-quebec.

Rogers, J.A. 2012. *Sex and Races: A History of White, Negro, and Indian Miscegenation in the Two Americas*. Vol. 2, *The New World*. St. Petersburg, FL: Helga M. Rogers.

Sabourin, Mathieu. 2010. "Les squatters de la rivière Gatineau entre 1812 et 1870." Master's thesis, Université Laval.

Scace, Robert, Charles Ramsay, Evelyn Siegfried, Andrea Klaiber, and Jordyce Malasiuk. 2005. *A Historical Profile of the Northeast Alberta Area's Mixed European–Indian Ancestry Community*. Discussion draft of report for Department of Justice Canada. n.p.: Stantec Consulting.

Schenck, Theresa M. 1994. "The Cadottes: Five Generations of Fur Traders on Lake Superior." In *The Fur Trade Revisited: Selected Papers of the Sixth North American Fur Trade Conference, Mackinac Island, Michigan, 1991*, edited by Jennifer S.H. Brown, W.J. Eccles, and Donald P. Heldman, 189–98. East Lansing: Michigan State University Press.

Senior, Nancy. 2004. "Of Whales and Savages: Reflections on Translating Louis Nicolas' *Histoire naturelle des Indes occidentales*." *Meta* 49 (3): 462–74. https://doi.org/10.7202/009372ar.

Sleeper-Smith, Susan. 2000. "Women, Kin, and Catholicism: New Perspectives on the Fur Trade." *Ethnohistory* 47 (2): 423–52. https://doi.org/10.1215/00141801-47-2-423.

Smallman, Shawn. 2010. "Spirit Beings, Mental Illness, and Murder: Fur Traders and the Windigo in Canada's Boreal Forest, 1774 to 1935." *Ethnohistory* 57 (4): 571–96. https://doi.org/10.1215/00141801-2010-037.

Smith, Derek G. 1975. *Canadian Indians and the Law: Selected Documents, 1663–1972*. Toronto: McClelland and Stewart.

Spraakman, Gary, and Julie Margret. 2005. "The Transfer of Management Accounting Practices from London Counting Houses to the British North American Fur Trade." *Accounting, Business and Financial History* 15 (2): 101–19. https://doi.org/10.1080/09585200500121108.

Spraakman, Gary, and Alison Wilkie. 2000. "The Development of Management Accounting at the Hudson's Bay Company, 1670–1820." *Accounting History* 5 (1): 59–84. https://doi.org/10.1177/103237320000500104.

Sprague, D.N. 1996. "Canada's Treaties with Aboriginal Peoples." *Manitoba Law Journal* 23 (1–2): 341–51.

Stocking, George W. Jr. [1968] 1982. *Race, Culture, and Evolution: Essays in the History of Anthropology*. Chicago: University of Chicago Press.

Stone Circle Consulting and Know History. 2015. *Mattawa Nipissing Métis Historical Research Project*. Final synthesis report for the Steering Committee. n.p.: Stone Circle Consulting and Know History.

St-Onge, Nicole. 2004. *Saint-Laurent, Manitoba: Evolving Métis Identities, 1850–1914*. Regina: Canadian Plains Research Center.

St-Onge, Nicole, and Carolyn Podruchny. 2012. "Scuttling Along the Spider's Web: Mobility and Kinship in Métis Ethnogenesis." In *Contours of a People: Metis Family, Mobility, and History*, edited by Nicole St-Onge, Carolyn Podruchny, and Brenda Macdougall, 59–92. Norman: University of Oklahoma Press.

Thistle, Paul C. 2007. "The Twatt Family, 1780–1840: Amerindian, Ethnic Category, or Ethnic Group Identity? (1997)." In *The Western Métis: Profile of a People*, edited by Patrick C. Douaud, 73–89. Regina: University of Regina Press.

Thorne, Tanis C. 1996. *The Many Hands of My Relations: French and Indians on the Lower Missouri*. Columbia: University of Missouri Press.

Tremblay, Fabien. 2009. "Mobilisation et exclusion chez les Métis de l'Abitibi." In *Histoires et identités métisses: Hommage à Gabriel Dumont/ Métis Histories and Identities: A Tribute to Gabriel Dumont*, edited by Denis Gagnon, Denis Combet, and Lise Gaboury-Diallo, 201–25. Winnipeg: Presses universitaires de Saint-Boniface.

Trigger, Bruce G. 1992. *Les Indiens, la fourrure et les Blancs: Français et Amérindiens en Amérique du Nord*. Translated by Georges Khal. Montréal/Paris: Boréal/Editions du Seuil.

Truth and Reconciliation Commission of Canada. 2015. *Canada's Residential Schools: The Final Report of the Truth and Reconciliation Commission of Canada*. Kingston and Montréal: McGill-Queen's University Press.

Turgeon, Laurier, Louis-Pascal Rousseau, Julie Lavigne, and Daniel Lessard. 2005. *Un profil historique des communautés d'ascendance mixte indienne européenne de la région de l'Outaouais*. Draft of report for Department of Justice Canada. n.p.: Circare Consultants.

Tylor, Edward B. 1871. *Primitive Culture: Researches into the Development of Mythology, Philosophy, Religion, Art and Custom*. 2 vols. London: Murray.

Van Kirk, Sylvia. [1980] 1999. *Many Tender Ties: Women in Fur-Trade Society, 1670–1870*. Winnipeg: J. Gordon Shillingford Publishing.

Vowel, Chelsea, and Darryl Leroux. 2016. "White Settler Antipathy and the Daniels Decision." *Topia: Canadian Journal of Cultural Studies* 36 (Autumn): 30–42. https://doi.org/10.3138/topia.36.30.

Watson, Bruce M. 2010. *Lives Lived West of the Divide: A Biographical Dictionary of Fur Traders Working West of the Rockies, 1793–1858*. Okanagan: Centre for Social, Spatial, and Economic Justice, University of British Columbia.

Willmot, Cory, and Kevin Brownlee. 2010. "Dressing for the Homeward Journey: Western Anishinaabe Leadership Roles Viewed through Two Nineteenth-Century Burials." In *Gathering Places: Aboriginal and Fur Trade Histories*, edited by Carolyn Podruchny and Laura Peers, 48–89. Vancouver: UBC Press.

Woodcock, George. 1985. "Grant, Cuthbert (d. 1854)." In *Dictionary of Canadian Biography*, vol. 8. Université Laval/University of Toronto, 2003–. http://www.biographi.ca/en/bio/grant_cuthbert_1854_8F.html.

# Index

*Note:* "(f)" after a page number indicates an illustration; "(m)," a map; "(t)," a table

Riel, Louis (resistance leader): attachment to, 169, 172, 209–12, 226; baptism, 105; blood quantum (ancestry),
48, 223, 245n5; father of, 165; flags
used, 26; identity fluidity, 228; letters,
47, 169–70, 210–11, 257n21; refuge (as
in exile), 3, 10, 133, 222–23; refuge
(oral account transcript), 37, 130, 163–
72, 210, 256nn1–2, 256n6, 256nn8–9,
257n12, 257n16, 257n18, 257n21; on
religion, 102, 104; resistance, 45, 222,
246n10; self-identification ethnonyms,
31, 47–48, 52–53, 55; as source of inspiration, 226; sovereignty, 247n2
Riel, Louis (son of Louis Riel), 45
Riel, Lucie (wife of John Lee), 165–66
Riel, Marie-Joseph, 210
Riel (Chipakijikokwe), Marie-Louise
(wife of Robert McGregor, File 12):
about, 164(f), 165–69, 239, 256n6,
256nn8–9; descendants, 34, 213, 215,
239; healer, 164(f), 223; hides tanning, 148, 254n5; mobility, 154, 158;
moccasin making, 110; refuge (Louis
Riel), 163, 223; traditional practices,
110, 148, 170–71, 223, 254n5
Riel, Patrick, 34
Riel, Paul (son of Émilien Riel and
Henriette McDougall), 178–80, 223,
238, 258n14
Riel, Sophie (daughter of Jean-Baptiste
Riel and Marguerite Boucher), 165–
66, 256n6
Rivard, Étienne (geographer), 7, 49
Rivière Désert (Desert River/Maniwaki):
band registry (identity and guardian-
ship), 187–88, 260nn40–41; illicit
trade, 162; mission, 177; trading post,
71. *See also* Maniwaki community;
Maniwaki Reserve
road allowances, 222, 263n1
Robert, Rose (wife of Joseph David, File
5), 233
Robertson, James (clerk), 102, 250n5
Robinson, William, 59, 126
Robinson Huron Treaty (1850), 59
Robinson Treaties, 44–45, 59–60, 126,
159, 221

Rocbrune (Larocque), Caroline (wife
of Joseph Foubert, File 6), 233–34,
254n1
Rouge River (Red River), 194, 199(f),
261n12, 261n21
Round Lake. *See* Lac-Sainte-Marie
(Round Lake) community
Roy, Jacques (father of James King),
248n5
Royal Commission on Aboriginal
Peoples (RCAP), 21, 57
Royal Proclamation (1763), 40

Sabourin, André (fur trader), 144,
160–61
Sainte-Geneviève-de-Berthier, 104–5,
165
Saint-Maurice, 93–94, 138, 250n12
Sault St. Louis, 89, 92
Sault Ste. Marie: agriculture, 149; cultural recognition (Métis), 14, 21, 95;
ethnocultural similarities (Métis kinship ties, Lac-Sainte-Marie), 62, 130,
149–52; population (Métis), 57,
248n15; treaty exclusion (Métis),
57, 59, 62, 126. *See also R. v. Powley*
decision
Saulteaux (Ojibwe) Nation, 166, 246n8,
261n21. *See also* Ojibwe Nation
*Sauvage/Sauvagesse* ethnonym, xiv, 15,
51–52, 151–52
Sauvagesse, Thérèse (wife of Neil
McKay), 105
Sawchuk, Joe: ethnogenesis, 21, 25, 27,
33, 39; family identity, 125; pemmican
trade war, 41
Sayer, Guillaume (Métis), 45
Schocier (Chaussé), Thomas (Métis),
178–79, 258n6
Schocier (Chaussé/Socière), Pierre
(Métis), 259n28. *See also* Chaussé,
Pierre Jr. (grandson of François
Vanasse and Louise Forcier, File 19)
Schultz, Dr. John Christian, 143
Scottish Métis: distinctions vs French
Métis/Canadien Métis, 45, 106–8, 202,
221; language and religion, 106–8, 141;
presence of and identity, 194–96, 224